MANHATTAN PREP

GMAT Advanced Quant

GMAT Strategy Guide

This supplemental guide provides in-depth and comprehensive
explanations of the advanced math skills necessary for the highest-level
performance on the GMAT.

GMAT Advanced Quant Strategy Guide, Second Edition

10-digit International Standard Book Number: 1-941234-35-6
13-digit International Standard Book Number: 978-1-941234-35-8
eISBN: 978-1-941234-36-5

Layout Design: Dan McNaney and Cathy Huang
Cover Design: Dan McNaney and Frank Callaghan
Cover Photography: Alli Ugosoli

INSTRUCTIONAL GUIDE SERIES

SUPPLEMENTAL GUIDE SERIES

May 19th, 2015

Dear Student,

Thank you for picking up a copy of *GMAT Advanced Quant*. This book is aptly titled—it's designed to provide you with the most advanced knowledge and skills you'll need to perform at the highest level on the GMAT quantitative section. Be sure that you have mastered the content found in our core strategy guides before tackling these tougher math concepts. We hope it ends up being the most challenging and rewarding GMAT quant book you'll put your hands on.

A great number of people were involved in the creation of the book you are holding. First and foremost is Zeke Vanderhoek, the founder of Manhattan Prep. Zeke was a lone tutor in New York City when he started the company in 2000. Now, well into its second decade, the company contributes to the successes of thousands of students around the globe every year.

Our Manhattan Prep Strategy Guides are based on the continuing experiences of our instructors and students. The original edition of this book was authored by Emily Meredith Sledge and edited by Tate Shafer, with questions written not only by Emily and Tate but also by many other instructors, including Josh Braslow, Matt Cressy, Steven Jupiter, Jad Lee, and Dave Mahler.

The Second Edition that you are holding brought even more talent to the table. This update was authored by Stacey Koprince and edited by Stephanie Moyerman. New questions were written by Stacey and Stephanie, as well as by Kim Cabot, Whitney Garner, Avi Gutman, Dave Mahler, Ron Purewal, Emily Meredith Sledge, Ryan Starr, and Patrick Tyrrell.

Meanwhile, Dan McNaney and Cathy Huang provided design and layout expertise as Dan managed book production. Liz Krisher made sure that all the moving pieces, both inside and outside of our company, came together at just the right time. Finally, we are indebted to all of the Manhattan Prep students who have given us feedback over the years. This book wouldn't be half of what it is without your voice.

At Manhattan Prep, we aspire to provide the best instructors and resources possible, and we hope that you will find our commitment manifest in this book. We strive to keep our books free of errors, but if you think we've goofed, please post to manhattanprep.com/GMAT/errata. If you have any questions or comments in general, please email our Student Services team at gmat@manhattanprep.com. Or give us a shout at 212-721-7400 (or 800-576-4628 in the U.S. or Canada). I look forward to hearing from you.

Thanks again, and best of luck preparing for the GMAT!

Sincerely,

Chris Ryan
Vice President of Academics
Manhattan Prep

HOW TO ACCESS YOUR ONLINE RESOURCES

IF YOU ARE A REGISTERED MANHATTAN PREP STUDENT

and have received this book as part of your course materials, you have AUTOMATIC access to ALL of our online resources. This includes all practice exams, question banks, and online updates to this book. To access these resources, follow the instructions in the Welcome Guide provided to you at the start of your program. Do NOT follow the instructions below.

IF YOU PURCHASED THIS BOOK FROM MANHATTANPREP.COM OR AT ONE OF OUR CENTERS

1. Go to: **www.manhattanprep.com/gmat/studentcenter**
2. Log in with the username and password you chose when setting up your account.

IF YOU PURCHASED THIS BOOK AT A RETAIL LOCATION

1. Go to: **www.manhattanprep.com/gmat/access**
2. Create an account or, if you already have one, log in on this page with your username and password.
3. Follow the instructions on the screen.

Your one year of online access begins on the day that you register your book at the above URL.

You only need to register your product ONCE at the above URL. To use your online resources any time AFTER you have completed the registration process, log in to the following URL:

www.manhattanprep.com/gmat/studentcenter

Please note that online access is nontransferable. This means that only NEW and UNREGISTERED copies of the book will grant you online access. Previously used books will NOT provide any online resources.

IF YOU PURCHASED AN EBOOK VERSION OF THIS BOOK

1. Create an account with Manhattan Prep at this website:

www.manhattanprep.com/gmat/register

2. Email a copy of your purchase receipt to **gmat@manhattanprep.com** to activate your resources. Please be sure to use the same email address to create an account that you used to purchase the eBook.

For any questions, email **gmat@manhattanprep.com** or call **800-576-4628**.

Please refer to the following page for a description of the online resources that come with this book.

YOUR ONLINE RESOURCES
YOUR PURCHASE INCLUDES ONLINE ACCESS TO THE FOLLOWING:

GMAT ADVANCED QUANT ONLINE QUESTION BANK

Purchase of GMAT Advanced Quant comes with access to two online question sets, each of 10 very hard problems, that test the variety of advanced math concepts and skills covered in this book. You can mimic test conditions by setting a timer for the entire set, allowing you to practice your time management skills. Then, review the in-depth explanations to learn the most effective and efficient approaches for each problem.

5 FREE INTERACT™ LESSONS

Interact™ is a comprehensive self-study program that is fun, intuitive, and directed by you. Each interactive video lesson is taught by an expert Manhattan Prep instructor and includes dozens of individual branching points. The choices you make define the content you see. This book comes with access to the first five lessons of GMAT Interact. Lessons are available on your computer or iPad so you can prep where you are, when you want. For more information on the full version of this program, visit **manhattanprep.com/gmat/interact**

ONLINE UPDATES TO THE CONTENT IN THIS BOOK

The content presented in this book is updated periodically to ensure that it reflects the GMAT's most current trends. You may view all updates, including any known errors or changes, upon registering for online access.

The above resources can be found in your Student Center at manhattanprep.com/gmat/studentcenter

TABLE *of* CONTENTS

Chapter *of* 0

GMAT Advanced Quant

Introduction

In This Chapter...

Introduction

A Qualified Welcome

Welcome to GMAT Advanced Quant! In this venue, we decided to be a little nerdy and call the introduction "Chapter 0." After all, the point (0, 0) in the coordinate plane is called the *origin*, right? (That's the first and last math joke in this book.)

Unfortunately, we have to qualify our welcome right away, because **this book isn't for everyone**. At least, it's not for everyone *right away*.

Who Should Use This Book

You should use this book if you meet the following conditions:

- You have achieved a raw score of at least 47 on the Quant section of either the Manhattan Prep or the GMATPrep® practice CATs.
- You have worked through the five math-focused Manhattan Prep Strategy Guides, which are organized around broad topics, or you have worked through similar material from another company:
  - Algebra
  - Fractions, Decimals, & Percents
  - Geometry
  - Number Properties
  - Word Problems
- You are already comfortable with the core principles in these topics.
- You want to raise your performance to a raw score of 49 or higher.
- You want to become a significantly smarter test-taker.

If you match this description, then please turn the page!

0

If you don't match this description, then you will probably find this book too difficult at this stage of your preparation.

For now, you are better off working on topic-focused material, such as our Strategy Guides, and ensuring that you have mastered that material *before* you return to this book.

Try Them

Take a look at the following three problems, which are very difficult. They are at least as hard as any real GMAT problem—probably even harder.

Go ahead and give these problems a try. You should not expect to solve any of them in two minutes. In fact, you might find yourself completely stuck. If that's the case, switch gears. Do your best to eliminate some wrong answer choices and take an educated guess.

Try-It #0-1

A jar is filled with red, white, and blue tokens that are equivalent except for their color. The chance of randomly selecting a red token, replacing it, then randomly selecting a white token is the same as the chance of randomly selecting a blue token. If the number of tokens of every color is a multiple of 3, what is the smallest possible total number of tokens in the jar?

(A) 9   (B) 12   (C) 15   (D) 18   (E) 21

Try-It #0-2

Arrow $\overline{AB}$, which is a line segment exactly 5 units long with an arrowhead at A, is to be constructed in the xy-plane. The x- and y-coordinates of A and B are to be integers that satisfy the inequalities $0 \leq x \leq 9$ and $0 \leq y \leq 9$. How many different arrows with these properties can be constructed?

(A) 50   (B) 168   (C) 200   (D) 368   (E) 536

Try-It #0-3

In the diagram to the right, the value of x is closest to which of the following?

(A) $2+\sqrt{2}$ (B) 2   (C) $\sqrt{3}$ (D) $\sqrt{2}$ (E) 1

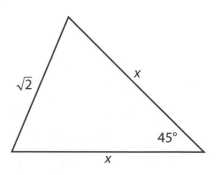

(Note: This problem does not require any non-GMAT math, such as trigonometry.)

The Purpose of This Book

This book is designed to prepare you for the *most difficult* math problems on the GMAT.

So…what *is* a difficult math problem, from the point of view of the GMAT?

A difficult math problem is one that most GMAT test-takers get wrong under exam conditions. In fact, this is essentially how the GMAT measures difficulty: by the percent of test-takers who get the problem wrong.

So, what kinds of math questions do most test-takers get wrong? What characterizes these problems? There are two kinds of features:

1. **Topical nuances or obscure principles**

   - Connected to a particular topic

   - Inherently hard to grasp, or simply unfamiliar

   - Easy to mix up

   These topical nuances are largely covered in the Extra sections of the Manhattan Prep Strategy Guides. The book you are holding includes many problems that involve topical nuances. However, the exhaustive theory of *Divisibility & Primes*, for instance, is not repeated here.

2. **Complex structures**

   - Based only on simple principles but have non-obvious solution paths

   - May require multiple steps

   - May make you consider many cases

   - May combine more than one topic

   - May need a flash of real insight to complete

   - May make you change direction or switch strategies along the way

   Complex structures are essentially *disguises* for simpler content. These disguises may be difficult to pierce. The path to the answer is twisted or clouded somehow.

   To solve problems that have simple content but complex structures, you need approaches that are both *more general* and *more creative*. This book focuses on these more general and more creative approaches.

   The three problems on the previous page have complex structures; the solutions are a bit later in this chapter. In the meantime, take a look at another problem.

An Illustration

Give this problem a whirl. Don't go on until you have spent a few minutes on it—or until you have figured it out!

Try-It #0-4

What should the next number in this sequence be?

1   2   9   64   —

Note: This problem is *not* exactly GMAT-like, because there is no mathematically definite rule. However, you'll know when you've solved the problem. The answer will be elegant.

This problem has very simple content but a complex structure. Researchers in cognitive science have used sequence-completion problems such as this one to develop realistic models of human thought. Here is one such model, simplified but practical.

Top-Down Brain and Bottom-Up Brain

To solve the sequence-completion problem above, you need two kinds of thinking:

You might even say that you need two types of brain.

The Top-Down brain is your conscious self. If you imagine the contents of your head as a big corporation, then your Top-Down brain is the CEO, responding to input, making decisions and issuing orders. In cognitive science, the Top-Down brain is called the "executive function." Top-Down thinking and planning is indispensible to any problem-solving process.

But the corporation in your head is a big place. For one thing, how does information get to the CEO? And how pre-processed is that information?

The Bottom-Up brain is your PRE-conscious processor. After raw sensory input arrives, your Bottom-Up brain processes that input extensively *before* it reaches your Top-Down brain.

For instance, to your optic nerve, every word on this page is simply a lot of black squiggles. Your Bottom-Up brain immediately turns these squiggles into letters, joins the letters into words, summons relevant images and concepts, and finally serves these images and concepts to your Top-Down brain. This all happens automatically and swiftly. In fact, it takes effort to *interrupt* this process. Also, unlike your Top-Down brain, which does things one at a time, your Bottom-Up brain can easily do many things at once.

How does all this relate to solving the sequence problem above?

0

Each of your brains needs the other one to solve difficult problems.

Your Top-Down brain needs your Bottom-Up brain to notice patterns, sniff out valuable leads, and make quick, intuitive leaps and connections.

But your Bottom-Up brain is inarticulate and distractible. Only your Top-Down brain can build plans, pose explicit questions, follow procedures, and state findings.

Imagine that you are trying to solve a tough murder case. To find all the clues in the woods, you need both a savvy detective and a sharp-nosed bloodhound.

> **Your Top-Down brain is the detective.**
>
> **Your Bottom-Up brain is the bloodhound.**
>
> } Be **organized**, **fast**, and **flexible** to crack the case.

To solve difficult GMAT problems, try to harmonize the activity of your two brains by following an organized, fast, and flexible problem-solving process.

| Organized | You need a general step-by-step approach to guide you. One such approach, inspired by the expert mathematician George Polya, is ***Understand, Plan, Solve***: |

1. ***Understand*** the problem first.

2. ***Plan*** your attack by adapting known techniques in new ways.

3. ***Solve*** by executing your plan.

You may never have thought explicitly about steps 1 and 2 before. It may have been easy or even automatic for you to *Understand* easier problems and to *Plan* your approach to them. As a result, you may tend to dive right into the *Solve* stage. This is a bad strategy. Mathematicians know that the real math on hard problems is not *Solve*; the real math is *Understand* and *Plan*.

| Fast | Speed is important for its own sake on the GMAT, of course. What you may not have thought as much about is that being fast can also lower your stress level and promote good process. If you know you can *Solve* quickly, then you can take more time to comprehend the question, consider the given information, and select a strategy. To this end, make sure that you can complete calculations and manipulations fairly rapidly so that you can afford to spend some time on the *Understand* and *Plan* stages of your problem-solving process. A little extra time invested up front can pay off handsomely later. |

| Flexible | To succeed against difficult problems, you sometimes have to "unstick" yourself. Expect to run into brick walls and encounter dead ends. Returning to first principles and to the general process (e.g., making sure that you fully *Understand* the problem) can help you back up out of the mud. |

0

Let's return to the sequence problem and play out a sample interaction between the two brains. The path is not linear; there are several dead ends, as you would expect. This dialogue will lead to the answer, so don't start reading until you've given the problem a final shot (if you haven't already solved it). The Top-Down brain is labeled TD; the Bottom-Up brain is labeled BU.

1	2	9	64	___	TD: "Okay, let's *Understand* this thing. At a glance, they've given me an increasing list of numbers, and they want me to find the number that 'should' go in the blank, whatever 'should' means. What's a good *Plan*? Hmm. No idea. Stare at the numbers given?" *BU notices that 9 = 3² and 64 = 8². Likes the two squares.*
1	2	3^2	8^2	___	TD: "Write in the two squares."
1	2	3^2	8^2	___	*BU notices that 1 is a square too.*
sq	no	sq	sq	___	TD: "Are they all perfect squares? No, since 2 isn't." *BU doesn't like this break in the pattern.*
1	2	3^2	2^6	___	TD: "Wait, back up. What about primes, factoring all the way. $8 = 2^3$, and so $8^2 = (2^3)^2 = 2^6$." *BU notices $6 = 2 \times 3$, but so what.*
1	2	3^2	$(2^3)^2$	___	TD: "Let's write 2^6 as $(2^3)^2$. Anything there?" *BU notices lots of 2's and 3's, but so what.*
					TD: "Okay keep looking at this. Are the 2's and 3's stacked somehow?" *BU notices no real pattern. There's 2–3–2 twice as you go across, but so what. And the 1 is weird by itself.*
1	2	9	64	___	TD: "No good leads there. Hmm... Time to go back to the original and try taking differences." *BU notices no pattern. The numbers look even uglier.*
1	2	9	64	___	TD: "Hmm. No good. Go back to original numbers again. What's going on there?" *BU notices that the numbers are growing quickly, like squares or exponentials.*
1^2	2	3^2	8^2	___	TD: "Must have something to do with those squares. I should look at those again." *BU notices a gap on the left, among the powers.*

(In the eighth row, below the original numbers: 1   7   55)

0

$1^?$	2^1	3^2	8^2	___	TD: "What about look at 2. Write it with exponents... $2 = 2^1$. Actually, 1 doesn't have to be 1^2. 1 can be to any power and still be 1. The power is a question mark." *BU notices 2^1 then 3^2. Likes the counting numbers.* *BU really wants 1, 2, 3, 4 somehow.*
$1^?$	2^1	3^2	$4^{??}$	___	TD: "Try 4 in that last position. Could the last term be 4 somehow?" *BU likes the look of this. 8 and 4 are related.*
$1^?$	2^1	3^2	4^3	___	TD: "64 is 4 to the what... $4^2 = 16$, times another 4 equals 64, so it's 4 to the third power. That fits." *BU is thrilled: 1, 2, 3, 4 below and 1, 2, 3 up top.*
1^0	2^1	3^2	4^3	___	TD: "Extend left. It's 1^0. Confirmed. The bases are 1, 2, 3, 4, etc. and the powers are 0, 1, 2, 3, etc." *BU is content.*
1^0	2^1	3^2	4^3	5^4	TD: "So the answer is 5^4, which is 25^2, or 625."

Your own process was almost certainly different in the details. Also, your internal dialogue was very rapid—parts of it probably only took fractions of a second to transpire. After all, you think at the speed of thought.

The important thing is to recognize how the Bottom-Up bloodhound and the Top-Down detective worked together in the case above. The TD detective set the overall agenda and then pointed the BU bloodhound at the clues. The bloodhound did practically all the "noticing," which in some sense is where all the magic happened. But sometimes the bloodhound got stuck, so the detective had to intervene, consciously trying a new path. For instance, 64 reads so strongly as 8^2 that the detective had to actively give up on that reading.

There are so many possible meaningful sequences that it wouldn't have made sense to apply a strict *recipe* from the outset: "Try X first, then Y, then Z…" Such an algorithm would require hundreds of possibilities. Should you always look for 1, 2, 3, 4? Should you *never* find differences or prime factors, because they weren't that useful here? Of course not! A computer can rapidly and easily apply a complicated algorithm with hundreds of steps, but humans can't. (If you are an engineer or programmer, maybe you *wish* you could program your own brain, but so far, that's not possible!)

What humans *are* good at, though, is noticing patterns. The Bottom-Up brain is extremely powerful—far more powerful than any computer yet built.

As you gather problem-solving tools, the task becomes **knowing when to apply which tool.** This task becomes harder as problem structures become more complex. But if you deploy your Bottom-Up bloodhound according to a general problem-solving process such as *Understand, Plan, Solve*, then you can count on the bloodhound to notice the relevant aspects of the problem—the aspects that tell you which tool to use.

0

You can break down *Understand, Plan, Solve* (UPS) into several discrete steps:

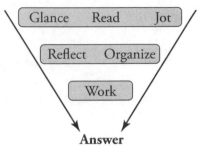

Understand   *Glance* at the problem briefly:
                    does anything stand out?

                    Read the problem.

                    Jot down any obvious formulas or numbers.

Plan   *Reflect* on what you were given:
                    what clues might help tell you
                    how to approach this problem?

                    Organize your approach:
                    choose a solution path.

Solve   *Work* the problem!

You'll get lots of practice using the UPS process throughout this guide.

Learning How To Think

This book is intended to make you smarter.

It is also intended to make you *scrappier*.

That description encompasses two main ideas: employing GMAT strategies as well as textbook solution methods and knowing when to let go.

If you have traditionally been good at paper-based standardized tests, then you may be used to solving practically every problem the *"textbook"* way. Problems that forced you to get down & dirty—to work backwards from the choices, to estimate and eliminate—may have annoyed you.

A major purpose of this book is to help you learn to choose the best GMAT approach. On the hardest quant problems, the textbook approach is often *not* the best GMAT approach.

Unfortunately, advanced test-takers are sometimes very stubborn. Sometimes they feel they *should* solve a problem according to some theoretical approach. Or they fail to move to Plan B or C rapidly enough, so they don't have enough gas in the tank to execute that plan. In the end, they might wind up guessing purely at random—and that's a shame.

GMAT problems often have **back doors**—ways to solve that don't involve crazy computation or genius-level insights. Remember that in theory, GMAT problems can all be solved in two minutes. Simply by searching for the back door, you might avoid all the bear traps that the problem writer set out by the front door!

In addition to learning alternative solution methods, you also need to learn when to *let go*. As you know, the GMAT is an adaptive test. If you keep getting questions right, the test will keep getting harder... and harder...and harder...

At some point, there will appear a monster problem, one that announces "I must break you." In your battle with this problem, you could actually *lose* the bigger war—even if you ultimately conquer this particular problem. Maybe it takes you eight minutes, or it beats you up so badly that your head starts pounding. This will take its toll on your score.

This will happen to *everyone*, no matter how good you are at the GMAT. Why?

The GMAT is not an academic test, though it certainly appears to be. Business schools are primarily interested in whether you're going to be an effective business person. Good business people are able to assess a situation rapidly, manage scarce resources, distinguish between good opportunities and bad ones, and make decisions accordingly.

The GMAT wants to put you in a situation where the best decision is, in fact, to guess and move on, because business schools are interested in learning whether you have the presence of mind to recognize a bad opportunity and the discipline to let that "opportunity" go.

Show the GMAT that you know how to manage your scarce resources (time and mental energy) and that you can recognize and cut off a bad opportunity!

Plan of This Book

The rest of this book has three parts:

Part I: Question Formats	Chapter 1 – Problem Solving: Advanced Principles Chapter 2 – Problem Solving: Strategies & Tactics Chapter 3 – Data Sufficiency: Principles Chapter 4 – Data Sufficiency: Strategies & Tactics
Part II: Cross-Topic Content	Chapter 5 – Pattern Recognition Chapter 6 – Common Terms & Quadratic Templates Chapter 7 – Visual Solutions Chapter 8 – Hybrid Problems
Part III: Workouts	Workouts 1–15: 15 sets of 10 problems each

The four chapters in Part I focus on principles, strategies, and tactics related to the two types of GMAT math problems: Problem Solving and Data Sufficiency. The next four chapters, Part II, focus on techniques that apply across several topics but are more specific than the approaches in Part I.

0

Each of the eight chapters in Part I and Part II contains

> **Try-It Problems**, embedded throughout the text, and
> **Problem Sets** at the end of the chapter.

Many of these problems will be GMAT-like in format, but many will not.

Part III contains sets of GMAT-like **Workout Problems**, designed to exercise your skills as if you were taking the GMAT and seeing its hardest problems. Several of these sets contain clusters of problems relating to the chapters in Parts I and II, although the problems within each set do not all resemble each other in obvious ways. Other Workout Problem sets are mixed by both approach and topic.

Note that these problems are *not* arranged in order of difficulty! Also, you should know that some of these problems draw on advanced content covered in the five Manhattan Prep Strategy Guides devoted to math.

Solutions to Try-It Problems

If you haven't tried to solve the first three *Try-It* problems on page 14, then go back and try them now. Think about how to get your Top-Down brain and your Bottom-Up brain to work together like a detective and a bloodhound. Come back when you've tackled the problems even if you don't get yourself to an answer (though, if so, do make a guess).

In these solutions, we'll outline sample dialogues between the Top-Down detective and the Bottom-Up bloodhound.

Try-It #0-1

> A jar is filled with red, white, and blue tokens that are equivalent except for their color. The chance of randomly selecting a red token, replacing it, then randomly selecting a white token is the same as the chance of randomly selecting a blue token. If the number of tokens of every color is a multiple of 3, what is the smallest possible total number of tokens in the jar?
>
> (A) 9   (B) 12   (C) 15   (D) 18   (E) 21

Solution to Try-It #0-1

… **jar** is filled with **red, white, and blue tokens** … **chance** of **randomly** selecting …	TD: "I need to *Understand* this problem first. There's a jar, and it's got red, white, and blue 'tokens' in it." *BU notices "chance" and "randomly." That's probability.* TD: "All right, this is a probability problem. Now, what's the situation?" *BU notices that there are two situations.*
… **chance of** randomly selecting **a red token**, replacing it, **then** randomly selecting **a white token** is the **same** as the **chance of** randomly selecting **a blue token**.	TD: "Let's rephrase. In simpler words, if I pick a red, then a white, that's the same chance as if I pick a blue. *Jot* that down. Okay, what else?"
… number of tokens of every color is a multiple of 3 …	*BU doesn't want to deal with this "multiple of 3" thing yet.*
… **smallest possible total number** of tokens in the jar?	TD: "Okay, what are they asking me?" *BU notices "smallest possible total number." Glances at answer choices. They're small, but not tiny. Hmm.*
$$\frac{R}{R+W+B} \times \frac{W}{R+W+B} = \frac{B}{R+W+B}$$ $$\frac{RW}{\left(R+W+B\right)^2} = \frac{B}{R+W+B}$$ $$RW = B\left(R+W+B\right)$$ $$RW = BR + BW + B^2$$	TD: "Let's *Reflect* for a moment to figure out a *Plan*. How can I approach this? How about algebra—if I name the number of each color, then I can represent each fact and also what I'm looking for. Okay, I use R, W, and B. Make probability fractions. Multiply red and white fractions. Simplify algebraically." *BU is now unsure. No obvious path forward.*
… The chance of randomly selecting a red token, replacing it, then randomly selecting a white token is the same as the chance of randomly selecting a blue token …	TD: "Let's start over conceptually. Reread the problem. Can I learn anything interesting?" *BU notices that blues are different.* TD: "How are blues different? Hmm. Picking a red, then a white is as likely as picking a blue. What does that mean?" *BU notices that it's unlikely to pick a blue. So there aren't many blues, compared to reds or whites.*

0

Fewer blues than reds or whites.

$B < R$ and $B < W$

In the very first equation above, each fraction on the left is less than 1, so their product is even smaller.

The denominators of the three fractions are all the same.

So the numerator of the product (B) must be smaller than either of the other numerators (R and W).

… If the number of tokens of every color is a multiple of 3, what is the smallest possible total number of tokens in the jar?

$$B = 3$$
$$RW = 3R + 3W + 9$$
$$1 = \frac{3}{W} + \frac{3}{R} + \frac{9}{RW}$$

Neither R nor W can equal 3 (since B is smaller than either).

Let $R = W = 6$.

(A) and (B) are out now. The smallest possible total is now 15.

$$\text{Is } 1 = \frac{3}{6} + \frac{3}{6} + \frac{9}{36}? \quad \text{No.}$$

Let $R = 6$ and $W = 9$.

$$\text{Is } 1 = \frac{3}{6} + \frac{3}{9} + \frac{9}{54}?$$
$$\text{Is } 1 = \frac{1}{2} + \frac{1}{3} + \frac{1}{6}? \quad \text{Yes.}$$

TD: "Are there fewer blues? Yes. Justify this. Focus on the algebraic setup."

BU notices fractions less than 1. All positive.

TD: "Two positive fractions less than 1, multiplied together, give an even smaller number."

TD: "Yes, there are fewer blues."

BU is quiet.

TD: "Time to go back and reread the rest of the problem."

BU again notices "multiple of 3," also in answer choices. Small multiples.

TD: "Change of *Plan*: Algebra by itself isn't getting me there. What about plugging in a number? Try the most constrained variable: B. Since it's the smallest quantity, but still positive, pretend B is 3. Execute this algebraically. Divide by RW."

BU likes having only 2 variables.

TD: "Need to test other numbers. Apply constraints I know—B is the smallest number. Rule out answer choices as I go."

TD: "6 and 6 don't work, because the right side adds up to larger than 1. (C) is out too. Try the next possibility."

BU doesn't like breaking the symmetry between R and W. They seem to be alike.

TD: "Does it matter whether $R = 6$ and $W = 9$ or the other way around? No, it doesn't. One is 6, the other is 9. Plug in and go."

TD: "This works. The answer is $3 + 6 + 9 = 18$."

The correct answer is **(D)**. Let's look at another pathway—one that moves more quickly to the back door.

Alternative Solution to Try-It #0-1

… **chance** of randomly selecting …	*BU notices "chance." BU doesn't like probability.* TD: "Oh man, probability. Okay, let's make sense of this and see whether there are any back doors. That's the *Plan*."
… the number of tokens of every color is a **multiple of 3** …	*BU notices that there are only limited possibilities for each number.* TD: "Okay, every quantity is a multiple of 3. That simplifies things. There are 3, 6, 9, etc. of each color."
	BU is alert—what about 0?
A jar is filled with red, white, and blue tokens …	TD: "What about 0? Hmm… The wording at the beginning assumes that there actually are tokens of each color. So there can't be 0 tokens of any kind."
(A) 9 (B) 12 (C) 15 (D) 18 (E) 21	TD: "Now let's look at the answer51 choices."
(A) 9	*BU notices that they're small.* TD: "Try plugging in the choices. Let's start at the easy end—in this case, the smallest number." *BU notices 9 = 3 + 3 + 3.*
Select a red: 3/9 = 1/3 Select a white: 3/9 = 1/3 1/3 × 1/3 = 1/9, which is not "select a blue" (3/9)	TD: "The only possible way to have 9 total tokens is to have 3 reds, 3 whites, and 3 blues. So…does that work? Plug into probability formula."
~~(A) 9~~ (B) 12 (C) 15 (D) 18 (E) 21 (B) 12	TD: "No, that doesn't work. This is good. Knock out (A). Let's keep going. Try (B)." *BU notices 12 = 3 + 3 + 6.*
	TD: "Only way to have 12 total is 3, 3, and 6. Which one's which… picking a red and then a white is the same as picking a blue, so the blue should be one of the 3's. Let's say red is 3 and white is 6."
Select a red: 3/12 = 1/4 Select a white: 6/12 = 1/2 1/4 × 1/2 = 1/8, which is not "select a blue" (3/12)	
~~(A) 9~~ ~~(B) 12~~ (C) 15 (D) 18 (E) 21	TD: "That doesn't work either. Knock out (B). Keep going."
(C) 15	*BU notices 15 has a few options.*

Select a red: 6/15 = 2/5 Select a white: 6/15 = 2/5 2/5 × 2/5 = 4/25, which is not "select a blue" (3/15)	TD: "I can make 15 by 3, 6, and 6 or by 3, 3, and 9. Try 3–6–6; make blue the 3."
3/15 × 9/15 = 3/25, which is not "select a blue" (3/15)	TD: "Nope. What about 3–3–9."
(A) 9 (B) 12 (C) 15 (D) 18 (E) 21 (D) 18	TD: "Knock out (C). Try (D)." TD: "Maybe 3-6-9 first. Make blue the 3."
6/18 × 9/18 = 1/3 × 1/2 = 1/6 = 3/18, which IS "select a blue"	TD: "Thank goodness! Answer's (D)."

Many people find this second approach less stressful and more efficient than the textbook approach. In fact, there is no way to find the right answer by pure algebra. Ultimately, you have to test suitable numbers.

Try-It #0-2

> Arrow $\overline{AB}$, which is a line segment exactly 5 units long with an arrowhead at A, is to be constructed in the xy-plane. The x- and y-coordinates of A and B are to be integers that satisfy the inequalities $0 \le x \le 9$ and $0 \le y \le 9$. How many different arrows with these properties can be constructed?
>
> (A) 50   (B) 168   (C) 200   (D) 368   (E) 536

Solution to Try-It #0-2

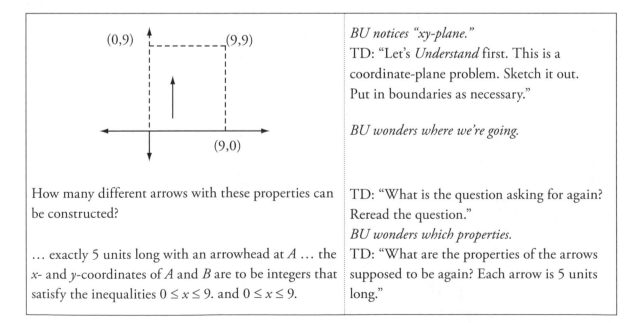

	BU notices "xy-plane." TD: "Let's *Understand* first. This is a coordinate-plane problem. Sketch it out. Put in boundaries as necessary." *BU wonders where we're going.*
How many different arrows with these properties can be constructed?	TD: "What is the question asking for again? Reread the question." *BU wonders which properties.*
… exactly 5 units long with an arrowhead at A … the x- and y-coordinates of A and B are to be integers that satisfy the inequalities $0 \le x \le 9$. and $0 \le x \le 9$.	TD: "What are the properties of the arrows supposed to be again? Each arrow is 5 units long."

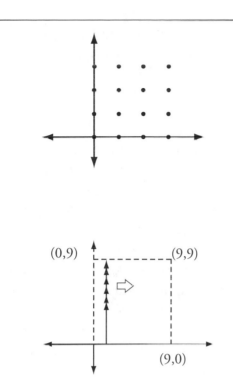

In one column, there are 5 positions for the arrowhead: $y = 5, 6, 7, 8,$ or 9. That's the same as $9 - 5 + 1$, by the way.

There are 10 identical columns: $x = 0$ through $x = 9$. $5 \times 10 = 50$ possible positions for the arrow pointing straight up.

$50 \times 2 = 100$ possible positions for the arrow if it points straight up or to the right.

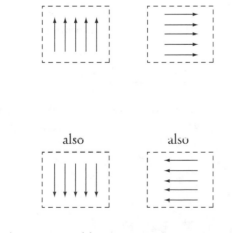

$50 \times 4 = 200$ possible positions

BU notices "integers" and "coordinates" and pictures a pegboard.

TD: "*Reflect.* The tip and the end of the arrow have to touch holes in the pegboard exactly. Okay. The *Plan* is to start counting. How to *Organize?*"

BU imagines many possible arrows. Brute force can't be the right way forward. The arrows can point in all sorts of different ways.

TD: "Let's simplify the *Plan.* Let's *focus* on just one orientation of arrows—pointing straight up. Draw this situation. How many places can the arrow be?"

BU wants to go up & down, then right & left.

TD: "Count the positions in *one* column, then multiply by the number of columns. Be careful to count endpoints."

TD: "Great. I've *Solved* one part. Other possibilities?"

BU notices the square is the same vertically as horizontally. Go right.
TD: "I get the same result for arrows pointing right. 50 more positions. Is that it? Am I done?"

BU wonders about "down" and "left"?
TD: "These arrows can point straight *down* or straight *left*, too. Those would have the same result. So there are 50 positions in each of the four directions. Calculate at this point and evaluate answers. Eliminate (A) and (B)."

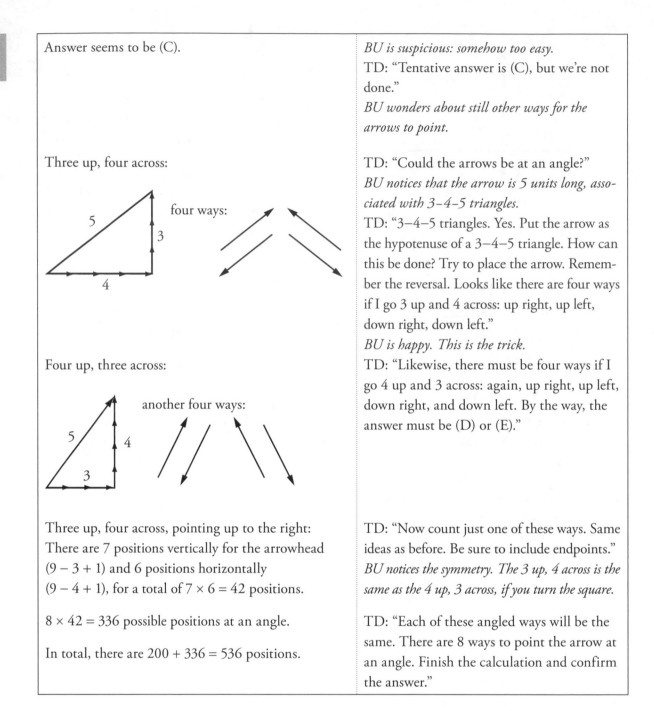

Answer seems to be (C).

Three up, four across:

four ways:

Four up, three across:

another four ways:

Three up, four across, pointing up to the right:
There are 7 positions vertically for the arrowhead
$(9 - 3 + 1)$ and 6 positions horizontally
$(9 - 4 + 1)$, for a total of $7 \times 6 = 42$ positions.

$8 \times 42 = 336$ possible positions at an angle.

In total, there are $200 + 336 = 536$ positions.

BU is suspicious: somehow too easy.
TD: "Tentative answer is (C), but we're not done."
BU wonders about still other ways for the arrows to point.

TD: "Could the arrows be at an angle?"
BU notices that the arrow is 5 units long, associated with 3–4–5 triangles.
TD: "3–4–5 triangles. Yes. Put the arrow as the hypotenuse of a 3–4–5 triangle. How can this be done? Try to place the arrow. Remember the reversal. Looks like there are four ways if I go 3 up and 4 across: up right, up left, down right, down left."
BU is happy. This is the trick.
TD: "Likewise, there must be four ways if I go 4 up and 3 across: again, up right, up left, down right, and down left. By the way, the answer must be (D) or (E)."

TD: "Now count just one of these ways. Same ideas as before. Be sure to include endpoints."
BU notices the symmetry. The 3 up, 4 across is the same as the 4 up, 3 across, if you turn the square.

TD: "Each of these angled ways will be the same. There are 8 ways to point the arrow at an angle. Finish the calculation and confirm the answer."

The correct answer is **(E)**. There isn't much of an alternative to the approach above. With counting problems, it can often be very difficult to estimate the answer or work backwards from the answer choices.

Try-It #0-3.

In the diagram to the right, the value of *x* is closest to which of the following?

(A) $2+\sqrt{2}$ (B) 2   (C) $\sqrt{3}$ (D) $\sqrt{2}$ (E) 1

Solution to Try-It #0-3

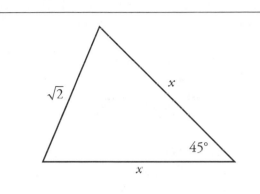

TD: "Okay, let's *Understand* this. Redraw the figure. The problem wants the value of *x*. Now… how about a *Plan*?"

BU notices this is an isosceles triangle, because there are two sides labeled x. How about the two equal angles?

$180° − 45° = 135°$.
Divide 135° equally across the two missing angles. So each angle is 67.5°.

TD: "Figure out the two missing angles. Use the 180° rule."

BU doesn't recognize this triangle.

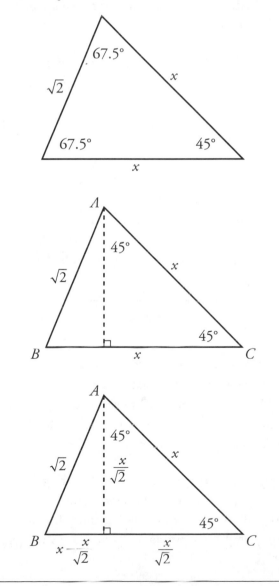

TD: "Hmm… Here's a *Plan*: add a perpendicular line to make right triangles. Drop the line from the top point. Let's label corners while we're at it. Now fill in angles."

BU notices 45−45−90 and is happy.

TD: "Use the 45−45−90 to write expressions for its sides. Then side $\overline{BC}$ can be split up into 2 pieces, and I can set up the Pythagorean theorem."

BU feels that this process is kind of ugly.

$$\left(\frac{x}{\sqrt{2}}\right)^2 + \left(x - \frac{x}{\sqrt{2}}\right)^2 = (\sqrt{2})^2$$

TD: "Let's push through. Write the Pythagorean theorem for the small triangle on the left, using the $\sqrt{2}$ as the hypotenuse."

BU thinks this equation is really ugly.

$$\frac{x^2}{2} + x^2 - \frac{2x^2}{\sqrt{2}} + \frac{x^2}{2} = 2$$

TD: "Push through. Expand the quadratic and simplify."

BU doesn't like the square root on the bottom.
TD: "Multiply by $\sqrt{2}$ to get rid of it on the bottom of the fraction."

$$2x^2 - \frac{2x^2}{\sqrt{2}} = 2$$

$$2x^2\sqrt{2} - 2x^2 = 2\sqrt{2}$$

$$x^2(2\sqrt{2} - 2) = 2\sqrt{2}$$

BU has no idea how to take the square root of this.

$$x^2 = \frac{2\sqrt{2}}{2\sqrt{2} - 2} = \frac{\sqrt{2}}{\sqrt{2} - 1}$$

$$x^2 = \frac{1.4}{1.4 - 1} = \frac{1.4}{0.4} = \frac{14}{4} = 3.5$$

TD: "Neither do I. Let's try estimating. If x^2 is about 3.5, then the square root must be a bit less than 2 (since the square root of 4 is 2). 18^2 is 324 and 19^2 is 361, so the answer is around 1.8 or 1.9.

(A) $2 + \sqrt{2}$

(B)   2

(C) $\sqrt{3}$

(D) $\sqrt{2}$

(E)   1

TD: "Answer (A) is about 3.5; that matches the squared value, not the square root. The answer needs to be less than 2, so (B) is also wrong. $\sqrt{3}$ is about 1.7. Answers (D) and (E) are too small, so the answer is (C)."

The correct answer is **(C)**.

The method you just saw is algebraically intensive, and so your Bottom-Up bloodhound might have kicked up a fuss along the way. Sometimes, your Top-Down brain needs to ignore the Bottom-Up brain. Remember, when you're actually taking the GMAT, you have to solve problems quickly—and you don't need to publish your solutions in a mathematics journal. What you want is to get the right answer as quickly and as easily as possible. In this regard, the solution above works perfectly well.

Alternatively, the question stem asks for an approximate answer, so you can also try estimating from the start. Draw the triangle *carefully* and start with the same perpendicular line as before. This line is a little shorter than the side of length $\sqrt{2}$ (which is about 1.4). Call the two shorter legs 1.2 and calculate the hypotenuse. It equals 1.2 multiplied by 1.4, or approximately 1.7. (Bonus question: how can you estimate that math quickly? Answer below.)

Now examine the answer choices, using 1.4 for $\sqrt{2}$ and 1.7 for $\sqrt{3}$.

(A) 3.4   (B) 2   (C) 1.7   (D) 1.4   (E) 1

They're all close, but you can pretty confidently eliminate answers (A) and (E). Furthermore, the answer needs to be less than 2, so (B) can't be it. Answer (C) is closer than (D), so (C) is probably it. Unfortunately, you might guess wrong at this point! But the odds are much better than they were at the outset.

It is worthwhile to look for multiple solution paths as you practice. Your Top-Down brain will become faster, more organized, and more flexible, enabling your Bottom-Up brain to have more flashes of insight.

That was a substantial introduction. Now, on to Chapter 1!

Chapter 1 *of*

GMAT Advanced Quant

Part 1

Problem Solving: Advanced Principles

In This Chapter...

Chapter 1
Problem Solving: Advanced Principles

Chapters 1 and 2 of this book focus on the more fundamental of the two types of GMAT math questions: Problem Solving (PS). Some of the content applies to any kind of math problem, including Data Sufficiency (DS). However, Chapters 3 and 4 deal specifically with DS issues.

This chapter outlines broad principles for solving advanced PS problems. You've already seen very basic versions of the first three principles in the Introduction, in the dialogues between the Top-Down and the Bottom-Up brain.

As mentioned earlier, these principles draw on the work of George Polya, who was a brilliant mathematician and teacher of mathematics. Polya was teaching future mathematicians, not GMAT test-takers, but what he said still applies. His little book *How To Solve It* has never been out of print since 1945—it's worth getting a copy.

In the meantime, keep reading!

Principle #1: Understand the Basics

Slow down on difficult problems. Keep three broad activities in mind while trying to *Understand* the problem:

> Glance   Read   Jot

Glance at the entire problem: is it PS or DS? If it's PS, glance at the answer choices to see what form they're in. If it's DS, glance at the statements: is most of the complexity in the question stem or in the statements?

Polya recommended that you ask yourself a few simple questions as you *Read* a problem. We wholeheartedly agree. Here are some great Polya-style questions that can help you *Understand:*

- **What exactly is the problem asking for?**
- **What are the quantities I care about?** These are often the *unknowns.*
- **What do I know?** This could be about certain quantities or about the situation more generally.
- **What *don't* I know?**
  - Sometimes you care about something you don't know. This could be an intermediate unknown quantity that you didn't think of earlier.
  - Other times, you don't know something, and you don't care. For instance, if a problem includes the quantity 11! (11 factorial), you will practically never need to know the exact value of that quantity.
- **What is this problem testing?** In other words, why is this problem on the GMAT? What aspect of math are they testing? What kind of reasoning do they want me to demonstrate?

Don't forget to *Jot* down any given numbers or formulas on your scrap paper.

The *Understand the Basics* principle applies later on as well. If you get stuck, go back to basics. Re-read the problem and ask yourself these questions again (within a reasonable amount of time, of course).

Start the following problem by trying to *Understand* what's going on.

Try-It #1-1

$x = 9^{10} - 3^{17}$ and $\dfrac{x}{n}$ is an integer. If n is a positive integer that has exactly two factors, how many different values for n are possible?

(A) One   (B) Two   (C) Three   (D) Four   (E) Five

Glance. This is a PS problem. The answers are numbers but in written form; this format is reserved for questions that ask for the number of numbers or number of possibilities for something. The numbers are small.

Read. Dive into the text. Here are some possible answers to the Polya questions.

What exactly is the problem asking for?	The number of possible values for n. This means that n might have multiple possible values. In fact, it probably can take on more than one value. I may not need these actual values. I just need to count them.
What are the quantities I care about?	I'm given x and n as variables. These are the quantities I care about.
What do I know?	$x = 9^{10} - 3^{17}$ That is, $x =$ a specific large integer, expressed in terms of powers of 9 and 3. $\dfrac{x}{n}$ is an integer. That is, x is divisible by n, or n is a factor of x. Finally, n is a positive integer that has exactly two factors. Prime numbers have exactly two factors. So I can rephrase the information: n is prime. (Primes are always positive.).
What *don't* I know?	Here's something I don't know: I don't know the value of x as a series of digits. Using a calculator or Excel, I could find out that x equals 3,357,644,238. But I don't know this number at the outset. Moreover, because this calculation is far too cumbersome, it must be the case that I don't *need* to find this number.
What is this problem testing?	From the foregoing, I can infer that this problem is testing *Divisibility & Primes*. I will probably also need to manipulate exponents, since I see them in the expression for x.

You can ask these questions in whatever order is most helpful for the problem. For instance, you might not look at what the problem is asking for until you've understood the given information.

Jot. As you decide that a piece of information is important, jot it down on your scrap paper. At this point, your scrap paper might look something like this:

$$\frac{x}{n} = \text{int} \quad n = \text{prime}$$
$$x = 9^{10} - 3^{17}$$

Principle #2: Build a Plan

Next, think about *how* you will solve the problem.

Reflect   Organize

Reflect. Here are some Polya questions that help you think about what you know and come up with a *Plan*.

Is a good approach already obvious?	From your answers above, you may already see a way to reach the answer. If you can envision the rough outlines of the right path, then go ahead and get started.
If not, what in the problem can help me figure out a good approach?	If you are stuck, look for particular *clues* to tell you what to do next. Revisit your answers to the basic questions. What do those answers mean? Can you rephrase or reword them? Can you combine two pieces of information in any way, or can you rephrase the question, given everything you know?
Can I remember a similar problem?	Try relating the problem to other problems you've faced. This can help you categorize the problem or recall a solution process.

Organize. For the Try-It #1-1 problem, some of the information is already rephrased (re-organized). Go further now, combining information and simplifying the question.

Given:	n is a prime number AND n is a factor of x
Combined:	**n is a prime factor of x**
Question:	How many different values for n are possible?
Combined:	How many different values for n, **a prime factor of x**, are possible?
Rephrased:	**How many distinct prime factors does x have?**

You need the prime factorization of x. Notice that n is not even in the question anymore. The variable n just gave you a way to ask this underlying question.

Consider the other given fact: $x = 9^{10} - 3^{17}$. It can be helpful initially to put certain complicated facts to the side. At this stage, however, you know that you need the prime factors of x. So now you have the beginning of a plan: factor this expression into its primes.

Principle #3: Solve—and Put Pen to Paper

The third step is to do the work: *Solve*.

Work

You'll want to execute that solution in an error-free way—it would be terrible to get all the thinking right, then make a careless computational mistake. That's why we say you should *Put Pen to Paper*.

In the expression $9^{10} - 3^{17}$, the 3 is prime but the 9 is not. Since the problem is asking about prime factors, rewrite the equation in terms of prime numbers:

$$x = (3^2)^{10} - 3^{17} = 3^{20} - 3^{17}$$

Next, pull out a common factor from both terms. The largest common factor is 3^{17}:

$$x = 3^{20} - 3^{17} = 3^{17}(3^3 - 1) = 3^{17}(27 - 1) = 3^{17}(26) = 3^{17}(13)(2)$$

Now you have what you need: the prime factorization of x. The number x has three distinct prime factors: 2, 3, and 13. The correct answer is (**C**).

The idea of putting pen to paper also applies when you get stuck *anywhere* along the way on a monster problem.

Think back to those killer Try-It problems in the introduction. Those are not the kinds of problems you can figure out just by looking at them.

When you get stuck on a tough problem, take action. Do not just stare, hoping that you suddenly "get" it.

Instead, ask yourself the Polya questions again and write down whatever you can:

- Reinterpretations of given information or of the question
- Intermediate results, whether specific or general
- Avenues or approaches that *didn't* work

This way, your Top-Down brain can help your Bottom-Up brain find the right leads—or help it let go. In particular, it's almost impossible to abandon an unpromising line of thinking without writing something down.

Think back to the sequence problem in the introduction. You'll keep seeing 64 as 8^2 unless you try *writing* it in another way.

Do not try to juggle everything in your head. Your working memory has limited capacity, and your Bottom-Up brain needs that space to work. A multi-step problem simply cannot be solved in your brain as quickly, easily, and accurately as it can be on paper.

As you put pen to paper, keep the following themes in mind:

1. Look for Patterns

Every quant GMAT problem has a two minutes-or-faster solution path, which may depend upon a pattern that you'll need to extrapolate. You'll know a pattern is needed when a problem asks something that would be impossible to calculate (without a calculator) in two minutes. When this happens, write out the first five to eight items in the sequence or list in order to try to spot the pattern.

Try-It #1-2

$$S_n = \frac{-1}{S_{n-1}+1}$$ for all integer values of n greater than 1. If $S_1 = 1$, what is the sum of

the first 61 terms in the sequence?

(A) −48   (B) −31   (C) −29   (D) 1   (E) 30

Nobody is going to write out all 61 terms and then add them up in two minutes. There must be a pattern. The recursive definition of S_n doesn't yield any secrets upon first glance. So write out the early cases in the sequence, starting at $n = 1$ and looking for a pattern:

$$S_1 = 1$$

$$S_2 = \frac{-1}{1+1} = -\frac{1}{2}$$

$$S_3 = \frac{-1}{-\frac{1}{2}+1} = \frac{-1}{\frac{1}{2}} = (-1)(2) = -2$$

$$S_4 = \frac{-1}{-2+1} = \frac{-1}{-1} = 1$$

$$S_5 = \frac{-1}{1+1} = -\frac{1}{2}$$

$$S_6 = \frac{-1}{-\frac{1}{2}+1} = -2$$

etc.

The terms of the sequence are 1, −1/2 , −2, 1, −1/2, −2 … Three terms repeat in this cyclical pattern forever; every third term is the same. Note: If you don't spot a pattern within the first five to eight terms, stop using this approach and see whether there's another way (including guessing!).

The question asks for the sum, so find the sum of each group of three consecutive terms: 1 + (−1/2) + (−2) = −3/2. There are 20 groups in the first 61 terms, and one additional term that hasn't been counted yet. So, the sum of the first 61 terms is:

(Number of groups)(Sum of one group) + (Uncounted terms) = (20)(−3/2) + 1 = −29

The correct answer is **(C)**.

It is almost impossible to stare at the recursive definition of this sequence and discern the resulting pattern.

The best way to identify the pattern is to calculate a few values of the sequence and look for the pattern. You will learn more about Pattern Recognition in Chapter 5.

2. Draw It Out

Some problems are much easier to solve if you draw out what's happening in the problem. Whenever a story problem describes something that could actually happen in the real world, you could try to draw out the solution. For instance, if a problem involves motion, you can draw snapshots representing the problem at different points in time.

Try-It #1-3

> Truck A is on a straight highway heading due south at the same time Truck B is on a different straight highway heading due east. At 1:00pm, Truck A is exactly 14 miles north of Truck B. If both trucks are traveling at a constant speed of 30 miles per hour, at which of the following times will they be exactly 10 miles apart?
>
> (A) 1:10pm   (B) 1:12pm   (C) 1:14pm   (D) 1:15pm   (E) 1:20pm

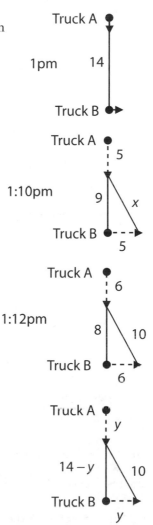

Represent Truck A and Truck B as of 1:00pm. How does the distance between Truck A and Truck B change as time goes by?

Try another point in time. Since the answers are all a matter of minutes after 1:00pm, try a convenient increment of a few minutes. After 10 minutes, each truck will have traveled 5 miles (30 miles per 60 minutes = 5 miles in 10 minutes). How far apart will the trucks be then? On the diagram to the right, the distance is represented by x.

Because Truck A is traveling due south and Truck B is traveling due east, the triangle must be a right triangle.

Therefore, $x^2 = 9^2 + 5^2$.

At this point, you could solve the problem in one of two ways. The first is to notice that once both trucks travel 6 miles, the diagram will contain a $6:8:10$ triangle. Therefore, $6/30 = 1/5$ of an hour later, at 1:12pm, the trucks will be exactly 10 miles apart.

Alternatively, you could set up an algebraic equation and solve for the unknown number of miles traveled, such that the distance between the trucks is 10. Call that distance y:

$$10^2 = y^2 + (14 - y)^2$$

$$100 = 2y^2 - 28y + 196$$

$$50 = y^2 - 14y + 98$$

$$0 = y^2 - 14y + 48$$

$$0 = (y - 6)(y - 8)$$

Therefore, *y* could equal 6 or 8 miles. In other words, the trucks will be exactly 10 miles apart at 1:12pm and at 1:16pm. Either way, the correct answer is **(B)**.

Notice how instrumental these diagrams were for the solution process. You may already accept that Geometry problems require diagrams. However, many other kinds of problems can benefit from visual thinking. You will learn more about advanced visualization techniques in Chapter 7.

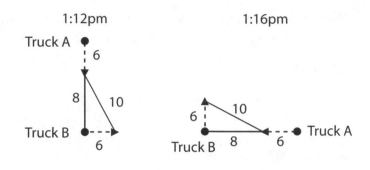

3. Solve an Easier Problem

A problem may contain large numbers or complicated expressions that actually distract you from the task at hand: finding a solution path.

When this happens, one tactic is to simplify part of the problem and solve that. Once you understand how the math works, return to the more complex problem and apply the same solution path.

Try-It #1-4

If x and y are positive integers and $\dfrac{1{,}620x}{y^2}$ is the square of an odd integer, what is the smallest possible value of xy?

(A) 1   (B) 8   (C) 10   (D) 15   (E) 28

As you read, jot down the given information.

Note that you might not immediately write down the *square of an odd integer* info if you still have to puzzle out what it means.

$$x, y = \text{int}$$

$$\frac{1{,}620x}{y^2}$$

What does the square of an odd integer look like? List out a few examples, on paper or in your head.

$$1^2 = 1$$
$$3^2 = 9$$
$$5^2 = 25$$
$$7^2 = 49$$

Are there any patterns or commonalities? All of the numbers are odd. All of the numbers are perfect squares. Therefore, $\dfrac{1{,}620x}{y^2}$ is an odd perfect square. Add that to your notes.

The question asks for the smallest possible value of *xy*. What do you need to figure out in order to find that?

If the $\dfrac{1,620x}{y^2}$ expression is distracting you, try figuring out what this would mean for a simpler version of the expression.

> *Simpler problem:* What if $\dfrac{20x}{y}$ is an odd perfect square?
>
> In order for the number to be odd, you have to get rid of the even number 20 (because an even number times any number equals an even number). The only way to get rid of the even part is to divide it out by y. If y is 4, then the expression would become
>
> $\dfrac{20x}{4} = 5x$. As long as x is an odd number, $5x$ will be odd, too.

Interesting. How can you apply that thinking to the real problem?

It's still true that, in order for $\dfrac{1,620x}{y^2}$ to be odd, you have to get rid of the even factors in the numerator.

In other words, y^2 must cancel out all the even factors in 1,620. The y^2 must contain at least two 2's, so y itself has to contain at least one 2.

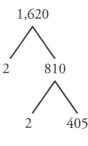

Okay, that takes care of y: at minimum, y must be 2. If so, then the expression

becomes $\dfrac{1,620x}{(2)^2} = 405x$.

Now, what about x? If you're not sure, return to your "simpler problem" thinking.

> *Simpler problem:* In the last step, in order to make $5x$ odd, x has to be odd. $5x$ also has to be a perfect square. If you make $x = 5$, then $5x = 25$, an odd perfect square.
>
> Why does that work? A perfect square must contain two of each factor: 5 and 5, for example. The expression $5x$, therefore, needs a second 5 to make this a perfect square.

Back to the real problem. Make sure that $405x$ has two pairs of every factor. 405 contains only one 5, so x must contain another 5. 405 also contains 81, which is 9^2. That set of factors already represents a perfect square, so the minimum requirement is that x equals 5.

If y must be 2, at minimum, and x must be 5, at minimum, then the smallest possible value of xy is 10.

MANHATTAN
PREP   43

You can generalize this approach. If a problem has many complexities, you can attack it by ignoring some of the complexities at first. Solve a simpler problem. Then see whether you can adjust the solution to the simpler problem in order to solve the original.

To recap, put your work on paper. Don't try to solve hard problems in your head.

- Find a pattern: write out the first few cases.
- Visualize a scene: draw it out!
- Solve an easier problem, then apply your method to the harder problem.

In general, jot down intermediate results as you go. You may see them in a new light and consider how they fit into the solution.

Also, try to be organized. For instance, make tables to keep track of cases. The more organized you are, the more insights you will have into difficult problems.

Principle #4: Review Your Work

When you are practicing under timed conditions, move on once you've found an answer or once you've decided to make a guess.

When you are done with that test or practice set, though, you are not really done! You're only just getting started. Eighty percent of your learning comes *after* you've finished the problem and picked your answer! Give yourself a *good deal of time* for thorough review, even if you answered the question correctly.

- Have I already seen a similar problem? What can I use from that problem to help on this one?
- What is the best pathway to the answer?
- What is the easiest and fastest way to complete each step?
- What are the alternative pathways? Could I have guessed effectively? If so, how?
- What traps or tricks are built into this problem?
- Where could I have made a mistake? If I did make a mistake, how can I avoid repeating that same type of mistake in the future?
- What are the key takeaways? What do I want to remember from this problem that I can apply to similar problems in the future?

Over time, this discipline will make you a better problem-solver.

For each of the five problems in the upcoming problem set, apply the principles from this chapter in the following order. Don't worry if your answers for each step don't match our explanations precisely—the point of this exercise is to get you to think *explicitly* about each step in the problem solving process:

a. While solving the problem, ask yourself:

- What exactly is the problem asking for?

- What are the quantities I care about?

- What do I know and what don't I know?

- Is a good approach jumping out at me?

- If not, what in the problem can help me figure out a good approach (including guessing)?

b. Afterwards, when reviewing, ask yourself:

- What can I re-use from past, similar problems?

- What is the best pathway to the answer? What problem clues signal this pathway? How can I work more efficiently?

- Could I have guessed effectively? If so, how?

- What traps or tricks are built into this problem? How can I avoid them? If I made a mistake, how can I avoid the same type of mistake in the future?

- What are the key takeaways? What can I learn from this problem?

Problem Set

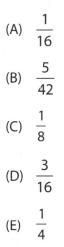

1. Each factor of 210 is inscribed on its own plastic ball, and all of the balls are placed in a jar. If a ball is randomly selected from the jar, what is the probability that the ball is inscribed with a multiple of 42?

    (A) $\dfrac{1}{16}$

    (B) $\dfrac{5}{42}$

    (C) $\dfrac{1}{8}$

    (D) $\dfrac{3}{16}$

    (E) $\dfrac{1}{4}$

2. If x is a positive integer, what is the units digit of $(24)^{5+2x}(36)^6(17)^3$?

    (A) 2
    (B) 3
    (C) 4
    (D) 6
    (E) 8

3. A baker makes a combination of chocolate chip cookies and peanut butter cookies for a school bake sale. His recipes only allow him to make chocolate chip cookies in batches of 7, and peanut butter cookies in batches of 6. If he makes exactly 95 cookies for the bake sale, what is the minimum number of chocolate chip cookies that he could make?

    (A)   7
    (B) 14
    (C) 21
    (D) 28
    (E) 35

4. A rectangular solid is changed such that the width and length are each increased by 1 inch and the height is decreased by 9 inches. Despite these changes, the new rectangular solid has the same volume as the original rectangular solid. If the width and length of the original rectangular solid are equal and the height of the new rectangular solid is 4 times the width of the original rectangular solid, what is the volume of the rectangular solid?

(A) 18
(B) 50
(C) 100
(D) 200
(E) 400

5. The sum of all distinct solutions for x in the equation $x^2 - 8x + 21 = |x - 4| + 5$ is equal to

(A) −7
(B) 7
(C) 10
(D) 12
(E) 14

MANHATTAN
PREP

Solutions

1. **(C)** $\frac{1}{8}$:

a. The problem is asking for the probability that the selected ball is a multiple of 42.

The quantities you care about are the factors of 210.

What you know: There are many balls, each with a different factor of 210. Each factor of 210 is represented. One ball is selected randomly. Some balls have a multiple of 42 (e.g., 42 itself); some do not (e.g., 1).

What you don't know: how many factors of 210 there are.

how many of these factors are multiples of 42.

What the problem is testing: *Probability; Divisibility & Primes*

The real question:

$$\text{Probability (multiple of 42)} = \frac{\text{\# of factors of 210 that are multiples of 42}}{\text{\# of factors of 210}} = ?$$

Plan: 210 to primes → Build full list of factors from prime components → Distinguish between multiples of 42 and non-multiples → Count factors → Compute probability.

Alternatively, you could list all the factors of 210 using factor pairs.

Solution:

1	**210**
2	105
3	70
5	**42**
6	35
7	30
10	21
14	15

There are 16 factors of 210, and two of them (42 and 210) are multiples of 42.

Alternatively, count the factors by finding 210's prime factorization = $(2)(3)(5)(7) = (2^1)(3^1)(5^1)(7^1)$.

Here's a shortcut to determine the number of distinct factors of 210. Add 1 to the power of each prime factor and multiply:

2^1: $1 + 1 = 2$
3^1: $1 + 1 = 2$
5^1: $1 + 1 = 2$
7^1: $1 + 1 = 2$

$2 \times 2 \times 2 \times 2 = 16$. There are 16 different factors of 210.

1

How many of these 16 factors are multiples of 42? 42 itself is a multiple of 42, of course. To find any others, divide 210 by 42 to get 5. This number is a prime, so the only other possible factor is 42 × 5, or 210. There are 2 multiples of 42 out of a total of 16 factors, so the probability is 2/16 = 1/8.

The correct answer is **(C)**.

b. The problem is straightforward in one sense: it says the word *factor* explicitly. Listing all the factors is feasible in two minutes, but you do need to be going down that solution path fairly quickly because it will take some time. It may be slightly faster to use the factor-counting shortcut, but only if you do know how to deal with the multiples of 42.

2. **(A) 2:**

a. The problem asks for the units digit. Because the problem talks about a product, you care only about the units digits, not the overall values. Furthermore, the problem provides crazy numbers; you are absolutely not going to multiply these out. There must be some kind of pattern at work. Use the *Last Digit Shortcut* (discussed in the *Fractions, Decimals, & Percents GMAT Strategy Guide*).

What jumps out? If x is a positive integer, then $2x$ must be even, and $5 + 2x$ must be odd.

Units digit of $(24)^{5 + 2x}$ = units digit of $(4)^{odd}$. The pattern for the units digit of $4^{integer}$ = [4, 6]. Thus, the units digit is 4.

Units digit of $(36)^6$ must be 6, as every power of 6 ends in 6.

Units digit of $(17)^3$ = units digit of $(7)^3$. The pattern for the units digit of $7^{integer}$ = [7, 9, 3, 1]. Thus, the units digit is 3.

The product of the units digits is $(4)(6)(3) = 72$, which has a units digit of 2. The correct answer is **(A)**.

b. Patterns were very important on this one! If you forget any of the units digit patterns, start listing out the early cases. At most, you'll need to list four cases to find the pattern.

3. **(E) 35:**

a. The problem asks for the minimum number of chocolate chip cookies.

Given: The baker only makes chocolate chip or peanut butter cookies. He can only make chocolate chip cookies in batches of 7; peanut butter cookies in batches of 6. He makes exactly 95 cookies total.

What jumps out? C and P must be integers.
$$95 = 7C + 6P$$

The answer choices are small multiples of 7, so work backwards from the answers on this problem. Because the problem asks you to minimize the number of chocolate chip cookies, start with the smallest answer choice.

Make a chart:

$7C$	$6P = 95 - 7C$	Is $6P$ a multiple of 6? (i.e., is P an integer?)
7	88	N
14	81	N
21	74	N
28	67	N
35	60	Y

Use the answer choices to calculate the value of $6P$. Cross off an answer choice if $6P$ is not a multiple of 6. The first answer choice that works is the last one, (E).

b. The two competing constraints made testing choices the most efficient method.

4. (E) 400:

a. The question asks for the volume of the box. Draw out the scenarios.

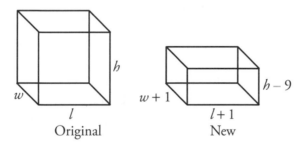

Original   New

Constraints: $w = l$

$$h - 9 = 4w$$
$$w \times l \times h = (w + 1)(l + 1)(h - 9) \qquad \text{(i.e., the volumes are equal)}$$

There are three equations and three variables. What is the easiest way to solve for the volume?

The width, w, appears in all three constraint equations, so solve for the other variables *in terms of w* and substitute into the longest constraint:

$$l = w$$
$$h = 4w + 9$$

Substitute:

$$w \times l \times h = (w + 1)(l + 1)(h - 9)$$
$$w(w)(4w + 9) = (w + 1)(w + 1)(4w) \qquad \text{Since } w \text{ can't be zero, you can divide it out safely.}$$
$$w(4w + 9) = 4(w + 1)(w + 1)$$
$$4w^2 + 9w = 4(w^2 + 2w + 1)$$
$$4w^2 + 9w = 4w^2 + 8w + 4$$
$$w = 4$$

Solve for all variables:

$$l = w = 4$$
$$h = 4w + 9 = 4(4) + 9 = 25$$
$$Volume = w \times l \times h = (4)(4)(25) = 400$$

The correct answer is **(E)**.

b. The question is complex enough that you could check your work at the end by also calculating the volume of the new solid $(w + 1)(l + 1)(h - 9)$. As always, you have to decide whether to spend that time here vs. elsewhere.

Notice that, though the initial volume formula seemed long and annoying, the calculations canceled out nicely in the end. This is common on the GMAT—common enough, in fact, to suspect that you may be doing something wrong if the algebra becomes very messy.

5. **(D) 12:**

a. The question asks for the sum of the distinct solutions. In other words, if the number 2 were to show up twice as a solution, you would count it only once.

The question implies that there may be multiple solutions, as does the non-linear given equation. What is the most efficient way to find those solutions?

There are actually two good approaches; choose the one that is easier for you.

Approach #1: do the algebra. Split into two equations, the "positive" version and the "negative" version.

Scenario 1: $x - 4 \geq 0$	Scenario 2: $x - 4 \leq 0$
$x^2 - 8x + 21 = \lvert x - 4 \rvert + 5$	$x^2 - 8x + 21 = -(x - 4) + 5$
$x^2 - 8x + 21 = x - 4 + 5$	$x^2 - 8x + 21 = -x + 4 + 5$
$x^2 - 9x + 20 = 0$	$x^2 - 7x + 12 = 0$
$(x - 5)(x - 4) = 0$	$(x - 4)(x - 3) = 0$
$x = 5 \ or \ 4$	$x = 4 \ or \ 3$

Sum of the different solutions: $5 + 4 + 3 = 12$. The correct answer is **(D)**.

Approach #2: simplify the equation and use theory to finish it off. Isolate the absolute value.

$$x^2 - 8x + 21 = |x - 4| + 5$$
$$x^2 - 8x + 16 = |x - 4|$$
$$(x - 4)(x - 4) = |x - 4|$$
$$(x - 4)^2 = |x - 4|$$

Think it through. You square a number and get the absolute value of that same number (not squared!). Only a few numbers can make that true: 1 squared equals $|1|$. 0 squared equals $|0|$. -1 squared equals $|-1|$. That's it!

$$x - 4 = -1, 0, \text{ or } 1$$
$$x = 3, 4, \text{ or } 5$$

Sum of the different solutions: $5 + 4 + 3 = 12$.

b. When a problem asks for distinct solutions, count each unique solution; ignore multiple instances of the same value. Consider whether you prefer the pure algebraic approach or the theoretical approach. Both are valid solution methods. Which one do you think you will be able to remember and use more easily?

Chapter *of* 2

GMAT Advanced Quant

Problem Solving:
Strategies & Tactics

In This Chapter...

Advanced Strategies

Advanced Guessing Tactics

Chapter 2

Problem Solving: Strategies & Tactics

Sometimes you will encounter a Problem Solving problem that you can't answer—either because its content is difficult or obscure, or because you don't have enough time to solve completely in two minutes.

This chapter describes a series of different methods you might try in these circumstances. Here, we make the distinction between **solution strategies** and **guessing tactics**.

Solution strategies are broad: they apply to a wide variety of problems, they provide a complete approach, and they can be used safely in most circumstances.

In contrast, *guessing tactics* can help you eliminate a few answer choices, but often leave a fair amount of uncertainty. Moreover, a particular tactic may only be useful in special situations or to parts of a problem.

The first section of this chapter outlines four Problem Solving strategies:

PS Strategy 1. **Choose Smart Numbers**

One of the most productive strategies on the GMAT is to pick good numbers and plug them into unknowns. Try this when the concepts are especially complex or when conditions are placed on key inputs that are otherwise unspecified (e.g., *n* is a prime number).

PS Strategy 2. **Work Backwards**

Another common approach is to work backwards from the answer choices, testing to see which one fits. Doing so can often help you avoid demanding calculations or the need to set up and solve complicated algebraic expressions.

PS Strategy 3. **Test Cases**

In certain circumstances, a problem allows multiple possible scenarios, or cases. On PS questions, the problem usually asks you to find something that *must be true or could be true*. On these problems, you can test different numbers to eliminate answers until only one remains.

PS Strategy 4. **Avoid Needless Computation**

The GMAT rarely requires you to carry out intensive calculations to arrive at an answer. Look for opportunities to avoid tedious computation by factoring, simplifying, or estimating.

The rest of the chapter is devoted to specialized tactics that can knock out answer choices or provide clues about how to approach the problem more effectively:

PS Tactic 1. **Look For Answer Pairs**

Some Problem Solving questions have answer choices that pair with each other in some way. The right answer may be part of one of these pairs.

PS Tactic 2. **Apply Cutoffs**

Sometimes a back-of-the-envelope estimation can help you eliminate any answer choice above or below a certain cutoff.

PS Tactic 3. **Look At Positive-Negative**

Some Problem Solving questions include both positive and negative answer choices. In such cases, look for clues as to the correct sign of the right answer.

PS Tactic 4. **Draw to Scale**

Many Geometry problems allow you to eliminate some answer choices using visual estimation, as long as you draw the diagram accurately enough.

Advanced Strategies

1. Choose Smart Numbers

Some types of problems allow you to pick real numbers and solve the problem arithmetically rather than algebraically. For instance, almost any Problem Solving problem that has variables in the answer choices gives you this opportunity. Likewise, you can often pick a smart number for a Fraction or Percent problem without specified absolute value amounts.

Other problem types allow this strategy as well. For instance, a problem may put *specific conditions* on the inputs but not give you exact numbers. In this case, you can go ahead and simply pick inputs that

fit the conditions. If a problem specifies that "*x* must be a positive even integer" but does not specify the value of *x*, simply picking 2 for *x* will probably get you to a solution quickly and easily.

The Official Guide for GMAT Review contains many problems that are difficult to solve algebraically but much easier to solve with real numbers. For instance, Problem Solving #26 in *The Official Guide for GMAT Review* 2015 edition asks about the remainder, after division by 12, of the square of any prime number greater than 3. Proving that there is a unique remainder in all cases is extremely tough. But the GMAT did the work for you: problem #26 couldn't work at all unless there existed just one remainder. All you have to do is plug in a prime number greater than 3.

Now, this particular problem is considered relatively easy, as demonstrated by its low number in the *Official Guide*. That's because almost everyone just goes ahead and plugs in a number. However, as an advanced test-taker, you might consider it a point of pride *not* to plug in a number. You might want to prove a "theoretically correct" answer. Overcome your pride! The GMAT is not a math test; the GMAT tests you on your flexibility of thinking and your ability to manage a very limited amount of time. Use the easiest and most efficient solution path, not the textbook math solution path!

Try-It #2-1

Andra, Elif, and Grady each invested in a certain stock. Andra invested *q* dollars, which was 40% more than Elif invested. If Elif invested 25% less than Grady invested, what was the total amount invested by all three, in terms of *q*?

(A) $2q$ (B) $\dfrac{41}{20}q$ (C) $\dfrac{12}{5}q$ (D) $\dfrac{18}{7}q$ (E) $\dfrac{8}{3}q$

This problem can be solved algebraically: write a couple of equations and solve for all three variables, then add them up. A glance at the answers, though, indicates that the algebra is likely to get messy.

Instead, choose a real number and solve the problem arithmetically.

If you've made it to the *GMAT Advanced Quant* book, then you have likely used this strategy before (or at least learned about it). At times, you may have been frustrated because this technique didn't actually seem easier than doing the math algebraically. If so, here's the missing piece: you need to learn how to *Choose Smart Numbers* in the best possible way.

Most of the time, you're going to choose for the variable given (in this case, *q*). In some cases, though, starting with the given variable doesn't make your life any easier. The problem above actually has three unknowns: one for Andra, one for Elif, and one for Grady. Take a look at the relationship between those unknowns before you decide which one is the best starting point.

Andra invests 40% more than Elif. For just these two, it would be easier to pick a number for Elif and then calculate Andra's amount.

Elif invested 25% less than Grady. For these two, it is easier to start with Grady and then calculate Elif. As a result, start with Grady, then find Elif, then find Andra.

If Grady invests $100, then Elif invests 25% less, or $75. Andra invests 40% more than Elif, or $75 + $30 = $105. Make sure to note on your scrap paper that $q = 105$.

Collectively, the three invest $100 + $75 + $105 = $280. Find the answer choice that matches $280.

(A) $2q = 2(105) = 210. Incorrect.

(B) $\dfrac{41}{20}q = \dfrac{41}{20}(105)$ = not an integer. Incorrect.

(C) $\dfrac{12}{5}q = \dfrac{12}{5}(105) = 12(21)$ = a number that ends in 2. Incorrect.

(D) $\dfrac{18}{7}q = \dfrac{18}{7}(105) = (18)(15) = 270$. Incorrect.

(E) $\dfrac{8}{3}q = \dfrac{8}{3}(105) = 8(35) = 280$. Correct!

The correct answer is **(E)**.

Note a few important aspects that will help you to *Choose Smart Numbers* efficiently and effectively.

First, if there are multiple unknowns and you have to choose where to start, pause to think about how to make the math as easy as possible. In the case of the problem above, if you had picked $q = 100$ for Andra, your next step would have been to figure out Elif's amount. It is *not* the case that Elif would be $60, or 40% less than Andra.

Rather, Andra is 40% more than Elif: $1.4e = 100, so $e = \dfrac{100}{1.4}$. Elif would actually equal approximately $71.42857. Nobody's going to want to go down that path! At this stage, you have two choices: you can go back and pick for someone else, or you can think about what numbers would make this particular path easier. For example, a value of $q = 140$ instead of 100 would result in an easier calculation, $\dfrac{140}{1.4}$, and a value of 100 for Elif. (In this case, that would still result in a messy number for the next calculation; on another problem that didn't have so many numbers, though, making one number adjustment can still leave you well within the two minute time frame.)

Second, you do not need to calculate the value of every answer choice. You can stop and eliminate a choice whenever you can tell that it will not equal $280. When you plug in 105 for q, answer (B) isn't an integer and answer (C)'s units digit isn't 0, so neither can be the right answer.

Third, practice this strategy extensively in order to expose yourself to these little variations and possible sticking points. As you become proficient with the strategy, you'll be amazed at how much time and mental effort it can save you on the GMAT.

2. Work Backwards

In a number of cases, the easiest way to solve a GMAT problem is to start from the answer choices and work backwards. Don't be too proud to try this technique either. The GMAT doesn't reward perfect math technique; it rewards finding the right answer as efficiently as possible or guessing when needed.

Try-It #2-2

If $\dfrac{2}{z} = \dfrac{2}{z+1} + \dfrac{2}{z+9}$, which of these integers could be the value of z?

(A) 0   (B) 1   (C) 2   (D) 3   (E) 4

Look at all of those fractions! Solving for z algebraically in this problem would not be easy. Instead, notice two important clues: the problem asks for the value of a single variable, and the answer choices offer nice-and-easy integers. *Work Backwards*! People often start at the beginning, with choice (A), but actually start with (B) or (D); you'll learn why in a moment.

(B) $\dfrac{2}{1} = \dfrac{2}{2} + \dfrac{2}{10}$ INCORRECT

The right side is smaller than the left. The numerators are always 2, so what needs to happen to bring the two halves of the equation together?

The left side needs to be made smaller, so the denominator needs to be bigger; eliminate answer choice (A) as well. This is why you start with choice (B) or (D)—you can eliminate other answer choices that are too small or too large without having to test them. Try answer (D) next.

(D) $\dfrac{2}{3} = \dfrac{2}{4} + \dfrac{2}{12}$ CORRECT

You can stop when you find an answer that works. If you are paying attention to how the math works as you solve, you can often get away with trying just two or three answer choices on these problems.

Try-It #2-3

A certain college party is attended by both male and female students. The ratio of male to female students is 3 to 5. If 5 of the male students were to leave the party, the ratio would change to 1 to 2. How many total students are at the party?

(A) 24   (B) 30   (C) 48   (D) 80   (E) 90

Of course, you could set up equations for the unknowns in the problem and solve them algebraically. However, the numbers in the answers are pretty straightforward integers. Try working backwards.

Again, begin with answer (B) or answer (D), whichever number looks easier for the problem.

> (B) In the original ratio, the total number of students would be represented as 3 + 5 = 8. If there are 30 students total, then the ratio multiplier is 30/8 = 3.75, leaving you with non-integer numbers for the students. This is impossible, so this answer must be wrong.

What characteristic must be true of the correct answer? It must be a multiple of 8, so eliminate answer (E). Try the remaining answers.

> (A) If there are 24 total students, then the ratio multiplier is 3; there are 9 male students and 15 female students at the party. If 5 males leave, there will be 4 left, leaving a ratio of 4 : 15. Eliminate answer (A). This ratio is also pretty far away from the correct ratio of 1 : 2, so consider trying the larger remaining answer, 80, next.

> (D) If there are 80 students total, then the ratio multiplier is 10, so there are 30 males and 50 females. If 5 males leave, the new ratio is 25 : 50, or 1 : 2. This is the correct answer!

Once you have found the answer using this technique, you can stop; you don't need to test any remaining answers. Also, you don't have to translate equations or figure out how to eliminate variables and solve. You just work each number through the problem until you're done.

As you work through an answer, think about how the math is playing out. Again, you will usually be able to eliminate some answers without actually having to try them.

3. Test Cases

Some problems allow you to choose real numbers to solve, but you can't choose just one set of numbers as you do when you *Choose Smart Numbers*. Rather, you have to test multiple scenarios to get yourself to the one right answer. On Problem Solving problems, this tends to occur with *must be true* or *could be true* problems.

Try It #2-4

> If n is a positive integer, what must be true of $n^3 - n$?
>
> (A) It is divisible by 4.
> (B) It is odd.
> (C) It is a multiple of 6.
> (D) It is a prime number.
> (E) It has, at most, two distinct prime factors.

This problem is asking about a theoretical concept: what mathematical characteristic must be true of this expression? In order to solve, you can test allowable cases to narrow down the answers until only one remains.

Note that in this Problem Solving problem, one of the answers must be correct. In this case, any positive integer n will help you get to the answer, so start with the simplest possible positive integer: 1. In general, when Testing Cases on PS or DS, start with the simplest number that fits the problem's parameters.

Try $n = 1$.

	$n =$	$n^3 - n$
Case 1	1	0

(A) Yes, 0 is divisible by 4. (0 is divisible by any number except 0.)
(B) No, 0 is not odd. Eliminate.
(C) Yes, 0 is a multiple of 6. (0 is a multiple of any number.)
(D) No, 0 is not a prime number. Eliminate.
(E) Yes, 0 does not have more than two prime factors.

Try your next case, ignoring answers (B) and (D) from now on:

	$n =$	$n^3 - n$
Case 2	2	6

(A) No, 6 is not divisible by 4. Eliminate.
(C) Yes, 6 is a multiple of 6.
(E) Yes, 6 does not have more than two distinct prime factors. (The prime factors are 2 and 3.)

You're down to (C) and (E). Because one of the statements talks about having more than a certain number of prime factors, try a larger number next.

	$n =$	$n^3 - n$
Case 3	5	120

(C) Yes, 120 is a multiple of 6.
(E) No. 120 does have more than two distinct prime factors. (The prime factors are 2, 3, and 5.) Eliminate.

The correct answer is **(C)**. You could save yourself some time on this one by recognizing that the expression $n^3 - n$ can be rewritten as:

$$n^3 - n$$
$$n(n^2 - 1)$$
$$n(n - 1)(n + 1)$$

In other words, the expression represents three consecutive integers. Test some cases to discover what must be true about the product of three consecutive integers.

Case 1: If $n = 1$, then the three consecutive integers are 0, 1, 2. This product is even and not prime, so eliminate answers (B) and (D).

Case 2: If $n = 2$, then the three consecutive integers are 1, 2, and 3. This product does not contain two 4's, so it is not a multiple of 4. Eliminate (A).

Case 3: If $n = 3$, then the three consecutive integers are 3, 4, and 5. You could multiply out the consecutive integers, but only go down the computation path if you must. In this case, you're trying to find factors and the three consecutive integers tell you that directly; you don't need to multiply them out. (You'll learn more about avoiding unnecessary computation in the next section.)

Instead, if possible, try to notice a pattern. In every set of three consecutive numbers, you will always have at least one even number. You will also always have a multiple of 3. (In Case 1, 0 is a multiple of 3.) As a result, the product will always be a multiple of 6.

You may also notice that the problem contains no upper limit. By choosing a large enough number, you're going to be able to create a number that contains more than two distinct prime numbers.

You can *Test Cases* directly to eliminate the four wrong answers, or you can use a few cases to help you figure out the theory underlying the problem, which will also get you to the answer.

4. Avoid Needless Computation

You won't see many GMAT questions that require substantial calculation to arrive at a precise answer. Rather, correct answers on difficult problems will generally be relatively easy to compute *once the difficult concept or trick in the problem has been correctly identified and addressed.*

On several types of GMAT problems, a significant amount of computation can be avoided. A simple rule of thumb is this: *if it seems that calculating the answer is going to take a lot of work, there's a good chance that a shortcut exists.* Look for the back door!

Estimation

Intelligent estimation can save you time and effort on many problems. For example, you can round to nearby benchmarks or be ready to switch a fraction to a decimal or percent, and vice versa.

Try-It #2-5

> The percent change from 29 to 43 is approximately what percent of the percent change from 43 to 57?
>
> (A) 50%　　　　(B) 66%　　　　(C) 110%　　　　(D) 133%　　　　(E) 150%

In this case, the question stem straight up tells you that you can estimate. Any time you see the word *approximately* (or a synonym), definitely do not try to solve for the exact answer.

The question stem is pretty complex. A direct translation would look like this:

$$\frac{\dfrac{43-29}{29}}{\dfrac{57-43}{43}}\times100=?$$

You can simplify things by solving the question in parts. First, it talks about *the percent change from 29 to 43*. What is this value?

$$\%\ \text{change}=\frac{\text{new}-\text{original}}{\text{original}}$$

The percent change, then, is $\dfrac{14}{29}$, but that number is very annoying. Estimate! This is approximately $\dfrac{1}{2}$.

The percent change from 43 to 57 is $\dfrac{14}{43}$. This is about $\dfrac{1}{3}$. The question asks:

$\dfrac{1}{2}$ is what percent of $\dfrac{1}{3}$?

$$\frac{1}{2}=\left(x\%\right)\left(\frac{1}{3}\right)$$

$$\frac{3}{2}=x\%$$

The fraction $\dfrac{3}{2}$ is equivalent to 150%. The correct answer is **(E)**.

The wording of the question can sometimes provide a strong clue that estimation should be used. Look for phrases such as these:

- "… the number is approximately equal to:"
- "… this result is closest to:"
- "Which of the following is most nearly equal to …?"

The test doesn't have to tell you that you can estimate, though! You can usually estimate when the answer choices are far apart.

Heavy Long Division

Very few problems on the GMAT truly require long division, even though it might appear otherwise. You can almost always approximate the answer or reduce the division by taking out common factors.

Try-It #2-6

$$\frac{3.507}{10.02} =$$

(A) 0.35   (B) 0.3505   (C) 0.3509   (D) 0.351   (E) 0.3527

At first glance, it appears that precise long division is necessary. The answer choices are very close together, making estimation difficult. However, with some manipulation and factoring, the solution is much more straightforward.

The key to factoring this fraction is to move the decimals of both the numerator and denominator three places to the right, so that you're dealing with integers. Then, you might notice that 3,507 is divisible by 7 (3,500 and 7 are both divisible by 7, providing a clue that you may be able to factor out 7). More-over, 10,020 is divisible by 10 and by 2 (10,020 ends in a 0, and 1,002 is even):

$$\frac{3.507}{10.02} = \frac{3,507}{10,020} = \frac{7(501)}{10(1,002)} = \frac{7(501)}{(10)(2)(501)} = \frac{7}{20} = 0.35.$$

The correct answer is **(A)**.

Alternatively, you might observe that 10.02 is very slightly larger than 10. Therefore, the correct answer will be slightly smaller than $\frac{3.507}{10} = 0.3507$. Guess between choices (A) and (B).

Try-It #2-7

What is the value of $\dfrac{81,918}{(10^5 - 10^2)}$?

(A) 8.19   (B) 8.02   (C) 0.89   (D) 0.82   (E) 0.81

10^2 is extremely small compared to 10^5, and the choices are somewhat spread out, so estimate:

$$\frac{81,918}{(10^5 - 10^2)} \approx \frac{81,918}{100,000} = 0.81918$$

Notice that by ignoring the 10^2 term, you made the denominator slightly larger than it originally was. Therefore 0.81918 is slightly *smaller* than the correct answer, 0.82. The correct answer is **(D)**.

Quadratic Expressions In Word Problems

Some Word Problems result in a quadratic equation. You are probably pretty good at solving quadratic equations, so your natural bias would be to set up and solve the equation. However, if the coefficients are huge, the equation may be very difficult to solve. In these cases, try testing the answer choices in the original problem (*not* in the translated and manipulated quadratic), especially when the answer choices contain easier numbers.

Try-It #2-8

> A shoe cobbler charges n dollars to repair a single pair of loafers. Tomorrow, he intends to earn 240 dollars repairing loafers. If he were to reduce his fee per pair by 20 dollars, he would have to repair an additional pair of the loafers to earn the same amount of revenue. How many pairs of loafers does he intend to repair tomorrow?
>
> (A) 1   (B) 2   (C) 3   (D) 4   (E) 5

The problem may not seem too bad…until you try to set it up algebraically. Assign x to represent the number of pairs of loafers the cobbler intends to repair tomorrow. Using the equation for revenue:

$$nx = 240$$

Furthermore, reducing his fee by $20 would result in the need to repair an additional pair of shoes for the same amount of revenue:

$$(n - 20)(x + 1) = 240$$

From here, the algebra gets complicated very quickly (the algebra is shown later, if you want to see!).

Switch to a different approach—working backwards from the answer choices. Start with (B) or (D):

The revenue in answer (B), $300, is too large. Do you need to make x larger or smaller? If you're not sure, try (D) next, and notice something very important. The revenue in (D), $200, is too small. The correct revenue, therefore, should fall between (B) and (D). The answer must be **(C)**!

	x	n	$x \times n$	$x + 1$	$n - 20$	$(x + 1) \times (n - 20)$
(A)	1	$240	$240	2	$220	$440
(B)	2	$120	$240	3	$100	$300
(D)	4	$60	$240	5	$40	$200
(E)	5	$48	$240	6	$28	$168

If you're not sure, try that answer:

	x	n	$x \times n$	$x + 1$	$n - 20$	$(x + 1) \times (n - 20)$
(C)	3	$80	$240	4	$60	$240

Here's the very annoying algebra:

$$nx = 240$$
$$(n - 20)(x + 1) = 240$$
$$x = \frac{240}{n}$$
$$(n - 20)\left(\frac{240}{n} + 1\right) = 240$$
$$240 + n - \frac{4,800}{n} - 20 = 240$$
$$n - \frac{4,800}{n} - 20 = 0$$

$$n^2 - 4,800 - 20n = 0$$
$$n^2 - 20n - 4,800 = 0$$
$$(n + 60)(n - 80) = 0$$
$$n = -60 \text{ or } 80 \text{ (price cannot be negative)}$$
$$80x = 240$$
$$x = 3$$

Advanced Guessing Tactics

To repeat, the tactics below are less universally useful than the strategies we just covered. However, when all else fails, "break the glass" and try one or more of these tactics. They're almost always better than guessing completely randomly. If you're way behind on time and you have to sacrifice a couple of problems, though, guess immediately and move on.

The examples below will not be too difficult, in order to illustrate the tactic clearly and not distract you with other issues. Of course, if you can solve the problem directly, do so! But also study the tactic, so you're ready to use it on a harder problem of the same type.

1. Look for Answer Pairs   *Certainty:* Moderate

GMAT answer choices are sometimes paired in a mathematically relevant way. Pairs of answers may:

- Add up to 1 on a probability or fraction question.
- Add up to 100% on questions involving percents.
- Add up to 0 (be opposites of each other).
- Multiply to 1 (be reciprocals of each other).

The right answer is sometimes part of such a pair. Why? The GMAT likes to put in a final obstacle. Say you do everything right, except you solve for the wrong unknown or forget to subtract from 1. Under the pressure of the exam, people make this sort of *penultimate error* all the time (*penultimate* means "next to last").

In order to catch folks in this trap, the GMAT has to make an answer choice that's paired to the right answer—it's right *except* for that one last step.

This means that you can often eliminate *unpaired* answer choices. Also, the way in which the answers are paired may provide clues about the correct solution method and/or traps in the problem.

Try-It #2-9

At a certain high school, the junior class is twice the size of the senior class. If $\frac{1}{3}$ of the seniors and $\frac{1}{4}$ of the juniors study Japanese, what fraction of the students in both classes do not study Japanese?

(A) $\frac{1}{6}$ (B) $\frac{5}{18}$ (C) $\frac{5}{12}$ (D) $\frac{7}{12}$ (E) $\frac{13}{18}$

Note that two pairs of answers each add up to 1: $\frac{5}{12} + \frac{7}{12}$, and $\frac{5}{18} + \frac{13}{18}$. Answer (A) is not likely to be correct, because it is not part of an answer pair. The fact that these pairs sum to 1 also provides a clue to double-check the wording of the question: *do* vs. *do not* study Japanese (the sum of the fractions of the students that *do* study Japanese and those who *do not* will equal 1).

To solve, you could use a double-set matrix that shows juniors vs. seniors and Japanese-studiers vs. non-Japanese-studiers. However, let's go back to the first strategy in this chapter and *Choose Smart Numbers*. Pick a smart number that is a multiple of the denominators in the problem: $3 \times 4 = 12$.

If the junior class has 12 people, then the senior class thus has 6. If 1/3 of the seniors study Japanese, then 1/3 × 6 = 2 seniors study Japanese. If 1/4 of the juniors study Japanese, then 1/4 × 12 = 3 junior study Japanese. There are 12 + 6 = 18 students total, and 2 + 3 = 5 of them study Japanese. Thus 5/18 of the students *do* study Japanese, so the fraction of the students that *do not* study Japanese is 13/18. The correct answer is **(E)**.

2. Apply Cutoffs   *Certainty:* High

You may be able to eliminate answers above or below some easily calculated threshold value. You may have to imagine that the problem is slightly different (and easier) to come up with that threshold value, but once you do, you can often get rid of two or three answer choices.

This strategy can sometimes be used in combination with an *Answer Pairs* strategy, as pairs of answers are often composed of a high and a low value.

In the previous problem, for example, 1/3 of the seniors and 1/4 of the juniors study Japanese. Therefore, somewhere between 1/3 and 1/4 of the students overall, or less than half, must study Japanese. This implies that the fraction of students who *do not* study Japanese must be more than half. You could eliminate answer choices (A), (B), and (C), because each of these answer choices is smaller than 1/2.

Try-It #2-10

The eSoroban device is available in two colors, orange and green. In 2013, 60% of the eSoroban devices sold were purchased by women, $\frac{5}{12}$ of whom purchased the orange device. If an equal number of orange and green eSoroban devices were sold in 2013, what fraction of men who purchased an eSoroban in 2013 purchased the green device?

(A) $\frac{3}{10}$ (B) $\frac{3}{8}$ (C) $\frac{5}{12}$ (D) $\frac{1}{2}$ (E) $\frac{5}{7}$

More than half of the people purchasing this device are women, and more than half of them buy the green version. If an equal number of green and orange devices are sold, then more than half of the men must buy the orange version. Therefore, less than half of men buy the green version: eliminate answers (D) and (E).

Furthermore, women represent 60% of purchases, while men represent just 40%. Pretend for a moment that there were equal numbers of men and women. If that were the case, then $\frac{5}{12}$ of women would buy orange and $\frac{7}{12}$ would buy green. On the flip side, $\frac{5}{12}$ of men would buy green and $\frac{7}{12}$ would buy orange.

In fact, there are more women than men, so the proportion of men buying orange devices has to be higher than $\frac{7}{12}$. Fewer than $\frac{5}{12}$ must buy the green version. Eliminate answer (C).

From here, if you have a strong number sense, you might guess that answer (B) is more likely the correct answer, because a $\frac{50}{50}$ split would have made the answer $\frac{5}{12}$. The actual split is $\frac{60}{40}$, so the correct value is not that much lower than $\frac{5}{12}$. But here's the actual solution, using a double-set matrix and a smart number of 100 total people:

	Men	**Women**	**Total**
Orange		(5/12)(60) = 25	50
Green	50 − 35 = 15	60 − 25 = 35	50
Total	40	60	100

15 men purchased a green device out of 40 men total, so the proportion is $\frac{15}{40} = \frac{3}{8}$. The correct answer is (**B**).

3. Look at Positive-Negative　　　*Certainty:* High

A special case of the *Cutoff Strategy* occurs when some of the answer choices are positive and others are negative. In this case, focus on figuring out the sign of the correct answer, then eliminate any answer choices of the opposite sign. (Again, this is something to do when you have run out of direct approaches or you are short on time!)

Try-It #2-11

If $x \,\square\, y$ is defined to equal $\dfrac{x^2}{y}$ for all x and y, then $(-1 \,\square\, 2) \,\square\, 3 =$

(A) $\dfrac{4}{3}$　　　(B) $\dfrac{1}{3}$　　　(C) $\dfrac{1}{12}$　　　(D) $-\dfrac{1}{12}$　　　(E) $-\dfrac{4}{3}$

The negative sign in the term -1 will be extinguished, because the term before the $\square$ symbol is squared when this function is calculated. Therefore, the correct answer will be positive. Eliminate (D) and (E).

4. Draw to Scale　　　*Certainty:* Moderate

The estimation technique can be extended to some Geometry problems.

You can approximate the length of a line segment, size of an angle, or area of an object by drawing it as accurately as possible on your scrap paper. When you take the GMAT, the laminated scratch booklet is printed with a light grid. This grid can help you draw very accurate scale pictures, and often the picture alone is enough to answer the question.

Try-It #2-12

In the diagram to the right, equilateral triangle *ADE* is drawn inside square *BCDE*. A circle is then inscribed inside triangle *ADE*. What is the ratio of the area of the circle to the area of the square?

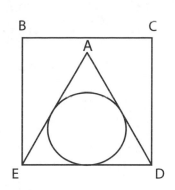

(A) $\dfrac{\pi}{12}$ (B) $\dfrac{\pi}{8}$ (C) $\dfrac{\pi}{6}$ (D) $\dfrac{\pi}{4}$ (E) $\dfrac{\pi}{2}$

2

If a Problem Solving question does not say that the diagram is *not* drawn to scale, then the diagram is drawn to scale. The circle is about $\dfrac{1}{2}$ the height of the square, and about $\dfrac{1}{2}$ the width. Therefore, the area of the circle should be approximately $\dfrac{1}{4}$ of the area of the square. Eliminate any answer choices that are far away from that estimate:

    (A) $\dfrac{\pi}{12} \approx \dfrac{3.1}{12} \approx \dfrac{1}{4}$ OK

    (B) $\dfrac{\pi}{8} \approx \dfrac{3.1}{8} \approx \dfrac{3}{8}$ ON THE HIGH SIDE

    (C) $\dfrac{\pi}{6} \approx \dfrac{3.1}{6} \approx \dfrac{1}{2}$ TOO HIGH

    (D) $\dfrac{\pi}{4} \approx \dfrac{3.1}{4} \approx \dfrac{3}{4}$ TOO HIGH

    (E) $\dfrac{\pi}{2} \approx \dfrac{3.1}{2} \approx \dfrac{3}{2}$ WAY TOO HIGH

Only answers (A) and (B) are remotely reasonable, and only (A) is really close to the estimate.

The most efficient way to solve this problem fully is to assign a radius of 1 to the circle. This way, the circle has an area of π. Now work outwards.

If the center of the circle is *O*, then *OF* = 1. Because *ADE* is an equilateral triangle, angle *ADE* = 60°. *OD* bisects angle *ADE*, so angle *ODE* = 30°. Therefore, triangle *OFD* is a 30:60:90 triangle, and *OD* must be twice the length of *OF*. Therefore, *OD* = 2, and *DF* = $\sqrt{3}$. *DE* must be twice the length of *DF*, meaning that *DE* = $2\sqrt{3}$, and the area of square *BCDE* = $\left(2\sqrt{3}\right)^2 = 12$.

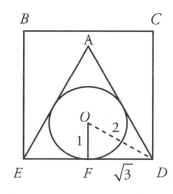

So the ratio of the area of the circle to the area of the square is $\dfrac{\pi}{12}$.

Notice how much easier the *Draw to Scale* tactic was! Will it work every time? No. But it works often enough that you want to think about using it.

Problem Set

Solve problems #1–12. In each case, identify whether you could use advanced strategies (*Choose Smart Numbers, Work Backwards, Test Cases,* or *Avoid Needless Computation*) and guessing tactics (*Look for Answer Pairs, Apply Cutoffs, Look at Positive-Negative,* or *Draw to Scale*) in any beneficial way. Of course, there are textbook ways to solve these problems directly; instead of trying the textbook method first, focus on applying the strategies and tactics described in this chapter.

1. A popular yoga studio that is always filled to capacity moves to a new location that is able to serve 45% more students. Unfortunately, 20% of the current students will no longer attend classes at the new location. If classes at the new location are also filled to capacity, what fraction of the students at the new location will be new students?

    (A) $\dfrac{25}{29}$

    (B) $\dfrac{20}{29}$

    (C) $\dfrac{16}{29}$

    (D) $\dfrac{13}{29}$

    (E) $\dfrac{9}{29}$

2. If $x < 10$, $y < 8$, and $y < x$, what must be true?

    I. $xy < 80$

    II. $\dfrac{x}{y} > 1$

    III. $x^2 + y^2 > 1$

    (A) None
    (B) II only
    (C) III only
    (D) I and II only
    (E) II and III only

3.   If $\dfrac{60}{x} + \dfrac{288}{x^2} = 7$, which of the following could be the value of x?

   (A) 6
   (B) 8
   (C) 9
   (D) 12
   (E) 15

2

4.   If $\left|x^2 - 6\right| = x$, which of the following could be the value of x?

   (A) −2
   (B) 0
   (C) 1
   (D) 3
   (E) 5

5.   If 154 is $\dfrac{37}{50}$ of x, approximately what is the value of $2x$?

   (A) 104
   (B) 114
   (C) 208
   (D) 228
   (E) 416

6. $\dfrac{1.206}{2.010} =$

   (A) 0.6
   (B) 0.603
   (C) 0.606
   (D) 0.615
   (E) 0.66

7.   In a certain clothing store, the most expensive pair of socks sells for one dollar less than twice the price of the cheapest pair of socks. A customer notices that for exactly $18, she can buy three fewer pairs of the most expensive socks than the cheapest socks. What could be the number of pairs of the cheapest socks she could have purchased?

   (A) 3
   (B) 5
   (C) 6
   (D) 12
   (E) 36

8. If $\dfrac{3}{\dfrac{m+1}{m}+1}=1$, then m must equal

    (A) −2
    (B) −1
    (C) 0
    (D) 1
    (E) 2

2

9. Simplify $\dfrac{\dfrac{35^3}{72}}{\left(\dfrac{7!}{3!\,4!}\right)^3}$

10. If $3^x + 3^x + 3^x = 1$, what is x?

    (A)   −1
    (B) $-\dfrac{1}{3}$
    (C)   0
    (D) $\dfrac{1}{3}$
    (E)   1

11. If a and b are integers, and a is a factor of b, what must be true?

    I. $a < b$

    II. The distinct prime factors of a^2 are also factors of b.

    III. $0 < \dfrac{a}{b} \leq 1$

    (A) None
    (B) II only
    (C) III only
    (D) I and II only
    (E) II and III only

12. The integer k is positive but less than 400. If $21k$ is a multiple of 180, how many unique prime factors does k have?

    (A) One
    (B) Two
    (C) Three
    (D) Four
    (E) Five

Without solving questions 13–16, which answers could you confidently eliminate and why?

13. $\dfrac{69,300}{10^5 - 10^3} =$

    (A) 0.693

    (B) 0.7

    (C) 0.71

    (D) 6.93

    (E) 7.1

2

14. $\dfrac{-(9.0)(0.25) - (1.5)(1.5)}{25} =$

    (A) −1.8

    (B) −0.18

    (C) 0

    (D) 0.18

    (E) 1.8

15. In the 7-inch square to the right, another square is inscribed. What fraction of the larger square is shaded?

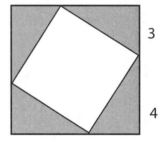

    (A) $\dfrac{3}{12}$

    (B) $\dfrac{24}{49}$

    (C) $\dfrac{1}{2}$

    (D) $\dfrac{25}{49}$

    (E) $\dfrac{7}{12}$

16. If Mason is now twice as old as Gunther was 10 years ago, and G is Gunther's current age in years, which of the following represents the sum of Mason's and Gunther's ages 4 years from now?

    (A) $\dfrac{3G}{2} + 3$

    (B) $3G + 28$

    (C) $3G - 12$

    (D) $8 - G$

    (E) $14 - \dfrac{3G}{2}$

MANHATTAN
PREP

Solutions

1. **(D)** $\dfrac{13}{29}$: (*Choose Smart Numbers*) Both the 45% figure and the answer choices look annoying, but the problem never provides a real value for the number of students, either before the move or after. *Choose a Smart Number* of 100 for this Percents problem.

> Old capacity: 100 students
> New capacity: 145 students
> Old students who will stay with the studio: 80

If the new studio is filled to capacity, at 145 students, but only 80 old students continue to attend, then the studio will have 65 new students.

The fraction of new students at the new location, then, is $\dfrac{65}{145} = \dfrac{13}{29}$.

2. **(A) None:** (*Test Cases*) Test real numbers to prove or disprove the statements. Make sure to choose only values that are allowed by the problem: $x < 10$, $y < 8$, and $y < x$.

Statement I: If $x = 9$ and $y = 7$, then $xy = 63$, which is less than 80. If, on the other hand, $x = -10$ and $y = -20$, then $xy = 200$, which is greater than 80. Statement I does not have to be true. Eliminate answer (D).

Statement II: Positive values for both x and y will make $\dfrac{x}{y} > 1$, but if $x = 9$ and $y = -1$, then $\dfrac{x}{y} = -9$, which is not greater than 1. Statement II does not have to be true. Eliminate answers (B) and (E).

Statement III: If $x = 3$ and $y = 2$, then $x^2 + y^2$ is 13, which is greater than 1. If $x = -2$ and $y = -3$, then $x^2 + y^2$ is still 13, which is still greater than 1. Don't forget about fractions! If $x = 0.3$ and $y = 0.2$, then $x^2 + y^2 = 0.09 + 0.04$, which is *not* greater than 1. Fractions between 0 and 1 get *smaller* when squared! Eliminate answers (C) and (E).

None of the statements must be true.

3. **(D) 12:** (*Work Backwards*) This problem can be solved algebraically, but not easily. You'd actually need to use the quadratic formula and the equation would turn out to be really nasty. No thank you!

Instead, notice that the problem asks for a single variable and the answer choices are decently small integers. Start with answer (B) or (D).

> (B) $\dfrac{60}{8} + \dfrac{288}{8^2} = 7$

That math looks annoying. Is answer (D) any easier? If so, start there.

> (D) $\dfrac{60}{12} + \dfrac{288}{12^2} = 7$

Yes! $12^2 = 144$, and that goes very nicely with 288. Start with answer (D).

$$5 + \frac{288}{144} = 7$$

This equation simplifies to $5 + 2 = 7$. Note that if (D) had not been the correct answer, you would have been able to tell whether to try a larger or smaller answer next based on whether (D) was too small or too large.

4. **(D) 3:** (*Work Backwards*) Typically, when working backwards, you start with answer (B) or (D). If you can tell that a problem isn't likely to have a consistent pattern, though, as with this absolute value equation, then just start at one end—answer (A) or answer (E)—and stop when you find the right answer.

	x	$x^2 - 6$	$\lvert x^2 - 6 \rvert$
(A)	-2	$(-2)^2 - 6 = 4 - 6 = -2$	2
(B)	0	$(0)^2 - 6 = 0 - 6 = -6$	6
(C)	1	$(1)^2 - 6 = 1 - 6 = 5$	5
(D)	3	$(3)^2 - 6 = 9 - 6 = 3$	**3**

The correct answer is **(D)**.

5. **(E) 416:** (*Avoid Needless Computation*) Not only do the numbers in the problem look ugly, but the problem asks for an approximate answer. Estimate.

It would be much easier if 154 were 150. What about that fraction? First of all, put it over 100: $\frac{74}{100}$. Much better! This is almost $\frac{3}{4}$, so use that fraction instead.

Translate the equation with the estimated values:

$$150 \approx \frac{3}{4}x$$

$$150\left(\frac{4}{3}\right) \approx x$$

$$x \approx 200$$

Finally, make sure to answer the right question! The answer is *not* (C), 208, because the question asks for the value of $2x$.

The correct answer is **(E)**.

MANHATTAN
PREP

6. **(A) 0.6:** (*Avoid Needless Computation*) $\dfrac{1.206}{2.010} = \dfrac{1,206}{2,010} = \dfrac{3(402)}{5(402)} = \dfrac{3}{5} = 0.6$.

Alternatively, note that 2.010 is very slightly larger than 2. Therefore the fraction is very slightly smaller than $\dfrac{1.206}{2} = 0.603$. Only (A) is smaller than 0.603. The correct answer is **(A)**.

7. **(D) 12:** (*Work Backwards*) This problem can be solved algebraically, but the math gets pretty ugly (see end of this explanation). It's easier to work from the answer choices. Start with (B) or (D).

Call the number of cheap pairs c and the number of expensive pairs e. Call the cost of a cheap pair $\$c$ and the cost of an expensive pair $\$e$.

# cheap pairs (c)	$\$ c$ pairs $\left(\dfrac{18}{c}\right)$	# e pairs ($c-3$)	$\$ e$ pairs $\left(\dfrac{18}{e}\right)$	Match? $\$e = 2(\$c) - 1$?
(B) 5	$\dfrac{\$18}{5}$	2	9	$9 = 2\left(\dfrac{18}{5}\right) - 1$ No ✗

Answer (B) is incorrect. Note that you don't actually have to figure out the value of the right-hand side of the equation, as long as you know that it will not equal 9. The two sides of the equation are pretty far apart, so (A) and (C) are also probably not the right answers. Try answer (D) next.

# cheap pairs (c)	$\$ c$ pairs $\left(\dfrac{18}{c}\right)$	# e pairs ($c-3$)	$\$ e$ pairs $\left(\dfrac{18}{e}\right)$	Match? $\$e = 2(\$c) - 1$?
(D) 12	$\$1.50$	9	$\$2$	$2 = 2(1.5) - 1$ Yes ✓

Answer **(D)** makes the final equation work, so it is the correct answer.

Here's how the algebra would have to be set up. Let c = the number of pairs of cheap socks, e = the number of pairs of expensive socks, x = the cost for one pair of cheap socks and y = the cost for one pair of expensive socks.

From sentence 1: $y = 2x - 1$

From sentence 2: $18 = cx$ and $18 = ey = (c - 3)y$

From here, you would solve the equations from sentence 2 for x and y, respectively, and plug them into the equation from sentence 1:

$$x = \dfrac{18}{c} \text{ and } y = \dfrac{18}{(c-3)}$$

Plug in to equation 1: $\dfrac{18}{(c-3)} = 2\left(\dfrac{18}{c}\right) - 1$

With the correct manipulation (over multiple, complicated steps!), that equation would eventually become $c^2 - 21 + 108 = 0$ and you could solve for the two solutions, $c = 9$ and $c = 12$. Only 12 is in the answer choices, so choice **(D)** is the correct answer.

8. **(D)** 1: (*Work Backwards*) In order for the left-hand side to equal 1, m has to be positive. Try only the three positive answer choices. In this circumstance, start with the middle number of the remaining choices. If $m = 1$, then the left-hand side simplifies to $\frac{3}{3} = 1$.

9. $\frac{1}{72}$: (*Avoid Needless Computation*)

$$\frac{\frac{35^3}{72}}{\left(\frac{7!}{3!4!}\right)^3} = \frac{\frac{5^3 7^3}{2^3 3^2}}{\left(\frac{(7)(6)(5)}{(3)(2)}\right)^3} = \frac{\frac{5^3 7^3}{2^3 3^2}}{7^3 5^3} = \frac{1}{2^3 3^2} = \frac{1}{72}$$

10. **(A)** –1: (*Work Backwards*) You might solve this one by inspection: three identical "somethings" sum to 1, so one of those "somethings" equals $\frac{1}{3}$, or $3^x = \frac{1}{3} = 3^{-1}$. Therefore, $x = -1$.

Testing choices is fast, too. In this case, (B) and (D) are both annoying numbers, so try testing (A), (C), and (E) instead. Stop when you find the right answer.

Many people would try (C) first because 0 is an easy number. Notice that it's too big. Which number should you try next, −1 or 1? Since 0 leads to a number that's too big, try −1 next.

	x	$3^x + 3^x + 3^x$
(C)	0	$1 + 1 + 1 = 3$
(A)	−1	$\frac{1}{3} + \frac{1}{3} + \frac{1}{3} = 1$

11. **(B)** II Only: (*Test Cases*) First, consider what the given information *a is a factor of b* tells you:

    2 is a factor of 6
    6 is not a factor of 2
    1, 2, 3, and 6 are all factors of 6.

Next, test the statements.

Statement I: $a < b$. A factor can be smaller than the main number, but a factor can also equal the main number: 6 is a factor of 6. Statement I does not have to be true. Eliminate answer (D).

Statement II: The distinct prime factors of a^2 are also factors of b. If $a = 2$, then $a^2 = 4$. There is just one distinct prime factor of a^2: 2. In this case, a is a factor of b, yes. If $a = 6$, then $a^2 = 36$. There are two distinct prime factors of a^2: 2 and 3. In this case, a is still a factor of b.

Notice any patterns? The distinct prime factors of a^2 are the same as the distinct prime factors of a, since a^2 is made up of a multiplied by itself. So, first, this statement is really saying that the distinct prime factors of a are also factors of b.

If a is a factor of b, then by definition all of a's prime factors also have to be factors of b. No matter what numbers you try for statement II, a will be a factor of b. Statement II must be true, so eliminate answers (A) and (C).

Statement III: $0 < \dfrac{a}{b} \le 1$. If b is 6, then a could be 6, in which case $\dfrac{a}{b} = 1$. Alternatively, if b is 6, then a could be 2, in which case $\dfrac{a}{b} = \dfrac{1}{3}$. So far, this statement looks good.

Don't forget about negative numbers! The problem doesn't specify positive integers. What if b is −6? In this case, a could still be 2, so $\dfrac{a}{b} = -\dfrac{1}{3}$. Statement III does not have to be true. Eliminate answer (E) and choose (**B**).

Note: The GMAT doesn't often test the factors of negative numbers, but the definitions provided in the math review of the *Official Guide* do allow for the possibility.

12. (**C**) **Three:** (*Choose Smart Numbers*) A laborious way to solve this problem would be to determine *all* the possible values for k and take a prime factorization of each value, counting the number of different prime factors that each value has. Ugh!

An easier technique is to pick a *smart number: one* value of k that satisfies the constraints. Any value of k that fits the constraints must have the same number of different prime factors as any other legal value of k. Otherwise, the problem could not exist as written! There would be more than one right answer.

The problem states that $21k$ is a multiple of 180, so $\dfrac{21k}{180} = \dfrac{7k}{60}$ must be an integer. In other words, k must be divisible by 60. The easiest number to choose is $k = 60$.

The prime factorization of 60 is $2 \times 2 \times 3 \times 5$, so 60 has the unique prime factors 2, 3, and 5. Thus, k has three unique prime factors. The correct answer is (**C**).

13. (**A**), (**D**), and (**E**) can be eliminated: If you ignore the 10^9 in the denominator, the division is $\dfrac{69,300}{10^5} = 0.693$. This is an approximation of the answer, not an exact computation of it, so eliminate (A). You have slightly overstated the denominator, thus slightly understated the result. Answers (B) and (C) are possibilities, but (D) and (E) are both too large. The correct answer turns out to be (**B**).

14. (A), (C), (D), and (E) can be eliminated: The numerator is negative, so eliminate (C), (D), and (E). The numbers in the numerator will add to more than −25 (i.e., closer to 0), so eliminate (A).

The correct answer must be **(B)**.

15. (A), (C), (D), and (E) can be eliminated: Ignoring the dimensions 3 and 4 for a moment, think about the types of squares that might be inscribed in the larger square:

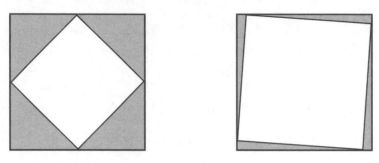

The shaded area can be at most $\frac{1}{2}$ of the larger square, which occurs when the smallest possible square is inscribed in the larger square. This gives you a great *Cutoff*.

The larger the inscribed square, the smaller the shaded area, and the more the inscribed square must be rotated from the vertical orientation of the minimum inscribed square.

Eliminate (D) and (E), since they are larger than $\frac{1}{2}$. Eliminate (C), since the labeled lengths of 3 and 4 are not equal, indicating that the inscribed square is rotated from the minimum square position.

Answer (B) is paired with (D) to sum to 1. Answer (A) is unpaired, so between (A) and (B), the more likely answer is (B). Choice **(B)** is in fact the correct answer.

There is a way to arrive at the exact answer: compute the relevant areas and take the ratio. The point of this exercise, though, is to practice guessing tactics.

16. (D) and (E) can be eliminated: Gunther must be at least 10 years old, in order for him to have had a non-negative age "10 years ago" and in order for Mason to have a non-negative age now. There-fore, eliminate (D) and (E), as both choices will give a negative result when $G > 10$. The correct answer is in fact **(C)**.

MANHATTAN
PREP

Chapter 3 of GMAT Advanced Quant

Data Sufficiency: Principles

In This Chapter...

Chapter 3

Data Sufficiency: Principles

The goal of every Data Sufficiency (DS) problem is the same: determine what information will let you answer the given question. This gives you a significant advantage. Once you know whether a piece of information lets you answer the given question, *you can stop calculating*. You do not have to waste time finishing that calculation.

However, this type of problem presents its own challenges. DS answer choices are never numbers, so you can't plug them back into the question to check your work. Also, answer choice (E)—that the two statements combined are NOT sufficient—leaves open the possibility that the embedded math question is not solvable even with *all* the information given. That is, unlike Problem Solving, DS may contain math problems that *cannot* be solved! This aspect of DS is simply unsettling. (Note: If you don't already have the five DS answer choices memorized, then you are not yet ready for this chapter. Practice with other material; then return here when you feel fully comfortable with how DS works.)

On DS problems, the issue being tested is *"answer-ability" itself*—can the given question be answered, and if so, with what information? So the GMAT disguises "answer-ability" as best it can. The given facts and the question itself are generally presented in ways that make this determination difficult.

For instance, information that *seems* to be sufficient may actually be insufficient, if it permits an alternative scenario that leads to a different answer. Likewise, information that seems to be *insufficient* may actually be sufficient, if all the possible scenarios lead to the same answer for the question.

Advanced DS problems require you to step up your game. You will have to get really good at elimination and testing cases, which are even more important for advanced DS than for advanced Problem Solving.

You will also have to get really good at simplifying the given facts and the given question. The GMAT increases the trickiness of the *phrasing* of the question and/or statements even more than the complexity of the *underlying concepts*.

So how do you approach advanced DS problems? Unfortunately, there is no "one size fits all" approach:

- The best approach may involve precise application of theory, *or* it may involve a "quick and dirty" approach.

- The statements may be easy *or* difficult to interpret.

- The question may require no rephrasing *or* elaborate rephrasing. In fact, the crux of the problem may rest entirely on a careful rephrasing of the question.

All that said, there are a few guiding principles you can follow.

Principle #1: Follow a Consistent Process

This is the most important principle. A consistent process will prevent most common errors. It will focus your efforts at any stage of the problem. Perhaps most importantly, it will reduce your stress level, because you will have confidence in the approach that you've practiced.

Follow these rules of the road:

- **Do your work on paper, not in your head.** This fits with the *Put Pen to Paper* concept discussed in Chapter 1. Writing down each thought as it occurs helps you keep track of the work you've done. Your mind is also freed up to think ahead. Many DS questions are *explicitly designed* to confuse you if you do all the work in your head.

- **Label everything and separate everything physically on your paper.** If you mix up the elements of the problem, you will often mess up the problem itself. Keep these four elements straight:

  - **Facts given in the question stem.** You can leave them unlabeled, or you can put them with each statement.

  - **Question.** Label the question with a question mark. Obvious, right? Amazingly, many people fail to take this simple step. Without a question mark, you might think the question is a fact—and you *will* get the problem wrong. Keep the question mark as you rephrase. It's also helpful to keep the helping verb in a Yes/No question:

    - Original question: Is $x = 2$?
    - You write down: Is $x = 2$?
    - You could just write down: $x = 2$?
    - DO NOT just write down: $x = 2$ ✗

  - **Statement (1).** Label this with a (1).

  - **Statement (2).** Label this with a (2).

It may be worth rewriting the facts from the question stem alongside each statement. Although this may seem redundant, the time is well spent if it prevents you from forgetting to use those facts.

- **Rephrase the question and statements whenever possible.** Question stems and statements are often more complex than they need to be; if you can simplify the information up front, you will save yourself time and effort later in the problem. In particular, try to rephrase the question *before* you dive into the statements.

- **Evaluate the easier statement first.** If the second statement looks much easier to you than the first, then start with the second statement.

- **Physically separate the work that you do on the individual statements.** Doing so can help reduce the risk of *statement carryover*—unintentionally letting one statement influence you as you evaluate the other.

Here is one sample schema for setting up your work on a Data Sufficiency question:

Scrapwork for Rephrasing: ~~~~		
Constraints: ~~~~		
	(1)	(2)
AD BCE	FACT from question stem: ~~~~ FACT from (1): ~~~~ *… and any work you do to combine these facts*	FACT from question stem: ~~~~ FACT from (2): ~~~~ *… and any work you do to combine these facts*
QUESTION: …?	ANSWER	ANSWER

Notice the *physical separation* between statement (1) and statement (2). You might even consider going so far as to cover up the statement (1) work when evaluating statement (2). Also observe that this schema explicitly parses out the facts given in the question stem and evaluates those facts *alongside* each statement.

Try this example problem, and then take a look at what the scrap paper would look like according to this schema.

Try-It #3-1

If x and y are integers and $4xy = x^2y + 4y$, what is the value of xy?

(1) $y - x = 2$
(2) $x^3 < 0$

Because the question stem contains an equation, evaluate it before considering the statements:

$$x^2y - 4xy + 4y = 0$$
$$y(x^2 - 4x + 4) = 0$$
$$y(x - 2)^2 = 0$$

Therefore, either $x = 2$ or $y = 0$, or both. One of the following scenarios must be true:

x	y	$xy = ?$
2	Not 0	$2y$
Not 2	0	0
2	0	0

Interesting. It turns out that you only need to know the value of y. If $y = 0$, then $xy = 0$. Otherwise, x must equal 2, in which case the value of xy is still determined by the value of y.

(1) INSUFFICIENT: Rather than trying to combine this algebraically with the equation in the question stem, try a couple of the possible scenarios that fit the statement $y - x = 2$. Construct scenarios using the earlier table as inspiration.

- If $x = 2$, then $y = 2 + x = 4$, so $xy = (2)(4) = 8$.
- If $y = 0$, then $x = y - 2 = -2$, so $xy = (-2)(0) = 0$.

Since there are two possible answers, this statement is not sufficient.

(2) SUFFICIENT: If $x^3 < 0$, then $x < 0$. If x does not equal 2, then y must equal 0, according to the fact from the question stem. Therefore, $xy = 0$.

Notice how valuable it was to evaluate the fact in the question stem first, and use it to rephrase the question. Then, when you reach the statements, your work is made much easier. Here is approximately how your paper could look:

Scrapwork for Rephrasing:	$4xy = x^2y + 4y$	Does $x = 2$ or does $y = 0$?
	$x^2y - 4xy + 4y = 0$	$x = 2$, $y = 0$, or both
	$y(x^2 - 4x + 4) = 0$	If $y = 0$, value of $xy = 0$.
	$y(x - 2)^2 = 0$	If $x = 2$, value of xy depends on y.
Constraints:	x and y <u>integers</u>	
	(1)	**(2)**
~~AD~~ ⒷCE	$x = 2$ or $y = 0$ or BOTH	$x = 2$ or $y = 0$ or BOTH
	$y - x = 2$	$x^3 < 0$
	$y = 2 + x$	$x < 0$
	Case 1: If $x = 2$, $y = 4$, so $xy = 8$.	If x is negative, y must equal 0.
	Case 2: If $y = 0$, $x = -2$, so $xy = 0$.	
QUESTION: Does $y = 0$? What is y?	INSUFFICIENT	$y = 0$ SUFFICIENT

The correct answer is **(B)**.

If you don't rephrase the question, it is easy to fall into the trap of thinking that statement (2) alone is not sufficient.

You can lay out your paper in many other ways. For instance, you might go with this version:

Stem:	Q: …?
1)	
2)	

In this second layout, facts go on the left, while the question and any rephrasing go on the right. Then the process is always to see whether you can bridge the gap, going from left to right.

The important thing is that you develop a consistent layout that you always use. Don't give away points on Data Sufficiency because your work is sloppy or you mix up the logic.

Principle #2: Never Rephrase Yes/No as Value

All Data Sufficiency questions can be divided into two types: **Value** questions (such as "What is a?") and **Yes/No** questions (such as "Is x an integer?"). Value questions and Yes/No questions are fundamentally different: they require different levels of information to answer the question. Therefore *never* rephrase a Yes/No question as a Value question. Value questions usually require more information than Yes/No questions.

Try-It #3-2

> Is the integer n odd?
>
> (1) $n^2 - 2n$ is not a multiple of 4.
> (2) n is a multiple of 3.

You don't need to know *which* value n might be, just *whether n is odd*. Therefore, do not rephrase this question to "What is integer n?" Doing so unnecessarily increases the amount of information you need to answer the question. Of course, if you happen to know what n is, then great, you can answer any Yes/No question about n. But you generally don't *need* to know the value of n to answer Yes/No questions about n, and the GMAT loves to exploit that truth at your expense.

(1) SUFFICIENT: $n^2 - 2n = n(n - 2)$. If n is even, both terms in this product will be even, and the product will be divisible by 4. Since $n^2 - 2n$ is not a multiple of 4, integer n cannot be even—it must be odd.

(2) INSUFFICIENT: Multiples of 3 can be either odd or even.

The correct answer is **(A)**.

Rephrasing a Yes/No question into a Value question makes the question *unnecessarily picky*. Yes/No questions can often be sufficiently answered despite having multiple possible values for the answer. In the last question, for example, n could be any odd integer. If you rephrased this question to "What is n?" you would *incorrectly* conclude that the answer is (E).

Note that the converse of this principle is *not* always true. Occasionally it's okay to rephrase a Value question as a Yes/No question—specifically, when it turns out that there are only two possible values.

Try-It #3-3

> If x is a positive integer, what is the remainder of $\dfrac{x^2 - 1}{4}$?

Some quick analysis will show that $x^2 - 1$ can be factored into $(x + 1)(x - 1)$. If x is odd, then both of these terms will be even and the product will be divisible by 4, yielding a remainder of 0 when divided by 4. If x is even, then x^2 will be divisible by 4, so the remainder of $x^2 - 1$ will be 3.

There are only two possible values of the remainder: 0 and 3. So this Value question can be rephrased as the Yes/No question "Is x odd?" or similarly, "Is x even?" Although this Value question seemed at first to have several different potential outcomes, only two are possible, so you are able to *change* the question to a Yes/No format by suitable rephrasing.

Principle #3: Work from Facts to Question

Especially for simple Yes/No questions, people often think, *"Could* the answer be yes?" or "Does the question fit the information in the statements?" They assume a "Yes" for the question, and then look at the statements.

This line of thinking is backwards—and tempting, because of the order in which things are presented.

Instead ask, "If I start with the applicable facts and consider *all* possibilities, do I get a *definitive* answer to the question?"

Always work from the given facts to the question—never the reverse! This is why you have to keep the facts separated from the question, and why you should always clearly mark the question on your paper.

Try-It #3-4

If $x \neq 0$, is $x = 1$?

(1) $x^2 = \dfrac{1}{x^2}$

(2) $x^2 = \dfrac{1}{x}$

If you work from the question to the facts, you would assume a "Yes" for the question, then plug into the statements. For instance, you would plug $x = 1$ into each statement. You would see that the value fits the equations in both statements, and you would pick (D) *incorrectly.* That's especially easy to do in this case, because this particular question is much simpler to think about than the statements (which are nasty little equations).

Don't start from the question! No matter what, when you are judging sufficiency, always proceed from the *facts* to the *question.* It doesn't matter how easy or hard the question is at that point. After you've rephrased, put the question on hold and work *from* the statements and any other given facts *to* the question:

	(1)	(2)
AD BCE	$x^2 = 1/x^2$ $x^4 = 1$ $x = 1$ or -1	$x^2 = 1/x$ $x^3 = 1$ $x = 1$
QUESTION: Is $x = 1$?	MAYBE	YES

The correct answer is **(B)**.

>
>
> In a Yes/No question, when evaluating the statements, always try to determine whether the question can be answered the same way under *any possibility* that is consistent with those facts. A *Yes* answer means Always Yes, for all allowed scenarios. Likewise, a *No* answer means Always No.

Principle #4: Be a Contrarian

To avoid statement carryover and to gain insight into the nature of a problem, *deliberately* try to violate one statement as you evaluate the other statement. This will make it much harder for you to make a faulty assumption that leads to the wrong answer. Think outside the first statement's box.

Try-It #3-5

> If $x \neq 0$, is $xy > 0$?
>
> (1) $x > 0$
>
> (2) $\dfrac{1}{x} < y$

The question is actually asking whether x and y have the same sign.

(1) INSUFFICIENT: This indicates nothing about the sign of y.

In evaluating statement (2), you might be tempted to assume that x must be positive. After all, you just read information in statement (1) that indicates that x is positive. Besides, it is natural to assume that a given variable will have a positive value, because positive numbers are much more intuitive than negative numbers.

Instead, follow Principle #4: *actively* try to violate statement (1), helping you to expose the trick in this question.

(2) INSUFFICIENT: Consider the possibility that x is negative. In this case, it is necessary to flip the sign of the inequality when you cross-multiply. That is, if $x < 0$, then $\dfrac{1}{x} < y$ means that $1 > xy$, and the answer to the question is MAYBE.

(1) & (2) SUFFICIENT: If x is positive, then statement (2) says that $1 < xy$ (do not flip the sign when cross-multiplying). Thus, $xy > 0$.

The correct answer is **(C)**.

>
>
> When evaluating individual statements, *deliberately* trying to violate the other statement can help you see the full pattern or trick in the problem. You will be less likely to fall victim to *statement carryover*.

Principle #5: Assume Nothing

This principle is a corollary of the previous principle: avoid assuming constraints that aren't actually given in the problem—particularly assumptions that seem natural to make.

Try-It #3-6

Is z an even integer?

(1) $\dfrac{z}{2}$ is an even integer.

(2) $3z$ is an even integer.

The wording of this question has a tendency to bias people towards integers. After all, the "opposite" of even is odd, and odd numbers are integers, too. However, the question does not state that z must be an integer in the first place, so *do not assume* that it is.

(1) SUFFICIENT: The fact that $\dfrac{z}{2}$ is an even integer implies that $z = 2 \times$ (an even integer), so z must be an even integer. (In fact, according to statement (1), z must be divisible by 4).

(2) INSUFFICENT: The fact that $3z$ is an even integer implies that $z =$ (an even integer)/3, so z might not be an integer at all. For example, z could equal $\dfrac{2}{3}$.

One way to avoid assuming is to invoke *Principle #3: Work from Facts to Question*. Statement (2) indicates that $3z =$ even integer $= -2, 0, 2, 4, 6, 8, 10$, etc. No even integers have been skipped over, nor have you allowed the question to suggest z values. That is how assumptions sneak in.

Next, divide the numbers in your list by 3: $z = -2/3, 0, 2/3, 4/3, 2, 8/3, 10/3$, etc. Is z an even integer? Maybe. [Note that you could have stopped computing after the second value, since you already achieved a Yes and a No.]

The correct answer is **(A)**.

> **!** If you had assumed that z must be an integer, you might have evaluated statement (2) with two cases:
>
> - $3 \times$ even $=$ even, so z could be even.
> - $3 \times$ odd $=$ odd, so z is definitely not odd.
>
> You would have *incorrectly* concluded that statement (2) was sufficient and therefore *incorrectly* selected answer (D).

Another common assumption is that a variable must be positive. Do not assume that any unknown is positive *unless it is stated as such* in the information given (or if the unknown counts physical things or measures some other positive-only quantity).

Problem Set

For problems #1–3, apply *Principle #1 (Follow a Consistent Process)* from this chapter to arrive at a solution to each problem. Note that the solutions presented later in this chapter for problems #1–3 are specific examples. Your process may be different.

1. There are 19 batters on a baseball team. Every batter bats either right-handed only, left-handed only, or both right-handed and left-handed. How many of the 19 batters bat left-handed?

    (1) 7 of the batters bat right-handed but do not bat left-handed.
    (2) 4 of the batters bat both right-handed and left-handed.

2. If a is a positive integer and 81 divided by a results in a remainder of 1, what is the value of a?

    (1) The remainder when a is divided by 40 is 0.
    (2) The remainder when 40 is divided by a is 40.

3. If a, b, c, d, and e are positive integers such that $\dfrac{a \times 10^d}{b \times 10^e} = c \times 10^4$, is $\dfrac{bc}{a}$ an integer?

    (1) $d - e \geq 4$
    (2) $d - e > 4$

Solve problems #4 and #5. Applying *Principle #2 (Never Rephrase Yes/No as Value)*, describe why these Yes/No questions cannot be rephrased as Value questions.

4. If a, b, and c are each integers greater than 1, is the product abc divisible by 6?

    (1) The product ab is even.
    (2) The product bc is divisible by 3.

5. If n is a positive integer, is $n - 1$ divisible by 3?

    (1) $n^2 + n$ is not divisible by 6.
    (2) $3n = k + 3$, where k is a positive multiple of 3.

6. Revisit problems #4 and #5 above, this time deliberately violating Principle #3 (*Work from Facts to Question*). Determine the incorrect answer you might have selected if you had reversed the process and worked from the *question* to the *facts*.

First, attempt to solve problem #7 by evaluating statement (1), and then evaluating statement (2) *without violating the information* in statement (1). Then, re-solve the problem by applying *Principle #4 (Be a Contrarian)*. Do you get the same answer? Verify that applying *Principle #4* leads to the correct answer, whereas not following the principle could lead to an incorrect answer.

7.   Is $m \neq 0$, is $m^3 > m^2$?

     (1) $m > 0$
     (2) $m^2 > m$

For problems #8 and #9, apply *Principle #5 (Assume Nothing)* by identifying the explicit constraints given in the problem. What values are still permissible? Next, solve using these constraints. Verify that different (incorrect) answers are attainable if incorrect assumptions about the variables in the problem are made, and identify examples of such incorrect assumptions.

8.   If $yz \neq 0$, is $0 < y < 1$?

     (1) $y = z^2$

     (2) $y < \dfrac{1}{y}$

9.   If x and y are positive integers, is y odd?

     (1) $\dfrac{(y+2)!}{x!}$ is an odd integer.

     (2) $\dfrac{(y+2)!}{x!}$ is greater than 2.

Solutions

(Note that the solutions presented for problems #1–3 are specific examples. Your notes may be different.)

1. (A):

Rephrasing:		L	not L	Total
19 batters total → integers only!	R			
some R only	not R		0	
some L only	Total	x		19
some R & L				
0 "neither"				

How many left-handed batters?   **What is the integer x?**

	(1)				(2)			
		L	not L	Total		L	not L	Total
Ⓐ D	R		7		R	4		
~~BCE~~	not R		0		not R		0	
	Total	x	7	19	Total	x		19
QUESTION: **Integer x = ?**	can find x (SUFFICIENT)				can't find x (INSUFFICIENT)			

2. (B):

Rephrasing:	81 divided by a → remainder of 1.
	a goes evenly into 80, and a ≠ 1.
	a is one of the factors of 80 other than 1.
	a = 2, 4, 5, 8, 10, 16, 20, 40, or 80.

Which of the numbers listed above is the value of a?

	(1)	(2)
	a/40 → remainder of 0.	40/a → remainder of 40.
~~AD~~	40 goes evenly into a.	a must be larger than 40.
Ⓑ CE	a is a multiple of 40.	
QUESTION: **Which of the listed numbers is a?**	a could be 40 or 80. (INSUFFICIENT)	a must be 80. (SUFFICIENT)

3. **(D):**

Rephrasing:	
$\dfrac{a \times 10^d}{b \times 10^e} = c \times 10^4$	Is $\dfrac{bc}{a}$ an integer?
$\dfrac{a}{b} \times 10^{d-e} = c \times 10^4$	Is 10^{d-e-4} an integer?
	Is $d - e - 4 \geq 0$?
$10^{d-e-4} = \dfrac{bc}{a}$	**Is $d - e \geq 4$?**

A~~B~~ⒹC~~E~~	(1) $d - e \geq 4$	(2) $d - e > 4$
QUESTION: **Is $d - e \geq 4$?**	YES (SUFFICIENT)	YES (SUFFICIENT)

4. **(C):** Each of the below is an accurate Yes/No rephrase:

- Is $\dfrac{abc}{6} = $ integer?
- Is $abc = 6, 12, 18, 24, 30, 36, 42, 48,$ etc.?
- Is abc divisible by 2 *and* by 3?

Alternatively, you could ask "Is there an even integer and a multiple of 3 among a, b, and c?"

(1) INSUFFICIENT: ab is divisible by 2, but it's unclear whether it is divisible by 3 (or whether c is divisible by 3).

(2) INSUFFICIENT: bc is divisible by 3, but it's unclear whether it is divisible by 2 (or whether a is divisible by 2).

(1) AND (2) SUFFICIENT: Statement (1) indicates that a or b is even, and statement (2) indicates that b or c is divisible by 3. Therefore abc is divisible by both 2 and 3.

The correct answer is **(C)**.

5. **(A):** An accurate Yes/No rephrase is the following:

Is $\dfrac{n-1}{3} = $ integer ?

Is $n - 1 = 3 \times$ integer?

Is $n = 3 \times$ integer $+ 1$?

Is the positive integer n one greater than a multiple of 3?

This narrows down the values of interest to a certain type of number, which follows a pattern: 1, 4, 7, 10, etc.

(1) SUFFICIENT: If $n^2 + n = n(n + 1)$ is not divisible by 6, you can rule out certain values for n.

n	$n + 1$	$n(n + 1)$ not divisible by 6
1	2	✓
2	3	✗
3	4	✗
4	5	✓
5	6	✗
6	7	✗
7	8	✓

The pattern from the rephrasing is apparent here: n can only be 1, 4, 7, 10, etc., all integers that are one greater than a multiple of 3.

Alternatively, use theory. The integers $n - 1$, n, and $n + 1$ must be consecutive. If $n(n + 1)$ is not divisible by 3, then $n - 1$ must be divisible by 3, since in any set of three consecutive integers, one must be divisible by 3.

(2) INSUFFICIENT: If $3n = 3 \times pos\ integer + 3$, then $n = pos\ integer + 1$. Therefore, n is an integer such that $n \geq 2$. This does not resolve whether n is definitely one greater than a multiple of 3.

The correct answer is **(A)**.

6. Revisiting #4, working incorrectly from the *Question* to the *Facts*:

Manipulating the question to $abc = 6 \times integer$ (and losing track of the question mark), someone might be tempted to check whether it is *possible* for abc to be a multiple of 6, instead of whether abc is *definitely* a multiple of 6:

> (1) $abc = 6 \times integer$, so ab is even. ✓
> (2) $abc = 6 \times integer$, so bc is divisible by 3. ✓

The *incorrect* thinking would lead someone to wrong answer (D). Be sure to revisit how to do this problem correctly!

Revisiting #5, working incorrectly from the *Question* to the *Facts*:

Someone working incorrectly might try multiples of 3 for $n - 1$ to see whether they "work" with the statements:

(1) SUFFICIENT:

$n - 1$	n	$n + 1$	$n^2 + n = n(n + 1)$	not divis by 6
3	4	5	20	✓
6	7	8	56	✓
9	10	11	110	✓

(2) SEEMS SUFFICIENT (*incorrectly*): If $3n = k + 3$, then $k = 3n - 3 = 3(n - 1)$.

$n - 1$	$k = 3n - 3 = 3(n - 1)$	pos mult of 3
3	9	✓
6	18	✓
9	27	✓

This *incorrect* work would lead you to wrong answer (D). Be sure to revisit how to do this problem correctly, so you are certain how to do so for the future!

7. **(C):**

Non-Contrarian Approach	Contrarian Approach
(1) INSUFFICIENT: $m > 0$ or $m =$ pos, so "Is $\text{pos}^3 > \text{pos}^2$?" • Yes, if $m > 1$. • No, if m is a proper fraction or 1. (That is, $0 < m \leq 1$).	(1) INSUFFICIENT: $m > 0$ or $m =$ pos, so "Is $\text{pos}^3 > \text{pos}^2$?" • Yes, if $m > 1$. • No, if m is a proper fraction or 1. (That is, $0 < m \leq 1$).
(2) SEEMS SUFFICIENT: $m^2 > m$ implies that m is *not* a fraction or 1, therefore $m^3 > m^2$. Or, if you *assume* that $m > 0$, carrying over from (1), you might do the following: $m^2 > m$ $m > 1$ (dividing by m) Therefore, $m^3 > m^2$.	(2) INSUFFICIENT: $m^2 > m$ implies that m is *not* a fraction or 1, so if $m > 1$ then the answer is Yes. BUT, contradicting (1), **what if m is negative**? That is possible according to (2), since $\text{neg}^2 >$ neg. Is $m^3 > m^2$? → Is $\text{neg}^3 > \text{neg}^2$? No!
	(1) AND (2) SUFFICIENT: Combined, the statements eliminate negative, zero, positive proper fractions, and 1 for the value of m. If $m > 1$, then $m^3 > m^2$. Definite Yes answer.
The (incorrect) answer is (B).	The correct answer is **(C)**.

Note that both solutions were hampered by inadequate rephrasing. Ideally, you would first rephrase as follows:

• Is $m^3 > m^2$?

• Is $m > 1$? (It's okay to divide by m^2, which must be positive: a square is never negative and m is also not 0, according to the question stem.)

Take-away: With proper rephrasing, other errors are less likely. But even with inadequate rephrasing, taking a Contrarian approach can save you from a wrong answer.

8. (C): The explicit constraint is $yz \neq 0$, which indicates that $y \neq 0$ and $z \neq 0$. Both y and z could be any non-zero value, including positive integer, negative integer, positive fraction, negative fraction, etc.

Making Faulty Assumptions:

For (1), a faulty assumption could be made by those who plug in values for z.

For example, if you plug $z = -2, -1, 1, 2, 3, 4$, etc., you would get $y = 1, 4, 9, 16$, etc. That would yield a definite No answer to the question, as all the y values are at least as great as 1. The (unverbalized) assumption is that z is an integer, but that's not necessarily so.

For (2), most people would want to cross-multiply, so a potential *false* assumption is that y is positive (and this is reinforced by the fact that, in statement (1), y is in fact positive):

$$y < \frac{1}{y}$$
$$y^2 < 1$$
$$0 < y^2 < 1$$
$$\sqrt{0} < \sqrt{y^2} < \sqrt{1}$$
$$0 < y < 1$$

Conclusion: SEEMS SUFFICIENT (incorrect)

These faulty assumptions would lead to the *incorrect* answers (A) or (D).

Correct solution:

(1) INSUFFICIENT: y must be positive, but is it a fraction or an integer?

If $z = 2$, then $y = 4$ and the answer is No.
If $z = 1/2$, then $y = 1/4$ and the answer is Yes.

(2) INSUFFICIENT:

	If $y > 0$:	If $y < 0$:
	$y < \dfrac{1}{y}$	$y < \dfrac{1}{y}$
	$y^2 < 1$	$y^2 > 1$
	$0 < y^2 < 1$	$\sqrt{y^2} > \sqrt{1}$
	$\sqrt{0} < \sqrt{y^2} < \sqrt{1}$	$|y| > 1$
	$0 < y < 1$	$y > 1$ or $y < -1$
		$y < -1$
		Since you're assuming $y < 0$, the rephrasing is $y < -1$.
Is $0 < y < 1$?	YES	NO

(1) AND (2) SUFFICIENT: Since y is positive, statement (1) indicates that $0 < y < 1$.

The correct answer is **(C)**.

9. **(C):** Both statements give number properties of the expression $\dfrac{(y+2)!}{x!}$, so you might glance ahead and then (correctly) rephrase the question with this in mind:

- Is y odd?
- Is $(y+2)$ odd?

A typical division of one factorial by another will involve canceling of terms, so you might try several numbers to see what the statements are really saying.

Making Faulty Assumptions:

(1) If $\dfrac{(y+2)!}{x!}$ = odd, all of the terms in the denominator cancel out, only one term can remain in the numerator, and that remaining term must be odd. For example:

$$\frac{3!}{2!} = 3 = odd \quad (okay)$$

$$\frac{5!}{4!} = 5 = odd \quad (okay)$$

$$\frac{6!}{4!} = (6)(5) = even \quad (not\ OK)$$

You might *incorrectly* conclude that $(y+2)$ must be odd, that $x = (y+2) - 1$, and that the answer is definitely Yes.

(2) If $\dfrac{(y+2)!}{x!}$ = 3, 4, 5, 6, 7, etc. then $(y+2)$ might be 3, 4, 5, 6, 7, etc., according to the test cases above in which $x = (y+2) - 1$. (This particular analysis is correct.)

Making assumptions might lead you to choose answer choice (A) incorrectly. However, you would have assumed that it could not be the case that $x = y + 2$. That assumption is unjustified.

Correct Solution:

(1) INSUFFICIENT:

$$\frac{3!}{3!} = 1 = odd \quad and \quad y = 0 \quad (okay)$$

$$\frac{4!}{4!} = 1 = odd \quad and \quad y = 1 \quad (okay)$$

Therefore, y might be either odd *or* even.

(2) INSUFFICIENT: If $\dfrac{(y+2)!}{x!} = 3, 4, 5, 6, 7$, etc. then $(y + 2)$ might be 3, 4, 5, 6, 7, etc., according to the test cases above in which $x = (y + 2) - 1$.

(1) AND (2) SUFFICIENT: If $\dfrac{(y+2)!}{x!} > 2$, then $\dfrac{(y+2)!}{x!} \neq 1$. The only way for $\dfrac{(y+2)!}{x!}$ to be odd is if $x = (y + 2) - 1$ and $(y + 2)$ is odd.

The correct answer is **(C)**.

3

Data Sufficiency:
Strategies & Tactics

In This Chapter...

Chapter 4
Data Sufficiency: Strategies & Tactics

Sometimes you will encounter a Data Sufficiency (DS) problem that you can't answer—either because its content is difficult or obscure, or because you don't have enough time to solve completely in two minutes.

Like Chapter 2, this chapter describes a series of different methods you might try in these circumstances. Again, this chapter distinguishes between **solution strategies** and **guessing tactics**.

Strategies are broad: they apply to a wide variety of problems, they provide a complete approach, and they can be used safely in most circumstances.

In contrast, *tactics* can help you eliminate a few answer choices, but often leave a fair amount of uncertainty. Moreover, a particular tactic may only be useful in special situations or for parts of a problem.

The first section of this chapter outlines six DS strategies:

DS Strategy 1. **Compute to Completion**
For some problems, you won't necessarily be able to tell whether the answer can be calculated until you follow through on the calculations *all the way*.

DS Strategy 2. **Extract the Equation**
For many Word Problems, you need to represent the problem with algebraic equations to avoid embedded tricks that can be difficult to spot otherwise.

DS Strategy 3. **Use the Constraints**
Many DS problems provide explicit constraints on the variables. In other problems, these constraints will be implicit (for example, "number of people" must be both positive and an integer). In either case, these constraints frequently determine the correct answer, so you *must* identify and use them.

DS Strategy 4. **Beware of Inequalities**

Whenever a DS problem involves inequality symbols, be especially careful—the GMAT loves to trick people with inequalities.

DS Strategy 5. **Use a Scenario Chart**

The given facts may suggest that only a handful of possible scenarios exist. In those cases, enumerate and test these scenarios in a systematic way. The Scenario Chart can help you organize your approach to these problems.

DS Strategy 6. **Test Cases**

For some one-variable DS problems, many possible values of a variable may exist, but underlying those values is some sort of pattern. You can often discover that pattern by intelligently testing numbers that cover a wide range of potential scenarios.

The remainder of the chapter is devoted to tactics that can knock out answer choices or provide clues as to how to approach the problem more effectively. These tactics are listed later in the chapter. As with Problem Solving tactics, some of these Data Sufficiency tactics work wonders when used correctly. Others only slightly improve your guessing odds.

Advanced Strategies

1. Compute to Completion

A general principle of Data Sufficiency is that once you have determined whether you can answer the question with a given set of information, you can stop calculating. For some problems, however, you cannot determine whether a single answer can be obtained until you've calculated the problem *all the way through*. This is particularly common in the following situations:

- Multiple equations are involved—particularly if they are non-linear.
- A complicated inequality expression is present.
- Variables hidden within a Geometry problem are related.

Try-It #4-1

What is the value of *ab*?

(1) $a = b + 1$
(2) $a^2 = b + 1$

(1) INSUFFICIENT: Statement (1) does not answer the question. For example, if $a = 2$ and $b = 1$, then $ab = 2$, and if $a = 3$ and $b = 2$, then $ab = 6$.

(2) INSUFFICIENT: Statement (2) does not answer the question. For example, if $a = 1$ and $b = 0$, then $ab = 0$, and if $a = 2$ and $b = 3$, then $ab = 6$.

(1) AND (2) SUFFICIENT: Evaluating both statements together is trickier, however.

$$b = a - 1$$
$$a^2 = (a - 1) + 1$$
$$a^2 - a = 0$$

$$a(a - 1) = 0$$
$$a = 0 \text{ or } 1$$

Based on this work, either $a = 0$ or $a = 1$. It would be tempting at this stage to decide that since a can have two different values, Statements (1) & (2) together are insufficient. However, this is *incorrect*.

Look at the values b can hold in these two scenarios:

a	b	ab
1	$= a - 1 = 0$	0
0	$= a - 1 = -1$	0

While it is true that a can take on different values, ab is equal to zero in *either case*. When $a = 1$, $b = 0$, and $ab = 0$. When $a = 0$, $b = -1$, and $ab = 0$. Therefore (1) & (2) combined are SUFFICIENT to answer this *specific* question: what is the value of ab?

The correct answer is (C).

> **!** In a multiple-scenario problem, be sure to compute for the specific question asked (in this case, ab) in order to determine whether the end result for each scenario is *actually different*.

2. Extract the Equation

For Word Problems, setting up an algebraic representation of the question is *essential*. It is very easy to get intellectually lazy and miss an embedded trick in the problem. These tricks are usually much easier to spot if you are looking at the underlying algebra behind the problem.

Try-It #4-2

A store sells two types of birdfeeders: Alphas and Bravos. Alphas feed 1 bird at a time, whereas Bravos feed 2 birds at a time. The total number of birds that can be fed at one time by birdfeeders sold last month is 50. What is the total revenue generated by birdfeeders sold last month?

(1) Last month, the price of each Alpha was $15, and the price of each Bravo was $30.
(2) 40 Alphas were sold last month.

From the words in the question stem, *Extract the Equation*. The problem indicates that Alphas can feed one bird at a time and Bravos two. The problem also indicates that last month 50 birds could be fed at a time, so you have this:

Total number of birds fed $= A + 2B = 50$, where A and B represent the number of birdfeeders of each type that have been sold.

To calculate the revenue, it seems you will need the prices of the birdfeeders and the number of bird-feeders, A and B.

(1) SUFFICIENT: Again *Extract the Equation* from the wording of the question:

$$\text{Total revenue} = \$15A + \$30B = \$15(A + 2B)$$

It turns out that you don't need to know A and B individually, since the question stem equation indicated that $A + 2B = 50$. Therefore total revenue equals $\$15(A + 2B) = \$15(50) = \$750$.

It's true that there are many possible values of A and B that satisfy the condition that $A + 2B = 50$. However, mathematically *every possible combination* that satisfies this equation would lead to the same revenue of $750. The number of each type of birdfeeder sold is irrelevant. In this sense, *Extract the Equation* can be similar to the *Compute to Completion* strategy, because once the equation has been extracted, you may find that the multiple possibilities for the variables might converge to a single answer to the specific question that's been asked.

(2) INSUFFICIENT: If there were 40 Alphas sold, there were 5 Bravos sold. But you still don't know the prices, so you can't compute revenue.

The correct answer is **(A)**.

> Relying on intuition, which indicates a need for the prices and number of the two birdfeeder types, someone might ultimately choose (C) *incorrectly*. Be sure to translate all Word Problems into math so they can be properly evaluated. These issues are sensitive to the exact numbers given.

3. Use the Constraints

Often, a DS question will provide relevant constraints on the variables in the problem—for example, that the variables must be integers or must be positive, or must be between 0 and 1. When this information is given, it is usually *essential* to the problem. If you don't *Use the Constraints*, you could easily end up choosing the wrong answer choice.

Try-It #4-3

If $8x > 3x + 4x$, what is the value of the integer x?

(1) $6 - 4x > -2$
(2) $3 - 2x \leq 4 - x \leq 5 - 2x$

Simplify the question stem:

$8x > 3x + 4x$
$8x > 7x$
$x > 0$ $8x$ can only be greater than $7x$ when x is positive.

On top of that, there is also another constraint given: x must be an integer. This limits the scope of the potential values of x even further. *Make note of this type of constraint in your work on paper.* Write "$x =$ int" or something similar. You could also incorporate this information by rephrasing the question to include the constraint: "If the integer x is positive, what is the value of x?"

(1) SUFFICIENT: Solve this inequality for x:

$$6 - 4x > -2$$
$$-4x > -8$$
$$x < 2$$

Since you know from the question stem that $x > 0$, you can conclude that $0 < x < 2$. The *only integer* between 0 and 2 is 1. Therefore, $x = 1$.

(2) SUFFICIENT: Manipulate this compound inequality as follows:

$$3 - 2x \le 4 - x \le 5 - 2x$$
$$\underline{+ 2x \quad + 2x \quad + 2x}$$
$$3 \quad\quad \le 4 + x \le 5$$
$$\underline{-4 \quad\quad -4 \quad\quad -4}$$
$$-1 \quad \le \quad\quad x \le 1$$

Note that it's fine to manipulate all the parts of the compound inequality at the same time as long as you perform each manipulation to *all three* parts of the inequality.

Since the question stem indicates that $x > 0$, it must be the case that $0 < x \le 1$. The only integer that fits this criteria is 1. Therefore, $x = 1$.

If you had overlooked the fact that x is an integer, you would have determined that there are many values between 0 and 1 or between 0 and 2. You might have chosen answer (E), incorrectly.

The correct answer is **(D)**.

!	Make a note of any additional information given to you in the question stem (for example, "x is positive" or "x is an integer"). You often will have to use this information properly to get the correct answer.
	Integer constraints in particular are very potent: they often limit the possible solutions for a problem to a small set. Sometimes this set is so small that it contains *only one item*.

Constraints will not always be explicitly given. The ones the GMAT doesn't explicitly give you can be called **hidden constraints**. Hidden constraints are most prevalent in Word Problems and Geometry questions. Here are some examples of hidden constraints that you should train yourself to take note of:

a) The number of *countable* items must be a *non-negative integer*. Note that zero is only a possibility if it is possible for the items not to exist at all—if the problem clearly assumes that the items exist, then the number of items must be *positive*. Examples:

- Number of people
- Number of yachts
- Number of books

b) Many *non-countable* quantities must be *non-negative numbers*, though not necessarily integers. Again, zero is only an option if the underlying object might not exist. If the problem clearly assumes the existence and typical definition of an object, then these quantities must be *positive*. Examples:

- The side of a triangle must have a positive length. (All geometric quantities shown in a diagram, such as lengths, areas, volumes, and angles, must be positive. The only exception is negative coordinates in a coordinate plane problem.)
- The weight of a shipment of products must be positive in any unit.
- The height of a person must be positive in any unit.

c) Many other *non-countable* quantities are theoretically allowed to take on *negative* values. Examples:

- The profit of a company (However, if a company *made a profit*, that profit is positive!)
- The growth rate of a population
- The change in the value of essentially any variable.

These sorts of constraints exist in Problem Solving, but they are even more important and dangerous on Data Sufficiency. If these constraints are important in a Problem Solving problem, then failing to take a constraint into account may make you unable to solve the problem. That will alert you to the existence of the constraints, since every Problem Solving problem must be solvable. In contrast, you will get no such signal on a DS problem. After all, solvability is the very issue that Data Sufficiency tests!

4. Beware of Inequalities

Whenever a Data Sufficiency question involves inequality symbols, be especially careful. The GMAT can employ a variety of different inequality-specific tricks. Here are a few examples:

1. One inequality can imply another seemingly unrelated inequality, depending on the situation. For example, if you need to know whether $x > 0$, then knowing that $x > 5$ is sufficient. If x is larger than 5 it must be positive, thus $x > 0$. However the opposite is *not* the case. If you knew that $x < 5$, you would *not* be able to determine whether $x > 0$. After all, x could be positive but less than 5, or x could be negative.

2. Inequalities can combine with integer constraints to produce a single value. For example, if $0 < x < 2$ and x is an integer, then x *must* equal 1.

3. Some Word Problems can create a hidden constraint involving inequalities. These inequalities may come into play in determining the correct answer. For example, a problem might read "The oldest student in the class … the next oldest student in the class … the youngest student in the class…." This can be translated to the following inequality: *Youngest < Middle < Oldest*.

4. Inequalities involving a variable in a denominator often involve two possibilities: a positive and a negative one. For example, if you know that $1/y < x$, you might be tempted to multiply by y and arrive at $1 < xy$. However, this may not be correct. It depends on whether y is a positive or negative number. If $y > 0$, then it is correct to infer that $1 < xy$. However, if $y < 0$, then $1 > xy$. Therefore, you'll need to test two cases (positive and negative) in this situation.

5. At the same time, hidden constraints may allow you to manipulate inequalities more easily. For instance, if a quantity must be positive, then you can multiply both sides of an inequality by that quantity without having to set up two cases.

6. Many questions involving inequalities are actually disguised positive/negative questions. For example, if you know that $xy > 0$, the fact that xy is greater than 0 is not in and of itself very interesting. What is interesting is that the product is positive, meaning both x and y are positive, or both x and y are negative. Thus x and y have the *same sign*. Here, the inequality symbol is used to disguise the fact that x and y have the same sign.

Take a look at some examples that illustrate these concepts.

Try-It #4-4

If $\sqrt{x}$ is a prime number, what is the value of x?

(1) $-16 < -3x + 5 < 22$
(2) x^2 is a two-digit number

If $\sqrt{x}$ is a prime number, then possible values are 2, 3, 5, and so on. Therefore, x must be a perfect square of a prime; possible values include 4, 9, 25, and so on.

(1) SUFFICIENT: Manipulate the inequality to isolate x:

$$-16 < -3x + 5 < 22$$
$$-21 < -3x < 17$$
$$7 > x > -\frac{17}{3}$$

Since x is the square of a prime, it can't be negative or zero; it has to be positive. The smallest possible square of a prime is 4 and the next smallest possible square of a prime is 9. This inequality allows just one possible value: $x = 4$.

(2) INSUFFICIENT: According to this statement, $10 \leq x^2 \leq 99$. In addition, from the question stem, $\sqrt{x}$ is a prime number. Determine the possible value(s) for x:

If $x = 4$, then $\sqrt{x}$ is a prime number, 2, and x^2 is a two-digit number, 16.

If $x = 9$, then $\sqrt{x}$ is a prime number, 3, and x^2 is a two-digit number, 81.

Because there are two possible values for x, this statement is not sufficient.

The constraints were so specific that statement (1), which looks at a glance as though it will allow more than one possible answer, turns out to be sufficient.

The correct answer is **(A)**.

Try-It #4-5

If $mn \neq 0$, is $m > n$?

(1) $\dfrac{1}{m} < \dfrac{1}{n}$

(2) $m^2 > n^2$

The constraint in the question stem indicates that neither m nor n equals zero.

(1) INSUFFICIENT: You can solve algebraically/theoretically or you can *Test Cases*. If you solve algebraically, be careful: you have to account for multiplying the inequality by a negative.

If m and n are both positive, then $m > n$.

If m and n are both negative, the sign flips twice, so $m > n$ again.

If only one is negative, then the sign flips once and $m < n$. In this case, m must be the negative number, since any positive is greater than any negative.

Alternatively, *Test Cases*:

If $m = 3$ and $n = 2$, then statement (1) is true and the answer to the question is Yes, $m > n$.

If $m = -3$ and $n = 2$, then statement (1) is true and the answer to the question is No, m is not greater than n.

(2) INSUFFICIENT: This statement indicates nothing about the signs of the two variables. Either one could be positive or negative.

(1) AND (2) INSUFFICIENT. If you are solving algebraically, test the scenarios that you devised for statement (1).

If m and n are both positive, then $m > n$ and $m^2 > n^2$. Both statements allow this scenario.

If m and n are both negative, then $m > n$ but and m^2 is *not* greater than n^2. Discard this scenario, since it makes statement (2) false.

If m is negative and n is positive, then $m < n$. It could also be true that $m^2 > n^2$, as long as m's magnitude is larger than n's. If you're not sure *Test Cases* (see below).

Alternatively, test cases. Start by testing whether the cases you already tried for statement (1) also apply to statement (2).

If $m = 3$ and $n = 2$, then $m > n$ and $m^2 > n^2$. Both statements allow this scenario.

If $m = -3$ and $n = 2$, then $m < n$ and $m^2 > n^2$. Both statements allow this scenario.

Because there are scenarios in which $m > n$ and $m < n$, both statements together are still insufficient to answer the question. If you forgot to account for the positive and negative cases, you may end up with (A) or (D) as your *(incorrect)* answer.

The correct answer is **(E)**.

5. Use a Scenario Chart

In many DS problems, the available information suggests that only a *handful* of possible scenarios exist. In other words, the possibilities *branch* into more than one possible outcome, but the number of total possible outcomes is limited. As a result, you can list them all out:

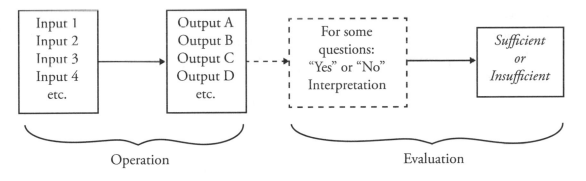

While it is always important to be organized when performing calculations on the GMAT, multiple-scenario problems require a *very* organized approach in your work on paper: the Scenario Chart. We suggest creating the following elements in your Scenario Charts, though you should be flexible in your implementation.

1. **ORGANIZE YOUR WORK** in a table. Each variable gets its own *column*. Each scenario gets it own *row*. Example: if the question involves odds/evens, you would create a column for each variable, and populate the rows with applicable *Odd* and *Even* scenarios *for each variable*.	**WHY?** • You have to consider *every possible combination* of inputs to determine the *possible outputs*. • There may be too many variables to track mentally. • Each variable individually may have too many possible values to track mentally. • Putting the inputs on paper makes it easier to evaluate the question for each scenario.

2. Consider **FACT CHECK COLUMNS.**

Easy facts/constraints such as "*x* is an integer" can be addressed by listing only integer scenarios for *x*—no separate fact check column is necessary. However, you might want to add a fact check column for *complicated* or *algebraic* constraints.

WHY?

- Ensures that you consider all the applicable constraints as you evaluate each statement
- Forces a check that the scenarios comply with more complicated constraints
- Minimizes the burden of implementing simple constraints, such as "*x* is positives"

3 Create a **QUESTION & ANSWER COLUMN.**

Clearly label the question with a question mark. For each scenario (row), check to see what the answer to the question is. For more complicated questions, you may want to create extra columns to act as subtotals.

WHY?

- Forces the generation of an answer for every allowable scenario
- Prevents confusion between the question and the facts
- Reduces the risk of becoming biased by the question (making unwarranted assumptions)

4. **MAKE SEPARATE CHARTS** for each statement.

You may also need to create a third chart for the combined statements. Or, you could circle the scenarios in one statement's chart that also exist in the other statement's chart.

WHY?

- To avoid *statement carryover*
- One big chart with (1), (2) and possibly (1) and (2) combined could be unwieldy and/or confusing.

Scenario Charts trade off *exhaustiveness* and *efficiency*. You will have to find your own balance, but we recommend that you work towards *efficiency* (i.e., evaluating only the scenarios that fit the given information) rather than *exhaustiveness* (i.e., evaluating all possible scenarios and then crossing out the scenarios that violate the given information). This helps keep you focused on the scenarios that remain possible, rather than wasting time on scenarios that are irrelevant.

Try-It #4-6

If *a*, *b*, and *c* are integers, is $abc > 0$?

(1) $ab > 0$
(…)

In this partial problem, there are three variables, each of which might be positive or negative. Therefore there are a total of $2^3 = 8$ possible positive/negative scenarios to evaluate. However, based on the information available in statement (1), you may realize early on that only 4 of the scenarios are possible (*a* and *b* have the same sign, so any combination involving *a* and *b* having different signs does not fit the statement). In an *exhaustive* Scenario Chart, you would write down 8 rows corresponding to each possible positive/negative combination, and cross out the 4 that violate this constraint. In an *efficient* Scenario Chart, you would only write the 4 scenarios that fit the constraint. Clearly, the efficient Scenario Chart will take less time to complete. For example, here are two examples of the chart you might set up for (1):

EXHAUSTIVE CHART

a	*b*	*c*	*abc* > 0?
+	+	+	Y
+	+	−	N
+	−		} invalid
+			
	+		
	+		
−	−	+	Y
−	−	−	N

EFFICIENT CHART

a	*b*	*c*	*abc* > 0?
+	+	+	Y
+	+	−	N
−	−	+	Y
−	−	−	N

In addition, you would stop the efficient chart at the point that you prove the statement not sufficient. In the case of the chart above, you only have to test the first two scenarios to get a Yes answer and a No answer.

That said, sometimes a problem might be so complex that you decide you'd be more comfortable evaluating all possible scenarios. Or perhaps at first you can't determine which scenarios fit the facts in the problem (and you would therefore need to use the Scenario Chart to determine which scenarios fit the problem). In these cases, an exhaustive approach is perfectly acceptable, as long as you are mindful of the amount of time it will take to complete.

Also, be sure to *cross out* or mark as invalid any scenarios that do not fit your facts, as soon as you discover them! You can't use these scenarios as "No" cases—they don't count at all.

Try-It #4-7

If *a*, *b*, and *c* are integers, is *abc* divisible by 4?

(1) $a + b + 2c$ is even.
(2) $a + 2b + c$ is odd.

Evaluate the possible odd/even combinations of *a*, *b*, and *c* using Scenario Charts to determine the answer to the question.

(1) INSUFFICIENT: $2c$ must be even because c is an integer. This statement implies that $a + b =$ Even, which occurs when a and b have the same odd/even parity. (There is no constraint on c.) An efficient Scenario Chart might look like this:

a	b	c	$a + b + 2c =$ **Even** (FACT CHECK)	Is abc divisible by 4? (QUESTION)
E	E	E	✓	Y
E	E	O	✓	Y
O	O	E	✓	Maybe (only if c is divis by 4)

Stop here! MAYBE indicates insufficient.

(2) INSUFFICIENT: $2b$ must be even because b is an integer. Thus, this statement implies that $a + c =$ Odd, which occurs when a and c have opposite odd/even parity. (There is no constraint on b.)

a	b	c	$a + b + 2c =$ **Odd** (FACT CHECK)	Is abc divisible by 4? (QUESTION)
E	E	O	✓	Y
E	O	O	✓	Maybe

Stop here! MAYBE indicates insufficient.

(1) AND (2) INSUFFICIENT: From (1) you know that a and b have the same odd/even parity, while from (2) you know that a and c have opposite odd/even parity.

a	b	c	$a + b + 2c =$ **Even** (FACT CHECK)	$a + 2b + c =$ **Odd** (FACT CHECK)	Is abc divisible by 4? (QUESTION)
E	E	O	✓	✓	Y
O	O	E	✓	✓	Maybe

Even with these constraints, you do not have a definitive answer to the question. The correct answer is **(E)**.

Notice that in evaluating statements (1) and (2) together, you would not need to write a completely new Scenario Chart. You can reuse the work from statement (1) and statement (2) to determine the answer (for instance, by circling the scenarios in one chart that also appear in the other chart). Just be careful as you do this! Know what case you're considering.

Try-It #4-8

If x and y are integers and $|xy| = 8$, what is the value of $|x + y|$?

(1) x and y are both divisible by 2,
(2) $xy > 0$

If the two variables must be integers and the absolute value of their product is 8, then x and y have to represent either the factor pair (1, 8) or the factor pair (2, 4), in either order and with either sign (positive or negative). This narrows the possible number of cases considerably.

(1) INSUFFICIENT: List out the possible cases allowed by this statement. If x and y are both divisible by 2, then you're dealing with the factor pair (2, 4). After you try your first case, ask yourself what different case would be most likely to return a *different* answer to the question.

x	y	$|xy| = 8$ (FACT CHECK)	$|x + y| = ?$ (QUESTION)
2	4	✓	6
−2	4	✓	2

In this case, simply reversing the numbers (4, 2) won't make a difference to the final question, so don't list that case second. Try one of the cases that allows a negative value. Now that you have two different values, you know the statement is not sufficient.

(2) INSUFFICIENT: Follow the same process. This statement indicates that the two values have the same sign: both positive or both negative.

x	y	$|xy| = 8$ (FACT CHECK)	$|x + y| = ?$ (QUESTION)
1	8	✓	9
2	4	✓	6

Again, list cases until you have two contradictory results (or until you've tried all cases and realized that there is only one possible answer).

(1) AND (2) SUFFICIENT:

x	y	Both divis by 2? Same signs?	$|xy| = 8$ (FACT CHECK)	$|x + y| = ?$ (QUESTION)
2	4	✓ ✓	✓	6
−2	−4	✓ ✓	✓	6

Only four possible cases are allowed: the variables must match the (2, 4) factor pair and the signs have to be the same. The chart above shows two of the four possible cases, but you could also reverse the order: (4, 2) and (−4, −2). Since you're just adding at the end, though, the order of the two variables doesn't matter. In all four cases, $|x + y| = 6$.

The correct answer is **(C)**.

Another concept related to Scenario Charts is **Flow Charts**. Flow charts are a visual way to track scenarios. They are most useful when there are *question* scenarios—i.e., the exact question being asked is dependent upon certain conditions. A flow chart allows you to divide the different question scenarios and evaluate them separately.

Try-It #4-9

If $a \neq 0$, is $\dfrac{1}{a} > \dfrac{a}{b^4 + 3}$?

(1) $a = b^2$
(2) $a^2 = b^4$

This problem would be easier to evaluate if you could cross-multiply the inequality to eliminate the fractions. But *watch out*! You can multiply by $(b^4 + 3)$, which is definitely positive because of the even exponent. But a could be either positive or negative—and depending on the sign of a, you may need to flip the inequality symbol. That is, the rephrasing of the question depends on the sign of a.

Flow charts can help you with this dilemma. Represent the scenarios this way:

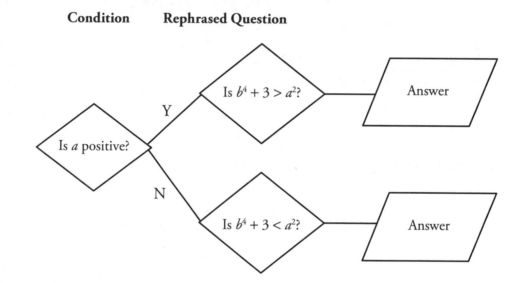

(1) SUFFICIENT: b^2 must be positive, so a must be positive. (Note: b can't be 0 because the question stem specifies that a does not equal 0.) Therefore, you have to evaluate only the top branch of the flow chart:

Is $b^4 + 3 > a^2$?
Is $b^4 + 3 > (b^2)^2$?
Is $b^4 + 3 > b^4$?
Is $3 > 0$?

The answer to the ultimate question is a definite Yes.

(2) INSUFFICIENT: $a^2 = b^4$ can be true with positive or negative values for a. You don't know the sign of a, so answer both questions that follow in the flow chart:

If a is positive:	If a is negative:
Is $b^4 + 3 > a^2$?	Is $b^4 + 3 < a^2$?
Is $b^4 + 3 > b^4$?	Is $b^4 + 3 < b^4$?
Is $3 > 0$?	Is $3 < 0$?
The answer to this question is Yes.	The answer to this question is No.

Alternatively, you might observe that the two questions are exact opposites, so even if you get a definite answer to either one, you will get the opposite answer to the other, for a net result of Maybe. The correct answer is **(A)**.

For an in-depth list of situations in which you might consider using Scenario Charts, please see the Appendix at the end of this chapter entitled "Selected Applications of Scenario Charts."

6. Test Cases

Scenario Charts can be both versatile and effective. For many problems, a full chart is not necessary, but you still need to consider a handful of possible values for the unknowns to identify an underlying pattern. In this case, you can *Test Cases*.

Again, as an advanced test-taker, you might be biased against number testing: it might somehow seem less advanced than theoretical approaches. However, the theory required to answer a question may be cumbersome to figure out in two minutes. If implemented correctly, testing cases can be fast, easy, and accurate, so it should be part of your toolbox.

Plugging random numbers as they come to mind is the most common approach to testing cases, and while this strategy can be successful, it is inherently ad hoc and therefore not the most reliable process. It's easy to overlook a salient scenario. The key is to have a *systematic approach* to testing cases. This relies on two approaches: The *Standard Number Set for Testing* and *Discrete Number Listing*.

Standard Number Set for Testing

The GMAT often tests odd/even rules, positive/negative rules, fraction/integer rules, proper vs. improper fractions, etc. On any given problem, you may have trouble identifying which rule is relevant, and in fact the GMAT may test more than one rule within a given question. Therefore, if you must pick and test numbers, consider a set of numbers that covers every possible combination of properties:

	Odd	**Even**	**Proper Fraction**	**Improper Fraction**
Negative	-1	-2	$-\dfrac{1}{2}$	$-\dfrac{3}{2}$
Zero		0		
Positive	1	2	$\dfrac{1}{2}$	$\dfrac{3}{2}$

This set includes integers, non-integers, positive and negative numbers, and numbers greater than and less than 1. Thus, a comprehensive set of test numbers (to memorize and apply) would be as follows:

$$\{-2, -\frac{3}{2}, -1, -\frac{1}{2}, 0, \frac{1}{2}, 1, \frac{3}{2}, 2\}$$

Remember this list as "every integer and half-integer between −2 and 2."

Not all of these numbers will be relevant or possible on every problem. For example, if the variable has to be positive, five of the nine values presented above can be ignored. The question itself may suggest certain values to test, but always keep in mind the *potential* need to test a value of each relevant type—and if a problem really might entail testing nine different cases, consider whether that problem is really worth your time.

Try-It #4-10

Is $a < 0$?

(1) $a^3 < a^2 + 2a$
(2) $a^2 > a^3$

This problem presents inequalities with non-linear terms, and the question asks whether a is negative. Therefore, test different values of a to see which values fit the statements.

The question stem doesn't provide any constraints, so begin by testing some easier integers and then move to fractions if needed.

(1) $a^3 - a^2 - 2a < 0$
(2) $a^2 - a^3 > 0$

(1) INSUFFICIENT: Test the possible integers from the *Standard Number Set*.

a	(1): $a^3 - a^2 - 2^a < 0$	$a < 0$?
−2	$(-2)^3 - (-2)^2 - 2(-2) = -8$ (valid)	YES
−1	$(-1)^3 - (-1)^2 - 2(-1) = 0$ (invalid)	
0	$(0)^3 - (0)^2 - 2(0) = 0$ (invalid)	
1	$(1)^3 - (1)^2 - 2(1) = -2$ (valid)	NO

Stop when you find two valid cases that return different answers to the question.

(2) INSUFFICIENT: Try integers first.

a	(2): $a^2 - a^3 > 0$	$a < 0$?
−2	$(-2)^2 - (-2)^3 = 12$ (valid)	YES
−1	$(-1)^2 - (-1)^3 = 2$ (valid)	YES
0	$(0)^2 - (0)^3 = 0$ (invalid)	
1	$(1)^2 - (1)^3 = 0$ (invalid)	
2	$(2)^2 - (2)^3 = -4$ (invalid)	

Careful: you're not done. Try a fraction. Because a positive and a negative number figured into the mix for statement (1), try one positive and one negative fraction.

a	(2): $a^2 - a^3 > 0$	$a < 0$?
-2	$(-2)^2 - (-2)^3 = 12$ (valid)	YES
-1	$(-1)^2 - (-1)^3 = 2$ (valid)	YES
0	$(0)^2 - (0)^3 = 0$ (invalid)	
1	$(1)^2 - (1)^3 = 0$ (invalid)	
2	$(2)^2 - (2)^3 = -4$ (invalid)	
$-1/2$	$(-1/2)^2 - (-1/2)^3 = 3/8$ (valid)	YES
$1/2$	$(1/2)^2 - (1/2)^3 = 1/8$ (valid)	NO

Statement (2) is *insufficient*. When $a = \dfrac{1}{2}$, the constraint is fulfilled, but a is positive.

Combining statements (1) and (2) shows that whenever $a = -2$, $-\dfrac{3}{2}$, or $\dfrac{1}{2}$, both conditions are fulfilled. The variable a could thus be positive or negative. The correct answer is **(E)**.

Notice that you did not need to test every possible value for a. For example, when $a = -2$, both conditions are easily satisfied. That means that testing $-\dfrac{3}{2}$ was unlikely to be necessary, since that value is not much different from -2. Furthermore, when you do find a contradictory answer, you can stop testing. For a Yes/No question, all you need to do is find *one* valid Yes and *one* valid No to prove insufficiency.

This problem can also be solved algebraically, but it takes more conceptual work. A number line would help keep track of signs.

(1) INSUFFICIENT: $a^3 - a^2 - 2a < 0$
                            $a(a^2 - a - 2) < 0$
                            $a(a - 2)(a + 1) < 0$
                            $a < 2$, 0, or -1.

	-1		0		2	
a	$-$		$-$		$+$	$+$
$a - 2$	$-$		$-$		$-$	$+$
$a + 1$	$-$		$+$		$+$	$+$
Product:	$\ominus$		$+$		$\ominus$	$+$

This chart demonstrates that either $a < -1$ *OR* $0 < a < 2$.

(2) INSUFFICIENT: $a^2 - a^3 > 0$
                            $a^2(1 - a) > 0$ Since a can't be zero, you can divide by a^2.
                            $1 - a > 0$
                            $a < 1$.

(1) AND (2) INSUFFICIENT: Overlapping the possible ranges, either $a < -1$ *OR* $0 < a < 1$. This is still not enough information to tell whether a is negative. The correct answer is **(E)**.

In some cases, the *standard number testing* list may not quite suffice; try the example below.

Try-It #4-11

If x is positive, is $x \leq 1$?

(1) $x^2 \leq 1.3$

...

If you used the standard number testing list of $\{\frac{1}{2}, 1, \frac{3}{2}, 2\}$ (ignoring the non-positive values in the set), all of the values for x above 1 would *fail* to fit statement (1) and all of the values for x equal to or below 1 would *fit* statement (1). Therefore, the standard number testing list would indicate that statement (1) is sufficient. However, x could be 1.1, in which case $x^2 = 1.21$, which is less than 1.3. So statement (1) is actually insufficient.

You could figure out that x *could* be greater than 1 upon a quick inspection of this problem. You might think to try a number slightly larger than 1. However, if the problem were more complicated, it might not be so obvious. In cases like these, use the **boundary principle**: test values that are *close to boundaries* given in the problem. In this case, the boundary value is 1, so add 0.9 and 1.1 to your list of numbers to test. You might even try 0.99 or 1.01. You should know that −1, 0, and 1 are natural boundaries, because numbers behave differently on either side of them (that's why the standard list contains numbers in the ranges defined by −1, 0, and 1).

Discrete Number Listing

In the previous problems, the variables a and x were not constrained, so you had to test a series of different numbers to solve the problem. By contrast, many questions suggest specific constraints: x must be odd, for example, or x must be a positive integer. In these cases, just *list* a series of consecutive numbers that fit these criteria and test them all. For example, if x must be positive and even, test $x = 2, 4, 6, 8, 10$.

Discrete Number Listing can be used whenever a problem specifies a sequence of discrete (separate) values that a variable or an expression can take on:

- Integers (the classic case): ... −3, −2, −1, 0, 1, 2, 3 ...
- Odd/even integers: ... −3, −1, 1, 3 ... or ... −4, −2, 0, 2, 4 ...
- Positive perfect squares: 1, 4, 9, 16, 25 ...
- Positive multiples of 5: 5, 10, 15, 20 ...
- Any set that is "integer-like," with well-defined, separated values

By contrast, some problems describe a *smooth range* of potential values for a variable or expression (for example, $0 < x < 1$ or x must be negative). In these cases, don't list consecutive values to test, because the set of possible values is *not* discrete. If the variable can take on any real number in a range, then rely on the standard number testing list, potentially with some modifications, as described in the previous section.

A key to the *Discrete Number Listing* process is to **test consecutive values** that fit the criteria—it would be too easy to leave out the one exception that proves insufficiency. Never skip numbers that fit the

constraint. This is especially important if you are listing discrete numbers to equal an expression, not just a variable. By the way, remember to work from the facts to the question, not the other way around! Don't assume that the question should be answered Yes and only test values that make it so.

Try-It #4-12

Is x a multiple of 12?

(1) $\sqrt{x-3}$ is odd.
(2) x is a multiple of 3.

Since statement (1) indicates that $\sqrt{x-3}$ is odd and the square root sign implies a positive answer, list 1, 3, 5, 7, 9, etc.

Notice that you're picking values for $\sqrt{x-3}$, *not x*. It would be far too much work to test different values for x to determine which make $\sqrt{x-3}$ odd, and you could potentially miss some values that fit the statement. Do not plug in numbers for x here! Instead, list consecutive odd values for $\sqrt{x-3}$, a quick and easy process. Then solve for x in each case.

For this problem, your work on paper may look something like this:

(1) INSUFFICIENT: $\sqrt{x-3}$ = odds = 1, 3, 5, 7, 9, etc.
   $x - 3 = 1, 9, 25, 49, 81$, etc.
   $x = 4, 12, 28, 52, 84$, etc.
   Is x divisible by 12? Maybe. For example, 12 is, while 28 is not.

(2) INSUFFICIENT: x = multiples of 3 = 3, 6, 9, 12, 15, etc.
   Is x divisible by 12? Maybe. For example, 12 is, while 15 is not.

(1) AND (2) SUFFICIENT: Combine these statements by selecting only the values for x that are in both lists. On your paper, circle the following values: $x = 12$ and $x = 84$. These are the values calculated in statement (1) that fit the criteria in statement (2). This seems to be SUFFICIENT—the values for x that fit both statements are multiples of 12. At this point, if you wanted to check another value, you could, or you could go with the trend, which is almost always going to be right after testing this many cases.

The correct answer is **(C)**.

> In retrospect, it may seem obvious that (1) indicates that x is a multiple of 4. But if you tried to evaluate (1) with algebra, you might reason that $\sqrt{x-3}$ is odd, so $(x-3)$ is odd^2, or an odd perfect square. Thus, x is an odd perfect square plus 3. One might conclude that x is even, which is a true but incomplete description! Listing numbers is an easy way to see that these numbers are all multiples of 4.

As in the previous example, trying to solve statement (1) algebraically is tricky. Yes, it's worth knowing how to do this algebra. The point is that a discrete number testing process is quick and simple, so it's also worth knowing how to do.

(1): INSUFFICIENT: $\sqrt{x-3} = 2k+1$, where k is an integer.

$x - 3 = (2k + 1)^2 = 4k^2 + 4k + 1$

$x = 4k^2 + 4k + 4 = 4(k^2 + k + 1)$

x must be divisible by 4.

(2) INSUFFICIENT: x is a multiple of 3, so x must be divisible by 3.

(1) AND (2) SUFFICIENT: x is divisible by 3 and by 4, so x is divisible by 12.

Advanced Guessing Tactics

The rest of this chapter is devoted to scrappy tactics that can raise your odds of success. There will be fewer opportunities to apply these tactics than the strategies mentioned previously. However, when all else fails, these tactics may be your only friend. The tactics are listed according to their reliability: the earlier tactics nearly always work, while the later tactics provide only a modest improvement over random guessing.

1. Spot Identical Statements   *Certainty:* Very High

| IF the two statements tell you exactly the same thing (after rephrasing)… | → | THEN the answer is either (D) or (E). |

(…)

(1) $3y - 6 = 2x$

(2) $y = \dfrac{2}{3}x + 2$

By adding 6 to both sides of statement (1) and multiplying statement (2) by 3, you can see that both statements indicate that $3y = 2x + 6$. Depending on the question, either each statement will be sufficient, or each will not—because they are identical, there cannot be any benefit from looking at the statements together. The answer must be (D) or (E).

2. Spot Clear Sufficiency   *Certainty:* Very High

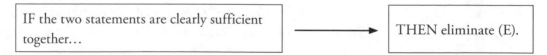

| IF the two statements are clearly sufficient together… | → | THEN eliminate (E). |

MANHATTAN
PREP

Try-It #4-13

If $Z = \dfrac{m + \dfrac{m}{3}}{n + \dfrac{2}{n^{-1}}}$ and $mn \neq 0$, what is the value of Z?

(1) $m = \dfrac{15}{n^{-1}}$

(2) $m = 5$

It is obvious that you could plug $m = 5$ into statement (1) to get a value for n, then plug values for m and n into the expression for Z. So you can knock out (E) for sure.

Note that this tactic does *not* imply that you should assume, or even *lean towards*, choosing answer choice (C). Many of these types of problems are trying to trap you into choosing (C) because it's so obvious that the two combined statements are sufficient. Quite often, some algebraic work will reveal that one or both of the statements will be sufficient on their own. Indeed, in the example problem given above, statement (1) alone is sufficient to answer the question, so the correct answer is **(A)**.

3. Spot One Statement Inside The Other   *Certainty:* Very High

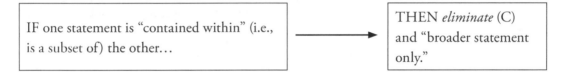

(Some question involving *x*)

(1) $x > 50!$
(2) $x > 10!$

This trick only shows up occasionally, but when it does, it's useful. Notice that narrow statement (1) is completely contained within broad statement (2). In other words, any value that satisfies statement (1) *also* satisfies statement (2). Therefore, if statement (2) is sufficient, statement (1) *must* be sufficient also. However, the reverse is not true. If (2) is insufficient, (1) could still possibly be sufficient on its own.

Either way, it is impossible for both of the statements to be required together to answer the question. It is also impossible for statement (2) to be sufficient without statement (1) being sufficient also. So you can definitively eliminate (B), as it corresponds to the broader statement, as well as (C) (the together option).

This situation can occur with inequalities. Whenever one statement defines a range that is completely encompassed by the other statement's range, you can eliminate (C), as well as the broader statement alone.

Be careful with this tactic, though. It can be easy to think—incorrectly—that one statement is a subset of the other.

(Some question involving *x*)

(1) *x* is an odd number
(2) *x* is a prime number

At first, it might seem that statement (2) is a subset of statement (1), but 2 is a prime number that is not odd. *Almost* every prime number is odd, but *not all*. Therefore statement (2) is *not* a subset of statement (1). Even if just one value escapes, you cannot use this tactic.

4. Spot One Statement Adding Nothing   *Certainty*: High

IF one statement adds no information to the other…	→	THEN eliminate (C).

(Some question involving x, y, and z)

(1) $y^x + (-y)^x = z$
(2) $y < 0$

This tactic may seem identical to the previous one, but it is not. Notice in this example that statement (1) does not determine whether y is positive or negative, and statement (2) does not even include z. Therefore, neither statement is a subset of the other.

That said, the fact that y is negative *does not change anything* in statement (1), because regardless of the value of y, z will remain the same if you swap y and $-y$. If $y = 4$, then you'd get $4^x + (-4)^x = z$. If $y = -4$, then you'd get $(-4)x + 4x = z$. Those equations are the same! The sign of y doesn't matter, because y and $-y$ are symmetric. So knowing the sign of y adds no information to statement (1).

Note that in this example, (A), (B), (D), and (E) are all still possible answers, depending upon the question. Only (C) can be eliminated.

5. Spot a (C) Trap   *Certainty:* Moderate

IF it is *very obvious* that the combined statements would be sufficient, but you can't eliminate the possibility that one statement alone is sufficient…	→	THEN eliminate (C) and (E).

This situation can occur when one statement is particularly tricky or when you didn't rephrase the question fully. The GMAT may be trying to trap you into concluding that both statements are needed to answer the question.

Try-It #4-14

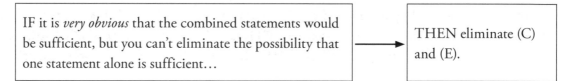

If $K = \dfrac{\dfrac{1}{3a} + \dfrac{1}{b}}{\dfrac{5}{ab}}$ and $ab \neq 0$, what is the value of K?

(1) $a = 3$
(2) $b - 3(5 - a) = 0$

MANHATTAN
PREP

It is evident that the two statements combined are sufficient to answer the question—you can plug the value of a from statement (1) into statement (2) to solve for the value of b; then you can plug those values into the question to solve for K.

Immediately be skeptical. Answer (C) should seem too easy. After all, you didn't do anything to the question stem. So you should do some work to determine whether one of the two statements *alone* (or, in some cases, each statement alone) is sufficient to answer the question.

Start by rephrasing the question:

$$K = \frac{\frac{1}{3a} + \frac{1}{b}}{\frac{5}{ab}} = \frac{\frac{b}{3ab} + \frac{3a}{3ab}}{\frac{5}{ab}} = \frac{b + 3a}{3ab} \times \frac{ab}{5} = \frac{b + 3a}{15}$$

"What is the value of K?" rephrases to "What is the value of $b + 3a$?" Statement (2) provides the answer:

$$b - 3(5 - a) =$$
$$b - 15 + 3a = 0$$
$$b + 3a = 15$$

The correct answer is **(B)**. In these cases, the more complicated statement may be enough.

This is not a tactic to use at lower levels of the test. On 500–600 level problems, the two statements may work together in straightforward ways to produce sufficiency. The (C) trap may be the (C) answer! This is one of many reasons why the material in this book is only appropriate if you have achieved a certain level of proficiency on the math side of the GMAT.

6. Use Basic Algebraic Reasoning   *Certainty:* Moderate

Quite often, basic intuition about algebra can lead you to the correct answer. For example, you might have the intuition on a problem that "I have two unknowns and only one equation, so I can't solve" or "this statement doesn't even mention the variable(s) that I care about." Often, you will discover that your intuition is correct.

Try-It #4-15

> A sales manager at an industrial company has an opportunity to switch to a new, higher-paying job in another state. If his current annual salary is $50,000 and his current state tax rate is 5%, how much income after state tax would he make at the new job?
>
> (1) His new salary will be 10% higher than his old salary.
> (2) His annual state taxes will total $2,200 in the new state at his new job.

You may reason that in order to answer this question, you need to know how much his new salary will be, and how much his taxes will increase by. This reasoning will lead you to conclude that the correct answer is **(C)**. And you'll be right.

Of course, you need to be *very careful* about using this tactic. Many problems on the GMAT are designed to hoodwink your algebraic reasoning—usually to make you think that you need to know every value precisely to answer the question.

For example, suppose the question in the previous problem were changed to "Will the manager make more money at the new job, after state taxes?" The correct answer in this case is **(B)**. The problem explicitly states that the new job is higher-paying, so you only need to check whether the change in state tax might lead to a lower after-tax compensation. Statement (2) indicates that his new state taxes ($2,200) will be lower than his current state taxes (5% of $50,000 = $2,500), so his after-state-tax compensation will definitely be higher in the new job. You do *not* need to find out how much higher his pre-tax salary would be to answer this question.

Because the GMAT frequently uses traps involving basic algebraic reasoning, you should only resort to using it if you are *truly stuck*.

7. Spot Cross-Multiplied Inequalities   *Certainty:* Low

When you are presented with an inequality problem in Data Sufficiency in which one or more variables appears in a denominator, you may need to know the sign of the variable or variables to answer the question. This might be the hidden trick.

Try-It #4-16

Is $xy < 1$?

(1) $\dfrac{2}{x} > 3y$

(2) $x > 0$

Statement (1) might imply that $xy < \dfrac{2}{3}$, but *only* if x is positive. If it is negative, you would need to flip the sign: $xy > \dfrac{2}{3}$. You need to know the sign of x—information that is provided in statement (2). The correct answer is **(C)**.

These types of questions may have an (A) or (B) trap, in that you might fail to realize that you have to set up negative and positive cases when you multiply or divide an inequality by a variable.

Watch out! In some GMAT problems, you *can* assume the sign of the variables, because the variables represent countable quantities of physical things. In those cases, you can assume that the variables are positive, and you can cross-multiply inequalities involving those variables at will.

8. Judge By Appearance   *Certainty:* Low

Sometimes a statement will leave you completely bewildered. In that case, the best (and only!) tactic is to guess whether it will be sufficient judging by how it looks:

- Does it simply look like it might be sufficient, even if you can't see how?
- Does it use the variables you are looking for?
- Could it likely be manipulated into a form *similar* to that of the question?

The general rule is this: if the information in a statement has a *structure* and *complexity* similar to the question, and has the right ingredients (variables, coefficients, etc.), it's more likely to be sufficient than otherwise. This won't crack every case by any means, but you'd be surprised at how much mileage you can get from this tactic.

Try-It #4-16

Does $4^a = 4^{-a} + b$?

(1) $16^a = 1 + \dfrac{2^{2a}}{b^{-1}}$

(2) $a = 2$

Depending on your level of comfort with exponent manipulations, you may be able to prove that statement (1) alone is sufficient:

$$16^a = 1 + \frac{2^{2a}}{b^{-1}}$$
$$16^a = 1 + \left(2^{2a}\right)b$$
$$4^{2a} = 1 + \left(4^a\right)b$$

$$\frac{4^{2a}}{4^a} = \frac{1 + \left(4^a\right)b}{4^a}$$
$$4^a = \frac{1}{4^a} + b$$
$$4^a = 4^{-a} + b$$

However, what if you find yourself at a temporary loss on the test? Your exponent engine may shut down for a problem or two. Then what do you do?

One line of reasoning might be as follows: "Statement (2) is clearly not sufficient, since it tells me nothing about b. Now let's look at statement (1). It's a very complicated expression, but it seems to have the right ingredients. It contains a and b, and uses a as an exponent. Also, the exponential terms in statement (1) are powers of 2 (2, 4, 16), just like the exponential terms in a. I'll bet if I manipulate this equation right, it will answer the question. I'll guess (A)." And you'd be right. The GMAT never needs to know that you guessed.

Summary

That was a lot of stuff! To summarize, the following advanced strategies and guessing tactics can be used to solve Data Sufficiency problems effectively or simply increase your chances of success:

Advanced Data Sufficiency Strategies

1. **Compute to Completion** – If you can't tell for certain whether the answer can be calculated in theory, keep going on the calculations *all the way*.

2. **Extract the Equation** – Represent Word Problems with algebraic equations to avoid embedded tricks that can be difficult to find otherwise.

3. **Use the Constraints** – Bring explicit and implicit constraints to the surface. These constraints will often be necessary to determine the correct answer.

4. **Beware of Inequalities** – Whenever a problem involves inequality symbols, *be careful*—there are many ways in which inequalities can be used to trick you.

5. **Use the Scenario Chart** – In problems with a limited number of potential outcomes, list those outcomes on paper and test them in a structured way.

6. **Test Cases** – In other Data Sufficiency problems, many possible values may exist, but underlying those values is some sort of pattern. Use the *Standard Number Set* to test the allowable cases. Use *Discrete Number Listing* when the values are "integer-like" (and thus can be listed consecutively).

Data Sufficiency Guessing Tactics

1. **Spot Identical Statements (High)** – If the two statements say the same thing (after rephrasing), then the answer must be (D) or (E).

2. **Spot Clear Sufficiency (High)** – If the two statements together are clearly sufficient, then eliminate (E).

3. **Spot One Statement Inside The Other (High)** – If a narrow statement is completely contained within a broader statement, then eliminate (C) and "broader statement only" (either (A) or (B)).

4. **Spot One Statement Adding Nothing (High)** – If one statement adds no value to the information given in the other statement, then eliminate (C).

5. **Spot a (C) Trap (Moderate)** – If the two statements together are *very* clearly sufficient and at least one of the statements is complex enough that it could be sufficient, then (C) could be a trap answer, so eliminate (C).

6. **Use Basic Algebraic Reasoning (Moderate)** – Apply basic knowledge of algebra, such as considering the number of unknowns relative to the number of known equations, to guide your thought process.

7. **Spot Cross-Multiplied Inequalities (Low)** – If a Yes/No question involves inequalities with variables in a denominator, then guess (C) or (E) if you must guess.

8. **Judge By Appearance (Low)** – If you're completely unsure what to do, then make your best guess as to whether it *appears* to be sufficient.

Selected Applications of Scenario Charts

	Trigger:	Reason:	Scenarios:	Example:
A	Even Exponents	Two solutions when you take the square root.	1. Negative root 2. Positive root	$x^2 = 9$: Case 1: $x = -3$ Case 2: $x = 3$
B	Inequalities: Multiplication or Division by a Variable	If you don't know the sign of the variable, then two possible inequalities result: one with a flipped inequality sign and one with the original sign.	1. Flipped sign 2. Original sign	$\dfrac{16}{x} > y$: Case 1: $16 < xy$ if $x < 0$ Case 2: $16 > xy$ if $x > 0$
C	Inequalities: Variables Raised to Powers	Numbers raised to powers become larger or smaller according to complicated rules: a. When raised to a power greater than 1, a fraction between 0 and 1 gets smaller. The numbers 0 and 1 stay the same. Numbers greater than 1 get larger. b. Even exponents make negative numbers positive, but odd exponents keep negative numbers negative.	For each variable: 1. greater than 1 2. between 0 and 1 3. between −1 and 0 4. less than −1 (and *possibly*) 5. equal to 1 6. equal to 0 7. equal to −1 (Some of the scenarios may be eliminated by the conditions given.)	a. Fractions vs. Integers: $(\frac{1}{2})^3 < \frac{1}{2}$ $\lvert(-\frac{1}{2})^3\rvert < \lvert-\frac{1}{2}\rvert$ *but* $2^3 > 2$ $\lvert(-2)^3\rvert > \lvert-2\rvert$ b. Positive vs. Negative: $(-3)^1 < (-3)^2$ *but* $(-3)^2 > (-3)^3$
D	Absolute Values	The expression within the absolute value bars could be positive or negative.	1. Expression is negative. 2. Expression is positive.	$\lvert x - 2\rvert = 3$: Case 1: $x - 2 = -3$ if $x - 2 < 0$ Case 2: $x - 2 = 3$ if $x - 2 > 0$
E	Zero Product	The product will be zero when any of the multiplied terms are zero	For each multiplied term: 1. Zero 2. Non-zero …as long as at least one of the terms is zero.	If $xy = 0$: Case 1: $x = 0$, or Case 2: $y = 0$, or Case 3: both $x = 0$ and $y = 0$

4

	Trigger:	Reason	Scenarios:	Example:
F	Odd/Even	Addition and multiplication rules allow for an output of a given parity (odd or even) to result from multiple scenarios.	For each variable: 1. Even 2. Odd There are a maximum of 2^n scenarios, where n is the number of variables.	Even results from: Case 1: Even ± Even Case 2: Odd ± Odd Case 3: Even × Even Case 4: Even × Odd Odd results from: Case 1: Even ± Odd Case 2: Odd × Odd
G	Positive/Negative	Multiplication rules (and addition rules, in certain cases) allow for an output of a given sign to result from multiple scenarios.	For each variable: 1. Positive 2. Negative There are a maximum of 2^n scenarios, where n is the number of variables.	Pos results from: Case 1: Pos × Pos Case 2: Neg × Neg Case 3: Pos + Pos Case 4: Pos − Neg Neg results from: Case 1: Pos × Neg Case 2: Neg + Neg Case 3: Neg − Pos Uncertain when you have: Pos + Neg (depends on absolute values)
H	High/Low	If an input variable can take on a range of values, then test the output at the extremes of the range.	1. High 2. Low	Gasoline costs between $3.50 and $4.00 per gallon. A trip requires 2–3 gallons of gasoline. High cost = $4.00 × 3 = $12 Low cost = $3.50 × 2 = $7
I	Remainder/Units Digit	Many different numbers give you the same remainder when divided by some number.	Each set of inputs	7 ÷ 5 → remainder 2 *or* 12 ÷ 5 → remainder 2

MANHATTAN PREP

Problem Set

For problems #1–3, list five values that satisfy each of the following constraints.

1. n is a prime number.

2. $x^2 > 0$

3. $\dfrac{M}{7} = N + \dfrac{3}{7}$, where M and N are positive integers.

For problems #4–6, solve the problem by Testing Cases. Be sure to note whether the *standard number set* (standard set of numbers to test, both integer and non-integer) or *Discrete Number Listing* (consecutive listing of discrete numbers that fit) is the appropriate method to use.

4.   If $a \neq 0$, is $a + a^{-1} > 2$?

   (1) $a > 0$
   (2) $a < 1$

5.   What is the value of positive integer x?

   (1) $x^4 < 1{,}000$
   (2) $2^x < x^2$

6.   Is $y^3 \leq |y|$?

   (1) $y < 1$
   (2) $y < 0$

For problems #7–9, use Scenario Charts to evaluate the possible scenarios for the problem and solve.

7.   If a, b, and c are positive integers, is abc an even integer?

   (1) $a + b$ is even.
   (2) $b + c$ is odd.

8.   28 students were each assigned to one of five classes: Anthropology, Biology, Geology, Musicology, and Sociology. Was at least one of the classes assigned fewer than 5 students?

   (1) At least 6 students were assigned to each of Biology, Geology, and Sociology.
   (2) Geology and Sociology were not assigned the same number of students.

9.   What is the value of xyz?

   (1) $xyz - xy = 0$
   (2) Either $x = 0$ or $y = 0$ or $z = 1$.

For problems #10–15, solve the problem. Note the **strategies** used to solve the problem, and also note any **guessing tactics** that could be employed to help eliminate answer choices. Even if you weren't certain as to the correct answer, which answer choices could you eliminate and why? Also, which guessing tactics would *not* work, and why?

The following Advanced Strategies and Guessing Tactics were discussed in this chapter:

Advanced Strategies	Guessing Tactics
(1) Compute to Completion	(1) Spot Identical Statements
(2) Extract the Equation	(2) Spot Clear Sufficiency
(3) Use the Constraints	(3) Spot One Statement Inside The Other
(4) Beware of Inequalities	(4) Spot One Statement Adding Nothing
(5) Use the Scenario Chart	(5) Spot a (C) Trap
(6) Test Cases	(6) Use Basic Algebraic Reasoning
	(7) Spot Cross-Multiplied Incqualities
	(8) Judge By Appearance

10. Jose purchased both large dressers and small dressers to add to his antique furniture collection. The large dressers cost $31 each, while the small dressers cost $25 each. If Jose did not purchase any other items, how many small dressers did he buy?

    (1) Jose purchased as many small dressers as large dressers.
    (2) In total, Jose spent $280 at the flea market.

11. Amanda and Todd purchase candy, popcorn, and pretzels at the stadium. If a package of candy costs half as much as a bag of popcorn, how much more money did Amanda and Todd spend on the candy than on the popcorn and pretzels combined?

    (1) The cost of a bag of popcorn is equal to the cost of a pretzel.
    (2) Amanda and Todd purchased 24 packages of candy, 6 pretzels, and 6 bags of popcorn.

12. What is the value of $|x + 4|$?

    (1) $x^2 + 8x + 12 = 0$
    (2) $x^2 + 6x = 0$

13. If $abcd \neq 0$, is $abcd < 0$?

    (1) $\dfrac{a}{b} > \dfrac{c}{d}$

    (2) $\dfrac{b}{a} > \dfrac{d}{c}$

14. If m and n are positive integers, is n a multiple of 24?

(1) $n = \dfrac{(m+7)!}{(m+3)!}$

(2) n is a multiple of $(m + 4)$

15. If $y \neq 0$, what is the value of $\dfrac{6^{(x-y)^2}}{6^{(x+3)(x-3)}}$?

(1) $y = 2x$
(2) $y = 2$

Solutions

1. $n = $ **2, 3, 5, 7, 11, 13, 17, 19, 23, etc.**

2. $x = $ **0.5, 2, 3, 6.7, 0, −1, etc.** (Note that the list should include integers and non-integers, positive and negative values—although the items you choose do not need to match these exact values. Anything other than 0 will work!)

3. $M = $ **10, 17, 24, 31, 38, etc. and $N = $ 1, 2, 3, 4, 5, etc.:**

 M must have a remainder of 3 when divided by 7:
 $M = 7 + 3, 14 + 3, 21 + 3, 28 + 3, 35 + 3$, etc.
 $M = 10, 17, 24, 31, 38$, etc.
 $N = 1, 2, 3, 4, 5$, etc.

Note that successive values of M differ by 7, and the corresponding values of N are consecutive integers.

One way to generate this list is to pick consecutive numbers for N and then calculate values for M:

$$\frac{M}{7} = N + \frac{3}{7}$$
$$M = 7N + 3$$

$N = 1, 2, 3, 4, 5$, etc.

$M = 7(1) + 3 = 10, 7(2) + 3 = 17, 7(3) + 3 = 24, 7(4) + 3 = 31, 7(5) + 3 = 38$, etc.

4. **(C):** Because there are no constraints on a, use the *Standard Number Set*. The inequality can be rephrased as follows:

Is $a + a^{-1} > 2$? → Is $a + \dfrac{1}{a} > 2$?

Statement (1): $a > 0$ (INSUFFICIENT)		
a	$a + \dfrac{1}{a}$	$> 2?$
$\dfrac{1}{2}$	$\dfrac{1}{2} + \dfrac{1}{1/2} = \dfrac{5}{2}$	Y
1	$1 + 1 = 2$	N

Statement (2): $a < 1$ (INSUFFICIENT)		
a	$a + \dfrac{1}{a}$	$> 2?$
-1	$-1 + (-1) = -2$	N
$-\dfrac{1}{2}$	$-\dfrac{1}{2} + \dfrac{1}{-1/2} = -\dfrac{5}{2}$	N
$\dfrac{1}{2}$	$\dfrac{1}{2} + \dfrac{1}{1/2} = \dfrac{5}{2}$	Y

Combining the two constraints, $0 < a < 1$. Within the *Standard Number Set*, only 1/2 is within this range. In addition, test numbers close to the boundaries of the range.

Statements (1) & (2): $0 < a < 1$ (SUFFICIENT)		
a	$a + \dfrac{1}{a}$	$> 2?$
$\dfrac{1}{10}$	$\dfrac{1}{10} + \dfrac{1}{^1/_{10}} = \dfrac{101}{10}$	Y
$\dfrac{1}{2}$	$\dfrac{1}{2} + \dfrac{1}{^1/_2} = \dfrac{5}{2}$	Y
$\dfrac{9}{10}$	$\dfrac{9}{10} + \dfrac{10}{9} = \dfrac{181}{90}$	Y

It seems that at the extreme edges, the values are greater than 2, so statements (1) & (2) appear to be SUFFICIENT.

The correct answer is **(C)**.

5. **(B):** Because x is a positive integer, employ *Discrete Number Listing*.

Statement (1): $x^4 < 1{,}000$ (INSUFFICIENT)		
x	x^4	< 1000
1	$1^4 = 1$	valid
2	$2^4 = 16$	valid
3	$3^4 = 81$	valid
4	$4^4 = 256$	valid
5	$5^4 = 625$	valid
6	$6^4 = 1{,}296$	invalid

Statement (2): $2^x < x^2$ (SUFFICIENT)			
x	2^x	x^2	$2x < x^2$
1	$2^1 = 2$	$1^2 = 1$	invalid
2	$2^2 = 4$	$2^2 = 4$	invalid
3	$2^3 = 8$	$3^2 = 9$	valid
4	$2^4 = 16$	$4^2 = 16$	invalid
5	$2^5 = 32$	$5^2 = 25$	invalid

Listing numbers for statement (2) indicates that 3 is the only integer for x such that $2^x < x^2$. Greater integers than 5 would only lead to a greater gap the other way.

The correct answer is **(B)**.

6. **(D):** Because there are no constraints on y, use the *Standard Number Set*, displayed here in Number Line graphic form:

	-2	$-3/2$	-1	$-1/2$	0	$1/2$	1	$3/2$	2
y^3	-8	$-27/8$	-1	$-1/8$	0	$1/8$	1	$27/8$	8
$|y|$	2	$3/2$	1	$1/2$	0	$1/2$	1	$3/2$	2
$y^3 \le |y|?$	Y	Y	Y	Y	Y	Y	Y	N	N

MANHATTAN
PREP

Statement (1): $y < 1$. If y is less than 1, all tested values show $y^3 \leq |y|$. SUFFICIENT.
Statement (2): $y < 0$. If y is less than 0, all tested values show $y^3 \leq |y|$. SUFFICIENT.

Notice that you could use Guessing Tactic 3: **Spot One Statement Inside the Other**. $y < 0$ is more limiting than $y < 1$, so if statement (1) is sufficient, statement (2) must be sufficient.

The correct answer is **(D)**.

7. **(B):** In order for abc to be even, what must be true? If just one of the numbers is even, then the product will be even. The only case that will produce an odd is when all three numbers are odd. Keep this in mind when testing the statements.

(1) INSUFFICIENT: If $a + b$ is even, then the two variables are either both even or both odd.

a	b	c	abc even?
Even	Even	Even	Y
Odd	Odd	Odd	N

(2) SUFFICIENT: $b + c$ is odd, so one of b and c is odd and the other is even. In other words, it is impossible for all three variables to be odd. Therefore, the product abc must be even.

The correct answer is **(B)**.

8. **(C):** Set up a table and try to find contradictory scenarios.

(1) INSUFFICIENT:

A	B	G	M	S	<5 in one class?
5	6	6	5	6	No
4	6	6	6	6	Yes

(2) INSUFFICIENT:

A	B	G	M	S	<5 in one class?
6	6	4	6	6	Yes
6	5	5	6	6	No

(1) AND (2) SUFFICIENT:

A	B	G	M	S	<5 in one class?
4	6	6	5	7	Yes

Since Geology and Sociology each have to have a minimum of 6 students, and they can't have the same number of students, one of the two classes has to have at least 7 students. Between Bio, Geo, and Soc, then, the minimum number of students is $6 + 6 + 7 = 19$, leaving 9 students to be split among the other two classes. In this case, it's impossible to have 5 or more students in both of those two remaining classes.

The correct answer is **(C)**.

9. (E):

(1) INSUFFICIENT: First, factor the equation:

$$xyz - xy = 0$$
$$xy(z - 1) = 0$$

For this product to equal zero, either $x = 0$, or $y = 0$, or $z = 1$. List the scenarios and test the possible values for xyz:

x	y	zs	xyz
0	any	any	0
any	0	any	0
any	any	1	xy (any value)

Thus if $x = 0$ or $y = 0$, then $xyz = 0$, but if $z = 1$, then xyz could take on any value.

(2) INSUFFICIENT: This statement indicates that either $x = 0$ or $y = 0$ or $z = 1$. This is the exact same information from statement (1), so eliminate (A), (B) and (C) by *Spotting Identical Statements*. Since statement (1) also proved to be insufficient, eliminate (D) as well.

The correct answer is **(E)**.

10. (B): The question stem indicates that Jose purchased both large ($31 each) and small dressers ($25 each), and asks how many small dressers he purchased.

Since this is an algebraic translations problem, assign variables to the unknowns in the problem:

L = Large dressers
S = Small dressers

(1) INSUFFICIENT: Jose purchased an equal number of small dressers and large dressers. This is not sufficient, because he could have purchased any number of dressers. For example, $L = 2$ and $S = 2$ is one possibility, while $L = 10$ and $S = 10$ is another.

(2) SUFFICIENT: Jose spent a total of $280 at the flea market. At first glance, this doesn't seem to be enough information, because there are 2 unknowns and 1 equation:

$$31L + 25S = 280$$

However, the problem contains the *hidden constraint* that L and S must be *positive integers*, since they represent countable things (the number of large and small dressers). It's possible that only one set of integers fulfills this constraint. Check possible values for L to see whether this leads to an integer solution for S:

#L	$L	$S (280 − $L)	$S = integer? ($S/25)
1	31	249	NO
2	62	218	NO
3	93	187	NO
4	124	156	NO
5	155	125	YES

You could continue with these calculations, but notice the pattern: every time you increase #*L* by one, the units digit of the $*S* decreases by 1, so the next time you'll reach a $*S* figure that could be a multiple of 25, #*L* would have to be 10. If #*L* = 10, then $*L* = $310, which is greater than the $280 that Jose spent. (In fact, if you notice the pattern earlier, you can save yourself a couple of calculations and jump straight to #*L* = 5.

The correct answer is (B).

11. (C): Assign variables to the unknowns in the problem.

C = packages of candy P_c = price of a package of candy
P = bags of popcorn P_p = price of a bag of popcorn
R = number of pretzels P_r = price of a pretzel

Algebraically, the question asks: what is $P_c \times C - (P_p \times P + P_r \times R)$?

The question stem indicates that $P_c = \dfrac{1}{2} \times P_p$.

(1) INSUFFICIENT: $P_r = P_p$. Substitute and rephrase the question:

What is $P_c \times C - (P_p \times P + P_r \times R)$?
What is $(\dfrac{1}{2} \times P_p) \times C - (P_p \times P + (P_p) \times R)$?
What is $P_p \times (\dfrac{1}{2} \times C - P - R)$?

There are four unknown variables, so statement (1) is not sufficient.

(2) INSUFFICIENT: $C = 24$, $P = 6$, and $R = 6$:

What is $P_c \times C - (P_p \times P + P_r \times R)$?
What is $(\dfrac{1}{2} \times P_p) \times 24 - (P_p \times 6 + P_r \times 6)$?
What is $12P_p - 6P_p - 6P_r$?
What is $6P_p - 6P_r$?

There are two unknown variables, so statement (2) is not sufficient.

(1) AND (2) SUFFICIENT:

From statement (2): What is $6P_p - 6P_r$?
From statement (1): What is $6P_p - 6(P_p)$?
Rephrased question: What is 0?

Given the relative prices of the candy, popcorn, and pretzels, and the quantity of each purchased, the cost of the candy will always equal the combined cost of the popcorn and pretzels, even though it's impossible to calculate the exact prices. Statements (1) and (2) combined are SUFFICIENT to answer the question.

The correct answer is (C).

12. (A): It's tempting to rephrase the question as "What is x?" but that is dangerous when the question contains absolute value symbols. It's possible that two different values of x would resolve to the same value of $|x + 4|$. Leave the question as it is.

(1) SUFFICIENT: $x^2 + 8x + 12 = 0$. Factor the equation:

$$(x + 2)(x + 6) = 0$$
$$x = -2 \text{ or } -6$$

Plug these answers into the question stem:

$$|(-2) + 4| = |2| = 2 \qquad\qquad |(-6) + 4| = |-2| = 2$$

The two different values resolve to the same final value for $|x + 4|$, so statement (1) is sufficient.

(2) INSUFFICIENT: $x^2 + 6x = 0$. Factor the equation:

$$x(x + 6) = 0$$
$$x = 0 \text{ or } -6$$

Plug both values into the question stem:

$$|(0) + 4| = 4 \qquad\qquad |(-6) + 4| = |-2| = 2$$

There are two different values for the expression $|x + 4|$, so statement (2) is not sufficient.

The correct answer is **(A)**.

13. (C): If $abcd \neq 0$, then none of the variables equals 0. In order for the product $abcd$ to be negative, you would need to have an odd number of negatives in the mix:

Scenario	Product $abcd$
all 4 positive or all 4 negative	+ product
3 positive, 1 negative	− product
2 positive, 2 negative	+ product
1 positive, 3 negative	− product

(1) INSUFFICIENT: Beware of inequalities.

If b and d are both positive or both negative, then $ad > bc$.

If one is positive and one is negative, then $ad < bc$.

This statement indicates nothing about a and c, though.

(2) INSUFFICIENT:

If a and c are both positive or both negative, then $bc > ad$.

If one is positive and one is negative, then $bc < ad$.

This statement indicates nothing about b and d, though.

(1) AND (2) SUFFICIENT: Here's where the trick comes in. The two statements allow two possible scenarios:

If $ad > bc$, then b and d have the same sign but a and c have opposite signs. In this case, three signs are the same and one is not, so there are an odd number of negatives in the mix and the product of all four variables must be negative.

If $ad < bc$, b and d have opposite signs, but a and c have the same signs. In this case, three signs are the same and one is not; as before, the product of all four variables must be negative.

Either way, the two statements together are sufficient to answer the question.

The correct answer is **(C)**.

14. **(A):** The question stem asks whether $n = 24$, 48, 72, …

(1) SUFFICIENT: Rewrite and simplify:

$$n = \frac{(m+7)(m+6)(m+5)(m+4)(m+3)!}{(m+3)!}$$

$$n = (m+7)(m+6)(m+5)(m+4)$$

In other words, n is the product of four consecutive integers. In any four consecutive integers, one number must be divisible by 3 and two numbers must be even. Furthermore, of the two even numbers, one must be divisible by 4. As a result, the product of any four consecutive integers is divisible by $(3)(2)(4) = 24$.

Alternatively, you could figure this out by testing a few cases:

$m = 1$: $(8)(7)(6)(5)$ which is divisible by $(8)(3) = 24$
$m = 2$: $(9)(8)(7)(6)$ which is divisible by $(8)(3) = 24$
$m = 3$: $(10)(9)(8)(7)$ which is divisible by $(8)(3) = 24$

(2) INSUFFICIENT: If $m = 1$, then n could equal 5, which is not a multiple of 24. If $m = 20$, then n could equal 24, which is a multiple of 24.

The correct answer is **(A)**.

15. **(A):** This problem's complexity resides almost entirely in the question stem; simplify it before moving to the statements.

$$\frac{6^{(x-y)^2}}{6^{(x+3)(x-3)}} = \frac{6^{x^2-2xy+y^2}}{6^{x^2-9}} = 6^{(x^2-2xy+y^2)-(x^2-9)} = 6^{-2xy+y^2+9}$$

You can therefore rephrase this Value question to, "What is the value of $y^2 - 2xy + 9$?"

Now check the statements. Statement (2) is simpler; start there.

(2) INSUFFICIENT: Even if you substitute $y = 2$ into the expression, you'll be left with an x.

(1) SUFFICIENT: Plug $y = 2x$ into the expression. Note that it's easier to plug in a y for the one occurrence of $2x$.

$$-2xy + y^2 + 9$$
$$-(y)y + y^2 + 9$$
$$-y^2 + y^2 + 9$$

Therefore, the value of the expression is 9.

The correct answer is **(A)**.

4

Chapter 5 *of* 5

GMAT Advanced Quant

Part 2

Pattern Recognition

In This Chapter...

Chapter 5
Pattern Recognition

Pattern Recognition Problems

In the context of the GMAT, *pattern recognition* involves spotting a repeating cycle or other simple relationship underlying a series of numbers. If you can grasp the rule, you can predict numbers that appear later in the series. The series may be part of a defined sequence, or it may arise from a general list of possibilities. Either way, if you can spot the pattern, you can eliminate a lot of unnecessary calculation. In fact, often the only feasible way to get the answer in two minutes (for example, finding the 100th number in some series) is to recognize the underlying pattern. Here's an example.

Try-It #5-1

> Each number in a sequence is 3 more than the previous number. If the first number is 4, what is the value of the 1,000th term in the sequence?

Obviously, finding the 1,000th number the long way (by computing every intervening number) is impossible in the time allotted on the GMAT. You can solve this problem in several ways, but one powerful way is to compute the first several terms, spot the underlying *pattern*, figure out *the rule*, and then apply it.

The first 5 terms of the sequence are 4, 7, 10, 13, 16. Notice that you repeatedly add 3 to get the next value. Repeated addition is simply multiplication, so match these numbers to the multiples of 3. The first 5 multiples of 3 are 3, 6, 9, 12, 15—all 1 less than the numbers in the sequence. Thus the rule for generating the sequence is "take the corresponding multiple of 3, and add 1." Therefore, the 1,000th term of the sequence is 1 more than the 1,000th multiple of 3, which is 3,000 + 1 = 3,001. Once you spot the pattern, you can skip over vast amounts of unnecessary work.

The two most basic patterns are these:

> 1. The *counting numbers* (1, 2, 3, 4, ...), also known as the *positive integers*. As simple as this pattern may seem, it is the basis for many other patterns. For instance, the sequence of the

multiples of 7 (7, 14, 21, 28, ...) can be derived from 1, 2, 3, 4, ... by multiplying by 7. You can write this sequence as $S_n = 7n$, where n is the basic sequence of positive integers.

2. A *repeating cycle* of numbers. For instance, the sequence 4, 2, 6, 4, 2, 6, 4, 2, 6... has a repeating cycle of three terms: 4, 2, 6. Repeating cycles can be derived in various ways from the counting numbers (for example, when you raise an integer to increasing powers, the units digits of the results repeat themselves). However, it is often easier to think of repeating cycles *on their own terms*, separately from the counting numbers and related patterns.

When you are examining a string of numbers for a pattern, do the following:

1. Compute the first five to eight terms and try to match them to a stock pattern that you already know. The most basic pattern is the counting numbers, but you should also have these related patterns up your sleeve:

   a. Multiples (e.g., $7 \times 1 = \mathbf{7}$, $7 \times 2 = \mathbf{14}$, $7 \times 3 = \mathbf{21}$, $7 \times 4 = \mathbf{28}$, $7 \times 5 = \mathbf{35}$, ..., $7n$, ...)
   b. Squares ($1^2 = \mathbf{1}$, $2^2 = \mathbf{4}$, $3^2 = \mathbf{9}$, $4^2 = \mathbf{16}$, $5^2 = \mathbf{25}$, ..., n^2, ...)
   c. Powers ($2^1 = \mathbf{2}$, $2^2 = \mathbf{4}$, $2^3 = \mathbf{8}$, $2^4 = \mathbf{16}$, $2^5 = \mathbf{32}$, ..., 2^n, ...)

For each of these stock sequences, notice exactly where the counting numbers come into play. For instance, in the squares series, the counting numbers are the *bases*, but in the powers series, the counting numbers are the *exponents*.

2. Look for repeating cycles. As soon as you generate a repeated term, see whether the sequence will simply repeat itself from that point onward. Repeating cycles on the GMAT typically begin repeating every four terms (or fewer), so five to eight terms should be sufficient to identify the pattern. Of course, some cycles repeat every single term—that is, it's the same number over and over again!

3. If you are stuck, look for patterns within *differences between terms* or *sums across terms*.

   a. Look at the difference between consecutive terms. For instance, this process can help you spot linear sequences (sequences of multiples plus a constant):

Sequence:	10	17	24	31	...	$7n + 3$ ...
Differences:	7	7	7	7	(constant difference)	

   b. Also look at the *cumulative sum* of all the terms up to that point. This is helpful if the terms get closer to zero or alternate in sign.

Sequence:	$\dfrac{1}{2}$	$\dfrac{1}{4}$	$\dfrac{1}{8}$	$\dfrac{1}{16}$	...	$\dfrac{1}{2^n}$	...
Cumulative Sum:	$\dfrac{1}{2}$	$\dfrac{3}{4}$	$\dfrac{7}{8}$	$\dfrac{15}{16}$	...	$\dfrac{(2^n - 1)}{2^n}$	...

   Notice that the cumulative sum for this sequence approaches 1.

c. Some sums involve *matching pairs* that sum to the same number (or even cancel each other out). Be on the lookout for such matching pairs.

What is the sum of 1, 5, 8, 10, 11, 11, 12, 14, 17, and 21?

You can of course sum these numbers in order, but look to make natural intermediate sums (subtotals) with matching pairs. In this example, spot the repeated 11's in the middle and sum them to 22. Working outward, 10 and 12 sum to 22 as well. So do 8 and 14, 5 and 17, and 1 and 21. In all, there are 5 subtotals of 22, for a grand total of 110.

4. Look at characteristics of the numbers: positive/negative, odd/even, integer/non-integer, etc. Once you have extended the pattern for several terms, these characteristics will generally repeat or alternate in some predictable way.

Perhaps the most important principle to apply on Pattern Recognition problems is to *Put Pen To Paper,* as discussed in Chapter 1. Often the pattern will be completely hidden until you actually compute the first several values of the sequence or other initial results.

Several types of problems frequently involve underlying patterns. When you see these types of problems on the GMAT, be ready to analyze the pattern so you can find the rule:

1. **Sequence problems** – Nearly all sequence problems involve a pattern in the elements (or terms) of the sequence. Sequences can be defined either directly (i.e., each value in the series is a function of its *location* in the order of the sequence) or recursively (i.e., each value is a function of the *previous items* in the sequence).

2. **Units (Ones) Digit problems** – Questions involving the last digit (sometimes called the *Units* or *Ones* digit) of an integer almost always involve some sort of repeating cycle pattern that can be exploited.

3. **Remainder problems** – Remainders from the division of one integer into another will result in a pattern. For example, when divided by 5, the counting numbers will exhibit the following repeating remainder pattern: 1, 2, 3, 4, 0, 1, 2, 3, 4, 0… The units digit of an integer is a special case of a remainder: it's the remainder after division by 10.

4. **Other pattern problems** – Some pattern problems do not involve deciphering a string of numbers and discovering the rule. For instance, you may have to count a set of numbers that all fit some constraint. The point is to discover a simple rule or group of rules that let you account for all the numbers — and therefore count them—without having to generate each one. Here are some ideas:

   • Break the problem into sub-problems. For instance, a sum may be split into several smaller sums. Or you might count a larger total, then subtract items that do not fit the constraint. You even might multiply a larger total by the proportion of suitable items, if that fraction is easy to calculate.

- Recall counting and summing methods from our Strategy Guides:

  a. Number of Choices: When you have a series of successive decisions, you multiply the number of choices you have at each stage to find the number of total choices you have. For instance, if you can choose 1 appetizer out of 6 possible appetizers and 1 main course out of 7 possible main courses, then you could have $6 \times 7 = 42$ possible meals.

  b. Number of items in a Consecutive Set of Integers: The number of integers in a consecutive set of integers equals the largest minus the smallest, plus 1.

  c. Sum of a Consecutive Set of Integers: The sum of a consecutive set of integers equals the number of integers (computed above) multiplied by the average, which is the average of the largest integer and the smallest integer. This is also equal to the median, or "middle," number in the set.

- As you go, always check that the extreme cases are still valid. Two or three constraints can interact in surprising ways, eliminating some of the values that would seem to work otherwise.

Sequence Problems

Any question that involves the definition of a sequence (usually involving subscripted variables, such as A_n and S_n) is very likely to involve patterns. These patterns can range from relatively straightforward linear patterns to much more complicated ones.

When you are given a sequence definition, list a few terms of the sequence, starting with any particular terms you are given, and look for a pattern.

Do not be intimidated by a *recursive* definition for a sequence, in which each term is defined using *earlier* terms. (By contrast, a direct definition defines each term using the *position* or *index* of the term.) To illustrate the difference, here are two ways to define the series of positive odd integers {1, 3, 5, 7, 9, etc.}:

Recursive definition	Direct definition
$A_n = A_{n-1} + 2$ where $n > 1$ and $A_1 = 1$ Translation: "This term = the *previous term* + 2, and the first term is 1."	$A_n = 2n - 1$, where $n \geq 1$ Translation: "This term = the *index number* $\times$ 2, minus 1. Thus the first term is $(2)(1) - 1 = 1$."

Try-It #5-2

The sequence X_n is defined as follows: $X_n = 2X_{n-1} - 1$ whenever n is an integer greater than 1. If $X_1 = 3$, what is the value of $X_{20} - X_{19}$?

The pattern underlying this sequence is not obvious, so begin computing a few of the terms in the set:

n	X_n
1	3
2	$2(3) - 1 = 5$
3	$2(5) - 1 = 9$
4	$2(9) - 1 = 17$
5	$2(17) - 1 = 33$
6	$2(33) - 1 = 65$
7	$2(65) - 1 = 129$

You might notice that there appears to be a repeating pattern among the units digits of the elements of X_n (3, 5, 9, 7, 3, 5, 9…). However, this does not help to answer the question, which asks about the *difference* between two consecutive elements later in the set. Instead, look at the differences between consecutive elements:

n	X_n	$X_n - X_{n-1}$
1	3	–
2	$2(3) - 1 = 5$	$5 - 3 = 2$
3	$2(5) - 1 = 9$	$9 - 5 = 4$
4	$2(9) - 1 = 17$	$17 - 9 = 8$
5	$2(17) - 1 = 33$	$33 - 17 = 16$
6	$2(33) - 1 = 65$	$65 - 33 = 32$
7	$2(65) - 1 = 129$	$129 - 65 = 64$

The pattern quickly emerges: the difference between consecutive terms in the sequence appears to always be a power of 2. Specifically, $X_2 - X_1 = 2 = 2^1$, $X_3 - X_2 = 4 = 2^2$, $X_4 - X_3 = 8 = 2^3$, etc.

You can determine the pattern for the sequence: $X_n - X_{n-1}$ equals 2^{n-1}. Therefore $X_{20} - X_{19} = 2^{19}$. This is a *difference pattern*—a pattern or rule that exists among the differences between consecutive terms in the sequence. Be careful at this last step! When you extrapolate the pattern, you might accidentally think that the number you want is 2^{20}. Always explicitly match to the index, and realize that you might be slightly shifted. In this case, the difference you want is *not* 2^n. The difference is 2^{n-1}.

Try-It #5-3

If $A_n = \dfrac{1}{n(n+1)}$ for all positive integers n, what is the sum of the first 100 elements of A_n?

Once again, compute the first few elements of A_n. Because you need to know the sum of the first 100 elements, also track the cumulative sum:

n	A_n	Sum through A_n:
1	$\dfrac{1}{1\times 2}=\dfrac{1}{2}$	$\dfrac{1}{2}$
2	$\dfrac{1}{2\times 3}=\dfrac{1}{6}$	$\dfrac{1}{2}+\dfrac{1}{6}=\dfrac{3+1}{6}=\dfrac{2}{3}$
3	$\dfrac{1}{3\times 4}=\dfrac{1}{12}$	$\dfrac{2}{3}+\dfrac{1}{12}=\dfrac{8+1}{12}=\dfrac{3}{4}$
4	$\dfrac{1}{4\times 5}=\dfrac{1}{20}$	$\dfrac{3}{4}+\dfrac{1}{20}=\dfrac{15+1}{20}=\dfrac{4}{5}$
5	$\dfrac{1}{5\times 6}=\dfrac{1}{30}$	$\dfrac{4}{5}+\dfrac{1}{30}=\dfrac{24+1}{30}=\dfrac{5}{6}$

The sum of the first n terms of A_n equals $\dfrac{n}{n+1}$. Therefore, the sum of the first 100 terms is $\dfrac{100}{101}$. This

5

is a *summing pattern*—a pattern or rule that exists among the cumulative sum of the terms in the sequence.

Units (Ones) Digit Problems

When you raise an integer to a power, the units digit always displays some kind of pattern as you increase the power.

Try-It #5-4

What is the units digit of 4^{674}?

Observe what happens to the units digit of the consecutive powers of 4, starting with 4^1:

$4^1 = 4$ → last digit of $4 = 4$
$4^2 = 4(4^1)$ → last digit of $4(4) =$ last digit of $16 = 6$
$4^3 = 4(4^2)$ → last digit of $4(6) =$ last digit of $24 = 4$
$4^4 = 4(4^3)$ → last digit of $4(4) =$ last digit of $16 = 6$

} Because the computations $(4 \times 4 = 16)$ and $(4 \times 6 = 24)$ keep repeating, the units digit will continue to alternate [4, 6].

Thus 4^x will have a units digit of 4 whenever x is odd, and a units digit of 6 whenever x is even (assuming, of course, that x is positive). The units digit of 4^{674} is therefore 6.

MANHATTAN
PREP

Also notice that in determining the value of the units digit of a product, *all of the other digits* besides the units digit are irrelevant. Therefore, 14^{674} and $3,184^{674}$ will both also have units digits of 6. This is also true for multiplication of *any* two integers, as well as the *addition* of any integers:

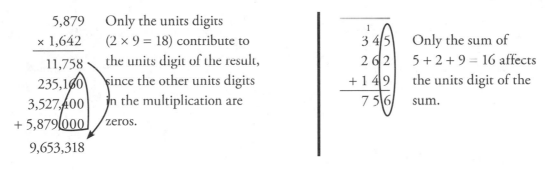

As mentioned earlier, every integer raised to different positive exponents has a units digit pattern. As an exercise, derive several of the patterns yourself for the units digits 2, 3, 5, 7, and 8; you can check your work using the table below.

Series	Consecutive Powers	Units digit pattern
1^x	**1**; **1**; **1**; **1**; **1**; **1**; etc.	[1]
2^x	**2**; **4**; **8**; **16**; **32**; **64**; etc.	[2, 4, 8, 6]
3^x	**3**; **9**; **27**; **81**; **243**; **729**; etc.	[3, 9, 7, 1]
4^x	**4**; **16**; **64**; **256**; **1,024**; **4,096**; etc.	[4, 6]
5^x	**5**; **25**; **125**; **625**; **3,125**; **15,625**; etc.	[5]
6^x	**6**; **36**; **216**; **1,296**; **7,776**; **46,656**; etc.	[6]
7^x	**7**; **49**; **343**; **2,401**; **16,807**; **117,649**; etc.	[7, 9, 3, 1]
8^x	**8**; **64**; **512**; **4,096**; **32,768**; **262,144**; etc.	[8, 4, 2, 6]
9^x	**9**; **81**; **729**; **6,561**; **59,049**; **531,441**; etc.	[9, 1]
10^x	**10**; **100**; **1,000**; **10,000**; **100,000**; **1,000,000**; etc.	[0]

You can either memorize this chart or know how to regenerate these patterns quickly. The units digits 1, 5, 6, and 0 just repeat the same digit forever; there's no real pattern to memorize. That leaves you with six possibilities to memorize (or to recreate when you need them). Note that no pattern goes beyond four numbers before repeating, so you don't have to check beyond the first four terms of any pattern.

Try-It #5-5

What is the units digit of 19^{40}?

As shown in the table above, $9^1 = 9$, $9^2 = 81$, $9^3 = 729$, etc., 19 will have the same units digit pattern as 9. Therefore the pattern is a two-term repeating pattern: 9, 1, 9, 1... This pattern alternates every two items, just like odd and even integers. Since 40 is an even number, the units digit of 19^{40} will equal 1.

What is the remainder when 19^{40} is divided by 10?

The remainder whenever an integer is divided by 10 will always be the same as the units digit of the original number. In effect, this alternative question is asking the exact same thing as the original question.

$$\frac{84}{10} = 8\frac{4}{10} \rightarrow 8 \text{ remainder } \mathbf{4} \qquad\qquad \frac{361}{10} = 36\frac{1}{10} \rightarrow 36 \text{ remainder } \mathbf{1}$$

$$\frac{7,819}{10} = 781\frac{9}{10} \rightarrow 781 \text{ remainder } \mathbf{9}$$

Remainder Problems

In general, remainders provide a means by which the GMAT can disguise an underlying pattern. For example, notice that when the positive integer n is divided by 4, the remainders follow a pattern as n increases consecutively:

1 div by 4 → remainder 1
2 div by 4 → remainder 2
3 div by 4 → remainder 3
4 div by 4 → remainder 0
5 div by 4 → remainder 1

} A *repeating cycle* of [1,2,3,0] emerges for the remainders when dividing the counting numbers by 4. The number of terms in the repeat equals the divisor in this case.

Surprising patterns can emerge in remainder problems as well.

Try-It #5-6

If x and y are positive integers, what is the remainder when 5^x is divided by y?

(1) $x = 3$
(2) $y = 4$

(1) INSUFFICIENT: $5^3 = 125$. The problem provides no information about the value of y, however. For example, if $y = 5$, then the remainder equals 0. If $y = 6$, then the remainder is 5.

(2) SUFFICIENT: This statement may not initially appear to be sufficient, but test some different values for x:

x	5^x	Remainder of $\dfrac{5^x}{4}$
1	5	1
2	25	1
3	125	1
4	625	1

The pattern is clear: no matter what exponent 5 is raised to, the remainder when divided by 4 will always equal 1—a fact that you probably did not expect before testing the rule for this problem.

The correct answer is **(B)**.

Do not fall into the easy trap of assuming that you need to know both x and y to solve this problem. Remainders can hide a wide array of underlying patterns. In this case, when $y = 4$, the answer will be the same no matter what value is chosen for x.

Other Pattern Problems

Many questions will not at first glance demonstrate an obvious pattern. For example, a Word Problem involving counting a collection of objects or maximizing some number may hide some sort of regularity. The point is to discover a simple rule or group of rules that let you account for all the possibilities—and therefore count or maximize them—without having to generate each possibility separately.

Try-It #5-7

> How many of the integers between 1 and 400, inclusive, are not divisible by 4 and do not contain any 4's as a digit?

This problem involves a *counting pattern*. It's clear that there are 400 integers between 1 and 400, inclusive. You'll need to subtract the integers that are divisible by 4 or contain a 4 as a digit. The tricky part is the overlap: some numbers, such as 64 and 124, violate both constraints.

It is easier to determine the number of multiples of 4. Since there are 400 integers in the set, and those 400 integers are consecutive, there must be 400/4 = 100 integers that are divisible by 4. There are 400 − 100 = 300 integers remaining.

Next, consider the numbers that have a 4 among their digits, but haven't already been eliminated. In other words, numbers with a 4 among their digits that *are not* themselves multiples of 4.

Only one of the integers between 1 and 400, inclusive, has a 4 in the hundreds place: 400. You have already eliminated that one from the count because it is a multiple of 4.

To eliminate integers with a 4 in the tens place, of the form $x4y$, count only those that are not multiples of 4. These are the numbers whose last two digits are 41, 42, 43, 45, 46, 47, or 49. There are 7 such numbers in each set of "hundreds," i.e., the 300's, the 200's, the 100's and the no hundreds. That is a total of 7 × 4 = 28 terms. There are 300 − 28 = 272 integers remaining.

Last, count and eliminate the integers with 4 in the units digit, of the form $xy4$, that have not already been subtracted. These are the numbers whose last two digits are 14, 34, 54, 74, or 94 (numbers with an even integer in the tens place and 4 in the units are all divisible by 4, so they have been eliminated already). There are 5 such numbers in each set of "hundreds," so that is a total of 5 × 4 = 20 terms. There are 272 − 20 = 252 integers remaining.

The correct answer is 400 − 100 − 28 − 20 = 252.

Try-It #5-8

$x = 10^{10} - z$, where z is a two-digit integer. If the sum of the digits of x equals 84, how many values for z are possible?

The first thing to do in solving this problem is to subtract any two-digit number from 10^{10} and look for a pattern. Try subtracting 24:

$$10^{10} = 10,000,000,000$$

$$
\begin{array}{r}
10,000,000,000 \\
-24 \\
\hline
9,999,999,976
\end{array}
$$

Notice the pattern: the first 8 digits of x are all 9's, so those digits sum to 72. This will be true no matter which two-digit integer you try for z. Therefore, the final two digits of x must sum to $84 - 72 = 12$.

What possibilities would work for these final two digits of x? 39, 48, 57, 66, 75, 84, and 93 all add to 12. When subtracted from 100, these numbers will have to produce a two-digit integer. Try subtracting from 100 to find the pattern:

$$100 - 39 = 61 \qquad\qquad 100 - 48 = 52$$

Hmm. Each successive number is larger, so it will result in a smaller two-digit integer. Do the numbers actually drop to one digit at some point? Jump to the other end of the scale: try 93.

$$100 - 93 = 7$$

In order for x to end in 93, z would have to be 7, which is not a two-digit integer. According to the GMAT, a two-digit integer must have a non-zero tens digit and zeros for all higher places. What about the next number up? If x ends in 84, then it would result in the two-digit integer $100 - 84 = 16$. All of the other numbers are two-digit integers; only 93 doesn't work.

Therefore, the final two digits of x can only be 39, 48, 57, 66, 75, and 84, resulting in six possible values for z.

As the two previous problems demonstrate, unusual patterns can appear in problems on the GMAT. Sometimes you must "think outside the box" to identify the wanted pattern.

Look for the examples in the following diagram:

Pattern Type	Example	Comments
Repeats	1, 3, –2, 1, 3, –2, 1, etc.	Often these repeating patterns can only be identified by listing out a few values in the pattern. On the GMAT, the cycle is usually 4 numbers or fewer (the cycle in the example shown is 3).
Consecutive integers	10, 11, 12, 13, 14, etc.	Can be defined as follows: $A_n - n + k$, where n and k are integers. In this example, $A_n = n + 9$, so that the first term is $1 + 9 = 10$. Note that the average term = the median term = $1/2 \times$ (First + Last).
Consecutive multiples	7, 14, 21, 28, etc.	Consecutive multiples of 7, for example, can be defined as follows: $A_n = 7n$, where n is a set of consecutive integers. The evens are just a special case (multiples of 2, or $2n$). Note that the average term = the median term = $1/2 \times$ (First + Last).
Evenly spaced sets	9, 16, 23, 30, etc. (Constant difference of 7 between consecutive terms.)	When dividing this series by 7, each of the terms leaves a remainder of 2. Can be defined as a multiple plus/minus a constant: $A_n = 7n + k$, where n is a set of consecutive integers, in this example. The odds are a special case (multiples of 2, plus 1, or $2n + 1$). Note that the average term = the median term = $1/2 \times$ (First + Last), as for consecutive multiples.
Non-uniform spacing that itself follows a pattern	0, 1, 3, 6, 10, 15, etc. (Spacing between terms follows 1, 2, 3, 4, 5, etc. pattern.)	Another example of this type is the perfect squares: 0, 1, 4, 9, 16, 25, etc. (Spacing between squares = 1, 3, 5, 7, 9, etc. = the odd integers!)
Alternating sign	–1, 1, –2, 2, –3, 3, etc.	Can result from a $(-1)^n$ term in a direct sequence definition, or a $(-(A_{n-1}))$ term in a recursive sequence definition.

In general, listing five to eight examples or terms will usually be sufficient to identify a pattern on the GMAT—you can stop with fewer examples if you've identified the pattern by that point.

Problem Set

For the following problems, use the Pattern Recognition techniques discussed in this chapter to solve.

1. In the sequence 4, 9, 14, 19, ..., each term is 5 greater than the previous term. What is the remainder when the 75th term is divided by 9?

2. If x and y are integers between 0 and 9, inclusive, and the units digit of x^y is 5, what are the possible values of x and y?

3. What is the remainder when $13^{17} + 17^{13}$ is divided by 10?

4. If y is a positive integer, what is the units digit of y?

    (1) The units digit of y^2 equals 6.
    (2) The units digit of $(y + 1)^2$ equals 5.

5. If y is a positive integer, what is the units digit of y?

    (1) The units digit of $y^2 = 1$.
    (2) The units digit of y does not equal 1.

6. If x is a positive integer and $<z>$ is the greatest multiple of ten less than or equal to z, what is the value of $x - <x>$?

    (1) $<x^{14}> + x^{15}$ has a units digit of 7.
    (2) $<x^{15}> + x^{16}$ has a units digit of 1.

7. If x is an integer, what is the remainder when x is divided by 5?

    (1) x^2 has a remainder of 4 when divided by 5.
    (2) x^3 has a remainder of 2 when divided by 5.

8. If x and y are positive integers, what is the remainder when 5^x is divided by y?

    (1) x is an even integer.
    (2) $y = 3$.

9. $a, b, c,$ and d are positive integers. If $\dfrac{a}{b}$ has a remainder of 9 and $\dfrac{c}{d}$ has a remainder of 10, what is the minimum possible value for bd?

10. What is the sum of the numbers in the grid below?

-2	-1	1	2	3	4
-4	-2	2	4	6	8
-6	-3	3	6	9	12
-8	-4	4	8	12	16
-10	-5	5	10	15	20
-12	-6	6	12	18	24

11. The sequence $a_1, a_2, a_3, \ldots, a_n$ is defined such that $a_n = 9 + a_{n-1}$ for all $n > 1$. If $a_1 = 11$, what is the value of a_{35}?

12. The sequence S is defined as follows for all $n \geq 1$:

$$S_n = (-1)^n \frac{1}{n(n+1)}$$

The sum of the first 10 terms of S is

(A) Between -1 and $-\frac{1}{2}$ (B) Between $-\frac{1}{2}$ and 0 (C) Between 0 and $\frac{1}{2}$

(D) Between $\frac{1}{2}$ and 1 (E) Greater than 1

13. In sequence Q, the first number is 3, and each subsequent number in the sequence is determined by doubling the previous number and then adding 2. How many times does the digit 8 appear in the units digit of the first 10 terms of the sequence?

14. $g(x)$ is defined as the product of all even integers k such that $0 < k \leq x$. For example, $g(14) = 2 \times 4 \times 6 \times 8 \times 10 \times 12 \times 14$. If $g(y)$ is divisible by 4^{11}, what is the smallest possible value for y?

(A) 22   (B) 24   (C) 28   (D) 32   (E) 44

15. Mitchell plans to work at a day camp over the summer. Each week, he will be paid according to the following schedule: at the end of the first week, he will receive $1. At the end of each subsequent week, he will receive $1, plus an additional amount equal to the sum of all payments he's received in previous weeks. How much money will Mitchell be paid in total during the summer, if he works for the entire duration of the 8-week-long camp?

MANHATTAN
PREP

Solutions

1. **5:** The sequence starts with the number 4, then adds 5 to each subsequent term. The math plays out in this way:

> 1st term: 4
> 2nd term: 4 + 5
> 3rd term: 4 + 5 + 5 = 4 + 5(2)
> 4th term: 4 + 5(3)

The sequence pattern is $4 + 5(n - 1)$, where n is the number of the term. The 75th term in the sequence is therefore $4 + 5(75 - 1) = 4 + 5(74) = 374$.

In order to find the remainder, first find the multiple of 9 closest to 374 but smaller than that number. 360 is a multiple of 9, and so is 369. Therefore, $\dfrac{369}{9}$ has a remainder of 0, so $\dfrac{374}{9}$ has a remainder of 5.

2. **$x = 5$; $1 \le y \le 9$:** Only the integer 5 can be raised to a power to result in a units digit of 5. Any power of 5 will have a units digit of 5, other than zero, because $5^0 = 1$. The integer y, on the other hand, can have any value except for 0.

3. **0:** The remainder when dividing an integer by 10 always equals the units digit. Ignore all but the units digits and rephrase the question: *What is the units digit of $3^{17} + 7^{13}$?*

The pattern for the units digits of 3 is [3, 9, 7, 1]. Every fourth term is the same. The 17th power is 1 past the end of the repeat. Since 3^{16} ends in 1, 3^{17} must end in 3.

The pattern for the units digits of 7 is [7, 9, 3, 1]. Every fourth term is the same. The 13th power is 1 past the end of the repeat. Since 7^{12} ends in 1, 7^{13} must end in 7.

The sum of these units digits is $3 + 7 = 10$. Thus, the units digit is 0.

For problems 4–6, reference the following chart:

Units Digit Patterns for Integers ending in:

	1	2	3	4	5	6	7	8	9	0
y^1	1	2	3	4	5	6	7	8	9	0
y^2	1	4	9	6	5	6	9	4	1	0
y^3	1	8	7	4	5	6	3	2	9	0
y^4	1	6	1	6	5	6	1	6	1	0

4. **(B):**

(1) INSUFFICIENT: According to the Units Digit Patterns chart above, both 4 and 6 yield a units digit of 6 when raised to the 2nd power. (Notice that you would only need to check even numbers for this statement, as odd numbers to any power cannot end in a 6, an even number.)

(2) SUFFICIENT: Only 5 yields a units digit of 5 when raised to *any* power. Since the units digit of $y + 1$ is 5, the units digit of y must be 4.

The correct answer is **(B)**.

5. **(C):** Begin with statement (2).

(2) INSUFFICIENT: The statement indicates only that the units digit does not equal 1, but it could still be any other digit.

(1) INSUFFICIENT: Because both 1 and 9 yield a units digit of 1 when raised to the 2nd power, there are two possible values for the units digit.

(1) AND (2) SUFFICIENT: The two statements together indicate that the units digit of y must be 9.

The correct answer is **(C)**.

6. **(A):** If you're not sure you understand what the function $<z>$ is describing, pick a random number for z and test it out to try to understand how it works. Because the problem mentions multiples of ten, pick a large-ish two-digit number.

If $z = 84$, then $<84>$ = the greatest multiple of ten less than 84. That is, $<84> = 80$.

The question asks for the value of $x - <x>$. No matter what the value of x, $<x>$ will always end in 0 (because it will always be a multiple of 10). Furthermore, the difference between x and $<x>$ must be between 0 and 9, inclusive. For example, if $x = 89$, then $<x> = 80$, but if $x = 90$, then $<x> = 90$).

As a result, if you can determine the units digit of x, you will know the difference $x - <x>$. The rephrased question is "What is the units digit of x?"

(1) SUFFICIENT: The units digit of $<x^{14}>$ must be 0, so if $<x^{14}> + x^{15}$ has a units digit of 7, then x^{15} must have a units digit of 7. Check the reference table: something raised to the 15th power corresponds to the x^3 row in the table. The only base that has a units digit of 7 is the base 3. Therefore, x must have a units digit of 3.

(2) INSUFFICIENT: The units digit of $<x^{15}>$ must be 0, so if $<x^{15}> + x^{16}$ has a units digit of 1, then x^{16} must have a units digit of 1. Check the reference table: something raised to the 16th power corresponds to the x^4 row in the table.

Four possible bases have a units digit of 1: 1, 3, 7, and 9. Since there isn't just one possible value for the units digit of x, this statement is not sufficient.

The correct answer is **(A)**.

7. **(B):** Because the question is asking about the remainder when x is divided by 5, you only need to check the units digits 0 through 4. The pattern will recycle for the next set of 5 (5 through 9) and for every set of 5 after that.

(1) INSUFFICIENT:

x	x^2	$\dfrac{x^2}{5}$ = remainder of 4	$\dfrac{x}{5}$ = remainder of?
0	0	No (invalid)	
1	1	No (invalid)	
2	4	Yes	2/5 = 0 remainder 2
3	9	Yes	3/5 = 0 remainder 3

There are at least two possible values for the remainder.

(2) SUFFICIENT:

x	x^3	$\dfrac{x^3}{5}$ = remainder of 2	$\dfrac{x}{5}$ = remainder of?
0	0	No (invalid)	
1	1	No (invalid)	
2	8	No (invalid)	
3	27	Yes	3/5 = 0 remainder 3
4	64	No (invalid)	

There is only one possible remainder: 3.

If you aren't sure that you only need to test these 5 cases, try the next 5 values for x. Note the repeat of the remainder pattern. Only every 3rd term (3, 8, 13, and so on) will be valid based on the information from statement (2) and will always have a remainder of 3.

The correct answer is **(B)**.

8. **(C):** 5^x will always end in 5.

(1) INSUFFICIENT: If x is even, then $5^x = 25$, 625, and so on. This statement provides no information about y, though. For example if $y = 5$, then $\dfrac{25}{5} = 5$ remainder 0. If $y = 4$, then $\dfrac{25}{4} = 6$ remainder 1.

(2) INSUFFICIENT: Test some different values for x.

x	5^x	Remainder of $\dfrac{5^x}{3}$
1	5	2
2	25	1
3	125	2
4	625	1

After testing the first two numbers, it's clear that statement (2) is not sufficient. Because you will have to test the two statements together, continue testing another couple of numbers to see whether there is a pattern. When 5 is raised to an odd power, the remainder is 2, but when 5 is raised to an even power, the remainder is 1.

(1) AND (2) SUFFICIENT: When $5^{\text{even integer}}$ is divided by 3, the remainder is always 1.

The correct answer is **(C)**.

9. 110: The remainder must always be smaller than the divisor. Thus b must be at least 10, and d must be at least 11. Therefore, bd must be at least 110. The purpose of this problem is to remind you of these constraints on remainders.

10. 147: There are several patterns in the grid, depending on whether you look by row or by column. Within each row, there are positive and negative terms at the beginning that cancel each other. For example, in the first row, $-2 + 2 = 0$ and $-1 + 1 = 0$. The only terms in the first row that contribute to the sum are 3 and 4, in the far-right columns. The same is true for the other rows.

Thus, the sum of the grid is equal to the sum of only the two far-right columns. The sum in the first row in those columns is $3 + 4 = 7$; the sum in the next row is $6 + 8 = 14$, etc. The sum in the final row is $18 + 24 = 42$. Because they are consecutive multiples of 7, use the consecutive multiples formula:

$$
\begin{aligned}
Sum &= \left(\frac{\text{Lowest Term} + \text{Highest Term}}{2} \right) (\text{Number of Terms}) \\
&= \left(\frac{7 + 42}{2} \right) (6) \\
&= \frac{(49)(6)}{2} \\
&= 147
\end{aligned}
$$

11. 317: Each term in the sequence is 9 greater than the previous term. To make this obvious, you may want to write a few terms of the sequence: 11, 20, 29, 38, etc.

a_{35} comes 34 terms after a_1 in the sequence. In other words, a_{35} is $34 \times 9 = 306$ greater than a_1.

Thus, $a_{35} = 11 + 306 = 317$.

12. **(B)** **Between** $-\dfrac{1}{2}$ **and 0:** Compute the first few elements of S_n:

n	S_n
1	$(-1)^1\dfrac{1}{1\times 2}=-\dfrac{1}{2}$
2	$(-1)^2\dfrac{1}{2\times 3}=\dfrac{1}{6}$
3	$(-1)^3\dfrac{1}{3\times 4}=\dfrac{1}{12}$
4	$(-1)^4\dfrac{1}{4\times 5}=\dfrac{1}{20}$
5	$(-1)^5\dfrac{1}{5\times 6}=-\dfrac{1}{30}$

Use a number line to track the sum:

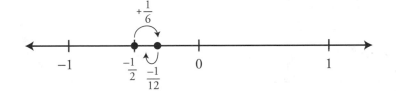

Place the first term, $-\dfrac{1}{2}$, on the number line. The second term is $+\dfrac{1}{6}$, so the sum will move to the right (closer to 0) on the number line. The third term is $-\dfrac{1}{12}$, so the sum will move to the left, but it can't go as far as $-\dfrac{1}{2}$ again, because you're only subtracting $\dfrac{1}{12}$ this time—the distance is smaller than the first $\dfrac{1}{6}$ hop that you made.

Each subsequent hop flips back and forth between positive and negative but also keeps getting smaller and smaller, so you'll never "break out" of the range $-\dfrac{1}{2}$ to 0.

The correct answer is **(B)**.

13. **9:** Calculate the first several terms of the sequence to find the pattern:

$$Q_1 = 3$$
$$Q_2 = 2(3) + 2 = 8$$
$$Q_3 = 2(8) + 2 = 18$$
$$Q_4 = 2(18) + 2 = 38$$
$$Q_5 = 2(38) + 2 = 78$$
$$\dots$$

The pattern should continue, so 8 will be the units digit nine out of the first ten times.

14. **(B) 24:** This is a counting pattern problem. In order for $g(y)$ to be divisible by 4^{11}, it must be divisible by $(2^2)^{11} = 2^{22}$. Thus $g(y)$ must contain 22 twos in its prime factorization.

If $y = 10$, for example, then g(y) equals $2 \times 4 \times 6 \times 8 \times 10$. The number 2 has one 2 in its prime factorization; 4 has two 2's; 6 has one 2 (and a 3); 8 has three 2's; 10 has one 2 (and a 5). This amounts to a total of only eight 2's:

Number	2	4	6	8	10
Prime Factors	2	2, 2	2, 3	2, 2, 2	2, 5
Total 2's in PF	1	2	1	3	1
Cumulative 2's	1	3	4	7	8

Keep adding even numbers to the result until you get to 22 twos in total:

Number	2	4	6	8	10	12	14	16	18	20	22	24
Prime Factors	2	2,2	2,3	2,2,2	2,5	2,2,3	2,7	2,2,2,2	2,3,3	2,2,5	2,11	2,2,2,3
Total 2's in PF	1	2	1	3	1	2	1	4	1	2	1	3
Cumulative 2's	1	3	4	7	8	10	11	15	16	18	19	22

Thus the smallest possible number for y is 24. Notice the pattern in the number of twos in each even number: 1, 2, 1, 3, 1, 2, 1, 4, 1, 2, 1 …

The correct answer is **(B)**.

15. **$255 (or $2^8 - 1$):** At the end of the first week, Mitchell receives $1. At the end of the second week, he gets $1, plus $1 for the total he had been paid up to that point, for a total of $2. At the end of the third week, he gets $1, plus ($1 + $2), or $3, for the total he had been paid up to that point, so this third week's total is $4. Put this in a table:

Week #	Paid this week($)	Cumulative Pay including this week ($)
1	1	1
2	1 + 1 = 2	1 + 2 = 3
3	1 + 3 = 4	3 + 4 = 7
4	1 + 7 = 8	7 + 8 = 15
5	1 + 15 = 16	15 + 16 = 31
6	1 + 31 = 32	31 + 32 = 63
7	1 + 63 = 64	63 + 64 = 127
8	1 + 127 = 128	127 + 128 = 255

This calculation is not so bad, but you may notice that this payment schedule is a geometric sequence, 2^{n-1}, where n is the number of the week in which Mitchell is being paid. Summing that sequence is equivalent to $2^t - 1$, where t is the total number of weeks. In other words, the cumulative pay is one less than the next power of 2.

The correct answer is $2^8 - 1 = 255.

5

Chapter 6

of

GMAT Advanced Quant

Common Terms & Quadratic Templates

In This Chapter...

Chapter 6

Common Terms & Quadratic Templates

You are probably already familiar with the *mechanics* of algebraic manipulations—what is allowed and what is not:

> You can substitute one expression for another if they are equal… You can add some number to one side of an equation as long as you do the same on the other side of the equation… You can cross-multiply to simplify fractions… and so on.

But of all the steps you *could* take, how do you decide which steps you *should* take?

Two indicators can often help you on the GMAT:

1. Common Terms
2. Quadratic Templates

Common Terms

If you spot Common Terms, you can often spot the path all the way to the solution. Common Terms appear on the GMAT in three typical ways:

1. Algebra

Look for terms that appear in the same form more than once. Those recurring expressions might also appear in slightly modified form such as reciprocal, negative, or raised to a power:

If $\left(\dfrac{a}{b}\right)=\dfrac{3}{5}$, then $\dfrac{b+a}{a}=$	$\dfrac{b}{a}$ is the reciprocal of $\dfrac{a}{b}$.	$\dfrac{b+a}{a}=\dfrac{b}{a}+\dfrac{a}{a}=\dfrac{5}{3}+1=\dfrac{8}{3}$
Is $\dfrac{1}{a^2-b^2}<b^2-a^2$?	b^2-a^2 is negative a^2-b^2.	Is $\dfrac{1}{x}<-x$? where $a^2-b^2=x$
$\left(\dfrac{x}{3y}\right)^2+2\left(\dfrac{x}{3y}\right)(3y)+(3y)^2$ $\underbrace{\qquad}_{a}\qquad\underbrace{\qquad}_{b}$	$\dfrac{x}{3y}$ and $3y$ appear both squared and multiplied together.	This expression is of the form: $a^2+2ab+b^2=(a+b)^2$ (More on Quadratic Templates later in this chapter)

Try-It #6-1

If $y\neq3$, simplify as much as possible: $\dfrac{2y^2(3-y)-3+y}{3-y}$

Spot the common term $(3-y)$. Note that $(-3+y)$ is $-(3-y)$, or $-1\times(3-y)$.

Factor out the common term $(3-y)$ and cancel: $\dfrac{(3-y)\left[2y^2-1\right]}{3-y}=2y^2-1$.

By the way, the condition that y could not equal 3 just prevented you from dividing by zero and ending up with an undefined number.

2. Exponents

Exponents can be manipulated when either bases or exponents are common. Also look for bases that have common factors, such as 3 and 12 (common factor of 3). You can often create a common base. For example:

$(16x)(4^2)=256$	4 is a factor of 4, 16, and 256. Similarly, 4, 16, and 256 are all powers of 4.	$\left(16^x\right)\left(4^2\right)=256$ $\left(4^2\right)^x\left(4^2\right)=4^4$ $4^{2x+2}=4^4$ $2x+2=4$ $x=1$

MANHATTAN
PREP

Try-It #6-2

If $3^x + 243 = 2(3^x)$, what is the value of x?

Note the common term "3^x," and note the fact that $243 = 3^5$:

$$\boxed{3^x} + \boxed{243} = 2\left(3^x\right)$$
$$3^x + 243 = 3^x + 3^x$$
$$243 = 3^x$$
$$3^5 = 3^x$$
$$5 = x$$

3. Factors and Multiples

When many terms share a factor, pull that shared factor *out to the side*. These can appear in algebraic or numerical expressions.

$$x^{18} + 2x^{16} + x^{14} \;\rightarrow\; x^{14} \text{ is a factor of each term} \;\rightarrow\; x^{14}(x^4 + 2x^2 + 1) = x^{14}(x^2 + 1)^2$$

$$\dfrac{\dfrac{8}{15} - \dfrac{2}{5}}{\dfrac{1}{3} + \dfrac{2}{15}} \;\rightarrow\; \text{get common denominators, then cross them all off} \;\rightarrow\; \dfrac{\dfrac{8}{15} - \dfrac{6}{15}}{\dfrac{5}{15} + \dfrac{2}{15}} = \dfrac{(8-6)}{(5+2)} = \dfrac{2}{7}$$

Factorials are particularly noteworthy, as they often have an abundance of shared factors. For any integer n, the factorial $n!$ is calculated as follows: $n! = n(n-1)(n-2)(n-3) \dots 1$. Thus, all the terms in $4! = (4)(3)(2)(1)$ are also common factors of $6! = (6)(5)(4)(3)(2)(1) = (6)(5)(4!)$.

More generally, factorials are "super-multiples." Without ever computing their precise value, you can tell that they're divisible by all sorts of numbers.

If x is an integer between $7! + 2$ and $7! + 4$, inclusive, is x prime?	x is one of the following integers:	x has one of the following factors, if x is:
	$7! + 2 = (7)(6)(5)(4)(3)(\mathbf{2})(1) + \mathbf{2}$ $7! + 3 = (7)(6)(5)(4)(\mathbf{3})(2)(1) + \mathbf{3}$ $7! + 4 = (7)(6)(5)(\mathbf{4})(3)(2)(1) + \mathbf{4}$	$7! + 2 = \mathbf{2} \times \text{Integer}$ $7! + 3 = \mathbf{3} \times \text{Integer}$ $7! + 4 = \mathbf{4} \times \text{Integer}$ $\dots$so x is not prime!

Sometimes a common factor is just a random number buried inside a couple of larger numbers. Find it and pull it out.

| $\dfrac{10.1010}{5.0505} =$ | 10's in the numerator line up with 5's in the corresponding digit place of the denominator:

$\dfrac{10.\ 10\ 10}{5.\ 05\ 05}$ | $\dfrac{10.1010}{5.0505} = \dfrac{10}{5}\left(\dfrac{1.0101}{1.0101}\right)$

$= \dfrac{10}{5}$

$= 2$ |

Try-It #6-3

If n is a positive integer, and $\sqrt{(45)(14)(7^n) - (15)(7^{n-1})(54)}$ is a positive integer, what is the value of n?

(1) n is prime
(2) $n < 3$

What would need to be true in order for the square root to be a positive integer? The number under the square root symbol would have to be a perfect square. Rearrange the expression to determine whether there are any restrictions that could help narrow down the possibilities before going to the statements. Try to break the numbers down into primes to locate and pull out any existing perfect squares.

$$\sqrt{(45)(14)(7^n) - (15)(7^{n-1})(54)}$$
$$\sqrt{(3^2)(5)(2)(7)(7^n) - (3)(5)(7^{n-1})(3^3)(2)}$$

Pull out Common Terms:

$$\sqrt{(3^2)(5)(2)[(7^{n+1}) - (7^{n-1})(3^2)]}$$

It turns out that you can also pull out the term 7^{n-1}. The term $7^{n+1} = (7^{n-1})(7^2)$:

$$\sqrt{(3^2)(5)(2)(7^{n-1})[7^2 - 3^2]}$$
$$\sqrt{(3^2)(5)(2)(7^{n-1})[49 - 9]}$$
$$\sqrt{(3^2)(5)(2)(7^{n-1})(40)}$$
$$\sqrt{(3^2)(400)(7^{n-1})}$$

The first two terms are both perfect squares and can be pulled out of the square root sign:

$$(3)(20)\sqrt{7^{n-1}}$$

What would need to be true in order for 7^{n-1} to be pulled out of the square root sign? It would also have to be a perfect square, so $n - 1$ must be even and n itself must be odd.

The question is "If n is odd, what is the value of n?"

(1) INSUFFICIENT: This statement allows multiple possible odd values of n.

(2) SUFFICIENT: The question stem indicates that n is a positive integer and this statement specifies that $n < 3$. The only odd, positive integer less than 3 is the number 1.

The correct answer is **(B)**.

Quadratic Templates

On the GMAT, quadratic expressions take three common forms called the Quadratic Templates. Memorize these templates, and get comfortable transforming back and forth between factored and distributed form.

	Factored	⟷	Distributed
Square of a sum	$(a + b)^2$	$=$	$a^2 + 2ab + b^2$
Square of a difference	$(a - b)^2$	$=$	$a^2 - 2ab + b^2$
Difference of two squares	$(a + b)(a - b)$	$=$	$a^2 - b^2$

Quick Manipulation

Expressions with both squared and non-squared Common Terms should make you suspect that you are looking at a Quadratic Template.

Try-It #6-4

Rewrite $\left(\dfrac{x}{3}\right)^2 + 2\left(\dfrac{x}{3}\right)(5y) + (5y)^2$ as a quadratic expression.

This problem requires you to manipulate a rather complicated expression. However, by using the Common Terms, you can put the problem in the more basic template form to solve.

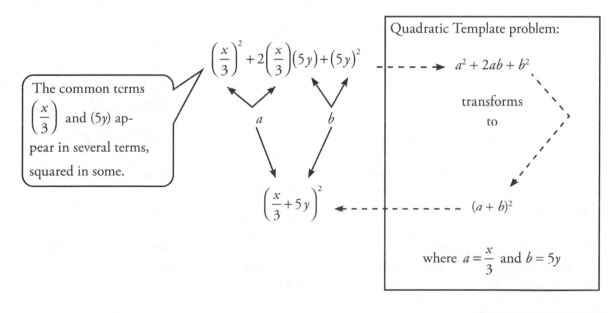

Once you are comfortable with Quadratic Templates, you can manipulate even complicated expressions quickly, as in the middle box above. Until then, write down the templates and the substitution of the Common Terms, as in the box on the right.

The very same problem could have been presented in disguise:

Rewrite $\dfrac{x^2}{9} + \dfrac{10xy}{3} + 25y^2$ as a quadratic expression.

The Common Terms are slightly harder to spot in this form. In such a case, start with the squared terms, $\dfrac{x^2}{9}$ and $25y^2$. Then try to untangle their square roots, $\dfrac{x}{3}$ and $5y$, from the remaining term. The factored form is:

$$\left(\frac{x}{3} + 5y\right)^2$$

Consider all three of the common Quadratic Templates before deciding which one(s) are most convenient to use.

The Middle Term: $2ab$

The "square of a sum" and "square of a difference" templates have something in common: the middle term is $\pm 2ab$. The only difference is the sign of that middle term.

When you *add* these two templates, the middle terms cancel, leaving the *end* terms:

		Factored	⟷	Distributed
	"Square of a sum"	$(a + b)^2$	=	$a^2 + 2ab + b^2$
+	"Square of a difference"	$(a - b)^2$	=	$a^2 - 2ab + b^2$
	Addition:	$(a + b)^2 + (a - b)^2$	=	$2a^2 + 0 + 2b^2$ $2(a^2 + b^2)$

In contrast, when you *subtract* these two templates, the end terms cancel, leaving the *middle* term:

		Factored	⟷	Distributed
	"Square of a sum"	$(a + b)^2$	=	$a^2 + 2ab + b^2$
+	"Square of a difference"	$(a - b)^2$	=	$a^2 - 2ab + b^2$
	Subtraction:	$(a + b)^2 - (a - b)^2$	=	$0 + 4ab + 0$

This is handy for simplification. Also, whenever you see the "Sum of two squares" $(a^2 + b^2)$, which is not itself a Quadratic Template, remember that it can be derived from this sum of two templates.

What is the sum of $9{,}999^2$ and $10{,}001^2$?

(A) 99,980,001
(B) 199,999,998
(C) 200,000,002
(D) 399,999,996
(E) 400,000,004

These numbers all look pretty annoying. If only they had given the easier number of 10,000 instead…

When "wishful thinking" pops up, try to use it to make the problem easier. If you changed both of these numbers to the form 10,000 plus or minus a number, what would that be?

$$(10{,}000 - 1)^2 + (10{,}000 + 1)^2 = ?$$

These are the Quadratic Templates! In this case, $a = 10{,}000$ and $b = 1$. If you've memorized the "sum" term, plug these in:

$$\text{sum} = 2(a^2 + b^2)$$

$$\text{sum} = 2(10{,}000^2 + 1^2)$$

Now, notice something: the part in the parentheses is going to have a units digit of 1. Multiple the number by 2 and the end result will have a units digit of 2. Only answer choice (C) fits.

Not sure about that? Go ahead and do the math.

$$2(100{,}000{,}000 + 1)$$
$$200{,}000{,}002$$

The correct answer is **(C)**.

Even if you don't memorize the "sum" term of the Quadratic Templates, the math is still far easier to do in this rewritten form:

$$(10{,}000 - 1)^2 + (10{,}000 + 1)^2$$
$$(100{,}000{,}000 - 20{,}000 + 1) + (100{,}000{,}000 + 20{,}000 + 1)$$
$$200{,}000{,}000 + 2$$
$$200{,}000{,}002$$

Quadratic Templates in Disguise

Quadratic Templates can be disguised in arithmetic computations.

Try-It #6-6

$$198 \times 202 =$$

You can round each number and quickly estimate the result to be about 200^2. Or you could laboriously multiply two 3-digit numbers by hand to get an exact result. But if you need an exact result quickly, you can use a quadratic template, as shown in the previous section. You just need to turn 198 into $(200 - 2)$ and 202 into $(200 + 2)$.

$$198 \times 202 = (200 - 2)(200 + 2) = 200^2 - 2^2 = 40{,}000 - 4 = 39{,}996$$

Another place to hide a Quadratic Template is in an advanced right-triangle problem.

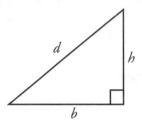

You know that Area $= \dfrac{1}{2}\, bh$ and $d^2 = b^2 + h^2$ (by the Pythagorean theorem). Do the Common Terms b^2, h^2, and bh look familiar? Use the "square of a sum" template:

$$\left(b + h\right)^2 = b^2 + 2bh + h^2 = (b^2 + h^2) + 4\left(\frac{bh}{2}\right)$$

$$\left(b + h\right)^2 = d^2 + 4(\text{Area})$$

Likewise, there is a similar relationship based on the "square of a difference" template.

$$\left(b - h\right)^2 = b^2 - 2bh + h^2 = (b^2 + h^2) - 4(\frac{bh}{2})$$

$$\left(b - h\right)^2 = d^2 - 4(\text{Area})$$

An advanced GMAT problem can draw on these complicated relationships. For instance, you can compute the area of a right triangle directly from the sum of the shorter sides and the hypotenuse:

$$\left(b + h\right)^2 = d^2 + 4(\text{Area})$$

$$\frac{\left(b + h\right)^2 - d^2}{4} = (\text{Area})$$

You should absolutely *not* memorize these particular formulas. Rather, be able to recognize when the GMAT is indirectly testing these generic Quadratic Templates.

Problem Set

For the following problems, use the Pattern Recognition techniques discussed in this chapter to solve.

1.   If $xy > 0$, is $(5^x)^{\frac{1}{y}} > 25$?

   (1) $2\left(\dfrac{xy^4}{x^2}\right)^2 = \dfrac{16y^5}{x^2}$

   (2) $x > 2y$

For problems #2–#4, if $x < -1$, which of the following inequalities must be true?

2. $x^4 > x^2$

3. $x^3 + x^4 > x^3 + x^2$

4. $x^6 - x^7 > x^5 - x^6$

5.   If, $\dfrac{(x+y)^2}{xy+y^2} = 3$ and $|x| \ne |y|$, what is the ratio of x to y?

   (A) 4 : 1
   (B) 3 : 1
   (C) 2 : 1
   (D) 3 : 2
   (E) 1 : 3

6.   If $\dfrac{a}{b} = \dfrac{1}{8}$, what is the value of $\dfrac{a^2+b^2}{ab}$?

7.   If n is an integer and $(-3)^{4n} = 3^{7n-3}$, then $n = $?

8.   Simplify: $\dfrac{(0.2^4)(0.05^2)(60^4)}{(0.08^2)(0.002^2)(900^2)}$

9.   If x and k are both integers, $x > k$, and $x^{-k} = 625$, what is x?

   (1) $|k|$ is a prime number
   (2) $x + k > 20$

Distribute the expression in problems #10–#14 without FOILing (doing the math the long way). Use the Quadratic Templates.

10. $\left(x+\dfrac{1}{x}\right)^2$

11. $(x^2 - y)^2$

12. $\left(z^2 + \dfrac{1}{z}\right)\left(z^2 - \dfrac{1}{z}\right)$

13. $\left(5-\sqrt{21}\right)\left(5+\sqrt{21}\right)$

14. $\left(a-\dfrac{b}{2}\right)^2$

Factor problems #15–#19 according to the Quadratic Templates.

15. $y^4 - 2 + \dfrac{1}{y^4}$

16. $4 + 4a + a^2$

17. $81 - x^4$

18. $x + 2\sqrt{xyz} + yz$

19. $4x^2 - 12xy + 9y^2$

For problems #20–#23, simplify the expressions completely.

20. $\left(\sqrt{x}+\sqrt{y}\right)^2 + \left(\sqrt{x}-\sqrt{y}\right)^2$

21. $\left(\sqrt{x}+\sqrt{\dfrac{1}{x}}\right)^2 - \left(\sqrt{x}-\sqrt{\dfrac{1}{x}}\right)^2$

22. $(111)(89)$

23. $350^2 - 320^2$

24. In the right triangle below, side a is 7 inches longer than side b. If the area of the triangle is 30 inches^2, what is the length of hypotenuse c?

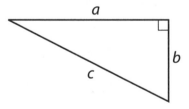

MANHATTAN
PREP

Solutions

1. **(C):** From $xy > 0$, you know that neither x nor y equals 0 and they must have the same sign
($++$ or $--$). Combine the exponent in the question to get $5^{\frac{x}{y}} > 25$.

What is the significance of the inequality in the question stem? If the exponent equals 2, then $5^2 = 25$.
In order to be greater than 25, the exponent has to be greater than 2. The question can be rephrased as
"Is $\frac{x}{y} > 2$?"

You may want to start with statement (2).

(2) INSUFFICIENT: If y is positive, then $\frac{x}{y} > 2$. If, on the other hand, y is negative, then $\frac{x}{y} < 2$.

(1) INSUFFICIENT: Simplify the equation:

$$2\left(\frac{xy^4}{x^2}\right)^2 = \frac{16y^5}{x^2}$$

$$2\left(\frac{y^8}{x^2}\right) = \frac{16y^5}{x^2}$$

$$2y^8 = 16y^5$$

$$y^8 = 8y^5$$

Therefore, y^3 must equal 8, so $y = 2$. This provides no information about x, however.

(1) AND (2) SUFFICIENT: If $y = 2$, then you can plug into statement (2) to find the range of
values for x. Since $x > 2y$ and y is positive, you can divide the expression by y, giving $\frac{x}{y} > 2$.

The correct answer is **(C)**.

For questions #2–#4: since $x \neq 0$, divide by the Common Terms, making sure to flip the
inequality sign if the common term is negative.

2. **TRUE:** $x^4 > \boxed{x^2}$ Note: x^2 is positive.

        $x^2 > 1$?   Divide both sides by x^2, leaving the sign as it is.

        True   The square of a number smaller than -1 will be greater than positive 1.

3. **TRUE:** $x^3 + x^4 > x^3 + \boxed{x^2}$ Note: x^2 is positive.

        $x + x^2 > x + 1$ Divide both sides by x^2, leaving the sign as it is.

        $x^2 > 1$ Subtract x from both sides.

        True   (Or you might have subtracted x^3 immediately.)

4. **TRUE:** $x^6 - x^7 > \boxed{x^5} - x^6$ Note: x^5 is negative.

        $x - x^2 < 1 - x$ Divide both sides by x^5, flipping the inequality sign.

        $2x - 1 < x^2$ Group like terms.

        neg < pos?

        True

5. **(C) 2 : 1**: Try to find like terms in order to simplify the left-hand side of the equation.

$$\frac{(x+y)^2}{xy+y^2} = 3$$

$$\frac{(x+y)^2}{y(x+y)} = 3$$

$$\frac{x+y}{y} = 3$$

$$\frac{x}{y} + \frac{y}{y} = 3$$

$$\frac{x}{y} + 1 = 3$$

$$\frac{x}{y} = 2$$

The ratio of x to y is 2 : 1.

The correct answer is **(C)**.

6. $\dfrac{\mathbf{65}}{\mathbf{8}}$: Since $\dfrac{a}{b} = \dfrac{1}{8}$, $\dfrac{a^2 + b^2}{ab} = \dfrac{a^2}{ab} + \dfrac{b^2}{ab} = \dfrac{a}{b} + \dfrac{b}{a} = \dfrac{1}{8} + 8 = \dfrac{65}{8}$

7. **$n = 1$**: Since n is an integer, $4n$ is even. An even exponent "hides the sign" of the base, so you can treat the (-3) base as a (3).

$$(-3)^{4n} = (3)^{7n-3}$$

$$(3)^{4n} = (3)^{7n-3}$$

$$4n = 7n - 3$$

$$3 = 3n$$

$$1 = n$$

8. **2,500**: Don't dive in and start doing long division or multiplication. Take a few moments to figure out how to make this math easier. The final pair (the 60 and the 900) look somewhat similar; start there.

$$\frac{60^4}{900^2}$$

$$\frac{60^4}{(30^2)^2}$$

$$\frac{2^4 30^4}{30^4}$$

Do you have your perfect squares memorized? It's a good idea to memorize up to 20^2, as well as 25^2 and 30^2. If you do have those memorized, then that 900 would be more likely to jump out at you and help you down the simplification path.

MANHATTAN
PREP

Can you use that same cancellation technique with any of the other numerators and denominators?

$$\frac{(0.2)^4}{(0.08)^2}$$

This might be easier to see using scientific notation. $0.2 = 2 \times 10^{-1}$ $(0.2)^4 = 2^4 \times 10^{-4}$.

Perform the same operation for the denominator to get:

$$\frac{2^4 \times 10^{-4}}{8^2 \times 10^{-4}}$$ Cancel out the 10^{-4} terms and continue to simplify.

$$\frac{2^4}{(2^3)^2} = \frac{2^4}{2^6} = \frac{1}{2^2}$$

Do the same with the middle pair of terms:

$$\frac{(0.05)^2}{(0.002)^2}$$

$$\frac{\left(5 \times 10^{-2}\right)^2}{\left(2 \times 10^{-3}\right)^2}$$

$$\frac{25 \times 10^{-4}}{4 \times 10^{-6}}$$

$$\frac{25 \times 10^2}{4}$$

Altogether, you have:

$$\left(\frac{1}{2^2}\right)\left(\frac{25 \times 10^2}{4}\right)\left(2^4\right)$$

$$25 \times 100 = 2,500$$

9. **(A):** The fact that x and k are both integers (and that $x > k$) significantly limits the possible values for x and k. The possible pairings are:

x	k
5	−4
25	−2
625	−1

(1) SUFFICIENT: If the absolute value of k is prime, then only the second possibility works: $x = 25$ and $k = -2$.

(2) INSUFFICIENT: The second and third possibilities both make this statement true, so it isn't possible to determine a single value for x.

6

10. $x^2 + 2 + \dfrac{1}{x^2}$

11. $x^4 - 2x^2y + y^2$

12. $z^4 - \dfrac{1}{z^2}$

13. $5^2 - \left(\sqrt{21}\right)^2 = 25 - 21 = 4$

14. $a^2 - ab + \dfrac{b^2}{4}$

15. $\left(y^2 - \dfrac{1}{y^2}\right)^2$

16. $(2 + a)^2$

17. $(9 + x^2)(9 - x^2) = (9 + x^2)(3 + x)(3 - x)$

18. $\left(\sqrt{x} + \sqrt{yz}\right)^2$

19. $(2x - 3y)^2$

20. $2(x + y)$

21. $4\sqrt{x}\sqrt{\dfrac{1}{x}} = 4\sqrt{\dfrac{x}{x}} = 4$

22. $(100 + 11)(100 - 11) = (100^2 - 11^2) = 10{,}000 - 121 = 9{,}879$

23. $(350 + 320)(350 - 320) = (670)(30) = 20{,}100$

24. $(a - b) = 7$ and $\dfrac{1}{2}ab = 30$. From the Pythagorean theorem, $a^2 + b^2 = c^2$.

Use the "square of a difference" template:
$$(a - b)^2 = a^2 - 2ab + b^2$$
$$= \left(a^2 + b^2\right) - 2ab$$
$$= \left(c^2\right) - 4\left(\dfrac{1}{2}ab\right)$$

Plug in the values:
$$7^2 = \left(c^2\right) - 4(30)$$
$$49 + 120 = c^2$$
$$169 = c^2$$
$$13 = c$$

MANHATTAN
PREP

Chapter 7
of
GMAT Advanced Quant

Visual Solutions

In This Chapter...

Chapter 7
Visual Solutions

Visual interpretations—good pictures, essentially—can help you solve certain types of GMAT problems. This chapter highlights some of these types of problems and demonstrates how you can use visual techniques to solve these problems more confidently, accurately, and quickly.

Many problems discussed in this chapter can be solved with other techniques. Still, visual thinking is a powerful tool. It can expand your comprehension of a topic. It may enable you to solve particular problem types more easily or "break through" on a difficult problem. In fact, visualization is the only realistic way to approach certain problems. So it's worth trying your hand with visual approaches.

In this chapter, we will discuss the following visual solution techniques:

Representing Objects With Pictures – Many Word Problems and Geometry problems do not provide a diagram alongside the problem. Drawing a good picture will make the problem-solving process easier and less error-prone.

Rubber Band Geometry – For Geometry questions involving both constraints and flexibility (especially in Data Sufficiency), drawing different "rubber band" scenarios according to those constraints and freedoms can often help you solve the problem without doing *any* computation.

Baseline Calculations for Averages – Visual techniques can help you compute averages (both basic and weighted) and can also foster a better understanding of those calculations.

Number Line Techniques for Statistics Problems – You can solve a variety of common problems involving statistics by using a number line to visualize and manipulate the problem.

Representing Objects with Pictures

For Word Problems that describe a physical object, or for Geometry problems that do not give a diagram alongside the problem, drawing a picture is often the best approach. Sometimes it's the *only* viable approach! Even if you are good at visualizing objects in your head, draw the picture anyway. It's just too easy to make a mistake on many of these questions.

Try-It #7-1

A rectangular wooden dowel measures 4 inches by 1 inch by 1 inch. If the dowel is painted on all surfaces and then cut into $\frac{1}{2}$-inch cubes, what fraction of the resulting cube faces are painted?

(A) $\frac{1}{3}$

(B) $\frac{3}{8}$

(C) $\frac{7}{16}$

(D) $\frac{1}{2}$

(E) $\frac{9}{16}$

If you draw a picture, this problem becomes a matter of counting:

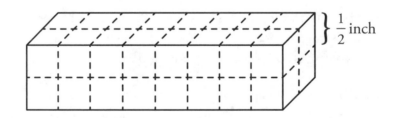

Total Cubes = (4 inches × 2 cubes per inch) × (1 × 2) × (1 × 2) = 32 cubes

Total Cube Faces = 32 cubes × 6 faces per cube = 192 faces total

Now consider the faces that were painted on the front and back of the dowel, the top and bottom of the dowel, and the ends of the dowel. In the diagram above, you can see 16 faces on the front, 16 faces on the top, and 4 faces on the end shown. Of course, there are other sides: the back, the bottom, and the other end.

Painted Cube Faces = (16 faces × 2) + (16 faces × 2) + (4 faces × 2) = 32 + 32 + 8 = 72 painted faces

                       ↗   ↗   ↗

    Front & Back   Top & Bottom   Ends

The fraction of faces that are painted $= \dfrac{72}{192} = \dfrac{24(3)}{24(8)} = \dfrac{3}{8}$. The correct answer is **(B)**.

Notice that there is no shortcut to solving this kind of problem, so don't waste time looking for one—just draw the diagram and count.

!	Even if you can easily picture 3-D shapes and objects in your head, it is still better to draw a picture on your scrap paper.
	Wrong answer choices are often those you might get by losing track of your progress as you process the object in your mind.

This kind of process can also help you with questions that deal with the relative size of different objects.

Try-It #7-2

Bucket A has twice the capacity of bucket B, and bucket A has $\dfrac{1}{3}$ the capacity of bucket C. Bucket B is full of water and bucket C is half full of water. When the water from bucket B is poured into bucket C, bucket C will be filled to what fraction of its capacity?

You could attempt to solve this problem algebraically, but the equations get messy very quickly. Instead, try drawing the buckets A, B and C in correct proportion to one another. Then think through the problem.

$$A_{\text{capacity}} = 2B_{\text{capacity}}$$

$$A_{\text{capacity}} = \frac{1}{3}C_{\text{capacity}}$$

$$B_{\text{water}} = B_{\text{capacity}}$$

$$C_{\text{water}} = \frac{1}{2}C_{\text{capacity}}$$

$$\frac{B_{\text{water}} + C_{\text{water}}}{C_{\text{capacity}}} = ?$$

—Alternatively—

$$A = 2B$$

$$A - \frac{1}{3}C$$

$$\frac{B + \frac{1}{2}C}{C} = ?$$

Algebra

Pour

B   A   C

size: $\times 2$ $\times 3$

Picture

The algebra and the picture say the same thing, but the picture has several advantages:

- It's much easier to comprehend at a glance.

- It's harder to mistake relative sizes (for example, accidentally thinking A is smallest).

- You can easily represent both total capacity and amount of water visually.

- It prompts you to pursue the smartest, easiest solution: picking numbers for the capacities of the buckets.

Based on this picture, you might pick a capacity of 1 for bucket B, yielding a capacity of 2 for bucket A and 6 for bucket C. Bucket B would contain 1 unit of water and bucket C, 3 units. When the contents of B are poured into C, bucket C would then be $\frac{4}{6} = \frac{2}{3}$ full.

Notice that the buckets are not labeled in alphabetical order, even though that would be easy to incorrectly assume. The GMAT frequently adds little layers of disguise and complexity such as this, to induce you to make a mistake. By drawing the buckets carefully, you minimize the chance that you will fall into a trap on a problem such as this one.

Rubber Band Geometry

Many Geometry problems—particularly of the Data Sufficiency (DS) variety—describe objects for which only partial information is known. We call these questions *Rubber Band Geometry* problems, because they simultaneously involve constraints and flexibility. Some parts of the diagram can stretch like a rubber band as you open or close angles.

Your job is to figure out what specifics in the problem are constrained, and what specifics are flexible.

For example, if a problem specifies that a line has a slope of 2, it will be steep and upward-sloping. In fact, it will always "rise" 2 units for every unit of "run." However, you don't know where the line will appear. The line is *constrained* in its slope, but it is *flexible* in that it can be moved up or down, right or left. You can draw many different lines with a slope of 2 (these lines will all be parallel, of course).

If, however, the problem only specifies that a line must go through the point (4, 0) in the coordinate plane, then the line is "fixed" at that point. However, the slope of the line would now be flexible. You could draw many different lines with different slopes that run through that point.

If you knew both of these specifications—that the line must have a slope of 2 and must run through the point (4, 0)—then you would be able to calculate the exact line that is being described. The slope of the line and a point that the line goes through specify the line precisely—there is no remaining flexibility for either the slope or the location of the line. (Note that in this example, the line is described by the equation $y = 2x - 8$.)

Given these specifications, every other feature of this line is also known: its x-intercept, its y-intercept, whether it goes through some fixed point, which quadrants it crosses, etc. Thus, in a DS problem, you could answer any such questions about this line without actually calculating the answer.

Thus, for these types of problems, your goal is to figure out what combination of information "cements" the problem in place—in other words, what combination of information removes all of the remaining flexibility. No flexibility means sufficiency. And by using *Rubber Band Geometry* thinking, you can often do this without using any calculation or algebra at all.

For each piece of information that you're given in this type of problem, think about what is *fixed* and what is *flexible*. Try to draw multiple versions of each object (if possible), testing the boundaries of this flexibility. The following everyday objects may be useful as analogies in your thinking:

- Rubber bands – Determines a straight line segment. Can stretch between any two points.
- Drinking straws – Determines a straight line segment, but with fixed length
- Thumbtacks – Fixes a point, but can allow rotations through that point in many cases.
- Wedge – Fixes an angle.

Here are some common examples of how these objects can be used to help you think through these problems:

Constrained	Flexible	Analogous Object(s)	Mental Picture / Simplified Sketch
A line passes through a specified point.	Slope of the line	Drinking straw = Line Thumbtack = Point	Line free to spin about a point.
Two lines intersect at a specified point.	Slope of the lines	Drinking straw = Line Thumbtack = Point	Both lines free to spin about a point. The angle is free to change.
A line passes through two points.	Nothing flexible	Drinking straw = Line Thumbtacks = Points	Two points pin down a line—no flexibility.

Constrained	Flexible	Analogous Object(s)	Mental Picture / Simplified Sketch
Specified distance between two points	Absolute or relative location of the points	Thumbtacks = Points Drinking straw = Distance between points	Fix one point temporarily. Line (straw) free to spin about one point, tracing the circle of possible locations of the other point.
Slope of a line	Location of the line, or points the line may pass through	Drinking straw = Line	Line is free to "float around" but not rotate.
Points are on a line (either in the coordinate plane or on a basic number line).	Distance between the points.	Rubber band = stretched between points	"Stretchy" distance between points.
Points on a line are a specified distance apart.	Order of the points (left-to-middle-to-right)	Drinking straws = fixed lengths between points Manipulation will be determined by other stated constraints, but thinking of the points as the endpoints of rigid straws will ensure that you do not forget the distance constraint.	A B (or) B A Lines could be laid end-to-end, overlapping, separated, and flipped right-to-left.
Triangle with a fixed area and a fixed base (and therefore a fixed height)	Position of the third vertex along a line parallel to the base	Straw = fixed base Rubber bands = other sides of the triangle Thumbtacks = endpoints of the base	B A

MANHATTAN
PREP

This is not intended to be an exhaustive list. The idea is simply to show you a new way of thinking through some difficult Geometry problems.

Try-It #7-3

A circle in a coordinate plane has a center at point A and a diameter of 6. If points B and C also lie in the same coordinate plane, is point B inside the circle?

(1) The distance between point A and point C equals 2.

(2) The distance between point B and point C equals 2.

The exact locations of points A, B, and C do not matter—only the relative locations of the points matter. Therefore, you can arbitrarily assign point A to a specific location (when possible, choose the origin of the coordinate plane), and draw a circle with a radius of 3 units around it.

Is B inside the circle?

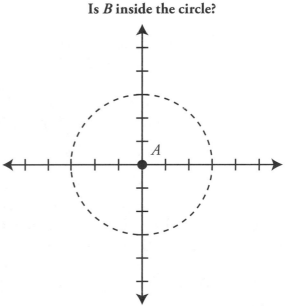

Statement (1) does not indicate anything about point B, so it is not sufficient. However, it does indicate that A and C are 2 units apart, so statement (1) enables you to place point C anywhere along the gray circle.

(1) The distance between A and C is 2.

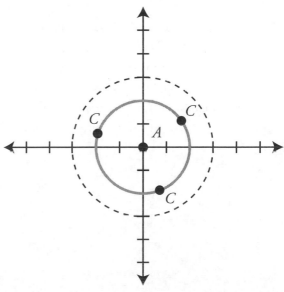

(2) The distance between *B* and *C* is 2.

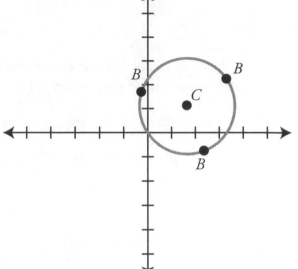

Statement (2) does not indicate anything about point *B* *relative* to point *A*, so it is not sufficient. However, it does constrain point *B* to be exactly 2 units away from wherever point *C* is. You could imagine point *C* at the center of a circle of size 2, with point *B* somewhere on the circle around it (and this circle could pick up and move anywhere on the coordinate plane).

(1) and (2) combined

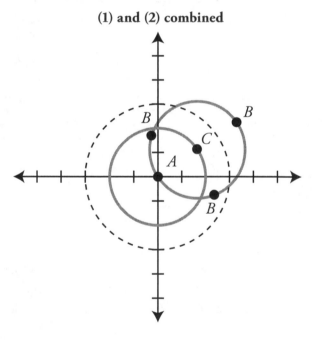

Finally, combine these two statements to see that depending upon where point *C* is drawn, point *B* may be inside the dotted circle, and it may not be.

The correct answer is **(E)**.

As long as you can achieve a visual proof of the answer, you don't need to prove it algebraically.

That's what *Rubber Band Geometry* is all about: testing scenarios for Geometry problems *without* the need to plug in numbers or use algebra. All you need is a visual environment that can be manipulated—one that preserves all key constraints and freedoms in the problem, and allows you to see and test them.

Baseline Calculations for Averages

Basic Averages

Try-It #7-4

> What is the average of 387, 388, and 389?

Without even calculating, you may be able to see that the average is 388. How did you arrive at that answer?

It's very unlikely that you calculated the average the classical way:

$$\text{Average} = \frac{\text{Sum}}{\text{Number of Terms}} = \frac{387 + 388 + 389}{3} = \frac{1{,}164}{3} = 388$$

You probably noticed that the numbers are very close together and evenly spaced. 387 is 1 less than 388, and 389 is 1 greater than 388. Thus the average must be 388—right in the middle.

Whether you realize it or not, you're using a relatively advanced technique to solve this problem: a **baseline calculation**. The baseline in this case is 388—the middle number. This concept can be applied to more difficult calculations of averages, making the calculation process much easier.

Try-It #7-5

> A consumer finds that five bags of popcorn contain 257, 261, 273, 280, and 259 corn kernels per bag, respectively. What is the average number of corn kernels per bag of popcorn?

First, note that all of the bags have at least 257 kernels, so the average must be greater than 257. How much greater than 257? First, consider how much each term differs from 257. Represent every number with a column rising above the baseline value (in this example, 257). The biggest numbers rise the highest; a number equal to the baseline has no height. The height of the column thus represents the difference between the number and the baseline value:

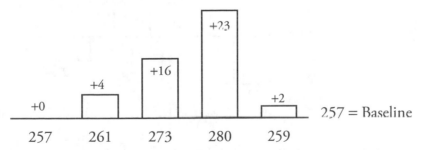

Calculate the sum of the differences: $0 + 4 + 16 + 23 + 2 = 45$.

Divide by the number of terms: the average difference is $45 \div 5 = 9$.

Therefore, the average number of kernels per bag equals baseline + average difference: $257 + 9 = 266$.

Simply put, a baseline picture is a column chart. The columns don't show the actual value of any number—rather, they show the difference between the baseline and the number.

> **!** The baseline can be *any* convenient number. Consider the following when choosing a baseline:
>
> - The smallest term in the set
> - The largest term in the set
> - The median term in the set
> - A round number near the range of values

For sets with apparent symmetry, choosing a baseline in the *middle* is a good way not only to confirm the symmetry, but also to compute the average. In this scenario, represent numbers lower than the baseline with columns that drop *below* the baseline. As before, the size of the column represents the difference between the number and the baseline.

Use trial and error to pick a possible average baseline, then adjust the drawing and calculations if necessary.

Try-It #7-6

If a small business paid quarterly taxes last year of $10,079, $10,121, $10,112, and $10,088, what was the average quarterly tax payment last year?

In this case, some of the numbers are below $10,100, and others are above $10,100, so $10,100 is a natural first guess:

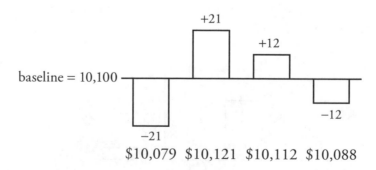

If the baseline is the average, then the sum of the differences from the baseline will be zero. Since the differences from the baseline do in fact sum to zero, $10,100 is indeed the average of this set.

Weighted Averages

Some sets may have many terms, but each of those terms has one of only two possible values. Rather than add each individual term together, simplify the calculations by using a *Weighted Average* calculation.

For weighted averages, use visualization to advance your understanding of the math. Two real-life analogies can make it easier to remember how the *relative weights* of high and low values determine where the weighted average falls.

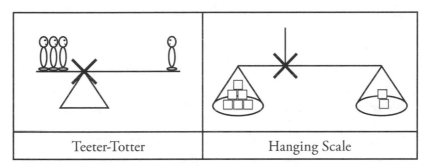

| Teeter-Totter | Hanging Scale |

These pictures represent the values in a set as horizontal positions—left-to-right, as on a number line, not as vertical columns. (It may help to imagine the balance beam or lever marked off in equal units like a number line.) Each pin or weight corresponds to the presence of a value in a set. The X in each picture marks the *equilibrium point*—in other words, the weighted average.

Both visual interpretations regard weighted averages as a kind of balancing act: *the weighted average will be closer to the end of the range that has more weight.* In the pictures, there are more instances of the left-hand side number in the set, so the X is relatively closer to the left-hand side. You can think of this point as the point where the weight would be "balanced" between the two sets.

Try-It #7-7

> A convenience store stocks soda in 12-ounce and 24-ounce bottles. If the average capacity of all the bottles in the store is 22 ounces, then what fraction of the bottles in the store are 12 ounces?

Note that 22 is much closer to 24 than to 12. This implies that there will be many more 24-ounce bottles than 12-ounce bottles. Because the question asks about 12-ounce bottles, you could strategically eliminate any answer greater than or equal to $\frac{1}{2}$.

Use your understanding of weighted averages as a balancing act to work backwards from the weighted average to the ratio of high to low terms.

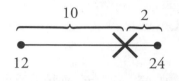

The total range between the high and low values (24 and 12) is 12 units. Mark off the distance from each end to the average of 22. Because the weighted average is closer to 24, that side of the teeter-totter is assigned the greater weight of 10 out of 12. The other side, 12, is assigned the smaller weight of 2 out of 12.

Therefore, the 24-ounce bottles constitute $\frac{10}{12} = \frac{5}{6}$ of the total number of bottles. The 12-ounce bottles constitute $\frac{2}{12} = \frac{1}{6}$ of the total number of bottles.

When using this technique, it is important to remember that the weighted average is *closer* to (i.e., *fewer* units away from) the side that has greater weight, so that side should always be assigned the higher fraction. It is easy to reverse this logic accidentally when solving a weighted average problem with this technique, so be very careful! Just remember: *the weighted average point will be closer to the side with* ***more*** *weight.*

Try-It #7-8

Darla decides to mix lemonade with limeade to make a new drink called citrusade. The lemonade is 50% water, 30% lemon juice, and 20% sugar. The limeade is 40% water, 28% lime juice, and 32% sugar. If the citrusade is more than 45% water and more than 24% sugar, which of the following could be the ratio of lemonade to limeade?

(A) 3 : 1
(B) 7 : 3
(C) 3 : 2
(D) 4 : 5
(E) 3 : 4

MANHATTAN
PREP

The citrusade is more than 45% water. The lemonade is 50% water and the limeade is 40% water, so the lemonade must be more heavily weighted:

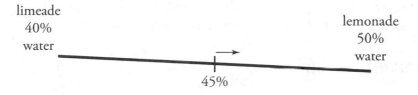

Therefore, the lemonade must make up more than 50% of the mixture. Eliminate answers (D) and (E).

Next, the citrusade is more than 24% sugar. The lemonade is 20% sugar and the limeade is 32% sugar, so what else can you figure out about the relative weighting?

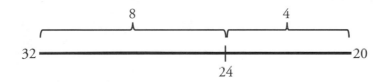

Since lemonade is more heavily weighted (the mixture is to the right of "50/50"), the weighting of the mixture is somewhere between 24% and the "50/50" weighting of the sugar, 26%. What weighting does the 24% figure represent?

$$
\begin{array}{c}
\overbrace{\hspace{2.5cm}}^{8}\quad\overbrace{\hspace{1.5cm}}^{4}\\
32\;\rule[0.5ex]{4cm}{0.4pt}\!\!\underset{24}{|}\!\!\rule[0.5ex]{2cm}{0.4pt}\;20
\end{array}
$$

The weighting is at most 8/12 lemonade, or 2/3. The weighting, then, must be between 1/2 and 2/3 lemonade and the rest limeade.

Answer (A) represents a weighting of 3/4 lemonade. Answer (B) represents a weighting of 7/10 lemonade. Only answer (C) offers a weighting in the right range: 3/5 or 3 : 5 lemonade.

The correct answer is **(C)**.

Number Line Techniques for Statistics Problems

Several other common types of questions involving statistics can be solved with visualization. Specifically, using a number line can help simplify the work for many of these problems.

Median Relative to Mean

Most questions involving the term *median* are really asking about the order of terms in a set: you line up the terms in a set in order of size, then select the middle term. By contrast, the *average* or arithmetic mean is the sum of all of the terms divided by the number of terms. It can be visualized as the balancing point of all the terms laid out on the number line, as in the discussion of the balancing point for weighted averages in the previous section. For Data Sufficiency questions involving median, you generally need to picture the placement of the unknown terms *relative to* the given terms in the problem.

This technique is similar to *Rubber Band Geometry* discussed earlier in this chapter, except this technique applies to problems involving sets rather than problems involving the coordinate plane. In this technique, you must place *fixed* terms in order from least to greatest (as you would on a number line), then move *variable* terms around according to the constraints. By doing so, you can visualize what impact these changes have on the answer.

Try-It #7-9

> If set S consists of the numbers n, -2, and 4, is the mean of set S greater than the median of set S?
>
> (1) $n > 2$
> (2) $n < 3$

The mean of set S is $\dfrac{n+(-2)+4}{3} = \dfrac{n+2}{3}$. The median depends on where n falls relative to -2 and 4: below -2, between -2 and 4, or above 4. One approach to this question is to think through the potential answers for all possible n values in the likely range (you can glance at the statements and other values in the list to get a sense of the relevant range) and draw the scenarios out on a number line. Try numbers around the relevant numbers, including a smaller and larger one at the far ends of the range; note that, by definition, all numbers in a set are different, so n cannot be -2 or 4.

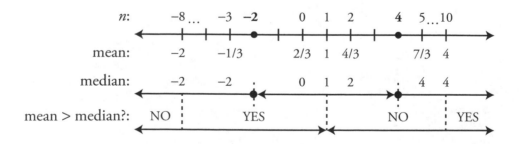

This requires a fair amount of up-front work, but evaluating the statements is fast as a result. Statement (1) indicates that $n > 2$, which is not sufficient. If $n = 5$, for example, the mean would equal 7/3 and the median would equal 4. By contrast, if $n = 10$, the mean would equal 4 and the median would still equal 4.

Similarly, statement (2) indicates that $n < 3$, which is not sufficient. If $n = -3$, for example, the mean would equal $-1/3$ and the median would equal -2. By contrast, if $n = -8$, the mean would equal -2 and the median would still equal -2.

Taken together, however, any number in the range of $2 < n < 3$ would feature a median greater than the mean.

The correct answer is (**C**).

Notice from this problem that as you move the variable terms, the mean *always* changes when the value of the variable terms change, but the median typically changes in *jumps*. The median can get stuck while the number you're changing doesn't affect *which* number is in the middle.

Changes in Standard Deviation

The GMAT will rarely (if ever) ask you to calculate the *standard deviation* of a list of numbers. However, the exam will expect you to have some intuition about standard deviations.

One way in which the GMAT might test your intuitive knowledge of standard deviations is by *changing numbers within a list* and asking you what the impact on standard deviation would be. The relationship is relatively straightforward:

- Moving terms away from the mean increases the standard deviation of the list
- Moving terms toward the mean decreases the standard deviation of the list

You might also see the term *variance*, which is also a measure of the spread of numbers in a set or list. Variance and standard deviation indicate the same information. A variance of 0 indicates that all of the numbers are identical, as does a standard deviation of 0. The larger the variance, or standard deviation, the more the numbers are spread out. (Variance and standard deviation are never negative.)

Try-It #7-10

Last Year	9	9.5	10	10	11	11	11	11	11	12.5	13	13
This Year	9	x	10	10	11	11	11	11	11	y	13	13

The monthly sales (in thousands of $) at a certain restaurant for the past two years are given in the chart above. If the standard deviation of the monthly sales is greater this year than last year, which of the following are possible values for *x* and *y*?

(A) 9 and 12.5
(B) 10 and 11
(C) 10 and 12.5
(D) 11 and 11
(E) 11 and 12.5

Except for *x* and *y*, the two lists of monthly sales numbers are identical, so focus exclusively on those terms that changed: 9.5 and 12.5 from last year were replaced by *x* and *y* this year. If this year's standard deviation is greater, then this year's numbers must be more spread out from the mean than last year's. The numbers are close enough together to indicate that the average should be somewhere around 11.

Visually, here are the interesting terms from last year:

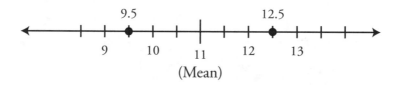

This problem does not require actual computation of the standard deviation using the new *x* and *y* values. The math would be too complex to complete in two minutes. Instead, determine visually which *x* and *y* values increase the standard deviation: the pair of *x* and *y* values *that are farther from the mean than are 9.5 and 12.5* will increase the standard deviation.

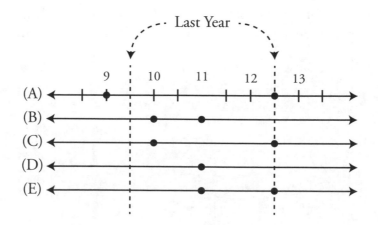

All of the sets have either one point or both points shifted in toward the mean EXCEPT (A), which has one of the points shifted away from the mean while the other is unchanged. Only in this case is the deviation greater.

The correct answer is **(A)**.

The GMAT may also test you on standard deviations by adding numbers to a list. When new terms are added, the GMAT will often ask you to compare the old list to the new list, or to compare various options for the new list, or to do both. You must have a technique to evaluate the standard deviation of different lists *relative to one another*. Again, pictures make for great comparison tools!

Try-It #7-11

> A list of 12 test scores has an average of 500 and a standard deviation of 50. Which of the following lists of additional test scores, when combined with the original list of 12 test scores, must result in a combined list with a standard deviation less than 50?
>
> (A) 6 test scores with average of 450 and standard deviation of 50.
> (B) 6 test scores with average of 500 and standard deviation of 25.
> (C) 6 test scores with average of 550 and standard deviation of 25.
> (D) 12 test scores with average of 450 and standard deviation of 25.
> (E) 2 test scores with average of 550 and standard deviation of 50.

It is not generally true that all of the terms in a list are within one standard deviation of the mean. However, standard deviation *is* a measure of the spread of the terms of a list, so you could represent the original list of scores this way:

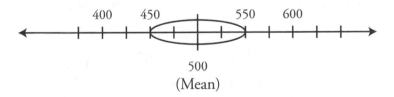

The oval spans ±1 standard deviation from the mean, where many of the scores will likely be. This simplification is acceptable as long as you represent all of the other lists the same way so that you can compare the *relative* effects of the new test scores systematically.

For each of the answer choices, overlay the representative ovals for the new data on top of the oval for the original data.

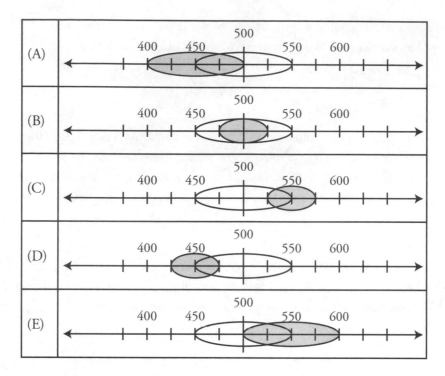

Only answer (B) concentrates the list of scores closer to the original average of 500. Thus, adding the data in answer (B) will result in a smaller standard deviation than that found in the original data. The correct answer is **(B)**.

In general, these are the rules for adding a single term to a list:

- Adding a new term *more than* 1 standard deviation from the mean generally *increases* the standard deviation.
- Adding a new term *less than* 1 standard deviation from the mean generally *decreases* the standard deviation.

Note that mathematically this is a slight oversimplification, but for the purpose of adding terms to a list of numbers on the GMAT, you can accept this simplification as true.

Floating Terms in a Set

On GMAT Statistics problems involving elements (i.e., terms) in a list, you can usually focus your attention on a single term or two. These terms could be considered the *floating terms*—the terms that are unknown or not completely defined among a list of more clearly defined terms.

As you approach a question of this type, try to rephrase the question quickly so that you focus on the unknown, or *floating*, terms rather than on the known terms.

Try-It #7-12

> List A contains 5 positive integers, and the average (arithmetic mean) of the integers in the list is 7. If the integers 6, 7, and 8 are in list A, what is the range of list A?
>
> (1) The integer 3 is in list A.
> (2) The largest term in list A is greater than 3 times and less than 4 times the size of the smallest term.

The average of all five integers in the list is 7. Three of the integers in the list are given (6, 7, and 8) and they all have an average of 7. Therefore, the *floating terms* in this problem must also have an average of 7. Assign x and y to represent these terms:

$$\frac{x+y}{2} = 7$$
$$x + y = 14$$

The rephrased question is thus, "Given that $x + y = 14$, what is either x or y?" Once you know one of the values, you can solve for the other and thereby determine the range of the list.

(1) SUFFICIENT: If 3 is one of the unknown integers, the other must be 11. The range is thus $11 - 3 = 8$.

(2) SUFFICIENT: This statement might seem a little too vague to be sufficient, but by visually listing the possible pairs that add up to 14, you can rule out pairs that don't fit the constraint from this statement:

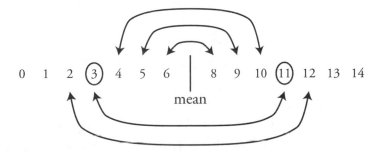

Notice that the pairings represent the constraint $x + y = 14$. Visually, this means that x and y are balanced around 7.

Among these pairs:

- 8 is 1.33 times the size of 6 (the ratio is too low).
- 9 is 1.8 times the size of 5 (the ratio is too low).
- 10 is 2.5 times the size of 4 (the ratio is too low).
- 11 is 3.66 times the size of 3 (an acceptable ratio).
- 12 is 6 times the size of 2 (the ratio is too high).

Only one pair of integers results in a ratio strictly between 3 and 4. The unknown terms must therefore be 3 and 11, and the range is $11 - 3 = 8$.

The correct answer is **(D)**.

7

In this problem the constraint $x + y = 14$ is a *fixed sum*. Another common constraint is a *fixed difference*, such as $a - b = 2$. A fixed difference can be represented visually as a fixed distance between a and b on the number line, with a to the right because it is larger. That distance could move left or right:

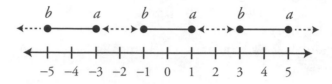

Maximizing (or Minimizing) One Term

Another visual technique for statistics involves maximizing (or minimizing) the value of a term in a set or list of numbers, subject to some constraints. Such problems will usually employ the word "maximum" or "minimum." For these problems, you often should maximize (or minimize) the term by minimizing (or maximizing) the *other* terms, because the constraints usually involve mathematical trade-offs.

Try-It #7-13

> In a certain lottery drawing, five balls are selected from a tumbler in which each ball is printed with a different two-digit positive integer. If the average (arithmetic mean) of the five numbers drawn is 56 and the median is 60, what is the greatest value that the lowest number selected could be?
>
> (A) 43
> (B) 48
> (C) 51
> (D) 53
> (E) 56

The goal is to maximize the value of the lowest-numbered ball. All balls contain a two-digit positive integer, and none of the balls have the same number. The problem provides enough info to calculate the sum and to lay out a visual listing of the numbers:

$$56 = \frac{\text{sum}}{5}$$

$$280 = \text{sum}$$

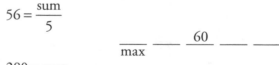

In order to maximize the value of the first (lowest) number in the set, what do you need to do to the other numbers?

You'd want to minimize them. Select the smallest numbers that you can for the remaining slots:

$$\underline{x} \quad \underline{x+1} \quad \underline{60} \quad \underline{61} \quad \underline{62}$$

In some problems, you might actually make different slots equal to each other (e.g., the three largest numbers could be 60, 60, and 60). This problem, though, specifies that the integers are all different.

MANHATTAN
PREP

The five numbers must sum to 280, so you can set up an algebraic equation and solve. Can you think of a way to minimize the arithmetic needed to solve in that way?

The three numerical values, 60, 61, and 62, are all larger than the average of 56. Specifically, they are +4, +5, and +6 away from that average.

The other two numbers, then, need to make up for that "overage" of 4 + 5 + 6 = 15.

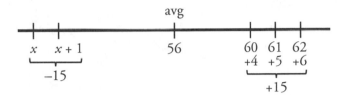

The numbers x and $x + 1$ are also consecutive, so they need to be −8 and −7 away from the average of 56. The two remaining numbers are 48 and 49. (We call this the *over-under approach*, by the way.)

The correct answer is **(B)**.

Try-It #7-14

> The average (arithmetic mean) of six numbers is 18 and the median of the six numbers is 16. What is the minimum possible value for the greatest number in the list?
>
> (A) 19
> (B) 20
> (C) 21
> (D) 22
> (E) 23

This time, the goal is to minimize the largest number:

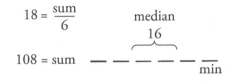

In order to minimize the final term, you'd want to maximize all of the other terms. This time, though, the list contains an even number of terms, so you can't just set the median to the middle number. The two middle numbers average to 16.

The pair (16, 16) averages to 16, as does the pair (15, 17). The first pair, though, is better when the goal is to minimize the final term, since the terms to the right have to be equal to or greater than the terms to the left.

In other words, when trying to minimize the final term, it's true that you want to maximize the earlier terms, but you also have to think about how to do so in a way that doesn't make the final term too large (since it has to be larger than the earlier terms).

$$\underline{16} \quad \underline{16} \quad \underline{16} \quad \underline{16} \quad \underline{} \quad \underline{}_{\text{min}}$$

Maximize the earlier terms as well, so the first four terms are all 16. In order to minimize the final term, set the last two terms equal to each other.

You can solve algebraically:

$108 - (16)(4) = 44$ and $44/2 = 22$

Or you can use the *over-under approach*:

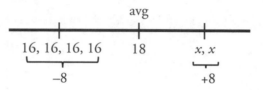

Those last two terms have to make up for the −8 on the other side, so each x must be 4 over the average, or 22.

Taking and Giving

Another common scenario involves taking value from one term in a list and giving it to another term. The relative value of the terms in the list will change, leading to some interesting results.

Try-It #7-15

Jake	51
Keri	63
Luke	15
Mia	38
Nora	22

The table above shows the number of points held by five players of a certain game. If an integer number of Keri's points were taken from her and given to Luke, and the median score of the five players increased, how many points were transferred from Keri to Luke?

(A) 23　　　(B) 24　　　(C) 25　　　(D) 26　　　(E) 27

The key to this problem is that by taking enough points from Keri and giving them to Luke, *the median of the list can change.*

Set it up visually. Order the scores from low to high on a number line, and represent the change in Luke's score with x:

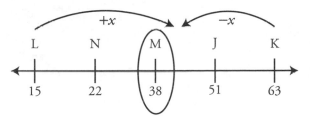

The current median is Mia's 38, circled in the diagram. In order for the median to change, Luke's score must leap-frog those of Nora and Mia, pushing Mia into the bottom two scores and making Luke's score the median. But be careful! You don't want to decrease Keri's score *so much* that Luke and Mia surpass her, leaving Mia once again in the median score position.

If $15 + x = 38$, Luke would *match* the current median score. That is $x = 23$, and Keri's new score would be $63 - 23 = 40$. However, the median score would remain 38, with both Luke and Mia having that score. Therefore, x must be greater than 23.

Try $x = 24$. Luke's new point value is $15 + 24 = 39$. Keri's new point value is $63 - 24 = 39$. Both Nora and Mia are below Luke (and Keri), so the new median is 39.

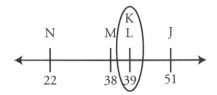

The correct answer is (**B**).

MANHATTAN
PREP

Problem Set

Use the Visual Solutions techniques discussed in this chapter to solve the following problems.

1. Does a rectangular mirror have an area greater than 10 cm²?

    (1) The perimeter of the mirror is 24 cm.
    (2) The diagonal of the mirror is less than 11 cm.

2. Distinct lines k and ℓ intersect in the coordinate plane at point (3, −2). Is the larger angle formed at the intersection between these two lines greater than 90°?

    (1) Lines k and ℓ have positive y-axis intercepts.
    (2) The distance between the y-axis intercepts of lines k and ℓ is 5.

3. If a, b, and c are positive, is $a > \dfrac{b+c}{2}$?

    (1) On the number line, a is closer to b than it is to c.
    (2) $b > c$

4. The length of one edge of a cube equals 4. What is the distance between the center of the cube and one of its vertices?

5. A test is taken by 100 people and possible scores are the integers between 0 and 50, inclusive. For each of the following scenarios, determine whether the average (arithmetic mean) score would be greater than 30 (answer Yes, No, or Uncertain).

    a) More than 70 people scored 40 or higher?
    b) 75 people scored 40 or higher?
    c) Fewer than 10 people scored 50?
    d) No more than 2 test-takers scored any given score?

6. As part of an experiment, a student repeatedly tests the temperature of a light bulb. The bar graph below displays the number of readings the student recorded at various temperatures, measured in degrees Fahrenheit. What was the average temperature reading of the light bulb?

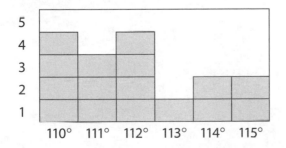

7. In a certain dance troupe, there are 55 women and 33 men. If all of the women are 62 inches tall and all of the men are 70 inches tall, what is the average height of the dancers in the troupe?

8. Five car salespeople reported their monthly car sales. The median number of sales was 21 cars.

   a) If the maximum number of cars sold by any one salesperson was 46 cars, what is the highest possible mean sales for the group?
   b) If the mean number of sales is equal to the median number of sales, what is the maximum number of cars that any one salesperson could have sold?
   c) If the highest number of sales by one person was twice the lowest number of sales by one person, what is the lowest possible number of cars that could have been sold in total?

9. Three people have $32, $72, and $98, respectively. If they pool their money then redistribute it among them, what is the maximum value for the median amount of money?

   (A) $72   (B) $85   (C) $98   (D) $101   (E) $202

10. List *A* consists of at least two different values and contains only positive multiples of 30. Which of the following cannot be true?

   I. The range of list *A* is twice as big as the median of list *A*.
   II. The variance of list *A* is less than the standard deviation of list *A*.
   III. The median of list *A* is the square of an integer but not an element in list *A*.

   (A) None
   (B) I only
   (C) II only
   (D) III only
   (E) II and III only

Solutions

1. **(C):** Because the formula for the area of a rectangle is $A = lw$ rephrase the question. Is $lw > 10$?

(1) INSUFFICIENT: The perimeter is 24 cm. The area of a quadrilateral is maximized when the quadrilateral is a square, so first try $l = w = 6$. In this case, the area is 36 cm² and the answer to the question is Yes.

If, on the other hand, $l = 11.5$ and $w = 0.5$, the perimeter is still 24, but the area is $(11.5)(0.5) = 5.75$ cm². In this case, the answer to the question is No.

(2) INSUFFICIENT. The diagonal of the rectangle is less than 11. If the diagonal is less than 11, then the sides must also be less than 11. If $l = w = 6$, then the diagonal is shorter than 11 and, as last time, the area is 36. In this case, the answer to the question is Yes.

If, on the other hand, $l = 3$ and $w = 1$, the diagonal is less than 11, but the area is $(3)(1) = 3$ cm². In this case, the answer to the question is No.

(1) AND (2) SUFFICIENT: The sides must be less than 11 and the perimeter must be 24. The case of the square still maximizes the area: $l = w = 6$ and the area is 36.

The largest possible length is just under 11, making the width just over 1. $(<11)(>1)$ = something larger than 10. The area must be greater than 10.

The correct answer is **(C)**.

2. **(D):** First, draw a picture of the coordinate plane, together with the point (3, −2) and two sample lines k and l.

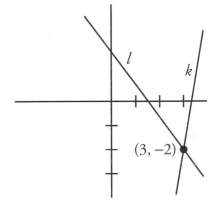

Stick a "thumbtack" at the point (3, −2). You can rotate lines k and l through any angle around this thumbtack.

The problem asks whether the larger of the two distinct angles formed between these lines is greater than 90°. Most of the time, when two lines intersect, they form two acute angles (less than 90°) and two obtuse angles (greater than 90°). The only case in which the two lines would *not* form any angle greater

than 90° is when the two lines are perfectly perpendicular to each other: then they form four 90° angles. The question can be rephrased as "Are the two lines *k* and *l* perpendicular to each other?" Use *Rubber Band Geometry* to try to force the lines to be perpendicular and non-perpendicular.

(1) SUFFICIENT. Both lines have positive *y*-axis intercepts. In other words, they both cross the *y*-axis above the origin (0, 0):

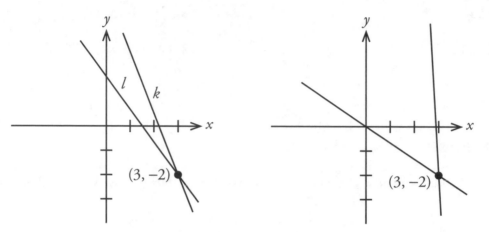

Both lines slope downward to the right (that is, they have negative slope). If you were to make one line very nearly vertical, with a very steep negative slope, the other line would still have to be angled to cross above the *x*-axis. There is no way to make the lines perpendicular to each other. (Another way to see this result is that any line perpendicular to a line with negative slope must have positive slope, so that their slopes can multiply together to −1, a condition of perpendicularity. If both lines have negative slope, they cannot multiply to −1.)

(2) SUFFICIENT. The distance between the *y*-intercepts of the two lines is 5. It's easy to generate a case in which the lines are not perpendicular. Can you also make the lines perpendicular?

To spread the lines as far apart as possible, center the distance of 5 directly opposite the thumbtack, like so:

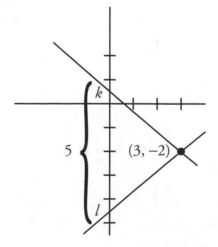

By symmetry, half of that distance of 5 will be above the thumbtack:

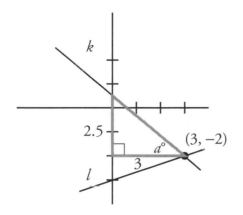

The legs of the two triangles have lengths 3 and 2.5. The angle opposite the 2.5, labeled $a°$ in the diagram, must be *less* than 45°, because it is opposite the smaller side. As a result, the angle between k and l cannot be 90°.

The correct answer is **(D)**.

3. **(C):** The problem indicates that a, b, and c are positive and asks whether a is greater than $\frac{b+c}{2}$, which is the *average* (or arithmetic mean) of b and c.

Draw a picture and rephrase the question: "On the number line, is a positioned to the right of the midpoint between b and c?"

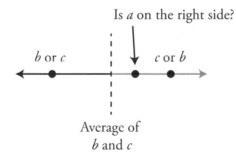

(1) INSUFFICIENT. It isn't clear whether b or c is the larger value—the point on the right—so a could be closer to the smaller number (making a less than the average) or the larger number (making a greater than the average).

(2) INSUFFICIENT. This statement indicates nothing about a, so it can't be sufficient.

(1) AND (2) SUFFICIENT. Together, the two statements indicate that b is the point on the right, so a must be on the right side of the midpoint.

The correct answer is **(C)**.

4. **$2\sqrt{3}$**: Draw it out!

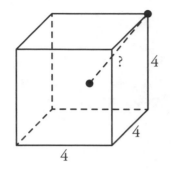

The length of any side of the cube is 4, and the problem asks for the distance between the center of the cube and any of its vertices (corners). Chop up the cube into 8 smaller cubes to see that the distance from the center of the 4 × 4 × 4 cube to any corner is the diagonal of a 2 × 2 × 2 cube.

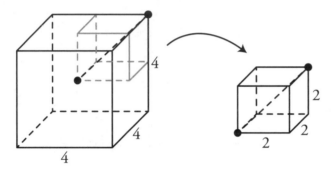

You can find the diagonal of a cube in a variety of ways. Probably the fastest (besides applying a memorized formula) is to use the "Super-Pythagorean" theorem, which extends to three dimensions:

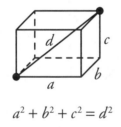

$$a^2 + b^2 + c^2 = d^2$$

In the special case when the three sides of the box are equal, as they are in a cube, use this equation:

$$s^2 + s^2 + s^2 = d^2$$
$$3s^2 = d^2$$
$$s\sqrt{3} = d$$

Since $s = 2$, $d = 2\sqrt{3}$.

5. To visualize this set of *Weighted Averages* problems, imagine a teeter-totter that is 50 meters long, marked off from 0 to 50 to represent scores. One hundred people of equal weight sit on the teeter-totter at their respective scores. The weighted average is the position where the teeter-totter would balance. Thus, to answer whether the average score is greater than 30, take extremes according to the given conditions and see whether you can swing the balance to either side of 30 (or whether you are forced to balance on one side of 30 only).

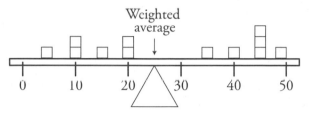

a) **Uncertain:** More than 70 people scored 40 or higher. If all 100 scored 40 (or higher), then the average is above 30.

If, on the other hand, 71 people score 40 and the other 29 score 0, does the average drop to 30 or lower?

Match up the 29 people who scored 0 with 29 of the people who scored 40. These 58 people together have an average score of 20. The other 42 people have a score of 40. If you average these two groups, the average must be below 30, since 58 is larger than 42.

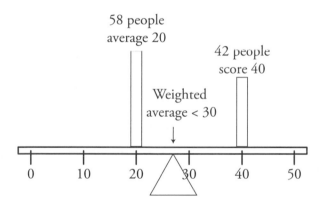

b) **Uncertain:** 75 people scored 40 or higher. If all 100 scored 40, then the average is higher than 30. If 75 scored 40 and the other 25 scored 0, then what?

Match the 25 people who scored 0 with 25 people who scored 40. These 50 people have an average score of 20. The remaining 50 people have an average score of 40, so the overall average is exactly 30. It is possible, therefore, to have an average that is higher than 30 or an average that is not higher than 30.

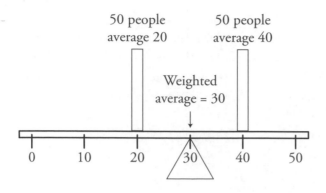

c) **Uncertain:** Fewer than 10 people scored 50. Say that 1 person scored 50 and other 99 scored 0. The average is definitely below 30. If on the other hand, 1 person scored 50 and the other 99 scored 40, then the average is definitely above 30.

d) **No:** Each score was achieved by no more than 2 people. There are 51 integers between 0 and 50, inclusive. In other words, there are 102 possible scores to spread among the test-takers. Since there are 100 test-takers, almost every score is taken.

The highest possible average will occur when nobody scores 0 points. If two test-takers score 1, two test-takers score 2, and so on up to 50, then the average score will be approximately 25. As this is the highest allowable average for this scenario, it's impossible for the average to be greater than 30.

6. **112°:** Eyeball the graph. The average looks like it's in the 112° range. Calculate the *over-under* with 112° as the assumed baseline.

The four 110° readings are each 2° below the baseline, and the three 111° readings are each 1° below the baseline, for a total of 11° below baseline.

On the other side, the 113°, 114°, and 115° readings are a total of 11° above the baseline. They balance perfectly! The average is exactly 112°.

7. **65 inches:** Algebraic solution:

$$\text{Average} = \frac{55(62 \text{ inches}) + 33(70 \text{ inches})}{(55 + 33)} = \frac{3,410 + 2,310}{88} \text{ inches} = \frac{5,720}{88} \text{ inches} = 65 \text{ inches}$$

Visual Solution:

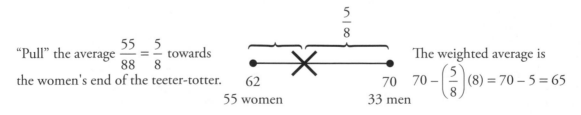

"Pull" the average $\frac{55}{88} = \frac{5}{8}$ towards the women's end of the teeter-totter.   The weighted average is $70 - \left(\frac{5}{8}\right)(8) = 70 - 5 = 65$

8. The median number of cars is 21. Lay this out visually: ___ ___ 21 ___ ___

    a) **31**: Add the new given information to your diagram: ___ ___ 21 ___ 46

You're asked to maximize the mean, so maximize all of the other numbers:

21 21 21 46 46

The mean is $\dfrac{155}{5}$ = 31.

    b) **63**: If the mean equals the median, then the mean is 21 and the sum of the numbers is
(21)(5) = 105. You're asked to maximize the largest number, so minimize the others and solve for x:

<u>0</u> <u>0</u> <u>21</u> <u>21</u> <u>x</u>

$42 + x = 105$
$x = 63$

    c) **86:** You're asked to minimize the overall sum. In order to do this, minimize the largest possible
number. That number must be even (because it is twice the lowest number sold) and it must be
greater than 21 (because it must to be greater than the median). Therefore, make the largest
number 22 and minimize the rest accordingly.

<u>11</u> <u>11</u> <u>21</u> <u>21</u> <u>22</u>

The sum is 86.

9. **(D) $101:** The pool of money is $32 + $72 + $98 = $202. After the redistribution, each person will
have an amount between $0 and $202, inclusive. Call the amounts L, M, and H (low, median, high).
To maximize M, minimize L and H.

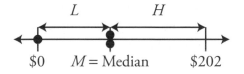

Minimum L = $0
Minimum $H = M$
Maximum M = Total pool of money – Minimum L – Minimum H
$M = $202 – $0 – M$
$2M = 202
$M = 101

The correct answer is **(D)**.

10. **(A) None:** The question stem doesn't specify which positive multiples of 30 are included in List A
(including the possibility of repeats).

I. The range represents the difference between the largest and smallest numbers in the list. Try to find a case in which the range is twice as large as the median. It's easiest to work with a 3-item list; the median is the middle number and the range equals the largest minus the smallest.

    If the median is 60, then the range would need to be 120. In this case, make the smallest number 30 and the largest 150. The list 30, 60, 150 fits statement I. Statement I can be true, so eliminate answer (B).

II. The variance is equal to the square of the standard deviation (SD). The variance is 0 when the SD is 0, but the SD is 0 only when all of the numbers in the list are identical. Because list *A* contains at least two different numbers, the variance cannot be 0. However, the standard deviation could be between 0 and 1. If so, then the square of the standard deviation (aka, the variance) would actually be less than the standard deviation. For instance, if you had 1,000 instances of the number 60 and one instance of the number 30, then the standard deviation would be about 0.95 and the variance would be about 0.9. (You do not, of course, need to calculate this! It's enough to know that an extreme case is a possibility.)

III. If the median is not an element in the list, then the list must have an even number of elements.

    Try to find the case in which the median is the square of an integer. The median is the average of the two middle numbers on the list; there are three possibilities:

    1. The two middle numbers are equal, in which case the median equals the two numbers; the statement does not allow this case.

    2. The two middle numbers are 30 apart, in which case the median must have a units digit of 5; for example, 30 and 60 result in a median of 45. This is true for any odd multiple of 30: 30, 90, 150, etc.

    3. The two middle numbers are 60 apart, in which case the median must have a units digit of 0 and be a multiple of 30. Use the perfect square of 30: 900. If the two middle numbers were 870 and 930, then the median would be 900.

    Therefore, the median needs to be a perfect square that ends in 5 or 0: 25, 100, 225, and so on. You can eliminate 25, since it is too small. If the median is 100, then the sum of the two middle numbers would have to be 200. This sum would be composed of two numbers that are multiples of 30, so it should be a multiple of 30, but 200 is not a multiple of 30.

    If the median is 225, then the sum of the two middle numbers would have to be 450. This sum is also a multiple of 30, so the pattern should work.

    (If you want to check: 210 and 240 average to 225. They are both multiples of 30, so List *A* could consist of the pair 210 and 240.) Eliminate answer (E).

The correct answer is (**A**).

Chapter 8

GMAT Advanced Quant

Hybrid Problems

In This Chapter...

Chapter 8
Hybrid Problems

Pop Quiz!

Try these four hybrid problems.

Try-It #8-1

A student cuts 80 rectangles from construction paper, all of which are at least 10 inches in length and in width, and 20 percent of the rectangles that are greater than 10 inches long are exactly 10 inches wide. If 40 of the rectangles have a length of exactly 10 inches and 50 of the rectangles are greater than 10 inches wide, how many rectangles have a perimeter of greater than 40 inches? (Note: Assume that width and length are interchangeable; in other words, width does not have to be shorter than length.)

(A) 18
(B) 22
(C) 32
(D) 58
(E) 66

Try-It #8-2

Set S contains 100 consecutive integers. If the range of the negative elements of Set S equals 80, what is the average (arithmetic mean) of the positive numbers in the set?

Try-It #8-3

If a and b are consecutive positive integers, and $ab = 30x$, is x an integer?

    (1) a^2 is divisible by 25.

    (2)   63 is a factor of b^2.

Try-It #8-4

A carnival card game gives the contestant a one in three probability of successfully choosing the right card and thereby winning the game. If a contestant plays the game repeatedly, what is the minimum number of times that he must play the game so that the probability that he never loses is less than 1%?

Hybrid Problems

Hybrid problems blend topics together. They contain two or more qualitatively different kinds of obstacles that you must surmount on the way to the answer.

Some hybrid problems feature content areas that are fairly closely related. Other hybrid problems feature content areas that share little in common; these problems must be solved in separate steps.

The difficulty of a hybrid problem is related to the following questions:

- **How closely related are the subjects being tested?** Are the content areas covered in the same Manhattan Prep Strategy Guide or different Strategy Guides? (The five Strategy Guides published by Manhattan Prep cover *Algebra; Fractions, Decimals, and Percents (FDPs); Geometry; Number Properties; and Word Problems.*) The more closely related the subjects, the easier it will be to navigate the problem.

- **How important are each of the subject areas?** Are each of the subject areas fundamental to the problem, or is one of them just a low-level disguise that can be quickly disposed of? The more important each topic is in solving the problem, the more difficult the problem will usually be.

Problems with minor additional content areas are generally easier to solve than hybrids that blend topics together in an *unusual, fundamental, and clever* way. The best hybrids are one of a kind. You will have to bring your A-game to solve them.

But solve them you can. That's why you're reading this chapter!

Identify and Sequence the Parts

When you encounter a hybrid problem, first pick out all of the topics tested. Take a look at the first problem from the pop quiz.

Try-It #8-1

> A student cuts 80 rectangles from construction paper, all of which are at least 10 inches in length and in width, and 20 percent of the rectangles that are greater than 10 inches long are exactly 10 inches wide. If 40 of the rectangles have a length of exactly 10 inches and 50 of the rectangles are greater than 10 inches wide, how many rectangles have a perimeter of greater than 40 inches? (Note: Assume that width and length are interchangeable; in other words, width does not have to be shorter than length.)
>
> (A) 18
> (B) 22
> (C) 32
> (D) 58
> (E) 66

This is obviously a Geometry problem but something else is going on as well. The 80 rectangles are split up into smaller sub-groups: those with lengths greater than 10 inches vs. exactly 10 inches, and those with widths greater than 10 inches vs. exactly 10 inches. In other words, this is really an Overlapping Sets problem.

This *Sets* problem comes with a twist though: the question doesn't ask about just one of the sub-categories; instead, you're going to have to figure out something to do with perimeter.

Which part should you tackle first?

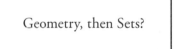

| Geometry, then Sets? | Sets, then Geometry? |

In this case, a good starting point is to begin by filling in a double-set matrix to sort out what information you know. Then you can think about what that might tell you about perimeter. In general, start with wherever you feel the logical beginning is or whichever part you feel is an easier, cleaner starting point.

Where to Start?

Starting at the Beginning

As you contemplate the logical order of steps, you might feel less confident with the second stage than with the first. If so, go ahead and start at the beginning. Just articulate very clearly, "What *intermediate result* will I get once I'm finished with the first part of the problem?"

If you begin with the double-set matrix, then when you're done, you'll know the number of rectangles that are assigned to the various length and width categories.

First, set up the matrix:

	10" long	> 10" long	Total
10" wide			
> 10" wide			
Total			

Next, fill in the given information (in bold, below) and calculate the values for the unknown cells:

	10" long	> 10" long	Total
10" wide		**$0.2x = 8$**	30
> 10" wide	18	$0.8x = 32$	**50**
Total	**40**	$x = 40$	**80**

Finally, move to the Geometry portion of the solution. How many rectangles have a perimeter greater than 40 inches?

The rectangles that are exactly 10 inches long and 10 inches wide have a perimeter of 40 inches, so any of the other rectangles will have a perimeter greater than 40 inches. (Note: One of the traps here is to assume that only the category "greater than 10 inches long *and* greater than 10 inches wide" leads to a perimeter greater than 40.)

The sum of the three categories—18, 32, and 8—is 58.

The correct answer is **(D)**.

Starting at the End

You might decide that it is easier to start at the end and work backwards. That's fine. Just ask yourself, "What information do I need to have as a *last step* before arriving at a solution to the question?"

In that case, the best strategy is to work through the final part of the problem as well as you can, with the hope that after that work is completed, you'll have a better sense of how to proceed on the earlier part of the problem.

In this example, you might first try to figure out what would be needed to determine perimeters greater than 40. The allowed measurements are: 10-inch length; 10-inch width; greater than 10-inch length; greater than 10-inch width.

Any rectangle with a 10-inch length and 10-inch width will have a perimeter of 40. Any rectangle with a 10-inch length and greater than 10-inch width will have a perimeter larger than 40, as will any rectangle with a 10-inch width and greater than 10-inch length. The same will be true of any rectangle with all dimensions greater than 10 inches.

Breaking down the problem into these sub-categories may provide the realization you need to set up the double-set matrix and solve.

Let's look at another example.

Try-It #8-2

> Set S contains 100 consecutive integers. If the range of the negative elements of
> Set S equals 80, what is the average (arithmetic mean) of the positive numbers in
> the set?

In this problem, information is given about the *range* of numbers in a set. Thus, knowing how to work with Statistics techniques will be important in solving the problem.

Solving this problem also requires using Consecutive Integers techniques—namely, counting consecutive integers and computing their average. These two topics are closely related but still cover different ideas.

If you start with the statistics piece of the problem, then you'll be able to find the highest and lowest negative numbers in the set of consecutive integers. This will act as an input to the formulas for computing the largest and smallest positive integers in the set, and subsequently the average of the positive integers in the set.

First, determine what set of consecutive negative integers will result in a range of 80. Range is defined as the difference between the highest and lowest numbers in a set:

High − Low = Range

The high number among the negative terms is the largest negative integer, −1:

$$-1 - \text{Low} = 80$$
$$-\text{Low} = 80 + 1$$
$$\text{Low} = -81$$

Therefore the lowest number in Set S is −81. Use this result to jump to the consecutive integers portion of the solution. In this case, −81 is the smallest or "First" element in the set:

8

$$Last - First + 1 = Count$$
$$Last - (-81) + 1 = 100$$
$$Last + 82 = 100$$
$$Last = 18$$

Therefore, the highest or "Last" number in Set S is 18.

Finally, calculate the average of the *positive* terms in the set using 1 as the smallest ("First Pos") positive integer and 18 as the largest ("Last Pos") positive integer:

$$\text{Average of Pos} = \frac{\text{Last Pos} + \text{First Pos}}{2} = \frac{18 + 1}{2} = \frac{19}{2} = 9.5$$

The average of the positive numbers in the set is 9.5.

If instead you decided to start with Step 2, you would write the formula for the average of consecutive integers first, focusing on the positive integers:

$$\text{Average of Pos} = \frac{\text{Last Pos} + \text{First Pos}}{2}$$

The two unknowns you need to solve for are the largest positive integer ("Last Pos") and the smallest positive integer ("First Pos"), because the question asks only about the *positive* integers in the set.

Some of the integers in Set S are negative and some are positive, so clearly the smallest positive integer will be 1. Therefore, you only need to figure out what the largest integer in the set will be. This is the information needed in the *last step* of solving the problem.

In order to calculate this number, you would now need to apply the definition of range:

$$High - Low = Range$$

The largest negative integer (the "High" number) is −1:

$$-1 - Low = 80$$
$$-Low = 80 + 1$$
$$Low = -81$$

Therefore the lowest number in the set is −81; plug this into the formula for counting consecutive integers:

$$Last - First + 1 = Count$$
$$Last - (-81) + 1 = 100$$
$$Last + 82 = 100$$
$$Last = 18$$

Therefore, the highest number in the set is 18.

Finally, plug 18 into the average formula:

$$\text{Average of Pos} = \frac{\text{Last Pos} + \text{First Pos}}{2} = \frac{18+1}{2} = \frac{19}{2} = 9.5$$

Whether you start solving this problem from the beginning or from the end, study how the steps hook together: the output of one step becomes the input to another. These are the "turns" you have to make in solving any hybrid problem. Often, a number that plays one role in a particular formula or calculation plays a completely different role in the next step.

Minor Hybrids

In minor hybrid problems, one of the following conditions applies:

- The content areas in the problem are closely related. For instance, they are covered in the same Manhattan Prep Strategy Guide, such as *Quadratic Equations* and *Inequalities* (in the *Algebra Strategy Guide*), or *Probability* and *Combinatorics* (in the *Number Properties Strategy Guide*).
- One of the content areas is simply a low-level disguise or some other minor feature.

These problems can be easier to solve than major hybrids. However, you will still benefit greatly from paying close attention to the turns as you move through the stages of the solution.

Try-It #8-3

If *a* and *b* are consecutive positive integers, and $ab = 30x$, is *x* an integer?

(1) a^2 is divisible by 25.
(2)   63 is a factor of b^2.

This problem tests your skill with both *Divisibility & Primes* and *Consecutive Integers*. Consecutive integers concepts often lend themselves well to questions about divisibility.

First, rephrase the wording of this question into something easier to handle. Isolate *x* by rewriting the given equation as follows:

$$x = \frac{ab}{30}$$

In order for *x* to be an integer, *ab* must be divisible by 30. To be divisible by 30, a number must have 2, 3, and 5 as prime factors. Thus the question becomes: "Does *ab* have 2, 3, and 5 as prime factors?"

Next, use a concept from consecutive integers: *a* and *b* are consecutive positive integers. Thus, either *a* or *b* is an even number, which means that the product *ab* is automatically divisible by 2. The question can be further simplified: "Does the product *ab* have 3 and 5 as prime factors?"

(1) INSUFFICIENT: Statement (1) indicates that 25 is a factor of a^2, meaning that 5 and 5 are prime factors of a^2. Knowing that 5 is a prime factor of *a* indicates that 5 is a factor of *ab*, but does not indicate whether 3 is a factor.

(2) INSUFFICIENT: Statement (2) indicates that 63 is a factor of b^2 which means that 3, 3, and 7 are prime factors of b^2 ($3 \times 3 \times 7 = 63$). Knowing that 3 is a prime factor of b indicates that 3 is a factor of ab, but does not indicate whether 5 is a factor.

(1) AND (2) SUFFICIENT: According to the combined statements, a is divisible by 5 and b is divisible by 3. This is sufficient information to answer the rephrased question.

The correct answer is **(C)**.

Notice that the solution never indicated exactly what consecutive integers a and b are—this isn't necessary. Also notice a potential trap in this problem—assuming that $a < b$ because of the way the question is phrased. This assumption would not be fatal in this case, but if you realize that a and b can come in *either* order, then it's easier to create an accurate list of different scenarios for a and b.

Try-It #8-4

> A carnival card game gives the contestant a one in three probability of successfully choosing the right card and thereby winning the game. If a contestant plays the game repeatedly, what is the minimum number of times that he must play the game so that the probability that he never loses is less than 1%?

This problem primarily tests *Probability* theory. In addition, *Exponents* are needed to represent the impact of playing multiple games on the probability of the outcomes. The probabilities are given in fractions, yet the question is asked in terms of percents, so *FDP Connections* are relevant. Finally, the question is phrased in terms of an inequality, so *Inequalities* come into play.

"The probability that he never loses" can be rephrased as "the probability that he always wins." This probability can be expressed as $(1/3)^n$, where 1/3 is the chance of winning on a single play and n is the number of times the contestant plays.

Track scenarios in a chart:

Number of Plays	P(all wins) = $(1/3)^n$	Approx. equivalent
1	1/3	$0.33 = 33\%$
2	1/9	$0.11 = 11\%$
3	1/27	$4/100 = 0.04 = 4\%$
4	1/81	$1/80 = 1.25/100 = 1.25\%$
5	1/243	$1/250 = 0.4/100 = 0.4\% < 1\%$

You might also have noticed that only the denominator in the probabilities mattered, as the numerator was always 1. To have a probability of less than 1%, the fractional probability must be "1 over something greater than 100." In order for $3^n > 100$, n must be at least 5.

The correct answer is **5**.

Conserving Time

Because hybrids contain multiple steps with twists and turns, you must complete each step quickly to finish the problem in under two minutes. Don't underestimate how much time it takes to mull over how the different parts fit together and to transition from one line of thinking to another; you may sometimes choose to guess immediately if the problem looks like it will take too much time.

If you try the problem but realize that it's taking far too long, be ready to bail out partway. For instance, you might be able to eliminate some choices using the work you've already completed. Let's look one last time at a problem discussed earlier in this chapter:

Try-It #8-1

> A student cuts 80 rectangles from construction paper, all of which are at least 10 inches in length and in width, and 20 percent of the rectangles that are greater than 10 inches long are exactly 10 inches wide. If 40 of the rectangles have a length of exactly 10 inches and 50 of the rectangles are greater than 10 inches wide, how many rectangles have a perimeter of greater than 40 inches? (Note: Assume that width and length are interchangeable; in other words, width does not have to be shorter than length.)

> (A)   18
> (B)   22
> (C)   32
> (D)   58
> (E)   66

If you were able to figure out that any rectangles with one dimension greater than 10 inches would have to have a perimeter greater than 40, you would be able to eliminate three answer choices! The problem states that 40 rectangles have a length of exactly 10 inches, so the other 40 rectangles must have a length greater than 10 inches. At least 40 rectangles, then, have a perimeter greater than 40 inches, so answers (A), (B), and (C) cannot be correct.

Also think back to Chapters 2 and 4, on Strategies and Guessing Tactics. Be ready to try those tactics out on hybrids that take excessively long. Don't be too proud! A single crazy hybrid problem can't hurt your performance if you get it wrong quickly and move on confidently. On the other hand, if you waste a lot of time and energy on the problem and become angry or upset, then even if you get it right, you'll have won a battle to lose the war.

MANHATTAN
PREP

Problem Set

Solve the following problems and identify the topics being tested.

1. The average of a list of six numbers is equal to 0. What is the positive difference between the number of positive numbers in the list and the number of negative numbers in the list?

    (1) Each of the positive numbers in the list equals 10.
    (2) Each of the negative numbers in the list equals −5.

2. Simplify: $\dfrac{2^2 + 2^3 + 2^4 + 2^5}{\left(\sqrt{5} + \sqrt{3}\right)\left(\sqrt{5} - \sqrt{3}\right)}$.

3. If a, b, and c are positive, is $a > b$?

    (1) $\dfrac{a}{b+c} > \dfrac{b}{a+c}$

    (2) $b + c < a$

4. If c is randomly chosen from the integers 20 to 99, inclusive, what is the probability that $c^3 - c$ is divisible by 12?

5. If x and y are positive integers greater than 1 such that $x - y$ and $\dfrac{x}{y}$ are both even integers, which of the following numbers must be non-prime integers?

    I. x

    II. $x + y$

    III. $\dfrac{y}{x}$

    (A) I only   (B) II only   (C) III only   (D) I and II only   (E) I, II and III

6   A number cube with faces numbered 1 through 6 has an equal chance of landing on any face when rolled. If the number cube is rolled twice, what is the probability that the sum of the two rolls is a prime number?

7. The function {x} is defined as the area of a square with diagonal of length x. If x > 0 and $\{x^2\} = x^2$, what is the value of x?

    (A) 1
    (B) $\sqrt{2}$
    (C) $\sqrt{3}$
    (D) 2
    (E) 4

8

8.   A circular microchip with a radius of 2.5 centimeters is manufactured following a blueprint scaled such that a measurement of 1 centimeter on the blueprint corresponds to a measurement of 0.05 millimeters on the microchip. What is the area of the blueprint, in square centimeters? (1 centimeter = 10 millimeters)

9.   Eight consecutive integers are selected from the integers 1 to 50, inclusive. What is the sum of the remainders when each of the integers is divided by x?

     (1) The remainder when the largest of the consecutive integers is divided by x is 0.
     (2) The remainder when the second largest of the consecutive integers is divided by x is 1.

10. If x, y, and z are all distinct positive integers and the percent increase from x to y is equal to the percent increase from y to z, what is x?

     (1) y is prime
     (2) $z = 9$

8

MANHATTAN
PREP

Solutions

1. **(E):** Since the average of the 6 numbers in the list is 0, the sum of the 6 numbers is 0. There could be positive numbers and negative numbers in the set. Zero is not mentioned, but this does not rule it out. In order for the sum of the numbers in the set to be 0, either all the terms are 0, or there are some positives and some negatives.

(1) INSUFFICIENT: Statement (1) indicates that the list contains at least one positive number, and that each positive term is 10. The list could be {−2, −2, −2, −2, −2, 10}, and the positive difference between the number of positive terms and the number of negative terms would be 4. Alternatively, the list could be {−20, 20, 10, 10, 10, 10}, and the positive difference would be 2.

(2) INSUFFICIENT: Statement (2) indicates that the list contains at least one negative number, and that each negative term is −5. The set could be {−5, 1, 1, 1, 1, 1}, and the positive difference between the number of positive terms and the number of negative terms would be 4. The set could be {−5, −5, −5, 5, 5, 5}, and the positive difference would be 0.

(1) AND (2) INSUFFICIENT: The statements together suggest that the set has twice as many −5 terms as 10 terms, in order to maintain a sum of 0. If every term is negative or positive, then the set would have to be {−5, −5, −5, −5, 10, 10} and the positive difference would be 2. However, zero terms are possible, so the set could be {−5, −5, 0, 0, 0, 10} and the positive difference would be 1.

2. **30:** You could simplify the numerator arithmetically (multiply out the terms and then add). Alternatively, factor a 2^2 out of the numerator. Then, distribute the denominator (which becomes the difference of squares).

$$\frac{2^2\left(1+2+2^2+2^3\right)}{\left[\left(\sqrt{5}\right)^2-\left(\sqrt{3}\right)^2\right]}=\frac{2^2\left(1+2+4+8\right)}{5-3}$$

$$=\frac{4(15)}{2}$$

$$=30$$

3. **(D):** Statement (2) appears to be a bit easier to work with so begin there.

(2) SUFFICIENT. If a, b, and c are all positive, then $a > b +$ positive. Therefore, a must be *even larger* than b. You could also prove this fact by testing cases.

Case	Statement (2): $b + c < a$	Is this case possible according to (2)?
$a > b$	$b +$ positive $<$ number greater than b	Possible
$a = b$	$b + c < b$	Impossible, since c is positive
$a < b$	$b + c <$ number less than b	Impossible, since c is positive

Only the $a > b$ case is possible, so the answer is a definite Yes.

(1) SUFFICIENT. Statement (1) can be cross-multiplied without flipping the inequality sign, since the denominators are positive.

$$a(a + c) > b(b + c)$$
$$a^2 + ac > b^2 + bc$$
$$a^2 + ac - b^2 - bc > 0$$
$$a^2 - b^2 + ac - bc > 0 \qquad \text{(Group similar terms to simplify)}$$
$$[a^2 - b^2] + [ac - bc] > 0 \qquad \text{(Note the Quadratic Template)}$$
$$(a - b)(a + b) + c(a - b) > 0$$
$$(a - b)[(a + b) + c] > 0 \qquad \text{(Factor out } a - b\text{)}$$

$a + b + c$ is positive, because all three additive terms are positive. So, $(a - b)(\text{positive}) > 0$. By Number Properties sign rules, $(a - b)$ must also be positive in order for the product to be greater than 0. Therefore, $a > b$.

This algebra is very tough; it is hard to see where to begin or what series of manipulations will be productive. If you did not see this, you could try testing cases to see which are allowed by Statement (1). Note: LT = less than and GT = greater than. GTb means "a number greater than b."

Case	(1) $\dfrac{a}{(b+c)} > \dfrac{b}{(a+c)}$	Is this case possible according to (1)?
$a > b$	$\dfrac{\text{GT}b}{(b+c)} > \dfrac{b}{\text{GT}(b+c)}$	Possible. The left is greater than the right.
$a = b$	$\dfrac{b}{(b+c)} > \dfrac{b}{(b+c)}$	Impossible; the two expressions are equal.
$a < b$	$\dfrac{\text{LT}b}{(b+c)} > \dfrac{b}{\text{LT}(b+c)}$	Impossible; the left side is actually less than the right side, not greater than as (1) requires.

The correct answer is **(D)**.

4. **3/4:** The words "divisible" and "probability" are used, so this question is about *Divisibility & Primes* and *Probability*.

Probability is $\dfrac{(\text{favorable outcomes})}{(\text{total \# of possibilities})}$. There are $99 - 20 + 1 = 80$ possible values for c, so the unknown is how many of these c values yield a $c^3 - c$ that is divisible by 12.

The prime factorization of 12 is $2 \times 2 \times 3$. There are at least two ways to think about this: numbers are divisible by 12 if they are divisible by 3 and by 2 twice, or if they are multiples of both 4 and 3.

The expression involving c can be factored.

$$c^3 - c = c(c^2 - 1) = c(c - 1)(c + 1)$$

These are consecutive integers. It may help to put them in increasing order: $(c - 1)c(c + 1)$. Thus, this question has a lot to do with Consecutive Integers, and not only because the integers 20 to 99 themselves are consecutive.

In any set of three consecutive integers, a multiple of 3 will be included. Thus, $(c - 1)c(c + 1)$ is always divisible by 3 for any integer c. This takes care of part of the 12. So the question becomes "How many of the possible $(c - 1)c(c + 1)$ values are divisible by 4?" Since the prime factors of 4 are 2's, it makes sense to think in terms of Odds & Evens.

$(c - 1)c(c + 1)$ could be (E)(O)(E), which is definitely divisible by 4, because the two evens would each provide at least one separate factor of 2. Thus, $c^3 - c$ is divisible by 12 whenever c is odd, which are the cases $c = 21, 23, 25, ..., 95, 97, 99$. That's $\left(\dfrac{99 - 21}{2}\right) + 1 = \left(\dfrac{78}{2}\right) + 1 = 40$ possibilities.

Alternatively, $(c - 1)c(c + 1)$ could be (O)(E)(O), which will only be divisible by 4 when the even term itself is a multiple of 4. Thus, $c^3 - c$ is also divisible by 12 whenever c is a multiple of 4, which are the cases $c = 20, 24, 28, ..., 92, 96$. That's $\left(\dfrac{96 - 20}{4}\right) + 1 = \left(\dfrac{76}{4}\right) + 1 = 20$ possibilities.

The probability is thus $\left(\dfrac{40 + 20}{80}\right) = \dfrac{60}{80} = \dfrac{3}{4}$.

5. **(D) I and II only:** x cannot equal y, as that would make $\dfrac{x}{y} = 1 \neq$ even. So either $x > y$ or $y > x$.

x and y are both positive, and $\dfrac{x}{y}$ is an integer, so $x > y$.

Since $x - y$ is even, either x and y are both even, or they are both odd.

Since $\dfrac{x}{y} =$ an even integer, $x = y \times$ (even integer).

Therefore, x is an even integer, as is y.

  I.   TRUE. x and y are both positive even integers, and $x > y$. No even number greater than 2 is prime, so x can't be prime.

  II. TRUE. x and y are each positive even integers and $x > y$. Thus, $x + y$ is even, and the smallest possible value of $x + y = 4 + 2 = 6$. All even numbers greater than or equal to 6 are non-prime.

  III. FALSE. It could be that $x = 4$ and $y = 2$, so $\dfrac{y}{x} = \dfrac{1}{2}$, which is not prime, but is also not an integer.

       In fact, if $\dfrac{x}{y} =$ an even integer, $\dfrac{y}{x} = \dfrac{1}{\text{an even integer}} =$ positive fraction.

The correct answer is **(D)**.

6. **5/12:** First think about the prime numbers less than 12, the maximum sum of the numbers. These primes are 2, 3, 5, 7, 11.

The probability of rolling 2, 3, 5, 7, or 11 = the number of ways to roll any of these sums, divided by the total number of possible outcomes. The total number of possible outcomes is $6 \times 6 = 36$.

Sum of 2 can happen 1 way: $1 + 1$

Sum of 3 can happen 2 ways: $1 + 2, 2 + 1$

Sum of 5 can happen 4 ways: $1 + 4, 2 + 3, 3 + 2, 4 + 1$

Sum of 7 can happen 6 ways: $1 + 6, 2 + 5, 3 + 4, 4 + 3, 5 + 2, 6 + 1$

Sum of 11 can happen 2 ways: $5 + 6, 6 + 5$

That's a total of $1 + 2 + 4 + 6 + 2 = 15$ ways to roll a prime sum.

Thus, the probability is $\dfrac{15}{36} = \dfrac{5}{12}$.

7. $\sqrt{2}$: The problem defines the function in words; you'll need to translate into math.

"The function $\{x\}$ is defined as the area of a square with diagonal of length x."

$\{x\} = s^2$, where s is the side of the square

If the diagonal $= x$, then the side of square $= \dfrac{x}{\sqrt{2}}$

Therefore

$$\{x\} = \left(\dfrac{x}{\sqrt{2}}\right)^2$$

$$\{x\} = \dfrac{x^2}{2}$$

The question stem also indicates that $\{x^2\} = x^2$. In other words, applying the defined function to x^2 will result in an answer of x^2. First, find $\{x^2\}$:

$$\left\{x^2\right\} = \dfrac{\left(x^2\right)^2}{2} = \dfrac{x^4}{2}$$

Now, set that equal to x^2 and solve:

$$\dfrac{x^4}{2} = x^2$$
$$x^4 = 2x^2$$
$$x^2 = 2$$

(Note: It is acceptable to divide by x^2 because the question stem indicates that $x \neq 0$.) Therefore, $x = -\sqrt{2}$, or $\sqrt{2}$. Since the question stem indicates that $x > 0$, only $x = \sqrt{2}$ is a valid solution.

Alternatively, you could work backwards from the answers. Start with (B) or (D).

(B) If $x = \sqrt{2}$, then $x^2 = 2$. Next, the question specifies that that $\{x^2\} = x^2$. $\left\{\left(\sqrt{2}\right)^2\right\}$ becomes $\{2\}$, so what does this function return?

"The function $\{x\}$ is defined as the area of a square with diagonal of length x."

The function $\{2\}$ is defined as the area of a square with diagonal length 2. The side length of this square is $\dfrac{2}{\sqrt{2}}$, so the area of this square is $\left(\dfrac{2}{\sqrt{2}}\right)^2 = \dfrac{4}{2} = 2$. Therefore $\{2\} = 2$, which matches the question stem specification that $\{x^2\} = x^2$.

The correct answer is **(B)**.

8. **$250{,}000\pi$:** Microchip radius = (2.5 cm)(10 mm/cm) = 25 mm

Blueprint radius = 1 cm per every 0.05 mm on the microchip
$$= 10 \text{ mm per every } 0.05 \text{ mm on the microchip}$$
$$= \left(\frac{10 \text{ mm}}{0.05 \text{ mm on microchip}}\right)\left(25 \text{ mm on microchip}\right)$$
$$= \left(\frac{10 \text{ mm}}{0.05}\right)(25)$$
$$= \left(\frac{1{,}000 \text{ mm}}{5}\right)(25)$$
$$= (1{,}000 \text{ mm})(5)$$
$$= 5{,}000 \text{ mm}$$
$$= \left(5{,}000 \text{ mm}\right)\left(\frac{1 \text{ cm}}{10 \text{ mm}}\right)$$
$$= 500 \text{ cm}$$

Blueprint area $= \pi \times r^2$
$$= \pi \times (500 \text{ cm})^2$$
$$= 250{,}000\pi \text{ cm}^2$$

8

9. **(C):** Recall that remainders follow a repeating pattern when x is divided into consecutive integers. For example, when the integers 1 to 50 are divided by $x = 4$, the remainders form a $[1, 2, 3, 0]$ repeating pattern, and the sum of any consecutive eight of these remainders would be $2 \times [1 + 2 + 3 + 0] =$ 12. However, when the integers 1 to 50 are divided by $x = 3$, the remainders are a $[1, 2, 0]$ repeating pattern, so the sum of any consecutive eight of these remainders would depend on which term of the pattern was the starting term.

(1) INSUFFICIENT: Statement (1) indicates that the largest of the eight consecutive integers is divisible by x. It does not indicate the value of x, which determines the remainder pattern and, indirectly, the sum of the remainders.

(2) INSUFFICIENT: Statement (2) indicates that the *third* largest of the eight consecutive integers is divisible by x. It does not indicate the value of x, which determines the remainder pattern and, indirectly, the sum of the remainders.

(1) & (2) SUFFICIENT: Together, the statements indicate a remainder pattern of $[1,0]$ repeating. Thus, x must be 2, and the sum of the remainders is $4 \times [1 + 0] = 4$.

10. **(A):** The question asks for the value of x. Translate the equation given in the question stem:

$$\frac{y - x}{x} = \frac{z - y}{y}$$
$$y^2 - xy = zx - xy$$
$$y^2 = zx$$
$$x = \frac{y^2}{z}$$

The problem stem specifies that x is an integer, so the right-hand side of the equation must also be an integer. Therefore, z must be a factor of y^2.

The question asks for the value of x.

(1) SUFFICIENT: If y is prime, then there are two possible scenarios:

Case 1: $y = z$. This isn't allowed, though, because the question stem indicates that the variables represent three different positive integers.

Case 2: $y^2 = z$, in which case x must equal 1. This is the only possible case, so statement (1) is sufficient.

(2) INSUFFICIENT: If $z = 9$, then y^2 is a multiple of 9, so z must be a multiple of 3. It's possible that $z = 9$, $y = 3$, and $x = 1$. It's also possible that $z = 9$, $y = 36$, and $x = 4$.

The correct answer is **(A)**.

8

MANHATTAN
PREP

Chapter 9 *of*

GMAT Advanced Quant

Part 3

Workout Sets

In This Chapter...

Workout Set 1–15

Workout Set 1

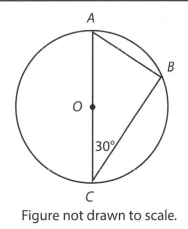

Figure not drawn to scale.

1. The circle with center *O* has a circumference of $6\pi\sqrt{3}$. If *AC* is a diameter of the circle, what is the length of line segment *BC*?

    (A) $\dfrac{3}{\sqrt{2}}$

    (B) 3

    (C) $3\sqrt{3}$

    (D) 9

    (E) $9\sqrt{3}$

2. A batch of widgets costs $p + 15$ dollars for a company to produce and each batch sells for $p(9 - p)$ dollars. For which of the following values of *p* does the company make a profit?

    (A) 3
    (B) 4
    (C) 5
    (D) 6
    (E) 7

9

3.   If K is the sum of the reciprocals of the consecutive integers from 41 to 60 inclusive, which of the following is less than K?

I. $\dfrac{1}{4}$

II. $\dfrac{1}{3}$

III. $\dfrac{1}{2}$

(A) None
(B) I only
(C) II only
(D) I and II only
(E) I, II, and III

4.   Triplets Adam, Bruce, and Charlie enter a triathlon. There are nine competitors in the triathlon. If every competitor has an equal chance of winning, and three medals will be awarded, what is the probability that at least two of the triplets will win a medal?

(A) $\dfrac{3}{14}$

(B) $\dfrac{19}{84}$

(C) $\dfrac{11}{42}$

(D) $\dfrac{15}{28}$

(E) $\dfrac{3}{4}$

5.   The expression $\sqrt{2+\sqrt{2+\sqrt{2+\sqrt{2+\sqrt{2+\cdots}}}}}$ extends to an infinite number of roots. Which of the following choices most closely approximates the value of this expression?

(A) $\sqrt{3}$
(B) 2
(C) $1+\sqrt{2}$
(D) $1+\sqrt{3}$
(E) $2\sqrt{3}$

9

MANHATTAN
PREP

6.   Half an hour after Car A started traveling from Newtown to Oldtown, a distance of
      62 miles, Car B started traveling along the same road from Oldtown to Newtown.
      The cars met each other on the road 15 minutes after Car B started its trip. If Car A
      traveled at a constant rate that was 8 miles per hour greater than Car B's constant
      rate, how many miles had Car B driven when they met?

      (A)   14
      (B)   12
      (C)   10
      (D)   9
      (E)   8

7.   If $x = 2^b - (8^8 + 8^6)$, for which of the following b values is x closest to zero?

      (A)   20
      (B)   24
      (C)   25
      (D)   30
      (E)   42

8.   If $k > 1$, which of the following must be equal to $\dfrac{2}{\sqrt{k+1}+\sqrt{k-1}}$?

      (A) 2

      (B) $2\sqrt{2k}$

      (C) $2\sqrt{k+1}+\sqrt{k-1}$

      (D) $\dfrac{\sqrt{k+1}}{\sqrt{k-1}}$

      (E) $\sqrt{k+1}-\sqrt{k-1}$

9.   If y is 20% less than 90% of x and z is 25% more than 130% of y, then z is what percent of x?

      (A)   72%
      (B)   92.5%
      (C)   108.5%
      (D)   117%
      (E)   135%

10.   *Let a be the sum of x consecutive positive integers. Let b be the sum of y consecutive*
      positive integers. For which of the following values of x and y is it NOT possible that $a = b$?

      (A) $x = 2; y = 6$
      (B) $x = 3; y = 6$
      (C) $x = 6; y = 4$
      (D) $x = 6; y = 7$
      (E) $x = 7; y = 5$

9

Workout Set 1 Answer Key

1. (D)
2. (B)
3. (D)
4. (B)
5. (B)
6. (A)
7. (B)
8. (E)
9. (D)
10. (C)

9

MANHATTAN
PREP

Workout Set 1 Solutions

1. **(D) 9:** If AC is a diameter of the circle, then triangle ABC is a right triangle, with angle $ABC = 90$ degrees. The shortest side of a triangle is across from its smallest angle, and the longest side of a triangle is across from its largest angle. Therefore, $AC > BC > AB$.

The circumference of the circle $= \pi d = 6\pi\sqrt{3}$, so $d = 6\sqrt{3} \approx 6(1.7) = 10.2$. Thus, $AC \approx 10.2$ and $BC < 10.2$. Answer (E) is too large and answer (D), while less than 10.2, is questionable, because side BC is opposite a 60° angle. The value should be smaller than 9.

Since angle ACB is 30°, angle CAB is 60°.

The sides in a 30–60–90 triangle have the ratio $x : x\sqrt{3} : 2x$, so use the ratio to compute the desired side, BC.

$$2x = 6\sqrt{3}$$
$$x = \frac{6\sqrt{3}}{2}$$
$$x = 3\sqrt{3}$$

Find the length of BC:

$$BC = x\sqrt{3} = (3\sqrt{3})(\sqrt{3})$$
$$BC = 9$$

Line segment BC has length 9.

The correct answer is **(D)**.

2. **(B) 4:** You can *Work Backwards* from the answers. Start with (B) or (D).

> (D) $p = 6$
> Cost: $6 + 15 = 21$
> Revenue: $6(9 - 6) = 18$
> Profit: $18 - 21 = -3$ loss, not profit!

Eliminate (D) and try (B) next.

> (B) $p = 4$
> Cost: $4 + 15 = 19$
> Revenue: $4(9 - 4) = 20$
> Profit: $20 - 19 = 1$

The company makes a profit when $p = 4$.

Alternatively, profit equals revenue minus cost. The company's profit is:

$$p(9 - p) - (p + 15) = 9p - p^2 - p - 15$$
$$= -p^2 + 8p - 15$$
$$= -(p^2 - 8p + 15)$$
$$= -(p - 5)(p - 3)$$

Profit will be zero if $p = 5$ or $p = 3$, which eliminates answers (A) and (C). For $p > 5$, both $(p - 5)$ and $(p - 3)$ are positive. In that case, the profit is negative (i.e., the company loses money). The profit is only positive if $(p - 5)$ and $(p - 3)$ have opposite signs, which occurs when $3 < p < 5$.

The correct answer is **(B)**.

3. **(D) I and II only:** The sum $(1/41 + 1/42 + 1/43 + 1/44 + \ldots + 1/57 + 1/58 + 1/59 + 1/60)$ has 20 fractional terms. It is impossible to compute this by hand in two minutes. Instead, look at the maximum and minimum possible values for the sum.

Maximum: The largest fraction in the sum is $1/41$. K is definitely smaller than $20 \times 1/41$, or $20/41$, which is smaller than $20/40 = 1/2$.

Minimum: The smallest fraction in the sum is $1/60$. K is definitely larger than $20 \times 1/60 = 1/3$.

Therefore, $1/3 < K < 1/2$.

  I.   YES: $1/4 < 1/3 < K$
 II.   YES: $1/3 < K$
III.   NO: $1/2 > K$

The correct answer is **(D)**.

4. **(B) 19/84:** With nine competitors and only three medals awarded, only 1/3 of the competitors will win overall. Although a simplification, it is reasonable for each competitor to see his or her chance of winning a medal as 1/3, or to expect to win 1/3 of a medal (pretending for a moment that medals can be "shared").

The question asks for the probability that *at least* two of the triplets will win a medal. In other words, you want 2/3 to 3/3 of the triplets to win medals, or for each triplet to win 2/3 to 3/3 of a medal. Since 2/3 and 3/3 are both greater than 1/3, you are looking for the probability that the triplets will win medals at a rate greater than that expected for competitors overall. In other words, this would be an unusual outcome. Thus, the probability should be less than 1/2. Eliminate (D) and (E). You could then guess from among the remaining answers with a 1 in 3 chance of guessing correctly.

To solve, use the probability formula and combinatorics:

$$\text{Probability} = \frac{\text{specified outcome}}{\text{all possible outcomes}} = \frac{\text{\# of ways at least 2 triplets win medal}}{\text{\# of ways 3 medals can be awarded}}$$

MANHATTAN
PREP

First, find the total number of outcomes for the triathlon. There are nine competitors; three will win medals and six will not. Set up an anagram grid where Y represents a medal, N no medal:

competitor:	C_1	C_2	C_3	C_4	C_5	C_6	C_7	C_8	C_9
medal:	Y	Y	Y	N	N	N	N	N	N

\# of ways three medals can be awarded $= \dfrac{9!}{3!6!} = \dfrac{(9)(8)(7)}{(3)(2)(1)} = (3)(4)(7) = 84$

Now, determine the number of instances when *at least two* brothers win a medal. Practically speaking, this could happen when (1) exactly three brothers win or (2) exactly two brothers win.

Start with *all three* triplets winning medals, where Y represents a medal:

triplet:	A	B	C	non-triplet:	C_1	C_2	C_3	C_4	C_5	C_6
medal:	Y	Y	Y	medal:	N	N	N	N	N	N

The number of ways this could happen is $\dfrac{3!}{3!} \times \dfrac{6!}{6!} = 1$. This makes sense, as there is only one instance in which all three triplets would win medals and all of the other competitors would not. (If you recognize this immediately, no need to write out the math.)

Next, calculate the instances when *exactly two* of the triplets win medals:

triplet:	A	B	C	non-triplet:	C_1	C_2	C_3	C_4	C_5	C_6
medal:	Y	Y	N	medal:	Y	N	N	N	N	N

Since both triplets and non-triplets win medals in this scenario, consider the possibilities for both sides of the grid. For the triplets, the number of ways that two could win medals is $\dfrac{3!}{2!1!} = 3$.

For the non-triplet competitors, the number of ways that one could win the remaining medal is $\dfrac{6!}{1!5!} = 6$.

Multiply these two numbers to get the total number of instances: $3 \times 6 = 18$.

The brothers win *at least two* medals in $18 + 1 = 19$ cases. The total number of cases is 84, so the probability is 19/84.

The correct answer is **(B)**.

9

5. **(B) 2:** Since the answer asks for an approximation, convert the answers to approximate decimal amounts to see how precisely you have to estimate.

(A) $\sqrt{3} \approx 1.7$

(B) 2

(C) $1 + \sqrt{2} \approx 1 + 1.4 = 2.4$

(D) $1 + \sqrt{3} \approx 1 + 1.7 = 2.7$

(E) $2\sqrt{3} \approx 2(1.7) = 3.4$

Note that there is a minimum difference of 0.3 between answer choices. If you can approximate to the nearest tenth, that should be sufficient.

$$\sqrt{2} \approx 1.4$$

$$\sqrt{2 + \sqrt{2}} \approx \sqrt{2 + 1.4} \approx \sqrt{3.4} \approx 1.8$$

$$\sqrt{2 + \sqrt{2 + \sqrt{2}}} \approx \sqrt{2 + 1.8} \approx \sqrt{3.8} \approx 1.9$$

$$\sqrt{2 + \sqrt{2 + \sqrt{2 + \sqrt{2}}}} \approx \sqrt{2 + 1.9} \approx \sqrt{3.9} \approx 2$$

$$\sqrt{2 + \sqrt{2 + \sqrt{2 + \sqrt{2 + \sqrt{2}}}}} \approx \sqrt{2 + 2} \approx \sqrt{4} = 2$$

The expression converges on 2.

Alternatively, an algebraic solution is possible if you recognize that the infinite expression is nested within itself:

$$x = \sqrt{2 + \left(\sqrt{2 + \sqrt{2 + \sqrt{2 + \sqrt{2 + \ldots}}}} \right)} = \sqrt{2 + x}$$

Solve for x as follows:

$$x = \sqrt{2 + x}$$
$$x^2 = 2 + x$$
$$x^2 - x - 2 = 0$$
$$(x - 2)(x + 1) = 0$$

This implies that $x = 2$ or $x = -1$. Since x is the square root of a real, positive number, it must be positive, so $x = 2$.

The correct answer is **(B)**.

6. **(A) 14:** Draw a diagram to illustrate the moment at which Car A and Car B pass each other moving in opposite directions:

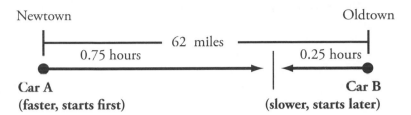

Try *Working Backwards* from the answers, starting with (B) or (D):

	B's distance (miles)	B's rate (mph) = D/T = D/0.25	A's rate (mph) = B's rate + 8	A's distance (miles) = R × T = R × 0.75	Total distance = 62?
(B)	12	48	56	42	54

The total distance is not 62, so answer (B) is incorrect. Furthermore, a distance of 54 is too short, so the answer must be (A). If you aren't sure, confirm by checking answer (A):

	B's distance (miles)	B's rate (mph) = D/T = D/0.25	A's rate (mph) = B's rate + 8	A's distance (miles) = R × T = R × 0.75	Total distance = 62?
(A)	**14**	**56**	**64**	**48**	**62**

Alternatively, you could solve algebraically, using an RTD chart. Note that you must convert 15 minutes to 1/4 (or 0.25) hours:

	Rate	Time	Distance
Car A	$(r + 8)$ mph	0.75 hours	$(0.75)(r + 8)$ miles
Car B	r mph	0.25 hours	$0.25r$ miles
Total			62 miles

Set up and solve an equation for the total distance:

$$(0.75)(r + 8) + (0.25r) = 62$$
$$0.75r + 6 + 0.25r = 62$$
$$r = 56$$

Therefore, in 15 minutes, Car B traveled a distance of $0.25r = (0.25)(56) = 14$ miles.

The correct answer is **(A)**.

7. **(B) 24:** Testing the choices would be a natural way to solve this problem, since the question doesn't ask you to solve for b in general, but rather "for which of the following is x closest to zero?" However, numbers between 2^{20} and 2^{42} are too large to plug and compute. Instead, manipulate the terms with base 8 to see how they might balance with 2^b:

$x = 2^b - (8^8 + 8^6)$
$0 \approx 2^b - (8^8 + 8^6)$
$2^b \approx (8^8 + 8^6)$
$2^b \approx (8^6)(8^2 + 1)$ Since 1 is very small in comparison to the other numbers, assume that $(8^2 + 1) \approx 8^2$.
$2^b \approx (8^6)(8^2)$
$2^b \approx 8^8$
$2^b \approx \left((2^3)^8\right)$
$2^b \approx 2^{24}$
$b \approx 24$

The correct answer is **(B)**.

8. **(E)** $\sqrt{(k+1)} - \sqrt{(k-1)}$: Since there are variables in the answer choices, *Choose a Smart Number* to solve. If $k = 2$, then $\dfrac{2}{\sqrt{k+1}+\sqrt{k-1}} = \dfrac{2}{\sqrt{3}+\sqrt{1}} \approx \dfrac{2}{1.7+1} = \dfrac{2}{2.7}$, which is less than 1. Now test the answer choices and try to match the target; stop if you can tell that an answer won't equal the target.

(A)   2   TOO HIGH

(B) $2\sqrt{2k} = 2\sqrt{4}$ TOO HIGH

(C) $2\sqrt{k+1}+\sqrt{k-1} = 2\sqrt{3}+\sqrt{1} \approx 2(1.7)+1$ TOO HIGH

(D) $\dfrac{\sqrt{k+1}}{\sqrt{k-1}} = \dfrac{\sqrt{3}}{\sqrt{1}} \approx 1.7$ TOO HIGH

(E) $\sqrt{k+1}-\sqrt{k-1} = \sqrt{3}-\sqrt{1} \approx 1.7-1 = 0.7$ OK

9

Alternatively, solve the problem algebraically. The expression given is of the form $\dfrac{2}{a+b}$, where $a = \sqrt{k+1}$ and $b = \sqrt{k-1}$.

You need to either simplify or cancel the denominator, as none of the answer choices have the starting denominator, and most of the choices have no denominator at all. First, try to eliminate the radical signs entirely, leaving only a^2 and b^2 in the denominator. To do so, multiply by a fraction that is a convenient form of 1:

$$\frac{2}{(a+b)} = \frac{2}{(a+b)} \times \frac{(a-b)}{(a-b)} = \frac{2(a-b)}{a^2 - b^2}$$

Notice the "difference of two squares" special product created in the denominator.

Substituting for a and b,

$$\frac{2}{\left(\sqrt{k+1}+\sqrt{k-1}\right)} \times \frac{\left(\sqrt{k+1}-\sqrt{k-1}\right)}{\left(\sqrt{k+1}-\sqrt{k-1}\right)} = \frac{2\left(\sqrt{k+1}-\sqrt{k-1}\right)}{(k+1)-(k-1)} = \frac{2\left(\sqrt{k+1}-\sqrt{k-1}\right)}{2} = \sqrt{k+1}-\sqrt{k-1}$$

The correct answer is **(E)**.

9. **(D) 117%:** An algebraic set-up would be fairly ugly on this problem, but a combination of two other techniques work quite nicely: *Choose Smart Numbers* and *Estimate*.

There are no real values for the variables, so *Choosing Smart Numbers* is a valid approach. Furthermore, the answer choices are far enough apart that you can *estimate* if the smart numbers get a little messy.

Of the three variables, it is easiest to pick for x. If you were to pick for y or z, you would have to do "reverse" calculations to find the other variables.

$x = 100$
90% of $x = 90$
y = 20% less than $90 = 90 - 18 = 72$

This number is a little ugly, so round down to 70. Therefore, $y = 70$.

130% of $y = 70 + 21 = 91$

The next step requires you to take 25% of that number, so 91 is going to get messy. Estimate again, but this time round up a little bit (to offset the error you introduced when you rounded down earlier). Round to the nearest number that is divisible by 4: 92.

z = 25% more than $92 = 92 + 23 = 115$

If $x = 100$ and $z \approx 115$, then the final calculation is $\dfrac{115}{100} \approx 115\%$ which is closest to 117%.

The correct answer is **(D)**.

10. **(C) $x = 6$; $y = 4$:** Consecutive integers have two defining characteristics tested most often by the GMAT: they differ by a known, constant value (i.e., 1), and they alternate odd, even, odd, even, etc. Use the odd/even property to evaluate these choices. This general approach is usually faster than considering specific values. It works particularly well for very general questions about whether something cannot or must be true.

(A)	$a = E + O = O$, or $a = O + E = O$	$b = 3$ pairs $(E + O) = O$, or $b = 3$ pairs $(O + E) = O$	a could equal b (both Odd)
(B)	$a = E + O + E = O$, or $a = O + E + O - E$	$b = 3$ pairs $(E + O) = O$, or $b = 3$ pairs $(O + E) = O$	a could equal b (both Odd)

(C)	$a = 3$ pairs $(E + O) = O$, or $a = 3$ pairs $(O + E) = O$	$b = 2$ pairs $(E + O) = E$, or $b = 2$ pairs $(O + E) = E$	$a \neq b$ (Odd $\neq$ Even)
(D)	$a = 3$ pairs $(E + O) = O$, or $a = 3$ pairs $(O + E) = O$	$b = O + 3$ pairs $(E + O) = E$, or $b = E + 3$ pairs $(O + E) = O$	a could equal b (both Odd)
(E)	$a = O + 3$ pairs $(E + O) = E$, or $a = E + 3$ pairs $(O + E) = O$	$b = O + 2$ pairs $(E + O) = O$, or $b = E + 2$ pairs $(O + E) = E$	a could equal b (both Odd or both Even)

Note: The solution shows the logic for all five answers but, on the test, stop when you find the right answer.

The correct answer is **(C)**.

9

MANHATTAN
PREP

Workout Set 2

11. If $a \neq b$, is $\dfrac{1}{a-b} > ab$?

    (1) $|a| > |b|$
    (2) $a < b$

12. $m = 4n + 9$, where n is a positive integer. What is the greatest common factor of m and n?

    (1) $m = 9s$, where s is a positive integer.
    (2) $n = 4t$, where t is a positive integer.

13. A museum sold 30 tickets on Saturday. Some of the tickets sold were $10 general exhibit tickets and the rest were $70 special exhibit tickets. How many general exhibit tickets did the museum sell on Saturday?

    (1) The museum's total revenue from ticket sales on Saturday was greater than $1,570 and less than $1,670.
    (2) The museum sold more than 20, but fewer than 25, special exhibit tickets on Saturday.

14. If x and y are integers, is $x^y = y^x$?

    (1) $x - y = 2$
    (2) $xy = 8$

15. If $ab^3c^4 > 0$, is $a^3bc^5 > 0$?

    (1) $b > 0$
    (2) $c > 0$

16. What is the perimeter of isosceles triangle ABC?

    (1) The length of side AB is 9.
    (2) The length of side BC is 4.

17. If x, y, and z are integers and $2^x\, 5^y\, z = 6.4 \times 10^6$, what is the value of xy?

    (1) $z = 20$
    (2) $x = 9$

18. If x and y are positive integers and $1 + x + y + xy = 21$, what is the value of x?

    (1) $y > 3$
    (2) $y = 6$

9

19. A school has a students and b teachers. If $a < 150$, $b < 25$, and classes have a maximum of 15 students, can the a students be distributed among the b teachers so that each class has the same number of students? (Assume that any student can be taught by any teacher.)

    (1) It is possible to divide the students evenly into groups of 2, 3, 5, 6, 9, 10, or 15.
    (2) The greatest common factor of a and b is 10.

20. If x and y are positive integers such that $x^2 + y^3$ is a prime number less than 18, what is the value of y?

    (1) $x^2 + y^2$ is a prime number.
    (2) $x^2 - y^2$ is a prime number.

Workout Set 2 Answer Key

11. (E)
12. (A)
13. (A)
14. (C)
15. (B)
16. (C)
17. (A)
18. (D)
19. (E)
20. (E)

Workout Set 2 Solutions

11. **(E):** You can cross-multiply the inequality, as long as you consider both cases:

> If $a - b$ is negative, the question becomes "Is $1 < ab(a - b)$?" (FLIPPED inequality sign)
> If $a - b$ is positive, the question becomes "Is $1 > ab(a - b)$?" (ORIGINAL inequality sign)

This is a conditional rephrased question—importantly, one with completely opposite questions as possibilities. *Any statement that doesn't at least answer the question of whether a – b is positive or negative is unlikely to be sufficient.* You would also have to carry each statement through both questions, so this path is not very efficient. It's better to use the original inequality to *Test Cases* in order to eliminate the wrong answers.

(1) INSUFFICIENT: *Test Cases* to determine whether this statement is sufficient:

	a	b	$\lvert a \rvert > \lvert b \rvert$	Is $\dfrac{1}{a - b} > ab$?
Case 1	2	1	✓	$\dfrac{1}{1} > 2$? NO
Case 2	2	−1	✓	$\dfrac{1}{3} > -2$? YES

(2) INSUFFICIENT: *Test Cases* again:

	a	b	$a < b$	Is $\dfrac{1}{a - b} > ab$?
Case 1	−2	1	✓	$\dfrac{1}{-3} > -2$? YES
Case 2	−2	−1	✓	$\dfrac{1}{-1} > 2$? NO

(1) AND (2) INSUFFICIENT: Whenever possible, re-use cases you've already tested (you can only do this when the case makes both statements true). The pairs tested for statement (2) are also valid for statement (1):

Case 1	−2	1	✓	$\frac{1}{-3} > -2$? YES
Case 2	−2	−1	✓	$\frac{1}{-1} > 2$? NO

Once again, two valid sets of numbers return two different answers, so even together, the statements are insufficient. The correct answer is **(E)**.

12. **(A):** The greatest common factor (GCF) of any two numbers is given by the product of the shared or overlapping primes in the two numbers. Any such question can be rephrased accordingly: "What exactly are the overlapping factors of m and n?"

(1) SUFFICIENT: This statement indicates that m must be a multiple of 9. If m is a multiple of 9 and $m = 4n + 9$, then this equation is really saying:

multiple of 9 = $4n + 9$

In order for this to be true, $4n$ must also be a multiple of 9. The number 4 does not contain any factors of 9, so n itself must be a multiple of 9.

If both m and n are multiples of 9, and m is exactly 9 units away from $4n$, then the largest possible common factor is 9, so this statement is sufficient.

(If you're not sure about the logic of that last part, test out a couple of real numbers. Remember that n must be a multiple of 9. If $n = 9$, then $m = 4(9) + 9 = 45$. The GCF of the numbers 9 and 45 is 9. If $n = 18$, then $m = 4(18) + 9 = 81$. The GCF of the numbers 18 and 81 is still 9.)

Alternatively, set up a Scenario Chart to track the allowed values of s, m, and n:

FACTS:				QUESTION:
s = pos int	$m = 9s$	$n = \dfrac{m-9}{4}$	n = pos int	GCF of m and n?
1	9	$\dfrac{0}{4}$	zero ✗	
2	18	$\dfrac{9}{4}$	fraction ✗	

3	27	$\dfrac{18}{4}$	fraction ✗	
4	36	$\dfrac{27}{4}$	fraction ✗	
5	**45**	$\dfrac{36}{4} = 9$	✓	**9**
6	54	$\dfrac{45}{4}$	fraction ✗	
7	63	$\dfrac{54}{4}$	fraction ✗	
8	72	$\dfrac{63}{4}$	fraction ✗	
9	**81**	$\dfrac{72}{4} = 18$	✓	**9**
10	90	$\dfrac{81}{4}$	fraction ✗	

In this case, n is only a positive integer when $(s - 1)$ is a multiple of 4. Also, m and n are both multiples of 9. Here's the proof:

$$n = \frac{m-9}{4} = \frac{9s-9}{4} = 9\frac{(s-1)}{4} = 9(\text{int})$$

Try the next number in the pattern, $9 + 4 = 13$, to be confident that the apparent GCF pattern will continue:

FACTS:				QUESTION:
s = pos int	$m = 9s$	$n = \dfrac{m-9}{4}$	n = pos int	GCF of m and n?
5	$(9)(5) = 45$	$\dfrac{36}{4} = 9 = (9)(1)$	✓	9
9	$(9)(9) = 81$	$\dfrac{72}{4} = 18 = (9)(2)$	✓	9
13	$(9)(13) = 117$	$\dfrac{108}{4} = 27 = (9)(3)$	✓	9

The variables m and n always share an overlapping factor of 9, but there is never any overlap between their remaining factors. The GCF is always 9.

(2) INSUFFICIENT: $n = 4t$, where t is a positive integer. In this case, n must be a multiple of 4. This does not allow you to deduce anything consistent about m, as statement (1) did.

FACTS:			QUESTION:
t = pos int	$n = 4t$	$m = 4n + 9$	GCF of m and n?
1	4	$16 + 9 = 25$	1
2	8	$32 + 9 = 41$	1
3	12	$48 + 9 = 57$	3

There is more than one possible GCF, so the statement is not sufficient.

The correct answer is **(A)**.

13. **(A):**

(1) SUFFICIENT: Use the integer constraint to test possible cases. Let g equal the number of general exhibit tickets sold. Because the special tickets are so much more expensive, begin by choosing numbers for which (70)(# of special tickets) is approximately $1,600.

If $g = 7$, total revenue = $10(7) + 70(23) = 70 + 1,610 = 1,680$. TOO HIGH
If $g = 8$, total revenue = $10(8) + 70(22) = 80 + 1,540 = 1,620$. OK
If $g = 9$, total revenue = $10(9) + 70(21) = 90 + 1,470 = 1,560$. TOO LOW

Only $g = 8$ gives a total revenue in the given range.

Don't Assume that having a *range* of values automatically means a statement is insufficient to answer a Value question. At times, a constraint (such as an integer constraint) may limit the number of cases to just one possibility.

Alternatively, you can use algebra, though that path is a bit long on this problem. Let g equal the number of general exhibit tickets sold. Then, $(30 - g)$ represents the number of special exhibit tickets sold. Set up and solve the following inequality:

$$1,570 < 10g + 70(30 - g) < 1,670$$
$$1,570 < 10g + 2,100 - 70g < 1,670$$
$$1,570 < -60g + 2,100 < 1,670$$
$$-530 < -60g < -430$$
$$\frac{-530}{-60} > \frac{-60g}{-60} > \frac{-430}{-60} \quad \text{(flip the direction of the inequality when dividing by a negative)}$$
$$8.8 > g > 7.2$$

The only integer between 7.2 and 8.8 is 8, so g must be 8. The museum sold 8 general exhibit tickets.

9

(2) INSUFFICIENT: This statement indicates that the museum sold 21, 22, 23, or 24 special exhibit tickets. Since the museum sold a total of 30 tickets, this means that it sold 9, 8, 7, or 6 general exhibit tickets.

The correct answer is **(A)**.

14. **(C):**

(1) INSUFFICIENT: *Test Cases* on this theory problem. If you can generate both Yes and No cases, you will prove insufficiency.

	x	y	x^y	y^x	Does $x^y = y^x$?
Case 1	2	0	$2^0 = 1$	$0^2 = 0$	N
Case 2	3	1	$3^1 = 3$	$1^3 = 1$	N
Case 3	4	2	$4^2 = 16$	$2^4 = 16$	Y

(2) INSUFFICIENT: Continue to test cases.

	x	y	x^y	y^x	Does $x^y = y^x$?
Case 1	8	1	$8^1 = 8$	$1^8 = 1$	N
Case 2	4	2	$4^2 = 16$	$2^4 = 16$	Y

(1) and (2) SUFFICIENT: Test whether any cases work for both statements. The case $x = 4$ and $y = 2$ was already used for both statements and returned a Yes answer. Can any of the No cases work for both statements?

They don't. Now you have a choice. If you are good with numbers, you can try to find another pair of integers that will work with both equations. Since x and y have to be integers, there are only a limited number of possibilities. The two numbers need to multiply to 4 and have a difference of 2. In addition to 4 and 2, the pair −4 and −2 fit the bill, as long as $x = -2$ and $y = -4$.

Alternatively, solve algebraically to determine the possible values for x and y.

$$xy = 8$$
$$(2 + y)y = 8$$
$$2y + y^2 = 8$$
$$y^2 + 2y - 8 = 0$$
$$(y + 4)(y - 2) = 0$$

$$y = -4 \text{ or } y = 2$$

Therefore, $x = -2$ or $x = 4$.

You have already tested the case where $x = 4$ (and $y = 2$), so test the other case.

x	y	x^y	y^x	Does $x^y = y^x$?
-2	-4	$(-2)^{-4} = 1/16$	$(-4)-2 = 1/16$	Y

In either case, $x^y = y^x$. The correct answer is **(C)**.

15. **(B):** Odd exponents do not "hide the sign" of the base. If $ab^3c^4 > 0$, then, a and b must have the same sign so that their product is positive. In that case, a^3b must also be positive. As a result, in order for the inequality a^3bc^5 to be positive, c^5 must be positive. The rephrased question is "Is $c > 0$?"

(1) INSUFFICIENT: No information about the sign of c.

(2) SUFFICIENT: Answers the rephrased question directly.

The correct answer is **(B)**.

16. **(C):** The perimeter of a triangle is equal to the sum of the three sides.

(1) INSUFFICIENT: Knowing the length of one side of the triangle is not enough to find the sum of all three sides.

(2) INSUFFICIENT: Knowing the length of one side of the triangle is not enough to find the sum of all three sides.

(1) AND (2) SUFFICIENT: Triangle ABC is an isosceles triangle which means that two of the sides are equal in length. The statements provide two of the side lengths, so the third side, AC, must equal one of the given sides.

There is a *hidden constraint* in this problem: the triangle must be valid. Recall that the sum of the lengths of any two sides of a triangle must be greater than the length of the third side.

AB	BC	AC	Perimeter	Valid Triangle?
9	4	4	$9 + 4 + 4 = 17$	NO: $4 + 4 < 9$
9	4	9	$9 + 4 + 9 = 22$	YES: $4 + 9 > 9$

A "triangle" with three sides of 4, 4, and 9 is not really a triangle, as it cannot be drawn with those dimensions.

Therefore the actual sides of the triangle must be $AB = 9$, $BC = 4$, and $AC = 9$. The perimeter is 22.

The correct answer is **(C)**.

17. **(A):** Express both sides of the equation in terms of prime numbers.

$$2^x 5^y z = 6.4 \times 10^6$$
$$= (64)(10^5)$$
$$= (2^6)(2^5 5^5)$$
$$= 2^{11} 5^5$$

The right side of the equation is composed of only 2's and 5's. The left side of the equation has x number of 2's and y number of 5's along with some factor z. This unknown factor z must be composed of only 2's and/or 5's, or it must be 1 (i.e., with no prime factors).

If $z = 1$, then $x = 11$ and $y = 5$.
If $z = 2^? 5^?$, where the exponents are not 0, then x and y will depend on the value of those exponents.

The rephrased question is thus, "How many factors of 2 and 5 are in z?"

(1) SUFFICIENT: If $z = 20 = 2^2 5^1$, then this answers the rephrased question. Incidentally, this implies that $2^x 5^y (2^2 5^1) = 2^{11} 5^5$, so $x = 9$ and $y = 4$, making $xy = 36$ (though you do not have to solve for x and y).

(2) INSUFFICIENT: $x = 9$, but the statement doesn't indicate anything about the value of y.

The correct answer is **(A)**.

18. **(D):** Factor $1 + x + y + xy = 21$ to determine that $(1 + x)(1 + y) = 21$. The product of the integers $(1 + x)$ and $(1 + y)$ is 21, which has the factors 1, 3, 7, and 21. The factor pair 1 and 21 is disqualified because neither $(1 + x)$ nor $(1 + y)$ could equal 1, as that would make x or y equal to zero (and they must be positive integers). Therefore, $(1 + x)$ could equal 3 or 7, and conversely, $(1 + y)$ could equal 7 or 3 such that their product is 21.

Knowing that x will equal either 2 or 6, rephrase the question: "Is the value of x equal to 2 or 6?"

(1) SUFFICIENT: If $y > 3$, then it must be true that $y = 6$ and $x = 2$.

(2) SUFFICIENT: If $y = 6$, then $x = 2$.

The correct answer is **(D)**.

19. **(E):** In order for the a students to be distributed evenly among the b teachers, a must be divisible by b. This is a factor question in disguise: "Is a divisible by b?"

(1) INSUFFICIENT: The given numbers represent factors of a. If the a students can be divided evenly into a group of 2, then 2 is a factor of a. Likewise, 3 and 5 must be factors of a.

If 2 and 3 are already factors of a, then 6 must also be a factor (since $2 \times 3 = 6$); you can ignore it. Likewise, you've already counted one factor of 3, so you need only one more factor of 3 to make 9. You already have the necessary factors to make both 10 and 15, so ignore those numbers as well. The final list of factors is: 2, 3, 5, and 3.

As a result, a must equal $(2)(3)(5)(3) = 90$ or a multiple of 90. Since the question stem indicated that $a < 150$, a must actually be 90. This statement provides no information about the teachers, however, so it is insufficient.

(2) INSUFFICIENT: If the greatest common factor (GCF) of a and b is 10, then a and b must both be multiples of 10. Since the question stem indicated that $b < 25$, b must be 10 or 20. The value of a is any multiple of 10 up to 140, inclusive. This is not enough to determine whether a is divisible by b. For example, if $a = 50$ and $b = 10$, then a is divisible by b. If $a = 50$ and $b = 20$, then a is not divisible by b.

(1) AND (2) INSUFFICIENT: From statement (1), $a = 90$. From statement (2), $b = 10$ or 20. If $b = 10$, then the 90 students can be divided up evenly, into classes of 9 students each. If $b = 20$, then the 90 students cannot be divided up evenly.

The correct answer is **(E)**.

20. **(E):** There are a limited number of primes that are less than 18: 2, 3, 5, 7, 11, 13, 17.

The sum $x^2 + y^3 \leq 17$, and the positive integers x and y each have a minimum value of 1, so $x^2 \leq 16$ and $y^3 \leq 16$. This implies that x can be 1, 2, 3, or 4 and y can be 1 or 2 (as $3^3 = 27 > 16$). Already this limits the possible (x, y) value pairs to $4 \times 2 = 8$ scenarios. Set up a chart to see whether the constraint that $x^2 + y^3$ is a prime number eliminates any of these scenarios.

x	y	$x^2 + y^3$	$x^2 + y^3$ is prime
1	1	$1 + 1 = 2$	✓
2	1	$4 + 1 = 5$	✓
3	1	$9 + 1 = 10$	✗
4	1	$16 + 1 = 17$	✓
1	2	$1 + 8 = 9$	✗
2	2	$4 + 8 = 12$	✗
3	2	$9 + 8 = 17$	✓
4	2	$16 + 8 = 24$	✗ (also, 24 >18 ✗)

This leaves only four basic scenarios that will need to be checked against the statement constraints. Here is a cleaned-up list, with invalid scenarios removed:

x	y	$x^2 + y^3$	$x^2 + y^3$ is prime
1	1	$1 + 1 = 2$	✓
2	1	$4 + 1 = 5$	✓
3	2	$9 + 8 = 17$	✓
4	1	$16 + 1 = 17$	✓

As you work through the statements, keep in mind that, in three scenarios, $y = 1$, and in just one scenario $y = 2$.

(1) INSUFFICIENT: Within a chart, determine which of the four basic scenarios also meet the constraint that $x^2 + y^2$ is a prime number; then answer the question for those that do. Given that $y = 2$ is an "odd man out" scenario, try it first.

x	y	$x^2 + y^2$	$x^2 + y^2$ is prime	$y = ?$
3	2	$9 + 4 = 13$	✓	2
1	1	$1 + 1 = 2$	✓	1

y could equal either 1 or 2.

(2) INSUFFICIENT: Now use the chart to determine which of the four basic scenarios also meet the constraint that $x^2 - y^2$ is a prime number; then answer the question for those that do.

x	y	$x^2 - y^2$	$x^2 - y^2$ is prime	$y = ?$
3	2	$9 - 4 = 5$	✓	2
1	1	$1 - 1 = 0$	✗	(discard case)
2	1	$4 - 1 = 3$	✓	1

y could equal either 1 or 2.

(1) AND (2) INSUFFICIENT: Both statements allow the scenario (3, 2), where $y = 2$. Try the scenario (2, 1) with statement (1) to see whether it works.

x	y	$x^2 + y^2$	$x^2 + y^2$ is prime	$y = ?$
2	1	$4 + 1 = 5$	✓	1

The pair (2, 1) also satisfies both statements. As a result, y can be both 1 and 2.

The correct answer is **(E)**.

Workout Set 3

21. Sequence S is defined as $S_n = (S_{n-1}+1) + \dfrac{1}{(S_{n-1}+1)}$ for all $n > 1$. If $S_1 = 100$, then which of the following must be true of Q, the sum of the first 16 terms of S?

    (A) $1{,}600 \leq Q < 1{,}650$
    (B) $1{,}650 \leq Q \leq 1{,}700$
    (C) $1{,}700 \leq Q \leq 1{,}750$
    (D) $1{,}750 \leq Q \leq 1{,}800$
    (E) $1{,}800 \leq Q \leq 1{,}850$

22. If x and y are positive integers, what is the remainder when x^y is divided by 10?

    (1) $x = 26$
    (2) $y^x = 1$

23. For all positive integers n, the sequence A_n is defined by the following relationship:

    $$A_n = \frac{n-1}{n!}$$

    What is the sum of all the terms in the sequence from A_1 through A_{10}, inclusive?

    (A) $\dfrac{9!+1}{10!}$

    (B) $\dfrac{9(9!)}{10}$

    (C) $\dfrac{10!-1}{10!}$

    (D) $\dfrac{10!}{10!+1}$

    (E) $\dfrac{10(10!)}{11!}$

24. If x and y are positive integers and $n = 5^x + 7^{y+3}$, what is the units digit of n?

    (1) $y = 2x - 16$
    (2) y is divisible by 4.

25. If $y + 1$ is the square of an integer, which of the following could NOT be y?

    (A) 3,024
    (B) 3,135
    (C) 3,246
    (D) 3,363
    (E) 3,480

26.   A certain sequence is defined by the following rule: $S_n = k(S_{n-1})$, where k is a constant. If $S_1 = 64$ and $S_{25} = 192$, what is the value of S_9?

   (A) $\sqrt{2}$

   (B) $\sqrt{3}$

   (C) $64\sqrt{3}$

   (D) $64\sqrt[3]{3}$

   (E) $64\sqrt[24]{3}$

27. n is a positive integer greater than 2. If $y = 9^0 + 9^1 + 9^2 + \ldots + 9^n$, what is the remainder when y is divided by 5?

   (1) n is divisible by 3.
   (2) n is odd.

28.   In the sequence S, each term after the first is twice the previous term. If the first term of sequence S is 3, what is the sum of the 14th, 15th, and 16th terms in sequence S?

   (A) $3(2^{16})$
   (B) $9(2^{15})$
   (C) $21(2^{14})$
   (D) $9(2^{14})$
   (E) $21(2^{13})$

29. n is an integer such that $n \geq 0$. For $n > 0$, the sequence t_n is defined as $t_n = t_{n-1} + n$. If $t_0 = 3$, is t_n even?

   (1) $n + 1$ is divisible by 3
   (2) $n - 1$ is divisible by 4

30.   What is the sum of the cubes of the first 10 positive integers?

9

   (A) 10^3
   (B) 45^2
   (C) 55^2
   (D) 100^2
   (E) 100^3

Workout Set 3 Answer Key

21. (C)
22. (A)
23. (C)
24. (B)
25. (C)
26. (D)
27. (B)
28. (E)
29. (B)
30. (C)

9

Workout Set 3 Solutions

21. **(C) $1,700 \le Q \le 1,750$:** To find each successive term in S, add 1 to the previous term; then add the reciprocal of that sum.

$S_1 = 100$

$$S_2 = (S_1 + 1) + \frac{1}{S_1 + 1}$$

$$= (100 + 1) + \frac{1}{100 + 1}$$

$$= 101 + \frac{1}{101}$$

$$S_3 = (S_2 + 1) + \frac{1}{S_2 + 1}$$

$$= \left(101 + \frac{1}{101} + 1\right) + \frac{1}{\left(101 + \frac{1}{101} + 1\right)}$$

$$= 102 + \frac{1}{102 + \frac{1}{101}}$$

Since each term is growing more complicated, stop computing exact numbers. Look at the answer choices. You are asked for a broad *range* within which the sum of the first 15 terms of S must fall; the fractional portion of each term is so small in relationship to these large numbers that you can safely ignore the fractional pieces.

$S_1 = 100$
$S_2 \approx 101$
$S_3 \approx 102$
$S_4 \approx 103$
$S_n \approx 100 + (n - 1)$

The sum of the first 16 terms of S will be approximately equal to the sum of the 16 consecutive integers 100, 101, ..., 115.

Form matching pairs and sum:

$100 + 115 = 215$
$101 + 114 = 215$
$102 + 113 = 215$
... etc.

There are 16 terms and therefore 8 pairs in the sum:

$215 \times 8 = 1,720$

The correct answer is **(C)**.

22. **(A):**

(1) SUFFICIENT: The tendency is to deem statement (1) insufficient because no information is given about the value of y. But 26 has a units digit of 6, and remember that $6^{\text{any positive integer}}$ has a units digit of 6 (the pattern is a single-term repeat).

$6^1 = \mathbf{6}$
$6^2 = 3\mathbf{6}$
$6^3 = 21\mathbf{6}$
etc.

Thus, 26 raised to ANY positive integer power will also have a units digit of 6 and therefore a remainder of 6 when divided by 10.

(2) INSUFFICIENT: Given that $y^x = 1$, there are a few possible scenarios:

x	y	Fact (2): $y^x = 1$
0	anything nonzero	$(\text{anything nonzero})^0 = 1$ ✓
anything	1	$1^{\text{anything}} = 1$ ✓
even	-1	$-1^{\text{even}} = 1$ ✓

However, the question stem indicates that x and y are POSITIVE integers, so eliminate the first and third scenarios.

The remaining scenario indicates that $y = 1$ and $x =$ any positive integer. Without more information about x, you cannot determine the remainder when x^y is divided by 10.

Since statement (1) indicates the value of x and statement (2) indicates the value of y ($y = 1$), the temptation might be to combine the information to arrive at an answer of (C). This is a common trap on difficult Data Sufficiency problems; in this case, you don't need both statements because statement (1) is sufficient by itself.

The correct answer is **(A)**.

23. **(C)** $\frac{10!-1}{10!}$: Set up a table to list the first few terms of the sequence and also the cumulative sum:

n	$A_n = \dfrac{n-1}{n!}$	Cumulative sum
1	$A_1 = \dfrac{1-1}{1!} = 0$	0
2	$A_2 = \dfrac{2-1}{2!} = \dfrac{1}{2}$	$\dfrac{1}{2}$
3	$A_3 = \dfrac{3-1}{3!} = \dfrac{2}{6} = \dfrac{1}{3}$	$\dfrac{5}{6}$
4	$A_4 = \dfrac{4-1}{4!} = \dfrac{3}{24} = \dfrac{1}{8}$	$\dfrac{23}{24}$

As you build the table, compare the input column values (n) with the output column values (cumulative sum), looking for a pattern. The denominator of the cumulative sum is $n!$ and the numerator is one less than $n!$.

$$\text{Sum of terms through } A_n = \frac{n!-1}{n!}$$

Substitute to find the sum through A_{10}:

$$\text{Sum of terms through } A_{10} = \frac{10!-1}{10!}$$

The correct answer is **(C)**.

24. **(B):** The units digit of n is determined solely by the units digit of the expressions 5^x and 7^{y+3}, because when two numbers are added together, the units digit of the sum is determined solely by the units digits of the added numbers.

Since x is a positive integer, and $5^{\text{any positive integer}}$ always has a units digit of 5, 5^x always ends in a 5. However, the units digit of 7^{y+3} is not certain, as the units digit pattern for the powers of 7 is a four-term repeat: [7, 9, 3, 1].

The question can be rephrased as "what is the units digit of 7^{y+3}?"

Note: Determining y would be one way of answering the question above, but don't rephrase to "what is y?" Because the units digits of the powers of 7 have a repeating pattern, you might get a single answer for the units digit of 7^{y+3} *despite* having multiple values for y.

(1) INSUFFICIENT: This statement indicates neither the value of y nor the units digit of 7^{y+3}, as y depends on the value of x, which could be any positive integer. For example, if $x = 9$, then $y = 2$ and 7^{y+3} has a units digit of 7. By contrast, if $x = 10$, then $y = 4$ and 7^{y+3} has a units digit of 3. (Note: The statement does indicate that y is an even number, so the exponent $y + 3$ must be odd. As a result, there are only

MANHATTAN
PREP

two possible values for the units digit of the desired term: 7 or 3. That could be useful to know if you later need to combine the two statements.)

(2) SUFFICIENT: Regardless of what multiple of 4 you pick, 7^{y+3} will have the same units digit:

y	$y + 3$	Units digit of 7^{y+3}
4	7	3
8	11	3
12	15	3

Ultimately this means that n has a units digit of $5 + 3 = 8$.

The correct answer is **(B)**.

25. (C) 3,246: The numbers in the answers are large; solving arithmetically would be pretty annoying without a calculator. Look for a shortcut.

Note that each answer choice has a different units digit. Perfect squares have a limited number of possibilities for their units digit. If you square 0, for example, you get a units digit of 0. Check the other digits:

$1^2 = 1$ $4^2 =$ units digit 6 $7^2 =$ units digit 9

$2^2 = 4$ $5^2 =$ units digit 5 $8^2 =$ units digit 4

$3^2 = 9$ $6^2 =$ units digit 6 $9^2 =$ units digit 1

The only possible units digits for perfect squares are 0, 1, 4, 5, 6, and 9.

The answer choices represent y; check the units digits of the perfect square $y + 1$.

(A) 3,024, so $y + 1 = 3,035$. Units digit okay.
(B) 3,135, so $y + 1 = 3,136$. Units digit okay.
(C) 3,246, so $y + 1 = 3,247$. Units digit NOT okay! This is the correct answer.
(D) 3,363, so $y + 1 = 3,364$. Units digit okay.
(E) 3,480, so $y + 1 = 3,481$. Units digit okay.

Only answer choice (C) results in a units digit that cannot reflect a perfect square. (You can stop checking the answers when you do find the correct answer.)

26. (D) $64\sqrt[3]{3}$: To form each new term of the sequence, multiply the previous term by k. If $S_1 = 64$, then $S_2 = 64k$, and $S_3 = 64k^2$, and $S_n = 64k^{n-1}$. Thus $S_{25} = 64k^{24}$. Since the problem indicates that $S_{25} = 192$, set up an equation to solve for k. Note that you need to find $S_9 = 64k^8$, so solve directly for k^8.

$64k^{24} = 192$

$k^{24} = 3$

$k^8 = 3^{\frac{1}{3}}$

Plug this value for k^8 into the expression for S_9

$$S_9 = 64\left(3^{\frac{1}{3}}\right) = 64\sqrt[3]{3}$$

The correct answer is **(D)**.

27. **(B):** Remember the units digit pattern for 9^x, where x is an integer. The units digit of 9^x is 9 if x is odd, but the units digit is 1 if x is even: a repeating pattern of [9, 1].

Now, consider the sums of the powers of 9 up to 9^n:

n	$y = 9^0 + 9^1 + 9^2 + \ldots + 9^n$	Units digit of y
1	$1 + 9 = \mathbf{10}$	0
2	$1 + 9 + 81 = 9\mathbf{1}$	1
3	$[1 + 9 + 81] + 729 =$ [units digit of 1] + units digit of 9	0
4	units digit of 0 + units digit of 1	1
odd	units digit: pairs of $(1 + 9)$	0
even	units digit: pairs of $(1 + 9)] + 1$	1

The alternating 1's and 9's in the units digits pair to a sum of 10, or a units digit of 0. Thus, the units digit of the sum displays another two-term repeating pattern. The units digit of y is 0 if n is odd, but 1 if n is even.

The remainder when y is divided by 5 depends only on the units digit and will be either 0 or 1 as well. The rephrased question is "Is n odd or even?"

(1) INSUFFICIENT: If n is a multiple of 3, it may be either odd or even.

(2) SUFFICIENT: If n is odd, the units digit of y is 0, and the remainder is 0 when y is divided by 5.

The correct answer is **(B)**.

28. **(E) $21(2^{13})$:** The sequence S is 3, 6, 12, 24, 48, and so on. You could write out the first 16 terms and add the 14th, 15th, and 16th together, but such an approach would be prone to error and time consuming. Additionally, you don't need to calculate the sum explicitly: the answer choices all have some power of 2 as a factor, providing a hint at the best solution method.

MANHATTAN
PREP

Write the sequence in terms of the powers of 2:

S: 3, 6, 12, 24, 48, and so on.
S: $3(2^0)$, $3(2^1)$, $3(2^2)$, $3(2^3)$, $3(2^4)$, and so on.

So S_n, the nth term of S, equals $3(2^{n-1})$.

Thus, the sum of the 14th, 15th, and 16th terms equals $3(2^{13}) + 3(2^{14}) + 3(2^{15})$.

All of the terms share the common factors 3 and 2^{13}, so factor those terms out:

$3(2^{13})(1 + 2^1 + 2^2)$
$3(2^{13})(1 + 2 + 4)$
$3(2^{13})(7)$
$21(2^{13})$

The correct answer is **(E)**.

29. **(B)**: Sequence problems are often best approached by charting out the first several terms of the given sequence. In this case, keep track of n, t_n, and whether t_n is even or odd.

n	t_n	Is t_n even or odd?
0	3	Odd
1	3 + 1 = 4	Even
2	4 + 2 = 6	Even
3	6 + 3 = 9	Odd
4	9 + 4 = 13	Odd
5	13 + 5 = 18	Even
6	18 + 6 = 24	Even
7	24 + 7 = 31	Odd
8	31 + 8 = 39	Odd

Notice that beginning with $n = 1$, a four-term repeating cycle of [even, even, odd, odd] emerges for t_n. Thus, a statement will be sufficient only if it indicates how n relates to a multiple of 4 (i.e., $n = $ a multiple of 4 ± known constant).

(1) INSUFFICIENT. This statement does not indicate how n relates to a multiple of 4. If $n + 1$ is a multiple of 3, then $n + 1$ could be 3, 6, 9, 12, 15, etc. This means that n could be 2, 5, 8, 11, 14, etc. From the chart, if $n = 2$ or $n = 5$, then t_n is even. However, if $n = 8$ or $n = 11$, then t_n is odd.

(2) SUFFICIENT: This statement indicates exactly how n relates to a multiple of 4. If $n - 1$ is a multiple of 4, then $n - 1$ could be 4, 8, 12, 16, 20, etc. and n could be 5, 9, 13, 17, 21, etc. From the chart (and the continuation of the four-term pattern), t_n must be even.

The correct answer is **(B)**.

30. **(C) 55²**: Set up a table to list the first few cubes and track the cumulative sum:

n	Cube	Cumulative sum
1	1	1
2	8	9
3	27	36
4	64	100

Interesting. The cumulative sums are all perfect squares. Extend the table to the right to list the square roots.

n	Cube	Cumulative sum	$\sqrt{\text{Cumulative Sum}}$
1	1	1	$1 = 1$
2	8	9	$3 = 1 + 2$
3	27	36	$6 = 1 + 2 + 3$
4	64	100	$10 = 1 + 2 + 3 + 4$
5	125	225	$15 = 1 + 2 + 3 + 4 + 5$
...			
n	n^3	(Sum of integers 1 through n, inclusive)²	Sum of integers 1 through n, inclusive.

A pattern emerges not only for the cumulative sum (always a perfect square), but also for the square root of the cumulative sum, which is always the sum of consecutive integers.

Therefore, the sum of the first 10 cubes will be the square of the sum of the first 10 positive integers:

$$1^3 + 2^3 + 3^3 + 4^3 + \ldots + 10^3 = (1 + 2 + 3 + 4 + \ldots + 10)^2$$

The sum of the first 10 positive integers can be computed by matching pairs:

$$
\begin{aligned}
1 + 2 + \ldots + 9 + 10 &= 11 + 11 + 11 + 11 + 11 \\
&= 5(11) \\
&= 55
\end{aligned}
$$

So, the sum of the first 10 cubes is 55^2.

The correct answer is **(C)**.

Workout Set 4

31. If $x^x y^y = \dfrac{24^3}{2}$, and x and y are integers such that $x < y$, what is the value of $y - x$?

   (A) -1
   (B) 1
   (C) 3
   (D) 5
   (E) 7

32. $S_n = n^2 + 5n + 94$ and $K = S_6 - S_5 + S_4 - S_3 + S_2 - S_1$. What is the value of K?

   (A) 67
   (B) 50
   (C) 45
   (D) 41
   (E) 36

33. Is $xy + xy < xy$?

   (1) $\dfrac{x^2}{y} < 0$

   (2) $x^3 y^3 < (xy)^2$

34. If $y \neq x$, then $\dfrac{x^3 + (x^2 + x)(1 - y) - y}{x - y}$

   (A) $(x - 1)^2 y$
   (B) $(x + 1)^2$
   (C) $x^2 + x + 1$
   (D) $(x^2 + x + 1)y$
   (E) $(x^2 + x + 1)(x - y)$

35. In the sequence g_n defined for all positive integer values of n, $g_1 = g_2 = 1$ and, for $n \geq 3$, $g_n = g_{n-1} + 2^{n-3}$. If the function $\psi(g_i)$ equals the sum of the terms $g_1, g_2, \ldots, g_i$, what is $\dfrac{\Psi(g_{16})}{\Psi(g_{15})}$?

   (A) g_3
   (B) g_8
   (C) $\psi(g_9)$
   (D) $\psi(g_{16}) - \psi(g_{15})$
   (E) $\dfrac{g_{16}}{2}$

9

36. If $3^k + 3^k = (3^9)^{3^9} - 3^k$, then what is the value of k?

   (A) $\dfrac{11}{3}$

   (B) $\dfrac{11}{2}$

   (C) 242

   (D) 3^{10}

   (E) $3^{11} - 1$

37. If x and y are positive integers, what is the value of xy?

   (1) $x! = 6y!$

   (2) $\dfrac{\dfrac{x!}{y}}{(x-2)!} = \dfrac{30}{y}$

38. If k is an integer and $\dfrac{33!}{22!}$ is divisible by 6^k, what is the maximum possible value of k?

   (A) 3
   (B) 4
   (C) 5
   (D) 6
   (E) 7

39. The sequence S is defined as $S_n = (n+1)!$ for all integers $n \geq 1$. Which of the following is equivalent to the difference between S_{100} and S_{99}?

   (A) 101!
   (B) 100!
   (C) $99^2(98!)$
   (D) $100^2(99!)$
   (E) $(100!)^2$

40. If $p = \dfrac{9^7 - 9^5}{7^5 + 7^3}$ and $q = \dfrac{9^5}{7^3}$, what is the value of $\dfrac{q}{p}$?

   (A) $\dfrac{2}{5}$

   (B) $\dfrac{1}{2}$

   (C) $\dfrac{5}{8}$

   (D) $\dfrac{8}{5}$

   (E) $\dfrac{5}{2}$

Workout Set 4 Answer Key

31. (B)
32. (E)
33. (E)
34. (C)
35. (A)
36. (E)
37. (C)
38. (D)
39. (D)
40. (C)

Workout Set 4 Solutions

31. **(B) 1:** Simplify the right side of the equation.

$$\frac{(24)(24)(24)}{2}$$

$(24)(24)(12)$
$(3)(8)(3)(8)(3)(4)$
$(3^3)(2^8)$

This still needs to be manipulated in order to match the left side of the equation, since the bases need to match their exponents. The number 3^3 is okay, but 2^8 is not. Try turning it into a base of 4 instead:

$$2^8 = 2^{2^4} = 4^4$$

That's it: $x = 3$ and $y = 4$, since the problem states that $y > x$. So $y - x = 4 - 3 = 1$.

The correct answer is **(B)**.

32. **(E) 36:** The expression for K becomes more manageable if you insert parentheses:

$$K = (S_6 - S_5) + (S_4 - S_3) + (S_2 - S_1)$$

K involves two expressions of the form $(S_{n+1} - S_n)$, so a general rule for $(S_{n+1} - S_n)$ might be helpful. The problem indicates that $S_n = n^2 + 5n + 94$, so

$S_{n+1} = (n + 1)^2 + 5(n + 1) + 94$
$S_{n+1} = (n^2 + 2n + 1) + (5n + 5) + 94$
$S_{n+1} = n^2 + 7n + 100$

In general, $(S_{n+1} - S_n) = (n^2 + 7n + 100) - (n^2 + 5n + 94) = 2n + 6$.

Apply this rule to the grouped terms in K:

$K = (S_6 - S_5) + (S_4 - S_3) + (S_2 - S_1)$
$\quad = (2 \times 5 + 6) + (2 \times 3 + 6) + (2 \times 1 + 6)$
$\quad = 16 + 12 + 8$
$\quad = 36$

MANHATTAN
PREP

Alternatively, plug into the S_n term definition, and identify common terms:

$$K = S_6 - S_5 + S_4 - S_3 + S_2 - S_1$$
$$= (6^2 + 5(6) + 94) - (5^2 + 5(5) + 94) + (4^2 + 5(4) + 94) - (3^2 + 5(3) + 94) + (2^2 + 5(2) + 94) - (1^2 + 5(1) + 94)$$
$$= (6^2 - 5^2 + 4^2 - 3^2 + 2^2 - 1^2) + 5(6 - 5 + 4 - 3 + 2 - 1)$$
$$= (36 - 25 + 16 - 9 + 4 - 1) + 5(3)$$
$$= (21) + (15)$$
$$= 36$$

The correct answer is **(E)**.

33. **(E):** First, rephrase the question stem by subtracting xy from both sides: "Is $xy < 0$?" The question is whether xy is negative, or "Do x and y have opposite signs?"

Be careful! Do not rephrase as follows:

Is $xy + xy < xy$?
Is $2xy < xy$?

Is $\dfrac{2xy}{xy} < \dfrac{xy}{xy}$? (Wrong! Dividing by variables is the mistake: What if $xy = 0$? What if $xy < 0$?)

Is $2 < 1$?   (Incorrect as a result of the mistake in the previous step.)

Not only does this rephrase make the statements moot (2 is definitely not less than 1, no matter what the statements say), but it also ignores some special cases. If $xy = 0$, then dividing by xy yields an undefined value. If $xy < 0$, you should have flipped the sign of the inequality.

Instead, use the correct rephrasing: "Do x and y have opposite signs?"

(1) INSUFFICIENT: If $\dfrac{x^2}{y} < 0$, then x^2 and y must have opposite signs. Since x^2 must be positive, y must be negative. However, x could be either positive or negative.

(2) INSUFFICIENT: If $x^3y^3 < (xy)^2$, then you can divide both sides by $(xy)^2$ (since that quantity is positive). The simplified inequality is $xy < 1$, which is not sufficient to answer the question.

(1) AND (2) INSUFFICIENT: Each statement indicates that xy could be either positive or negative. The statements are equally insufficient, and neither provides any additional information to the other.

The correct answer is **(E)**.

34. **(C)** $x^2 + x + 1$: First, distribute the numerator:

$$\frac{x^3 + (x^2 + x)(1-y) - y}{x - y} = \frac{x^3 + x^2 + x - x^2 y - xy - y}{x - y}$$

None of the answer choices are fractions, so the $x - y$ in the denominator must be cancelled by a $x - y$ in the numerator. Group the numerator terms with x and $-y$ in mind:

$$\frac{(x^3 + x^2 + x) - (x^2 y + xy + y)}{x - y} = \frac{x(x^2 + x + 1) - y(x^2 + x + 1)}{x - y}$$

$$= \frac{(x^2 + x + 1)(x - y)}{x - y}$$

$$= x^2 + x + 1$$

Alternatively, you could *Choose Smart Numbers*. If $x = 2$ and $y = 3$, then:

$$\frac{x^3 + (x^2 + x)(1-y) - y}{x - y} = \frac{8 + (4+2)(1-3) - 3}{2 - 3}$$

$$= \frac{8 + (6)(-2) - 3}{-1}$$

$$= \frac{8 - 12 - 3}{-1}$$

Plug the selected values into the choices. The choice that equals 7 is the correct answer.

(A) $(x-1)^2 y = (2-1)^2(3) = 3$
(B) $(x+1)^2 = (2+1)^2 = 9$
(C) $x^2 + x + 1 = 4 + 2 + 1 = 7$
(D) $(x^2 + x + 1)y = (4 + 2 + 1)(3) =$ too large
(E) $(x^2 + x + 1)(x - y) = (4 + 2 + 1)(2 - 3) =$ a negative number

The correct answer is **(C)**.

35. **(A)** g_3: Begin by listing some values of g_n, in order to get a sense for how g_n progresses:

$g_1 = 1$
$g_2 = 1$
$g_3 = g_2 + 2^0 = 1 + 1 = 2 = 2^1$
$g_4 = g_3 + 2^1 = 2 + 2 = 4 = 2^2$
$g_5 = g_4 + 2^2 = 4 + 4 = 8 = 2^3$
$g_6 = g_5 + 2^3 = 8 + 8 = 16 = 2^4$

For $n \geq 3$, $g_n = 2^{n-2}$.

Now look for a pattern in the sums defined by $\Psi(g_n)$:

$$\Psi(g_3) = g_1 + g_2 + g_3 = 1 + 1 + 2 = 4 = 2^2$$
$$\Psi(g_4) = (g_1 + g_2 + g_3) + g_4 = \Psi(g_3) + g_4 = 4 + 4 = 8 = 2^3$$
$$\Psi(g_5) = (g_1 + g_2 + g_3 + g_4) + g_5 = \Psi(g_4) + g_5 = 8 + 8 = 16 = 2^4$$

Each value is double the previous value: $\Psi(g_n) = 2 \times \Psi(g_{n-1})$. This means that:

$$\frac{\Psi(g_{16})}{\Psi(g_{15})} = \frac{2 \times \Psi(g_{15})}{\Psi(g_{15})} = 2$$

Now all you need to do is scan the answer choices to find an expression that equals 2. You have already discovered that $g_3 = 2$, so you can select g_3 as the answer.

The correct answer is **(A)**.

36. **(E) $3^{11}-1$:** The common term in this problem is the recurring base of 3. Group like terms (i.e. all the terms with k on the left side, all the other powers of 3 on the right side), then simplify each power of 3 using exponent rules.

$$3^k + 3^k = \left(3^9\right)^{3^9} - 3^k$$
$$3^k + 3^k + 3^k = \left(3^9\right)^{3^9}$$
$$3(3^k) = \left(3^9\right)^{3^9}$$
$$3^{k+1} = 3^{9 \times 3^9}$$
$$k + 1 = 9 \times 3^9$$
$$k + 1 = 3^2 \times 3^9$$
$$k = 3^{11} - 1$$

The correct answer is **(E)**.

37. **(C):** Note the constraints that x and y are positive integers.

(1) INSUFFICIENT: If $y = 5$ and $x = 6$, then this statement is true: $6! = 6 \times 5!$. Are these the only possible positive integer values for x and y?

The constant 6 is equal to 3!, so there's one more: when $y = 1$ and $x = 3$, the statement is also true: $3! = 6 \times 1!$.

(2) INSUFFICIENT: You can multiply both sides by y to eliminate that variable entirely; in other words, this statement doesn't indicate anything about y.

$$\frac{\frac{x!}{y}}{(x-2)!} = \frac{30}{y}$$

$$\frac{x!}{(x-2)!} = 30$$

(1) AND (2) SUFFICIENT: Continue to simplify the equation from statement (2):

$$\frac{x!}{(x-2)!} = 30$$
$$\frac{x(x-1)(x-2)!}{(x-2)!} = 30$$
$$x(x-1) = 30$$
$$x^2 - x - 30 = 0$$
$$(x+5)(x-6) = 0$$

The quadratic produces two solutions, but only $x = 6$ is valid, since x must be a positive integer. From statement (1), if $x = 6$, then $y = 5$. This is sufficient to calculate a value for xy.

The correct answer is **(C)**.

38. **(D) 6:** The question asks for the largest value of k such that $\frac{33!}{22!}$ is divisible by 6^k. Since $6 = 3 \times 2$, the largest value of k will equal the number of 3×2 pairs among the prime factors of $\frac{33!}{22!}$.

To count the number of times 3 appears as a factor of $\frac{33!}{22!}$, rewrite the expression, pulling out any factor(s) of 3 from each term:

$(33)(32)(31)(30)(29)(28)(27)(26)(25)(24)(23)$
$= (\mathbf{3} \times 11)(32)(31)(\mathbf{3} \times 10)(29)(28)(\mathbf{3^3})(26)(25)(\mathbf{3} \times 8)(23)$

There are six factors of 3 in $\frac{33!}{22!}$.

To count the number of times 2 appears as a factor of $\frac{33!}{22!}$, rewrite the expression, pulling out any factor(s) of 2 from each term:

$(33)(32)(31)(30)(29)(28)(27)(26)(25)(24)(23)$
$= (33)(\mathbf{2^5})(31)(\mathbf{2} \times 15)(29)(\mathbf{2^2} \times 7)(27)(\mathbf{2} \times 13)(25)(\mathbf{2^3} \times 3)(23)$

There are twelve factors of 2 in $\frac{33!}{22!}$.

Since there are twelve 2's but only six 3's, there are only six 3×2 pairs among the prime factors of $\frac{33!}{22!}$. In general, focus on the largest prime in the divisor (in this case, the six maximum possible factors of 3 in 6^k), as it will be the limiting factor.

The correct answer is **(D)**.

39. (D) $(100^2)(99!)$: $S_{100} = 101!$ and $S_{99} = 100!$

Factor the difference as follows:

$$
\begin{aligned}
S_{100} - S_{99} &= (101!) - (100!) \\
&= (101)(100!) - 100! \\
&= (100!)(101 - 1) \\
&= (100!)(100) \\
&= (100)(99!)(100) \\
&= (100^2)(99!)
\end{aligned}
$$

The correct answer is **(D)**.

40. (C) $\dfrac{5}{8}$: Not only does $q = \dfrac{9^5}{7^3}$, but you can also factor $\dfrac{9^5}{7^3}$ out of p:

$$
p = \frac{9^7 - 9^5}{7^5 + 7^3} = \left(\frac{9^5}{7^3}\right)\left(\frac{9^2 - 9^0}{7^2 + 7^0}\right) = \left(\frac{9^5}{7^3}\right)\left(\frac{81 - 1}{49 + 1}\right) = \left(\frac{9^5}{7^3}\right)\left(\frac{80}{50}\right) = \left(\frac{9^5}{7^3}\right)\left(\frac{8}{5}\right)
$$

Thus, $p = q\left(\dfrac{8}{5}\right)$, and $\dfrac{p}{q} = \dfrac{8}{5}$. Watch out! This is one of the incorrect answers.

The question asks for $\dfrac{q}{p}$, which is $\left(\dfrac{p}{q}\right)^{-1} = \left(\dfrac{8}{5}\right)^{-1} = \dfrac{5}{8}$.

The correct answer is **(C)**.

9

Workout Set 5

41. If x and y are positive integers, what is the value of $\dfrac{x}{y}$?

    (1) $x^2 = 2xy - y^2$
    (2) $2xy = 8$

42. What is the remainder when $(47)(49)$ is divided by 8?

    (A) 1
    (B) 3
    (C) 4
    (D) 5
    (E) 7

43. If $a = 4x^2 + 4xy$ and $b = 4y^2 + 4xy$, which of the following is equivalent to $x + y$?

    (A) $\sqrt{a+b}$

    (B) $2\sqrt{ab}$

    (C) $\dfrac{a+b}{\sqrt{2}}$

    (D) $2\sqrt{a} - 2\sqrt{b}$

    (E) $\dfrac{\sqrt{a+b}}{2}$

44. What is the value of $\dfrac{3^{(a+b)^2}}{3^{(a-b)^2}}$?

    (1) $a + b = 7$
    (2) $ab = 12$

45. What is the value of $\left(\sqrt{24 + 5\sqrt{23}}\right)\left(\sqrt{24 - 5\sqrt{23}}\right)$?

    (A) 48

    (B) $\sqrt{24}$

    (C) $5\sqrt{2}$

    (D) 1

    (E) $24 - 5\sqrt{23}$

46. If $x > 0$ and $y > 0$, what is the value of $x - 2y$?

    (1) $16y^2 = \dfrac{x^4 - 240}{y^2}$

    (2) $x^2 + 4y^2 = \dfrac{120}{x + 2y}$

MANHATTAN
PREP

47. If x and y are positive integers such that $x > y$ and $2\sqrt{x} - 2\sqrt{y} = \dfrac{(x-y)}{b}$, which of the following is equivalent to $2b$?

(A) $\sqrt{x} - \sqrt{y}$

(B) $\sqrt{x} + \sqrt{y}$

(C) $\dfrac{\sqrt{x}}{\sqrt{y}}$

(D) $2\sqrt{xy}$

(E) $2\sqrt{x-y}$

48. If $(x+y)^2 = 16$ and $x^2 - y^2 = 16$, what is the value of $2x^2$?

(A) 8
(B) 16
(C) 18
(D) 32
(E) 50

49. What is the value of $38^2 + 39^2 + 40^2 + 41^2 + 42^2$?

(A) 7,950
(B) 7,990
(C) 8,010
(D) 8,050
(E) 8,070

50. If $8xy^3 + 8x^3 y = \dfrac{2x^2 y^2}{2^{-3}}$, what is the value of xy?

(1) $y > x$
(2) $x < 0$

9

Workout Set 5 Answer Key

41. (A)
42. (E)
43. (E)
44. (B)
45. (D)
46. (C)
47. (B)
48. (D)
49. (C)
50. (A)

9

MANHATTAN
PREP

Workout Set 5 Solutions

41. (A):

(1) SUFFICIENT: Move all terms to one side:

$$x^2 = 2xy - y^2$$
$$x^2 - 2xy + y^2 = 0$$

Factor this "square of a difference" special product and simplify:

$$x^2 - 2xy + y^2 = 0$$
$$(x - y)^2 = 0$$
$$x - y = 0$$

Since $x = y$, the value of $\frac{x}{y}$ is 1.

(2) INSUFFICIENT: If $2xy = 8$, then $xy = 4$. Consider different values for x and y:

x (positive)	y (positive)	Fact (2): $xy = 4$	Question: $\frac{x}{y} = ?$
2	2	$2 \times 2 = 4$ ✓	1
1	4	$1 \times 4 = 4$ ✓	1/4

Alternatively, manipulate the equation $xy = 4$ to get $\frac{x}{y}$ on one side:

$$xy = 4$$
$$\frac{xy}{y^2} = \frac{4}{y^2}$$
$$\frac{x}{y} = \frac{4}{y^2}$$

The expression $\frac{x}{y}$ does not equal a constant, so $\frac{x}{y}$ could take on many different values.

The correct answer is **(A)**.

42. (E) 7: One way to solve would be to multiply (47)(49), then either divide the result by 8 or repeatedly subtract known multiples of 8 from the result until you are left with a remainder smaller than 8.

An alternative is to rewrite the given product as an equivalent yet easier-to-manipulate product. Note that 47 and 49 are equidistant from 48, a multiple of 8. Write each of the original factors as terms in the form $(a + b)$ or $(a - b)$.

$$(47)(49) = (48 + 1)(48 - 1)$$

This form is the *difference of two squares* special product, $(a + b)(a - b) = a^2 - b^2$; continue to simplify:

$(48 + 1)(48 - 1) = (48^2 - 1^2)$

48 is a multiple of 8, and therefore so is 48^2. Thus, $(48^2 - 1^2)$ is 1 less than a multiple of 8. All such numbers (e.g., 7, 15, 23, 31, etc.) have a remainder of 7 when divided by 8.

The correct answer is **(E)**.

43. **(E)** $\dfrac{\sqrt{a+b}}{2}$: Add a and b to get $a + b = 4x^2 + 8xy + 4y^2 = 4(x^2 + 2xy + y^2)$.

The right side is of the "square of a sum," so factor and solve:

$$a + b = 4(x^2 + 2xy + y^2)$$
$$a + b = 4(x + y)^2$$
$$\frac{a+b}{4} = (x+y)^2$$
$$\sqrt{\frac{a+b}{4}} = (x+y)$$
$$\frac{\sqrt{a+b}}{2} = (x+y)$$

Note that you could safely take the square root of both sides because any square is non-negative.

Alternatively, *Choose Smart Numbers*. For example, if $x = 2$ and $y = 3$, then the final answer $x + y = 5$.

For values to plug into the choices, first compute a and b:

$a = 4x^2 + 4xy = 4(2^2) + 4(2)(3) = 16 + 24 = 40$ and $b = 4y^2 + 4xy = 4(3^2) + 4(2)(3) = 36 + 24 = 60$

Next, test each answer choice; the one that equals 5 is the correct answer.

(A) $\sqrt{a=b} = \sqrt{40+60} = 10$

(B) $2\sqrt{ab} = 2\sqrt{(40)(60)} = 2\sqrt{(400)(6)}$ = not an integer

(C) $\dfrac{a+b}{\sqrt{2}} = \dfrac{40+60}{\sqrt{2}}$ = not an integer

(D) $2\sqrt{a} - 2\sqrt{b} = 2\sqrt{40} - 2\sqrt{60}$ = not an integer

(E) $\dfrac{\sqrt{a+b}}{2} = \dfrac{\sqrt{40+60}}{2} = \dfrac{10}{2} = 5$

The correct answer is **(E)**.

44. **(B):** Manipulate the question expression, noting the special products in the exponents:

$$\frac{3^{(a+b)^2}}{3^{(a-b)^2}} = \frac{3^{(a^2+2ab+b^2)}}{3^{(a^2-2ab+b^2)}}$$

$$= 3^{(a^2+2ab+b^2)-(a^2-2ab+b^2)}$$

$$= 3^{4ab}$$

The rephrased question is "What is the value of ab?" Knowing the values of a and b individually would be sufficient, of course, but the individual values are not required as long as you can determine ab.

(1) INSUFFICIENT: It is impossible to manipulate $a + b = 7$ to get ab, nor can you solve for a and b individually.

(2) SUFFICIENT: This statement answers the rephrased question directly.

The correct answer is **(B)**.

45. **(D) 1:** $\left(\sqrt{24+5\sqrt{23}}\right)\left(\sqrt{24-5\sqrt{23}}\right) = \sqrt{\left(24+5\sqrt{23}\right)\left(24-5\sqrt{23}\right)}$

Notice the special product of the form $(a + b)(a - b) = a^2 - b^2$ under the square root symbol.

$$\sqrt{\left(24+5\sqrt{23}\right)\left(24-5\sqrt{23}\right)} = \sqrt{24^2-\left(5\sqrt{23}\right)^2} = \sqrt{24^2-(25)(23)} = \sqrt{576-575} = 1$$

The correct answer is **(D)**.

46. **(C):** The constraints that x and y are greater than 0 eliminate the possibility of a 0 in the denominator of the fractions in the statements. That may be the only reason that this information is specified, but still write it down.

(1) INSUFFICIENT: Multiply both sides by y^2 to get rid of the fraction and then see whether you can manipulate to solve for $x - 2y$:

$$16y^2 = \frac{x^4 - 240}{y^2}$$

$$16y^4 = x^4 - 240$$

$$240 = x^4 - 16y^4$$

$$240 = (x^2 + 4y^2)(x^2 - 4y^2)$$

$$240 = (x^2 + 4y^2)(x + 2y)(x - 2y)$$

While the term $x - 2y$ does appear in the equation, it isn't possible to solve for a specific value.

(2) INSUFFICIENT: Multiplying by $x + 2y$ to eliminate the fraction makes the equation more complicated, not less:

$$\left(x^2 + 4y^2\right)(x + 2y) = 120$$

Multiplying this out would result in terms of x^3 and y^3. Moreover, there is no way to introduce a negative sign between the x and $2y$ terms (in a way that would also allow you to solve for a single value).

(1) AND (2) SUFFICIENT: Notice that the two equations contain similar expressions. In fact, the second equation contains exactly two of the three expressions from the first equation. Substitute the value 120 into the first equation:

$$240 = (x^2 + 4y^2)(x + 2y)(x - 2y)$$
$$240 = (120)(x - 2y)$$

It is possible to solve for a single value of $x - 2y$. (It turns out to equal 2.)

The correct answer is **(C)**.

47. **(B)** $\sqrt{x} + \sqrt{y}$: To solve this problem, isolate b in the equation:

$$2\left(\sqrt{x} - \sqrt{y}\right) = \frac{(x - y)}{b}$$

$$2b\left(\sqrt{x} - \sqrt{y}\right) = x - y$$

$$2b = \frac{(x - y)}{\left(\sqrt{x} - \sqrt{y}\right)}$$

Note that it is OK to divide by $\sqrt{x} - \sqrt{y}$, since $x > y$, which implies that $\sqrt{x} - \sqrt{y} \neq 0$.

The question asks for $2b$, but the result does not match any of the answer choices. Most of the choices are not fractions, so try to cancel the denominator. Since $x - y$ is a well-disguised "difference of two squares," factor the numerator and denominator:

$$2b = \frac{\left(\sqrt{x} - \sqrt{y}\right)\left(\sqrt{x} + \sqrt{y}\right)}{\left(\sqrt{x} - \sqrt{y}\right)}$$

Cancel $\left(\sqrt{x} - \sqrt{y}\right)$ in the numerator and denominator to get $2b = \sqrt{x} + \sqrt{y}$.

The correct answer is **(B)**.

MANHATTAN
PREP

48. **(D) 32:** Each of the expressions given is equal to 16, so set them equal to each other. Note that you have the "square of a sum" and the "difference of two squares" special products. Put them both in distributed form, then simplify:

$$(x + y)^2 = x^2 - y^2$$
$$x^2 + 2xy + y^2 = x^2 - y^2$$
$$2xy + y^2 = -y^2$$
$$2xy + 2y^2 = 0$$

Since $2y(x + y) = 0$, it must be true that either $2y$ or $(x + y)$ is equal to 0. However, $(x + y)$ cannot equal 0, since the problem indicates that $(x + y)^2 = 16$. So it must be that $2y = 0$ and therefore $y = 0$.

Plug 0 in for y in $x^2 - y^2 = 16$ to get $x^2 = 16$. Thus $2x^2 = 2(16) = 32$.

Alternatively, you can solve this problem by *Working Backwards* from answer choices. Try (B) or (D) first.

(D) If $32 = 2x^2$ then $x = \pm 4$. Use this to solve for y in the second equation:

$$16 - y^2 = 16$$
$$y = 0$$

Do $x = \pm 4$ and $y = 0$ also work in the first equation? Yes!

The correct answer is **(D)**.

49. **(C) 8,010:** When a problem looks like it requires large amounts of arithmetic computation, look for a shortcut. Here you can use the fact that the numbers being squared are five consecutive integers. Let $x = 40$ and the original expression becomes $(x - 2)^2 + (x - 1)^2 + x^2 + (x + 1)^2 + (x + 2)^2$.

For each of the pairs $(x - k)^2$ and $(x + k)^2$, the sum is:

$$(x - k)^2 + (x + k)^2$$
$$(x^2 - 2kx + k^2) + (x^2 + 2kx + k^2)$$
$$2(x^2 + k^2)$$

Thus, the sum of all five terms in the original expression is

$$2(x^2 + 2^2) + 2(x^2 + 1^2) + x^2$$
$$2x^2 + 2(2^2) + 2x^2 + 2(1^2) + x^2$$
$$5x^2 + 8 + 2$$
$$5x^2 + 10$$

Since $x = 40$, the sum is $5(40)^2 + 10 = 5(1,600) + 10 = 8,010$.

Alternatively, use the same idea to solve arithmetically:

$(40 - 2)^2 + (40 - 1)^2 + 40^2 + (40 + 1)^2 + (40 + 2)^2$

$(40^2 - 2(80) + 4) + (40^2 - 2(40) + 1) + 40^2 + (40^2 + 2(40) + 1) + (40^2 + 2(80) + 4)$

$5(40^2) + 4 + 1 + 1 + 4$

$5(16{,}000) + 10 = 8{,}010$

The correct answer is **(C)**.

50. **(A):** Begin by simplifying the equation given in the question:

$$8xy^3 + 8x^3 y = \frac{2x^2 y^2}{2^{-3}}$$

$$2^{-3}(8xy^3 + 8x^3 y) = 2x^2 y^2$$

$$\frac{1}{8}\left(8xy^3 + 8x^3 y\right) = 2x^2 y^2$$

$$xy^3 + x^3 y = 2x^2 y^2$$

At this stage, you might be tempted to divide both sides of the equation by xy, in order to arrive at the simpler equation $y^2 + x^2 = 2xy$. However, that would be a mistake—never divide both sides of an equation by an unknown (in this case xy), unless you are certain that the unknown cannot equal zero. (Division by zero is undefined, and can lead to nonsensical results.) So, rather than divide by xy, subtract $2x^2 y^2$ from both sides in order to group all terms on one side of the equal sign:

$$xy^3 + x^3 y - 2x^2 y^2 = 0$$

$$(xy)(y^2 + x^2 - 2xy) = 0$$

$$(xy)(y - x)^2 = 0$$

This last line implies that either $xy = 0$ or $y - x = 0$. In other words, either $xy = 0$ or $y = x$.

(1) SUFFICIENT. If $y > x$, then it is impossible that $y = x$. Therefore, $xy = 0$.

(2) INSUFFICIENT. If $x < 0$, then it is possible that $xy = 0$ (i.e., if $y = 0$) or that $y = x$ (i.e., y is negative too). If $y = x =$ any negative number, then there are infinitely many solutions for xy.

The correct answer is **(A)**.

Workout Set 6

51. Triangles *ABC* and *DEF* are similar right triangles. If the hypotenuse of triangle *DEF* has a length of 20, what is the length of the hypotenuse of triangle *ABC*?

    (1) The ratio of the perimeter of *ABC* to the area of *ABC* is the reciprocal of the ratio of the perimeter of *DEF* to the area of *DEF*.
    (2) One of the legs in triangle *DEF* has a length of 12.

52. Three of the four vertices of a rectangle in the *xy*-coordinate plane are (−5, 1), (−4, 4), and (8, 0). What is the fourth vertex?

    (A) (−4.5, 2.5)
    (B) (−4, 5)
    (C) (6, −2)
    (D) (7, −3)
    (E) (10, 1)

53. A student draws 35 lines in the *xy*-plane, none of which are vertical and 15 of which have a positive slope. Of those with positive slope, $\frac{1}{3}$ also have a positive *y*-intercept. If 23 lines have a *y*-intercept less than or equal to zero, how many lines contain no point in Quadrant I?

    (A) 0
    (B) 7
    (C) 13
    (D) 20
    (E) 35

54. A group of men and women gathered to compete in a marathon. Each competitor was weighed before the competition; the average weight of the females was 120 pounds and the average weight of the males was greater than 120 pounds. What percentage of the competitors were women?

    (1) The average weight of the men was 150 pounds.
    (2) The average weight of the entire group was twice as far from the average weight of the women as it was from the average weight of the men.

55. What is the average of these numbers: 12; 13; 14; 510; 520; 530; 1,115; 1,120; and 1,125?

    (A) 419
    (B) 551
    (C) 601
    (D) 620
    (E) 721

9

56. A set of 5 numbers has an average of 50. The largest element in the set is 5 greater than 3 times the smallest element in the set. If the median of the set equals the mean, what is the largest possible value in the set?

   (A) 85
   (B) 87
   (C) 88
   (D) 92
   (E) 93

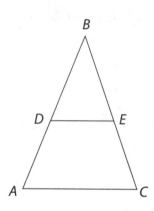

57. In the triangle above, *DE* is parallel to *AC*. What is the length of *DE*?

   (1) $AC = 14$
   (2) $BE = EC$

58. 5, 2, 4, *m*, 9, 5
    For the list of numbers above, what is the median?

   (1) The median is an integer.
   (2) $m = 8$

59. Set *M* contains seven consecutive integers and set *N* contains three values chosen from set *M*. Is the standard deviation of set *N* greater than the standard deviation of set *M*?

   (1) Set *N* contains the median of set *M*.
   (2) The range of set *M* and set *N* are equal.

60. Four different children have jelly beans: Aaron has 5, Bianca has 7, Callie has 8, and
     Dante has 11. How many jelly beans must Dante give to Aaron to ensure that each
     child has within one jelly bean of all other children.

     (A) 2
     (B) 3
     (C) 4
     (D) 5
     (E) 6

9

Workout Set 6 Answer Key

51.　(C)
52.　(D)
53.　(C)
54.　(B)
55.　(B)
56.　(D)
57.　(C)
58.　(D)
59.　(B)
60.　(B)

9

Workout Set 6 Solutions

51. (C): If the two triangles are similar, then their side lengths are in the same ratio. The problem indicates the length of the hypotenuse of triangle *DEF*, so one way to find the hypotenuse of triangle *ABC* would be to know the ratio of sides between the two triangles.

Statement (2) is much easier, so start with that one.

(2) INSUFFICIENT: This statement does allow you to determine the lengths of all three sides of *DEF* (it must be a 12–16–20 triangle, a multiple of the 3–4–5 right triangle). No information is provided about triangle *ABC*, though.

(1) INSUFFICIENT: This statement does provide information about the relationship between the two triangles. Call the sides of triangle *ABC* *a*, *b*, and *c* (with *c* the hypotenuse) and the sides of triangle *DEF* *d*, *e*, and *f* (with *f* the hypotenuse).

$$\frac{a+b+c}{0.5ab} = \frac{0.5de}{d+e+f}$$

The problem indicates that $f = 20$, but otherwise there are two many unknowns to determine the ratio between the sides of *ABC* and the sides of *DEF*.

(1) AND (2) SUFFICIENT: Combine the information.

$$\frac{a+b+c}{0.5ab} = \frac{0.5(12)(16)}{12+16+20}$$

$$\frac{a+b+c}{0.5ab} = \frac{96}{48}$$

$$(0.5)\left(\frac{a+b+c}{0.5ab} = 2\right)(0.5)$$

$$\frac{a+b+c}{ab} = 1$$

$$a+b+c = ab$$

Because triangle *DEF*'s sides are 12–16–20, similar triangle *ABC* must also be a variation of a 3–4–5 triangle. Substitute this information

$$3x + 4x + 5x = (3x)(4x)$$
$$12x = 12x^2$$
$$x^2 - x = 0$$
$$x(x-1) = 0$$
$$x = 0, 1$$

Length must be positive, so $x = 1$. The hypotenuse of triangle $ABC = (5)(1) = 5$.

The correct answer is **(C)**.

52. **(D) (7, −3):** Your GMAT scratchpad has a grid; use it to plot the diagram to scale.

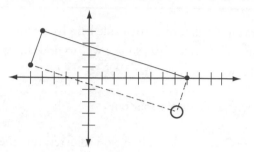

"Eyeball" solution: Complete the rectangle with the dashed lines shown. The 4th point must be located approximately where the bigger dot is drawn. Answers (A), (B), and (E) must be incorrect. The closest answer choice is the point (7, −3). Alternatively, you could plot the remaining two answer choice points to see which one "works" with the three given points.

Alternatively, compute the location of the 4th point, using the fact that the short sides have the same slope. The known short side connects the points (−5, 1) and (−4, 4). In other words, the bottom left corner is 1 to the left and 3 down from the top left corner. The unknown bottom right corner should therefore be 1 to the left and 3 down from the top right corner, or $x = 8 − 1 = 7$ and $y = 0 − 3 = −3$, corresponding to the point (7,−3).

The correct answer is **(D)**.

53. **(C) 13:** The problem describes several categories for the 35 lines drawn: positive slope vs. non-positive slope; positive y-intercept vs. non-positive y-intercept. Use a double-set matrix to keep track of the various categories:

	+ slope	neg or 0 slope	total
+ y-int	5		
neg or 0 y-int			23
total	15		35

Next, calculate the remaining numbers:

	+ slope	neg or 0 slope	total
+ y-int	5	7	12
neg or 0 y-int	10	13	23
total	15	20	35

Finally, what characteristics are necessary for a line that does not cross into Quadrant I, the (+, +) quadrant?

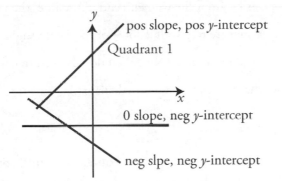

The only way to avoid Quadrant I is to have a line with negative or 0 slope that does not have a positive *y*-intercept. The matrix indicates that 13 lines fit this category.

The correct answer is **(C)**.

54. **(B):** The question stem indicates that the average weight of the women was 120 and the average weight of the men was greater than 120. In order to determine what percentage of the competitors were women, you would need to know more about the weight of the men and you'd also need to know something about the relative number of women vs. men. If there were not an equal number of each, then this is a weighted average question.

(1) INSUFFICIENT: Statement (1) provides the average weight of the men but does not indicate whether there were an equal number of men and women.

(2) SUFFICIENT: This does not provide the weight of the men or even the weighted average, but it does indicate where the weighted average falls between the two values.

	Women	Men	Difference
Weight	120	m	$m - 120$
# of people	?	?	
Fraction of people	$\dfrac{x}{3x} = \dfrac{1}{3}$	$\dfrac{2x}{3x} = \dfrac{2}{3}$	

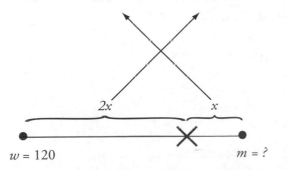

If the weighted average is twice as far from the women's end of the line, then the men are responsible for $\frac{2}{3}$ of the total weight and the women are responsible for $\frac{1}{3}$ of the total weight. Therefore, $\frac{1}{3}$, or approximately $33\frac{1}{3}$% of the competitors were women. (Note: You do not need to calculate this figure. You can stop whenever you understand that this figure can be calculated.)

The correct answer is **(B)**.

55. **(B) 551:** The simple average formula (Average = Sum/Number of terms) applies to this problem. However, the chance of computational error is high on a problem with this many terms of such a large size.

Try grouping the similar terms:

Group *A*: 12, 13, 14 (equidistant terms with an average of 13, the middle term)
Group *B*: 510, 520, 530 (equidistant terms with an average of 520, the middle term)
Group *C*: 1,115, 1,120, 1,125 (equidistant terms with an average of 1,120, the middle term)

Since each group of terms consists of three values (and are therefore equally weighted in the set of nine terms), the average of all nine original terms is the average of the respective averages of Groups *A*, *B*, and *C*:

$$
\begin{array}{r}
13 \\
520 \\
+\,1{,}120 \\
\hline
1{,}653
\end{array}
$$

$$
\text{Average} = \frac{1{,}653}{3} = 551
$$

You can make that division easier by breaking 1,653 into smaller numbers that are divisible by 3: 1653 = 1500 + 150 + 3. Divide each separately by 3 to get 500 + 50 + 1 = 551.

The correct answer is **(B)**.

56. **(D) 92:** Two techniques will help you efficiently interpret the information given in the question. First, draw a number line with five dots representing the five numbers in the set. Second, label these numbers *A*, *B*, *C*, *D*, and *E*, with the understanding that $A \le B \le C \le D \le E$.

The problem indicates that:

$A + B + C + D + E = 250$ (The set of five numbers has an average of 50.)
$E = 5 + 3A$ (The largest element is five greater than three times the smallest element in the set.)
$C = 50$ (The median of the set equals the mean.)

You're asked to maximize E. Arrange the dots on the number line such that you obey the constraints, yet also note where you have some flexibility.

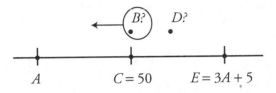

Point D can be anywhere on the line from point C to point E. Given the information from the question stem, you can maximize E by minimizing D. Therefore, make $D = C = 50$.

Similarly, point B can be anywhere on the line from point A to point C. Maximize E by minimizing B, so make $B = A$.

$$A + B + C + D + E = 250$$
$$A + (A) + 50 + 50 + (5 + 3A) = 250$$
$$105 + 5A = 250$$
$$5A = 145$$
$$A = 29$$

$E = 5 + 3A = 5 + 3(29) = 5 + 87 = 92$.

The correct answer is **(D)**.

57. **(C):**

(1) INSUFFICIENT: Many elements in this triangle could vary; you don't even know the placement of B relative to AC, so the triangle itself might stretch. Even for a fixed triangle, DE could slide up or down, so various lengths are possible for DE.

(2) INSUFFICIENT: You don't know the lengths of any sides of the triangle. The side that most affects the length of *DE* is *AC*, so stretch that side. Stretching the triangle out to the right stretches *DE*.

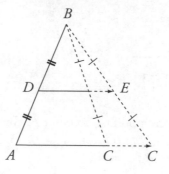

(1) AND (2) SUFFICIENT: *AC* must be 14, and *DE* must be parallel to *AC* and halfway between *AC* and *B*, in order to maintain *BE* = *EC*. Even though vertex *B* is free to move, *DE* will always be the average of the width of the triangle at *AC* (14) and the width at *B* (0). Thus, *DE* must be 7, no matter how the picture shifts.

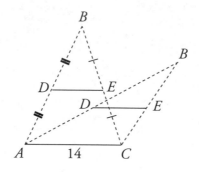

The correct answer is **(C)**.

58. **(D):** To find the median of a set of numbers, line them up in order of value. The question of interest is "Where is *m* relative to the other values?" This set has six values, an even number of terms, so the median is the average of the two middle terms.

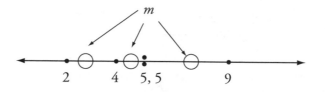

There are three scenarios:

If $m \leq 4$, then the two middle terms are 4 and 5, and the median is 4.5.

If $4 < m < 5$, then the two middle terms are *m* and 5, and the median is $\dfrac{m+5}{2}$.

If $m \geq 5$, then the two middle terms are 5 and 5, and the median is 5.

(1) SUFFICIENT: For the case where $4 < m < 5$, the median is $\dfrac{m+5}{2} = \dfrac{\text{non-integer} + odd}{2} = $ non-integer. Thus, if the median is an integer, it must be 5.

(2) SUFFICIENT: If $m = 8$, then $m \geq 5$, and the median is 5.

The correct answer is **(D)**.

59. **(B):** Standard deviation is a measure of the "spread" of a group of numbers.

(1) INSUFFICIENT: If set M contains the numbers {1, 2, 3, 4, 5, 6, 7}, then 4 is the median. Set N could be {3, 4, 5}, which has a smaller standard deviation than set M because the two sets have the same average but N is not as spread out as M.

Alternatively, N could be {1, 4, 7}, which has a larger standard deviation than set M because the two sets still have the same average, but N is now more spread out than M. (It doesn't have additional values that are closer to the average.)

(2) SUFFICIENT: If set M contains the numbers {1, 2, 3, 4, 5, 6, 7}, and set N has the same range, then N must contain 1 and 7. If set N contains {1, 4, 7}, then N has a larger standard deviation than M. If set N contains {1, 2, 7}, the standard deviation actually increases even more (because the numbers are no longer evenly distributed}. No matter what combination you try, the standard deviation of N has to be greater than the standard deviation of M.

The correct answer is **(B)**.

60. **(B) 3:** Conceptually, the transfer of jelly beans from Dante to Aaron reduces the range of the number of jelly beans held by individual children. The constraint is that the final distribution represents a range of just one jelly bean, a condition Bianca and Callie already satisfy.

Draw a picture (a number line) to visualize the scenario:

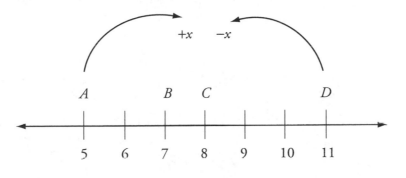

Aaron and Dante must end up with a number of jelly beans that is either 7 or 8. If either Aaron or Dante has a number of jelly beans *other than* 7 or 8, he will differ too much from either Bianca's or Callie's number. You can count out the necessary change on the number line above or you can write out the algebra.

$$A + x = 7 \text{ or } 8$$
$$5 + x = 7 \text{ or } 8$$
$$x = 2 \text{ or } 3$$

$$D - x = 7 \text{ or } 8$$
$$11 - x = 7 \text{ or } 8$$
$$x = 3 \text{ or } 4$$

The solution to both equations is $x = 3$: Add 3 to Aaron to get 8, and subtract 3 from Dante to get 8. The resulting number of jelly beans is $A = 8$, $B = 7$, $C = 8$, and $D = 8$.

The correct answer is (**B**).

9

Workout Set 7

61. A room is 480 centimeters wide and 520 centimeters long. If *n* identical square tiles are arranged in a grid pattern so as to cover the entire floor of the room, what is the value of *n*?

    (1)   A whole number of tiles fit exactly along the length and width of the room, and no tiles had to be cut in order to cover the entire floor.

    (2)   12 tiles placed adjacent to one another span the width of the room.

62. A group of friends charters a boat for $540, and each person contributes equally to the cost. They determine that if they can get three more of their friends to join them, every person in the group will pay $9 less. If they find three more friends to join them, what is the total number of people renting the boat?

    (A) 6
    (B) 9
    (C) 15
    (D) 18
    (E) 21

63. In Smithtown, the ratio of right-handed people to left-handed people is 3 to 1 and the ratio of men to women is 3 to 2. If the number of right-handed men is maximized, then what percent of all the people in Smithtown are left-handed women?

    (A) 50%
    (B) 40%
    (C) 25%
    (D) 20%
    (E) 10%

64. The sum of the interior angle measures for any *n*-sided polygon equals $180(n - 2)$. If Polygon *A* has interior angle measures that correspond to a set of consecutive integers, and if the median angle measure for Polygon *A* is 140°, what is the smallest angle measure in the polygon?

    (A) 130°
    (B) 135°
    (C) 136°
    (D) 138°
    (E) 140°

9

65. When the positive integer x is divided by the positive integer y, the quotient is 2 and the remainder is z. When x is divided by the positive integer a, the quotient is 3 and the remainder is b. Is $z > b$?

    (1) The ratio of y to a is less than 3 to 2.
    (2) The ratio of y to a is greater than 2 to 3.

66. If a and b are odd integers, $a \Delta b$ represents the product of all odd integers between a and b, inclusive. If y is the smallest prime factor of $(3 \Delta 47) + 2$, which of the following must be true?

    (A) $y > 50$
    (B) $30 \leq y \leq 50$
    (C) $10 \leq y < 30$
    (D) $3 \leq y < 10$
    (E) $y = 2$

67. Set S is the set of all prime integers between 0 and 20. If three numbers are chosen randomly from set S, and no number is chosen more than once, what is the probability that the sum of all three numbers is odd?

    (A) $\dfrac{15}{56}$

    (B) $\dfrac{3}{8}$

    (C) $\dfrac{15}{28}$

    (D) $\dfrac{5}{8}$

    (E) $\dfrac{3}{4}$

68. Sets A and B each consist of three terms selected from the first five prime integers. No term appears more than once within a set, but any integer may be a term in both sets. If the average of the terms in Set A is 4 and the product of the terms in Set B is divisible by 22, how many terms are shared by both sets?

    (1) The product of the terms in Set B is not divisible by 5.
    (2) The product of the terms in Set B is divisible by 14.

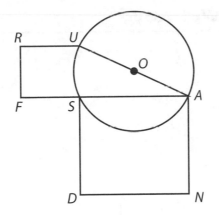

69. In the figure above, *SAND* and *SURF* are squares, and *O* is the center of the circle. If *Q* is the sum of the areas of squares *SAND* and *SURF* and *C* is the area of the circle, then the fraction $\frac{C}{Q}$ is

  (A) less than $\frac{5}{8}$

  (B) between $\frac{5}{8}$ and $\frac{3}{4}$

  (C) between $\frac{3}{4}$ and $\frac{7}{8}$

  (D) between $\frac{7}{8}$ and 1

  (E) greater than 1

70. Set *S* consists of *n* consecutive positive integers. If $n > 3$, what is the value of *n*?

  (1) The number of multiples of 2 contained in set *S* is equal to the number of multiples of 3 contained in set *S*.
  (2) *n* is odd.

9

Workout Set 7 Answer Key

61.　(B)
62.　(C)
63.　(C)
64.　(C)
65.　(A)
66.　(A)
67.　(D)
68.　(D)
69.　(C)
70.　(E)

9

Workout Set 7 Solutions

61. (B):

(1) INSUFFICIENT: There are several square tile sizes that can be placed as described. Consider these example values for *s*, the length of a side of the square tile:

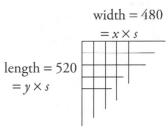

width = 480
= *x* × *s*

length = 520
= *y* × *s*

If $s = 40$, then $x = \dfrac{480}{40} = 12$ and $y = \dfrac{520}{40} = 13$, so $n = xy = (12)(13)$

If $s = 20$, then $x = \dfrac{480}{20} = 24$ and $y = \dfrac{520}{20} = 26$, so $n = xy = (24)(26)$. This second

number is clearly larger than the first, (12)(13).

(2) SUFFICIENT: The width of the room is 480 centimeters, so the side of the square tile must be $\dfrac{480}{12} = 40$ centimeters. Therefore, the exact number of tiles needed can be calculated.

The correct answer is **(B)**.

62. (C) 15: Call the initial number of friends in the group *f* and the initial cost *c*. The problem allows you to write two equations:

$fc = \$540$
$(f + 3)(c - 9) = \$540$

The question asks for $f + 3$. These equations can be solved algebraically, but the math is going to result in having to solve a quadratic. The numbers in the answer choices are fairly small; try plugging them into the problem to find the right answer. Start with (B) or (D).

	$f+3$	f	Orig cost (540/f)	New cost 540/($f+3$)	Are the costs $9 apart?
(B)	9	6	540/6 = 90	540/9 = 60	No

The two costs are much too far apart. More people need to join the group in order to bring the costs closer together. Eliminate (A) and (B). Try (D) next.

9

	$f+3$	f	Orig cost (540/f)	New cost 540/($f+3$)	Are the costs $9 apart?
(D)	18	15	540/18 = 30	540/15 = 36	No

This time, the two costs are only $6 apart. They're too close. The answer must be between 9 and 18; therefore, the answer must be (C).

Check the math if you're not sure, but do practice this technique enough that you know when you can actually tell what the answer must be (without doing the math).

The correct answer is **(C)**.

63. **(C) 25%:** Use a double-set matrix to solve this problem:

	Right-handed	Left-handed	Total
Men			$3x$
Women			$2x$
Total	$3y$	y	$4y = 5x$

There is a *hidden constraint:* the number of people must be an integer. Thus, both x and y are integers. Moreover, the total number of people must be a multiple of 4 and of 5 in order for the given ratios to be possible. From this constraint, there are two ways to solve.

Algebraic Solution
Since the question specifies that the number of right-handed men be as large as possible, assume that all the men are right-handed; of course that means that none of the men are left-handed. Because each column in a double-set matrix must total, you can also fill in the number of left-handed women (the group you want):

	Right-handed	Left-handed	Total
Men	$3x$	0	$3x$
Women		y	$2x$
Total	$3y$	y	$4y = 5x$

Thus, left-handed women represent $\dfrac{y}{4y} = \dfrac{1}{4} = 25\%$ of the total population.

Smart Number Solution
Since the total number of people in Smithtown must be a multiple of 20, set the total to 20 and determine the subtotals of men, women, left-handed and right-handed based on the ratios given in the problem:

	Right-handed	Left-handed	Total
Men			12
Women			8
Total	15	5	20

To maximize the number of right-handed men, assign all the men to the "right-handed men" cell and fill in the remaining cells:

	Right-handed	Left-handed	Total
Men	12	0	12
Women	3	5	8
Total	15	5	20

Therefore, left-handed women represent 5/20 = 1/4 = 25% of the population.

The correct answer is **(C)**.

64. **(C) 136°:** If the median angle measure is 140 degrees and the interior angle measures correspond to a set of consecutive integers, then the average (arithmetic mean) angle measure must equal 140 degrees. Since the sum of the angles must equal $180(n-2)$, the average angle must equal $\dfrac{180(n-2)}{n}$:

$$140 - \frac{180(n-2)}{n}$$
$$140n = 180n - 360$$
$$360 = 40n$$
$$n = 9$$

Therefore, the polygon has nine sides and nine interior angles, and the measures of these angles are equal to a set of consecutive integers *centered at* 140. The set of nine consecutive integers must therefore be:

$$\text{Set} = \{136, 137, 138, 139, 140, 141, 142, 143, 144\}$$

The smallest angle measure is 136°.

The correct answer is **(C)**.

65. **(A):** If x/y has a quotient of 2 and a remainder of z, then x is z more than $2y$. Mathematically, $x = 2y + z$. Therefore, $z = x - 2y$.

If x/a has a quotient of 3 and a remainder of b, then x is b more than $3a$. Mathematically, $x = 3a + b$. Therefore, $b = x - 3a$.

The question asks whether $z > b$, and the statements give information about y/a. Simplify the question by replacing z and b with their equivalents, and solving for the combination y/a:

$$z > b?$$
$$x - 2y > x - 3a?$$
$$-2y > -3a?$$
$$\frac{y}{a} < \frac{3}{2}?$$

9

Note that the inequality sign flipped in the last step because of the division by −2. The variable a is a positive integer, so no additional flip is required for that manipulation. Rephrase the question as "Is $\dfrac{y}{a} < \dfrac{3}{2}$?"

(1) SUFFICIENT: This directly answers the rephrased question: "Yes, $\dfrac{y}{a} < \dfrac{3}{2}$." Therefore, $z > b$.

(2) INSUFFICIENT: This indicates only that $\dfrac{y}{a} > \dfrac{2}{3}$. The answer might be "yes," if $\dfrac{2}{3} < \dfrac{y}{a} < \dfrac{3}{2}$. However, the answer might be "no," if $\dfrac{y}{a}$ is greater than 3/2.

The correct answer is **(A)**.

66. **(A)** $y > 50$: The function $(3 \, \Delta \, 47)$ equals the product $(3)(5)(7) \dots (43)(45)(47)$. This product is a very large odd number, as it is the product of only odd numbers and thus does not have 2 as a factor. Therefore, $(3 \, \Delta \, 47) + 2 = $ Odd + Even = Odd, and $(3 \, \Delta \, 47) + 2$ does not have 2 as a factor either.

Every odd prime number between 3 and 47 inclusive is a factor of $(3 \, \Delta \, 47)$, since each of these primes is a component of the product. For example, $(3 \, \Delta \, 47)$ is divisible by 3, since dividing by 3 yields an integer — the product $(5)(7)(9) \dots (43)(45)(47)$.

Now consider the sum $(3 \, \Delta \, 47) + k$, where k is an integer. The sum will only be divisible by 3 if k is also divisible by 3. In other words, when you divide $(3 \, \Delta \, 47) + k$ by 3, you are evaluating $(3 \, \Delta \, 47)/3 + k/3$. Because $(3 \, \Delta \, 47)/3$ is an integer, $k/3$ must also be an integer to yield an integer sum.

In this problem, $k = 2$, which is not divisible by any of the odd primes between 3 and 47. Since $(3 \, \Delta \, 47)$ IS divisible, but 2 is NOT divisible, the sum $(3 \, \Delta \, 47) + 2$ is NOT divisible by any of the odd primes between 3 and 47.

So, $(3 \, \Delta \, 47) + 2$ is not divisible by any prime number less than or equal to 47. The smallest prime factor of $(3 \, \Delta \, 47) + 2$ must be greater than 47. Thus, the minimum possible prime factor is 53, since that is the smallest prime greater than 47.

The correct answer is **(A)**.

67. **(D)** $\dfrac{2}{\sqrt{k+1}+\sqrt{k-1}} = \dfrac{2}{\sqrt{3}+\sqrt{1}} \approx \dfrac{2}{1.7+1} = \dfrac{2}{2.7}$: If set S is the set of all prime integers between 0 and 20 then $S = \{2, 3, 5, 7, 11, 13, 17, 19\}$.

There are seven odd terms and one even term in Set S. If the even term is among those selected, the sum will be even (E + O + O = E). The sum will be odd if all three terms selected are odd (O + O + O = O).

The probability of selecting three odd terms is $\dfrac{7}{8} \times \dfrac{6}{7} \times \dfrac{5}{6} = \dfrac{5}{8}$.

The correct answer is **(D)**.

68. **(D):** The first five prime integers are 2, 3, 5, 7, and 11. These are the only terms that can appear in Sets *A* and *B*. There are some other restrictions on the sets:

Set *A*: The average of the terms in Set *A* is 4, so the sum of the terms is (4)(3) = 12. There is only one way for three of the first five primes to sum to 12: 2 + 3 + 7. Set *A* is {2, 3, 7}.

Set *B*: The product of the terms in Set *B* is divisible by 22, so 2 and 11 are terms in Set *B*. Set *B* is {2, 11, *x*}, where *x* can be 3, 5, or 7, but *not* 2 or 11 (no duplicates).

Sets *A* and *B* share at least one term: the 2. If *x* is either 3 or 7, the sets will share two terms. If *x* is 5, the sets will only share one term.

The rephrased question is "Is *x* = 5?" A definite Yes or No answer leads to a definite value answer for the number of shared terms (that is, Yes = one shared term, No = two shared terms).

(1) SUFFICIENT: If the product of the terms in Set *B* is not divisible by 5, *x* ≠ 5 and the answer to the rephrased question is a definite No.

(2) SUFFICIENT: If the product of the terms in Set *B* is divisible by 14, then 2 and 7 are terms in *B*. Therefore, *x* = 7 and the answer to the rephrased question is a definite No.

The correct answer is **(D)**.

69. **(C) between $\dfrac{3}{4}$ and $\dfrac{7}{8}$:** The area of a square is equal to the length of one side squared. The area of a circle is equal to πr^2. The question asks for the fraction *C/Q*:

$$\frac{C}{Q} = \frac{\text{area of circle}}{\text{sum of areas of squares}}$$

Inscribed angle *USA* cuts off a diameter (*UA*) of the circle, so angle *USA* must be a right angle. Therefore, the triangle is a right triangle with hypotenuse *UA*.

The Pythagorean theorem indicates that $US^2 + SA^2 = UA^2$.

US^2 also represents the area of the smaller square. SA^2 also represents the area of the larger square. The sum of the two equals the quantity *Q* mentioned in the question stem, so $Q = UA^2$.

UA is a diameter of the circle, so the quantity $Q = (2r)^2 = 4r^2$. The fraction is:

$$\frac{C}{Q} = \frac{\pi r^2}{4r^2} = \frac{\pi}{4}$$

The value of π is approximately 3.14, which falls between 3 and 3.5. Therefore:

$$\frac{3}{4} < \frac{\pi}{4} < \frac{3.5}{4}$$

$$\frac{3}{4} < \frac{\pi}{4} < \frac{7}{8}$$

The correct answer is (C).

70. (E): The value of n must be 4 or greater. Start with statement (2), as it is much easier than statement (1).

(2) INSUFFICIENT: If n is odd, it could equal 3, 5, 7, or so on.

(1) INSUFFICIENT: *Test Cases* to figure out what is possible.

n	Set S	# multiples 2 = # multiples 3?
4	3, 4, 5, 6	Yes: 2 multiples of each
5	3, 4, 5, 6, 7	Yes: 2 multiples of each

(1) AND (2) INSUFFICIENT: The case of $n = 5$ was already proven in the last step. Is there a way to have n = another odd number? Keep testing.

n	Set S	# multiples 2 = # multiples 3?
5	3, 4, 5, 6, 7	Yes: 2 multiples of each
7	3, 4, 5, 6, 7, 8, 9	Yes: 3 multiples of each

Since there are still at least two possible values for n, none of the information is sufficient to answer the question.

The correct answer is (E).

9

MANHATTAN
PREP

Workout Set 8

Energy usage (units)	11	10	8	7
Number of days	4	5	n	3

71. The table above shows daily energy usage for an office building and the number of days that amount of energy was used. If the average (arithmetic mean) daily energy usage was greater than the median daily energy usage, what is the smallest possible value for n?

   (A) 2
   (B) 3
   (C) 4
   (D) 5
   (E) 6

72. A painting crew painted 80 houses. They painted the first y houses at a rate of x houses per week. Then more painters arrived and everyone worked together to paint the remaining houses at a rate of $1.25x$ houses per week. How many weeks did it take to paint all 80 houses, in terms of x and y?

   (A) $\dfrac{320-y}{5x}$

   (B) $\dfrac{y+320}{5x}$

   (C) $\dfrac{5(80-y)}{4x}$

   (D) $\dfrac{y+400}{4x}$

   (E) $\dfrac{4y+320}{5x}$

73. $a = x + y$ and $b = x - y$. If $a^2 = b^2$, what is the value of y?

   (1) $\sqrt{x} + \sqrt{y} > 0$

   (2) $\sqrt{x} - \sqrt{y} > 0$

74. A herd of 33 sheep is sheltered in a barn with 7 stalls, each of which is labeled with a unique letter from A to G, inclusive. Is there at least one sheep in every stall?

   (1) The ratio of the number of sheep in stall C to the number of sheep in stall E is 2 to 3.
   (2) The ratio of the number of sheep in stall E to the number of sheep in stall F is 5 to 2.

9

75. If $(x \times 10^q) - (y \times 10^r) = 10^r$, where q, r, x, and y are positive integers and $q > r$, then what is the units digit of y?

(A) 0
(B) 1
(C) 5
(D) 7
(E) 9

76. Is $\sqrt{(y-4)^2} = 4 - y$?

(1) $|y - 3| \leq 1$
(2) $y \times |y| > 0$

77. What is the greatest prime factor of $2^{10}5^4 - 2^{13}5^2 + 2^{14}$?

(A) 2
(B) 3
(C) 7
(D) 11
(E) 13

78. If the function $f(n)$ is defined as $f(n) = \dfrac{n}{n+1}$, for all integer values of n such that $n \neq -1$, which of the following must be true?

I. $f(x + 1) > f(x)$
II. $f(x) > 0$
III. $f(x) \neq 0$

(A) None
(B) I only
(C) II only
(D) I and III only
(E) I, II, and III

79. If x and y are positive integers and $x + y = 3^x$, is y divisible by 6?

(1) x is odd.
(2) x is a multiple of 3.

80. An (x, y) coordinate pair is to be chosen at random from the *xy*-plane. What is the probability that $y \geq |x|$?

    (A) $\dfrac{1}{10}$

    (B) $\dfrac{1}{8}$

    (C) $\dfrac{1}{6}$

    (D) $\dfrac{1}{5}$

    (E) $\dfrac{1}{4}$

9

Workout Set 8 Answer Key

71. (E)
72. (B)
73. (B)
74. (C)
75. (E)
76. (A)
77. (C)
78. (B)
79. (C)
80. (E)

9

MANHATTAN
PREP

Workout Set 8 Solutions

71. **(E) 6:** Here's what you know about the arithmetic mean:

$$\text{Mean} = \frac{4(11) + 5(10) + n(8) + 3(7)}{4 + 5 + n + 3}$$

$$\text{Mean} = \frac{44 + 50 + 8n + 21}{12 + n}$$

$$\text{Mean} = \frac{115 + 8n}{12 + n}$$

In contrast, the median depends on n, but not in a linear way. To find the median, you order the terms and pick the middle one, so try various n values (i.e., vary the number of 8's in the list). This implies the eventual need to plug n values into the mean formula above, so draw a picture to help eliminate some answers first.

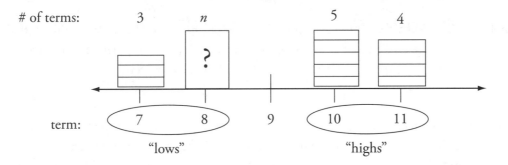

The "low" and "high" grouping is a fast way to find the relationship between median and mean for this set.

If the number of "lows" and "highs" are equal, the median is the average of the middle terms. That is, if $n = 6$, then the median = 9.

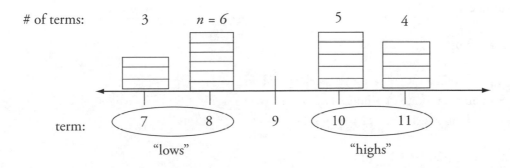

When $n = 6$, the mean must be greater than 9. Why? Pairs of 8 and 10 terms average to 9, but there is one "extra" 8. Pairs of 7 and 11 terms average to 9, but there is one "extra" 11. These "extra" terms differ from 9 by −1 and +2 respectively, for a total difference of +1. That positive difference implies that (mean > 9), or (mean > median).

To prove that $n = 5$ is too low, you could take a more conventional approach. If $n = 5$, the number of terms is $3 + 5 + 5 + 4 = 17$. The median is the 9th term in this ordered set: 7, 7, 7, 8, 8, 8, 8, 8, **10**, 10, 10, 10, 10, 11, 11, 11, 11. Thus, the median is 10, while the mean is closer to 9:

$$\text{Mean} = \frac{115 + 8n}{12 + n} = \frac{115 + 8(5)}{12 + 5} = \frac{155}{17} \approx 9$$

That is, if $n = 5$, then median > mean.
If $n = 6$, then mean > median.

The correct answer is **(E)**.

72. **(B) $y + 320$ divided by $5x$:** This is a combined work problem, so use the work formula: *rate × time = work*. The work and rates are given, but you need to calculate time, so manipulate the formula: *time = work/rate*. This problem also has variables in the answer choices, so it is efficient to *Choose Smart Numbers*.

There are 80 houses, y houses are painted at a rate of x houses per week, and the rate increases to $1.25x$ houses per week for the remaining $80 - y$ houses. To make the math easier, choose values such that x and $1.25x$ are integers (i.e., x is a multiple of 4) and y and $80 - y$ are divisible by x and $1.25x$, respectively.

	Variable	Value	Units
Total houses	80	80	houses
Houses painted at slower rate	y	20	houses
Houses painted at faster rate	$80 - y$	60	houses
Initial rate	x	4	houses/week
Increased rate	$1.25x$	5	houses/week

The total painting time is:

20 houses painted at a rate of 4 houses/week = 5 weeks
60 houses painted at a rate of 5 houses/week = 12 weeks
Total time for 80 houses = 5 + 12 = 17 weeks

(A) $\dfrac{320 - y}{5x} = \dfrac{320 - 20}{5(4)} = \dfrac{300}{20} = 15$

(B) $\dfrac{y + 320}{5x} = \dfrac{20 + 320}{5(4)} = \dfrac{340}{20} = 17$

MANHATTAN
PREP

(C) $\dfrac{5(80)-y}{4x} = \dfrac{5(80-20)}{4(4)} = \dfrac{300}{16} =$ not an integer

(D) $\dfrac{y+400}{4x} = \dfrac{20+400}{4(4)} = \dfrac{420}{16} = \dfrac{105}{4} =$ not an integer

(E) $\dfrac{4y+320}{5x} = \dfrac{4(20)+320}{5(4)} = \dfrac{20+80}{5} = 20$

The correct answer is **(B)**.

73. **(B):** If $a^2 = b^2$, then $(x+y)^2 = (x-y)^2$. Distribute both sides using the "square of a sum" and "square of a difference" special products, then simplify:

$$x^2 + 2xy + y^2 = x^2 - 2xy + y^2$$
$$2xy = -2xy$$
$$4xy = 0$$
$$xy = 0$$

There are three basic scenarios:

x	y	$xy = 0$
0	any non-zero	✓
any non-zero	0	✓
0	0	✓

(1) INSUFFICIENT: This statement indicates that x and y must be non-negative, in order for their square roots to be real values. The statement also eliminates the last scenario, in which $x = y = 0$. But y could still be 0 or any positive value.

x	y	$xy = 0$	(1): $\sqrt{x} + \sqrt{y} > 0$
0	any positive	✓	✓
any positive	0	✓	✓
0	0	✓	✗ invalid

(2) SUFFICIENT: This statement indicates that x and y must be non-negative, in order for their square roots to be real values. This statement eliminates the last scenario. If x and y were both 0, $\sqrt{x} - \sqrt{y}$

9

would equal 0. It also eliminates the first scenario. If $\sqrt{x} - \sqrt{y} > 0$, then $\sqrt{x} > \sqrt{y}$. Therefore $x > y$. Thus you can conclude that $y = 0$.

x	y	$xy = 0$	(2): $\sqrt{x} - \sqrt{y} > 0$
0	any positive	✓	✗ invalid
any positive	0	✓	✓
0	0	✓	✗ invalid

The correct answer is **(B)**.

74. **(C):**

(1) INSUFFICIENT: Set up a table and assign sheep to stalls.

Stall:	A	B	C	D	E	F	G
# of sheep:			2x		3x		

Since a fractional sheep is not possible in this problem, x must be a positive integer. Suppose $x = 2$, so there are 4 sheep in C and 6 sheep in E. With 23 sheep remaining, it is possible for each of the other stalls to hold at least 1 sheep (a Yes answer). However, the 23 other sheep might all be in stall B, leaving stalls A, D, F, and G empty (a No answer).

(2) INSUFFICIENT: Set up a table and assign sheep to stalls.

Stall:	A	B	C	D	E	F	G
# of sheep:					5y	2y	

If $y = 1$, there are 5 sheep in E and 2 sheep in F. With 26 sheep remaining, it is possible for each of the other stalls to hold at least 1 sheep (a Yes answer). However, 13 sheep might be in both stalls A and B, leaving stalls C, D, and G empty (a No answer).

(1) & (2) SUFFICIENT: Set up a table and assign sheep to stalls.

Stall:	A	B	C	D	E	F	G
# of sheep:			2x		3x = 5y	2y	

Since a fractional sheep is not possible in this problem, x and y must both be positive integers that satisfy the equation $3x = 5y$. The only possibility is $x = 5$ and $y = 3$, since higher multiples would require more than 33 sheep total. Thus, 31 sheep are allocated among these stalls as follows:

Stall:	A	B	C	D	E	F	G
# of sheep:			10		15	6	

31 of the 33 sheep are in three of the 7 pens. With only 2 sheep unaccounted for, there is no way to place at least 1 sheep in each of the remaining four pens (a definite No answer).

The correct answer is (C).

75. (E) 9: Group the 10^r terms together.

$$(x \times 10^q) - (y \times 10^r) = 10^r$$
$$x \times 10^q = (y \times 10^r) + (1 \times 10^r)$$
$$x \times 10^q = (y + 1) \times 10^r$$

Now, solve for y.

$$x \times 10^q = (y + 1) \times 10^r$$
$$x \times \frac{10^q}{10^r} = y + 1$$
$$x \times 10^{q-r} = y + 1$$
$$x \times 10^{q-r} - 1 = y$$

Since $q > r$, the exponent on 10^{q-r} is positive. Since x is a positive integer, $x \times 10^{q-r}$ is a multiple of 10 and therefore ends 0. Any multiple of 10 minus 1 yields an integer with a units digit of 9.

The correct answer is (E).

76. (A): The complicated expression in the question stem leads to a disguised Positive/Negative problem. In general, $\sqrt{x^2} = |x|$. Think about this relationship with a real example:

$$\sqrt{3^2} = \sqrt{9} = 3 \qquad\qquad \sqrt{(-3)^2} = \sqrt{9} = 3$$

In both cases (positive or negative 3), the end result is 3. Thus in general, $\sqrt{x^2}$ will always result in a positive value, or $|x|$. Rephrase the original question using the absolute value symbol in place of the "square root of the square" symbols; then try to make the right-hand side look more like the left:

Is $|y - 4| = 4 - y$?   becomes   Is $|y - 4| = -(y - 4)$?

Since the absolute value of $y - 4$ must be positive or zero, you can rephrase the question further:

Is $-(y - 4) \geq 0$?   becomes   Is $(y - 4) \leq 0$?   and then   Is $y \leq 4$?

(1) SUFFICIENT: The absolute value $|y - 3|$ can be interpreted as the distance between y and 3 on a number line. Thus, y is no more than 1 unit away from 3 on the number line, so $2 \leq y \leq 4$. Thus, $y \leq 4$.

9

(2) INSUFFICIENT: If $y \times |y| > 0$, then $y \times |y|$ is positive. This means y and $|y|$ must have the same sign. The term $|y|$ is non-negative, so y must be positive. However, knowing that y is positive is not enough to indicate whether $y \leq 4$.

The correct answer is **(A)**.

77. **(C) 7:** A base of 2 is common to each term, and 10 is the smallest exponent appearing with that base. Factor 2^{10} out from all of the terms in the expression:

$2^{10}5^4 - 2^{13}5^2 + 2^{14}$
$2^{10}(5^4 - 2^3 5^2 + 2^4)$

Clearly, 2 is a prime factor, but is it the greatest? Examine $(5^4 - 2^3 5^2 + 2^4)$ to determine whether it has a larger prime factor. The expression is of the form $x^2 - 2xy + y^2$, where:

$x^2 = 5^4$, so $x = 5^2$
$y^2 = 2^4$, so $y = 2^2$

Write the expression in factored form:

$(5^2)^2 - 2(2^2)(5^2) + (2^2)^2 = (5^2 - 2^2)^2$
$= (25 - 4)^2$
$= 21^2$

The prime factors of 21 are 3 and 7, so the largest prime factor of the original expression is 7.

Alternatively, if you did not see the quadratic template in $(5^4 - 2^3 5^2 + 2^4)$, you could also perform the computation and factor the result:

$(5^4 - 2^3 5^2 + 2^4)$
$(625 - (8)(25) + 16)$
$(625 - 200 + 16)$
(441)
$(3)(147)$
$(3)(3)(49)$
$(3)(3)(7)(7)$

The correct answer is **(C)**.

78. **(B) I only:** Set up a chart to test a representative set of possible x values, including positives, negatives, and zero. Try an easier number first, such as 0.

x	$f(x)$	$f(x+1)$	$f(x+1) > f(x)$?	$f(x) > 0$?	$f(x) \neq 0$?
0	0	1/2	Y	N	N

When $x = 0$, roman numerals II and III are not true, so cross off answers (C), (D), and (E). Next, test additional values with roman numeral I.

x	$f(x)$	$f(x+1)$	$f(x+1) > f(x)$?
1	1/2	2/3	Y
2	2/3	3/4	Y
3	3/4	4/5	Y
−2	2	undefined	
−3	3/2	2	Y

The patterns indicate that, whether zero, positive, negative, odd, or even, statement I always returns a Yes answer. Therefore, statement I must be true.

The correct answer is **(B)**.

79. **(C):** *Test Cases.*

(1) INSUFFICIENT. If $x = 1$, then $y = 2$, which is not divisible by 6. If $x = 3$, then $y = 24$, which is divisible by 6.

(2) INSUFFICIENT: If $x = 3$, then, as before, y is divisible by 6. If $x = 6$, then $x + y = 729$, and $y = 723$. This number is not even, so it is not divisible by 6.

(1) AND (2) SUFFICIENT: The two *No* cases ($x = 1$ and $x = 6$) are not allowed by the combined statements. The one *Yes* case ($x = 3$) is. Are there other possible numbers that would return a *No* answer?

Think about the math that you had to do. The value of y will always have to equal $3^x - x$. In order for y to be a multiple of 6, $3^x - x$ would also have to be a multiple of 6; that is, it must be even and a multiple of 3. Is it?

Since 3^x is always odd, and x must also be odd, the difference $3^x - x$ does have to be even. Since both 3^x and x are multiples of 3, $3^x - x$ must also be a multiple of 3. The two statements together are sufficient.

Alternatively, you can solve using theory alone:

$x + y = 3^x$
$y = 3^x - x$

In order for y to be divisible by 6, it must be divisible by both 2 and 3.

All of the positive powers of 3 (3^x, where x is a positive integer) are divisible by 3. Thus, y will be divisible by 3 only when x is also divisible by 3 (because a multiple of 3 − a multiple of 3 = a multiple of 3).

Moreover, all of the positive powers of 3 (3^x, where x is a positive integer) are odd. Thus, y will be even only when x is also odd (because odd − odd = even).

9

Combine these number properties to rephrase the question as, "Is x an odd multiple of 3?"

(1) INSUFFICIENT: x is odd, but nothing indicates whether it is a multiple of 3 (i.e., x could be 3 or 5).

(2) INSUFFICIENT: x is a multiple of 3, but nothing indicates whether it is odd (i.e., x could be 3 or 6).

(1) AND (2) SUFFICIENT: x is an odd multiple of 3: 3, 9, 15, etc.

The correct answer is **(C)**.

80. **(E)** $\frac{1}{4}$: Graph the equation $y = |x|$

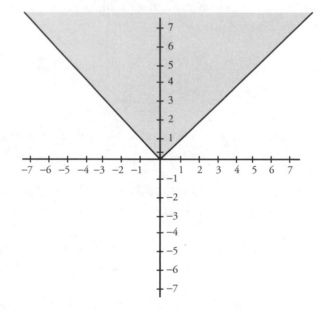

The inequality $y > |x|$ represents everything *above* the line (on either side of the y-axis)—i.e., the shaded region. Since the equation $y = |x|$ forms a 45-degree angle from the x-axis, there are 90 degrees above the line (on both sides of the y-axis). This represents one-fourth of the xy-plane. Therefore, if a random pair of (x, y) coordinates is chosen from the plane, the probability is 1/4 that the point will fit the criterion $y \geq |x|$.

The correct answer is **(E)**.

9

MANHATTAN
PREP

Workout Set 9

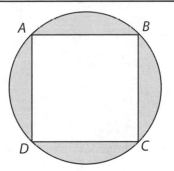

81.   *ABCD* is a square inscribed in a circle with circumference $2\pi\sqrt{x}$. What is the area of the shaded region in the diagram above?

   (A) $2x$

   (B) $\pi x - 2x$

   (C) $\pi x - x\sqrt{2}$

   (D) $1 - \dfrac{2}{\pi}$

   (E) $1 - \dfrac{2}{x}$

82.   If $3^a + 3^{a-2} = (90)(3^b)$, what is b in terms of a?

   (A) $a - 4$
   (B) $a - 2$
   (C) $a + 4$
   (D) $3a + 2$
   (E) $3a + 4$

83.   If $xy \neq 0$, what is the value of $\dfrac{x}{y}$?

   (1) $y = 4 - x$
   (2) $x(x - 6y) = -9y^2$

84.   When one new integer is added to an existing list of six integers, does the median of the list change?

   (1)   The mean of the original six numbers is 50.
   (2)   At least two of the numbers in the original list were 50.

9

85. Let *abc* and *dcb* represent three-digit positive integers. If $abc + dcb = 598$, then which of the following must be equivalent to *a*?

    (A) $d - 1$
    (B) d
    (C) $3 - d$
    (D) $4 - d$
    (E) $5 - d$

86. For non-zero integers *a, b, c* and *d*, is $\dfrac{ab}{cd}$ negative?

    (1) $ad + bc = 0$
    (2) $abcd = -4$

87. Set *A* consists of 8 distinct prime numbers. If *x* is equal to the range of set *A* and *y* is equal to the median of set *A*, is the product *xy* even?

    (1)   The smallest integer in the set is 5.
    (2)   The largest integer in the set is 101.

88. If $x^3 < 16x$, which of the following includes at least some of the possible solutions for *x*, but no values that are not solutions?

    (A) $|x| < 4$
    (B) $x < 4$
    (C) $x > 4$
    (D) $x < -4$
    (E) $x > 0$

89. Is the two-digit positive integer *n* divisible by 3?

    (1)   If the digits of *n* are reversed to produce the two-digit integer *m*, then *m* is divisible by 3.
    (2)   If the digits of *n* are reversed to produce the two-digit integer *m*, then $m + n$ is divisible by 3.

90. Twenty percent of all the sheets of paper in the tray of Printer A are removed and transferred to the tray of Printer B. After the transfer, are there more sheets of paper in the tray of Printer B than in the tray of Printer A?

    (1)   The transfer increases the number of sheets of paper in the tray of Printer B by more than 25 percent.
    (2)   The transfer increases the number of sheets of paper in the tray of Printer B by less than 30 percent.

Workout Set 9 Answer Key

81. (B)
82. (A)
83. (B)
84. (E)
85. (D)
86. (D)
87. (A)
88. (D)
89. (D)
90. (B)

9

Workout Set 9 Solutions

81. **(B)** $\pi x - 2x$: The circumference of the circle $= 2\pi r = 2\pi\sqrt{x}$, so $r = \sqrt{x}$.

The area of the circle $= \pi r^2 = \pi(\sqrt{x})^2 = \pi x$.

The area of a square is side². The diagonal of this square is the diameter of the circle $= 2r = 2\sqrt{x}$. The diagonal of a square is always $\sqrt{2}$(side), so side $= \dfrac{\text{diagonal}}{\sqrt{2}}$. Therefore, side $= \dfrac{2\sqrt{x}}{\sqrt{2}}$ and the area of square $ABCD$ is:

$$\text{side}^2 = \left(\frac{2\sqrt{x}}{\sqrt{2}}\right)^2 = \frac{4x}{2} = 2x$$

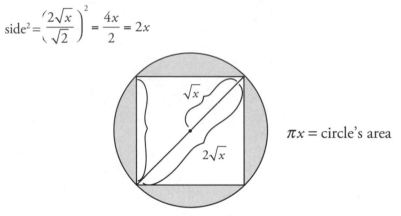

$\pi x =$ circle's area

The shaded area is the area of the circle minus the area of the square $= \pi x - 2x$.

The correct answer is **(B)**.

82. **(A)** $a - 4$: Because the problem never provides real values for a or b, you can *Choose Smart Numbers* to solve. Choose something for a that will make both exponents on the left side positive. If $a = 3$, then:

$$3^a + 3^{a-2} = (90)(3^b)$$
$$3^3 + 3^{3-2} = (90)(3^b)$$
$$27 + 3 = (90)(3^b)$$
$$\frac{1}{3} = 3^b$$
$$3^{-1} = 3^b$$

Therefore, $b = -1$. Plug $a = 3$ into the answers and look for -1.

(A) $3 - 4 = -1$ This works!
(B) $3 - 1 = 1$
(C) $3 + 4 =$ too big
(D) $3(3) + 2 =$ too big
(E) $3(3) + 4 =$ too big

MANHATTAN
PREP

Alternatively, you can solve algebraically. Some manipulation is required to determine b in terms of a, but spend a minute thinking strategically about what manipulations to do. It would help to isolate terms with an a, by factoring 3^a out on the left side. This will let you compare 3^a to 3^b, and thus compare a to b, once you clean up the constant terms that are left over. Also, 90 is a multiple of 9, which is a power of 3. 90 is also the sum of 81 and 9, both powers of 3 themselves. It is likely that some constant terms will cancel.

$3^a + 3^{a-2} = (90)(3^b)$	
$3^a (1 + 3^{-2}) = (90)(3^b)$	Factor out 3^a on the left side.
$3^a (3^2 + 1) = (90)(3^b)(3^2)$	Multiply both sides by 3^2 to cancel the negative exponent.
$3^a (10) = (90)(3^b)(3^2)$	Compute: $3^2 + 1 = 9 + 1 = 10$.
$3^a = (9)(3^b)(3^2)$	Divide both sides by 10.
$3^a = (3^2)(3^b)(3^2)$	Express 9 in terms of the common base: 3^2.
$3^a = 3^{b+4}$	Combine terms on the right side.
$a = b + 4$	Set the exponents on each side equal.

Therefore, $b = a - 4$.

The correct answer is **(A)**.

83. **(B):** The constraint in the question stem indicates that neither x nor y equals zero.

(1) INSUFFICIENT. You can prove insufficiency by testing cases. If $y = 1$, then $x = 3$, in which case $\frac{x}{y}$ is 3. If $y = 2$, then $x = 2$, in which case $\frac{x}{y}$ is 1.

(2) SUFFICIENT. Testing cases might not be such a great idea for this statement because there are multiple instances of each variable. Begin by distributing the left-hand side of the equation.

$$x^2 - 6xy = -9y^2$$

Now you've got a quadratic, so solve that way:

$$x^2 - 6xy + 9y^2 = 0$$
$$(x - 3y)^2 = 0$$
$$x - 3y = 0$$
$$x = 3y$$
$$\frac{x}{y} = 3$$

The correct answer is **(B)**.

84. **(E):** You can *Test Cases* to try to prove or disprove the statements.

(1) INSUFFICIENT: If the original set is 50, 50, 50, 50, 50, 50, the mean and median were 50 originally. The new term may be any value and the median will not change.

If, on the other hand, the original set is 0, 0, 0, 100, 100, 100, the mean and median were 50 originally. If the new term is 75, the median increases to 75. More generally for this set, if the new term is not equal to the original median of 50, the median will change.

(2) INSUFFICIENT: If the original set is 50, 50, 50, 50, 50, 50, the median was 50 originally. The new term may be any value and the median will not change.

If, on the other hand, the original set is 0, 0, 0, 50, 50, 50, the median was 25 originally. If the new term is 40, the median increases to 40. More generally for this set, if the new term is not equal to the original median of 25, the median will change.

(1) AND (2) INSUFFICIENT: The mean must be 50, and at least two terms in the original set must be 50.

If the original set is 50, 50, 50, 50, 50, 50, the mean and median were 50 originally. The new term may be any value and the median will not change.

If the original set is 0, 0, 0, 50, 50, 200, the mean was 50 and the median was 25 originally. If the new term is greater than 25, the median increases. If the new term is less than 25, the median decreases.

The correct answer is **(E)**.

85. **(D)** $4 - d$: Start with $\begin{array}{r} abc \\ +dcb \\ \hline 598 \end{array}$ and extract several equations by summing each digit place individually.

Note that both the ones digit and tens digit sum $c + b$. Since the result is different in the ones digit (8) and the tens digit (9), a 1 must be carried from the ones to the tens digit. Thus, $c + b \neq 8$; instead, $c + b = 18$.

If $c + b = 18$, then both c and b must be 9 (the largest digit). Place an 8 in the ones digit of the sum, and carry a 1 to the tens place. The sum in the tens digit is thus $1 + b + c = 1 + 18 = 19$. Next, place a 9 in the tens digit of the sum and carry a 1 to the hundreds place.

In the hundreds place, the sum is $1 + a + d = 5$.

Now solve for a:

$1 + a + d = 5$
$a + d = 4$
$a = 4 - d$

The correct answer is **(D)**.

86. (D): If an even number (0, 2, or 4) of the integers *a*, *b*, *c* and *d*, are negative, each pair of negatives will cancel, because $(-1)(-1) = +1$ and $\dfrac{(-1)}{(-1)} = +1$. This would yield a positive result for $\dfrac{ab}{cd}$.

Thus, a way to rephrase the question is "Among the integers *a*, *b*, *c* and *d*, are an odd number (*one or three*) of them negative?"

(1) SUFFICIENT: This statement can be rephrased as $ad = -bc$.

a	*d*	*b*	*c*	$ad = -bc$	Odd number of negatives?
+	+	−	+	✓	YES
+	−	+	+	✓	YES
−	−	−	+	✓	YES
+	−	−	−	✓	YES

Though the table doesn't list all possibilities, it lists enough to realize that, in order for the signs of *ad* and *bc* to be opposite one another, either one or three of the four integers must be negative.

(2) SUFFICIENT: You might recognize that the $(-1)(-1) = +1$ property implies that *abcd* is only negative when there are non-paired negatives among the integers. That is, an odd number (one or three) of the integers *a*, *b*, *c* and *d* must be negative. If not, you could list a few cases to see the pattern.

a	*b*	*c*	*d*	*abcd* = negative	Odd number of negatives?
+	+	−	+	✓	YES
+	−	+	+	✓	YES
−	+	−	−	✓	YES
−	−	+	−	✓	YES

The correct answer is **(D)**.

87. (A): The product *xy* will be even if *x* is even, *y* is even, or both are even.

The prime numbers include 2, 3, 5, 7, 11, 13, 17, 19, etc. The smallest possible term in Set *A* is 2, which is the only even prime.

x = the range of Set *A* = largest term − smallest term in Set *A*. If the smallest term in Set *A* is 2, then *x* = odd − even = odd. If the smallest term in set *A* is odd (i.e., not 2), then *x* = odd − odd = even.

The median of Set *A* is the average of the two middle terms, since the number of terms in the set is even. Thus, $y = \dfrac{\text{odd} + \text{odd}}{2} = \dfrac{\text{even}}{2} = \text{integer}$. However, *y* could be either even (e.g., when the middle terms are 11 and 13) or odd (e.g., when the middle terms are 7 and 11).

A useful rephrase of this question is "Is either *x* or *y* even?"

(1) SUFFICIENT: If the smallest prime in the set is 5, x = even and therefore xy is even.

(2) INSUFFICIENT: If the largest integer in the set is 101, the range of the set can be odd or even (e.g., $101 - 3 = 98$ or $101 - 2 = 99$). The median of the set can also be odd or even, as discussed. Therefore, xy can be either odd or even.

The correct answer is **(A)**.

88. **(D) $x < -4$:** It may be tempting to simplify this way:

$$x^3 < 16x$$
$$x^2 < 16$$
$$-4 < x < 4$$

This solution is wrong because you can't divide by x without *knowing its sign*. If x is negative, you would have to flip the sign.

Check both cases:

x	$x^3 < 16x$ becomes:	Take square root:	Solve for x:
Positive	$x^2 < 16$ (don't flip)	$|x| < 4$	$0 < x < 4$
Negative	$x^2 > 16$ (flip)	$|x| > 4$	$x < -4$

There are two ranges of solutions for x. Check the answer choices to see which one agrees with at least some of these solution ranges but does not include numbers that are not solutions.

	Positive solutions only possible are: $0 < x < 4$	Negative solutions only possible are: $x < -4$	Conclusion
(A) $|x| < 4$	All agree ($0 < x < 4$)	All disagree ($-4 < x < 0$)	Disagree
(B) $x < 4$	All agree ($0 < x < 4$)	Some disagree ($-4 < x < 0$)	Disagree
(C) $x > 4$	All disagree ($x > 4$)	*not applicable*	Disagree
(D) $x < -4$	*not applicable*	All agree ($x < -4$)	Agree
(E) $x > 0$	Some disagree ($x > 4$)	*not applicable*	Disagree

Alternatively, you could solve the problem algebraically:

$$x^3 - 16x < 0$$
$$x(x^2 - 16) < 0$$
$$x(x - 4)(x + 4) < 0$$

In order for the product of three numbers to be negative, either all three need to be negative, in which case $x < -4$, or one out of the three needs to be negative, in which case $x - 4$ is negative, but x and $x + 4$ are not. In this case, x must be between 0 and 4.

MANHATTAN
PREP

Of the given answers, only (D) covers an included range without mistakenly included values that are invalid.

The correct answer is **(D)**.

89. **(D):** Before diving into the statements, remind yourself of the divisibility rules. One way to check for divisibility by 3 is to add the digits. If their sum is divisible by 3, then the number itself is divisible by 3.

(1) SUFFICIENT: If m is divisible by 3, then the sum of the digits of m must be divisible by 3 as well. Since m has the same digits as n, the sum of the digits of n must also be a multiple of 3. Therefore, n itself is divisible by 3.

(2) SUFFICIENT: This statement requires a bit more work because it's not immediately clear what would happen when you add m and n. Because the question asks you to move digits around to different places (the tens place, the units place), rewrite the information using place value notation, where a = the tens digit of n and b = the units digit of n:

$n = 10a + 1b$
Therefore, $m = 10b + 1a$
The sum $m + n = 11a + 11b = 11(a + b)$

The statement indicates that the sum $m + n$ is divisible by 3, so $11(a + b)$ must also be divisible by 3. 11 itself is not divisible by 3, so the sum $a + b$ must be divisible by 3. This sum represents the sum of the two digits of the number m as well as the sum of the two digits of the number n; if the sum of n's two digits is divisible by 3, then n is also divisible by 3.

The correct answer is **(D)**.

90. **(B):** You can solve this problem algebraically or by *Testing Cases*. Both methods are shown.

(1) INSUFFICIENT: If Printer A starts out with 100 sheets, then 20 sheets are moved to Printer B, and A ends up with 80 sheets. If B started out with 75 sheets, then an increase of 20 sheets would be more than 25% of the starting number, and B would end up with 95 sheets. In this case, B has more sheets than A after the transfer.

If, instead, B started out with 40 sheets, then an increase of 20 sheets would be more than 25% of the starting number, and B would end up with 60 sheets. In this case, B has fewer sheets than A after the transfer.

(2) SUFFICIENT: If Printer A starts out with 100 sheets and 20 are moved to Printer B, then A ends up with 80 sheets. If B started out with 2,000 sheets, then an increase of 20 sheets would be less than 30% of the starting number, and B would end up with many more sheets than A.

9

If B started out with 80 sheets, then a 20-sheet increase would still be less than 30% of the starting number and again B would end up with more sheets than A.

How low can B go? If the 20 sheets represent a less-than-30% increase, then use 30% as the limiting figure. If 20 represented exactly 30% of B's sheets, then B would have to start with $66\frac{2}{3}$ sheets (ignore the fact that this isn't an integer). In this case, B would end up with $88\frac{2}{3}$ sheets, which is still greater than A's 80 sheets. After the transfer, B can't drop below A.

Algebraically, use a for the original number of sheets in Printer A and use b for the original number of sheets in Printer B.

After the transfer, A has $a - 0.2a = 0.8a$ sheets. B has $b + 0.2a$ sheets. Rephrase the question: "Is $b + 0.2a > 0.8a$?" Or "Is $b > 0.6a$?"

(1) INSUFFICIENT: Translate the statement into algebra.

$$b + 0.2a > 1.25b$$
$$0.2a > 0.25b$$
$$0.8a > b$$

Flip the statement around to compare it more easily to the rephrased question: $b < 0.8a$. Is it true that $b > 0.6a$? Maybe.

(2) SUFFICIENT: Translate the statement into algebra.

$$b + 0.2a < 1.3b$$
$$0.2a < 0.3b$$
$$2a < 3b$$

$$\frac{2a}{3} < b \text{ or } b > \frac{2a}{3}$$

The decimal equivalent of $\frac{2}{3}$ is $0.\overline{6}$ so b is indeed always greater than $0.6a$.

The correct answer is **(B)**.

MANHATTAN
PREP

Workout Set 10

91. If $|x| \neq |y|$, $xy \neq 0$, $\dfrac{x}{x+y} = n$, and $\dfrac{x}{x-y} = m$, then $\dfrac{x}{y} =$

   (A) $\dfrac{3mn}{2}$

   (B) $\dfrac{3m}{2n}$

   (C) $\dfrac{n(m+2)}{2}$

   (D) $\dfrac{2nm}{(m-n)}$

   (E) $\dfrac{n^2 - m^2}{nm}$

92. If a certain culture of bacteria increases by a constant factor of x every y minutes, how long will it take for the culture to increase to 10,000 times its original size?

   (1) $\sqrt[y]{x} = 10$
   (2) In two minutes, the culture will increase to 100 times its original size.

93. A cylinder of height h is $\dfrac{3}{4}$ full of water. When all of the water is poured into an empty cylinder whose radius is 25 percent larger than that of the original cylinder, the new cylinder is $\dfrac{3}{5}$ full. The height of the new cylinder is what percent of h?

   (A) 25%
   (B) 50%
   (C) 60%
   (D) 80%
   (E) 100%

94. If a and b are distinct positive integers, what is the units digit of $2^a 8^b 4^{a+b}$?

   (1) $b = 24$ and $a < 24$
   (2) The greatest common factor of a and b is 12.

95. Employees of a certain company are each to receive a unique 7-digit identification code consisting of the digits 0, 1, 2, 3, 4, 5, and 6 such that no digit is used more than once in any given code. In valid codes, the second digit in the code is exactly twice the first digit. How many valid codes are there?

    (A)   42
    (B)   120
    (C) 210
    (D) 360
    (E) 840

96. If x, y, and z are positive integers such that $x < y < z$, is x a factor of the even integer z?

    (1) x and y are prime numbers whose sum is a factor of 57.
    (2) y is not a factor of z.

97. If w, x, y, and z are positive integers and $\dfrac{w}{x} < \dfrac{y}{z} < 1$, what is the proper order, increasing from left to right, of the following quantities: $\dfrac{x}{w}, \dfrac{z}{y}, \dfrac{x^2}{w^2}, \dfrac{xz}{wy}, \dfrac{x+z}{w+y}, 1$?

    (A) $1, \dfrac{z}{y}, \dfrac{x}{w}, \dfrac{x+z}{w+y}, \dfrac{x^2}{w^2}, \dfrac{xz}{wy}$

    (B) $1, \dfrac{z}{y}, \dfrac{x+z}{w+y}, \dfrac{x}{w}, \dfrac{xz}{wy}, \dfrac{x^2}{w^2}$

    (C) $1, \dfrac{z}{y}, \dfrac{x}{w}, \dfrac{x+z}{w+y}, \dfrac{xz}{wy}, \dfrac{x^2}{w^2}$

    (D) $1, \dfrac{z}{y}, \dfrac{x}{w}, \dfrac{xz}{wy}, \dfrac{x+z}{w+y}, \dfrac{x^2}{w^2}$

    (E) $1, \dfrac{z}{y}, \dfrac{x+z}{w+y}, \dfrac{xz}{wy}, \dfrac{x^2}{w^2}, \dfrac{x}{w}$

98. What is the value of $|a + b|$?

    (1) $(a + b + c + d)(a + b - c - d) = 16$
    (2) $c + d = 3$

99. Set A consists of all the integers between 10 and 21, inclusive. Set B consists of all the integers between 10 and 50, inclusive. If x is a number chosen randomly from set A, y is a number chosen randomly from set B, and y has no factor z such that $1 < z < y$, what is the probability that the product xy is divisible by 3?

(A) $\dfrac{1}{4}$

(B) $\dfrac{1}{3}$

(C) $\dfrac{1}{2}$

(D) $\dfrac{2}{3}$

(E) $\dfrac{3}{4}$

100. At a birthday party, x children will be seated at two different tables. At the table with the birthday cake on it, exactly y children will be seated, including the birthday girl, Sally. How many different groups of children may be seated at the birthday cake table?

(A) $\dfrac{(x-1)!}{(y-1)!(y-1)!}$

(B) $\dfrac{x!}{y!(x-y)!}$

(C) $\dfrac{y!}{x!(x-y)!}$

(D) $\dfrac{(y-1)!}{(x-y)!(y-1)!}$

(E) $\dfrac{(x-1)!}{(x-y)!(y-1)!}$

9

Workout Set 10 Answer Key

91. (D)
92. (D)
93. (D)
94. (B)
95. (D)
96. (A)
97. (B)
98. (C)
99. (B)
100. (E)

9

Workout Set 10 Solutions

91. **(D)** $\dfrac{2nm}{m-n}$: If $x = 2$ and $y = 3$, then $n = \dfrac{2}{5}$ and $m = \dfrac{2}{-1} = -2$. The target number for testing the answer choices is $\dfrac{x}{y} = \dfrac{2}{3}$.

(A) $\dfrac{3mn}{2} = negative$

(B) $\dfrac{3m}{2n} = negative$

(C) $\dfrac{n(m+2)}{2} = 0$

(D) $\dfrac{2nm}{(m-n)} = \dfrac{2\left(\frac{2}{5}\right)(-2)}{-2-\frac{2}{5}} = \dfrac{\frac{-8}{5}}{\frac{-10}{5}-\frac{2}{5}} = \dfrac{\frac{-8}{5}}{\frac{-12}{5}} = \dfrac{8}{12} = \dfrac{2}{3}$

(E) $\dfrac{n^2 - m^2}{nm} = \dfrac{\frac{4}{25}-4}{\frac{-4}{5}} = \dfrac{\frac{4}{25}-\frac{100}{25}}{\frac{-20}{25}} = \dfrac{-96}{-20} = \dfrac{24}{5}$

This problem can be solved algebraically, but this path is not recommended.

$$\dfrac{x}{x+y} = n \qquad\qquad \dfrac{x}{x-y} = m$$

$$\left(\dfrac{x}{x+y}\right)^{-1} = n^{-1} \quad \text{and} \quad \left(\dfrac{x}{x-y}\right)^{-1} = m^{-1}$$

$$\dfrac{x+y}{x} = \dfrac{1}{n} \qquad\qquad \dfrac{x-y}{x} = \dfrac{1}{m}$$

Now that the fractions have a common denominator of x, subtract one from the other:

$$\left(\dfrac{x+y}{x}\right) - \left(\dfrac{x-y}{x}\right) = \dfrac{1}{n} - \dfrac{1}{m}$$

$$\dfrac{x+y-x-(-y)}{x} = \dfrac{m}{nm} - \dfrac{n}{nm}$$

$$\dfrac{2y}{x} = \dfrac{m-n}{mn}$$

$$\dfrac{y}{x} = \dfrac{m-n}{2mn}$$

$$\dfrac{x}{y} = \dfrac{2mn}{m-n}$$

You are not alone if the algebraic solution was not obvious to you! Algebraic "false starts" are common in this type of problem. In addition, there are other, equally valid algebraic paths whose final forms would not match any of the answers.

When you encounter a tough "pure algebra" problem that has variables in the answer choices, picking numbers and testing the answer choices is often the best approach; it's fast, easy, and correct.

The correct answer is **(D)**.

92. **(D):** To understand the question stem, pick some numbers: the bacteria culture begins with an initial quantity of $I = 100$ and increases by a factor of $x = 2$ every $y = 3$ minutes. Construct a table to track the growth of the bacteria:

Time (min.)	Bacteria
3	$100(2) = 100(2)^1$
6	$100(2)(2) = 100(2)^2$
9	$100(2)(2)(2) = 100(2)^3$
12	$100(2)(2)(2)(2) = 100(2)^4$
...	...
$3n = t$	$100(2)^n$

n represents the number of growth periods, and $n = t/y$ where t is time in minutes. For example, the 4th growth period in the table above ended at 12 minutes, and $4 = 12$ minutes/3 minutes.

From this example, construct a general formula for the quantity of bacteria, F:

$$F = I(x)^{t/y}$$

This question asks how long it will take for the bacteria to grow to 10,000 times their original amount. In other words, "What is t when $F = 10,000I$?"

$$F = 10,000I = I(x)^{\frac{t}{y}}$$

$$10,000 = (x)^{\frac{t}{y}}$$

The rephrased question is "What is t when $10,000 = (x)^{\frac{t}{y}}$?"

(1) SUFFICIENT: Note that the yth root of x is equivalent to x to the $1/y$ power. This statement indicates that $x^{1/y} = 10$. If you plug this value into the equation, you can solve for t (though stop the calculation at the point that you can tell that you can solve for t):

MANHATTAN
PREP

$$10,000 = (x)^{\frac{t}{y}}$$

$$10,000 = \left[(x)^{\frac{1}{y}}\right]^{t}$$

$$10,000 = 10^{t}$$

$$10^{4} = 10^{t}$$

$$t = 4$$

(2) SUFFICIENT: The culture grows one-hundredfold in 2 minutes. In other words, the sample grows by a factor of 10^{2}. Since exponential growth is characterized by a constant factor of growth (i.e., by a factor of x every y minutes), in another 2 minutes, the culture will grow by another factor of 10^{2}. Therefore, after a total of 4 minutes, the culture will have grown by a factor of $10^{2} \times 10^{2} = 10^{4}$, or 10,000.

The correct answer is **(D)**.

93. **(D) 80%:** The answer choices contain percentages and the problem never offers a real value for h. *Choose a Smart Number!*

Also note that the problem mentions the volume of the cylinder ($V = \pi r^{2} h$), so you're going to need a radius. That radius needs to be increased by 25% later in the problem, so pick a small integer that is easy to increase by 25%, such as 4.

$$r = 4$$

The problem also contains two fractions, 3/4 and 4/5. Since one number is already a multiple of 4, make the other number a multiple of 5:

$$h = 5$$

Now, solve the problem using these numbers. Remember that the original cylinder is only 3/4 full:

Three-quarters of original cylinder volume $= (3/4)[\pi(4^{2})(5)]$
$$= 60\pi$$

New radius $= 4 + (0.25)4 = 5$

The amount of water in the new cylinder has to be the same 60π. Remember that it is only 3/5 full:

$$60\pi = \pi(5^{2})(h)(3/5)$$
$$60 = 15h$$
$$4 = h$$

The new height is 4. The original height was 5, so the new height is 4/5, or 80%, of the original height.

The correct answer is **(D)**.

9

94. **(B):** This problem contains a common trap seen in many difficult DS questions. Answer choice (C) is a tempting short-cut answer, as the combined statements would provide the values of both a and b, which could be plugged into the expression to answer the question.

Rephrase the question:

$$2^a 8^b 4^{a+b} = 2^a (2^3)^b (2^2)^{a+b}$$
$$= 2^a (2^{3b})(2^{2a+2b})$$
$$= 2^{3a+5b}$$

Remembering the units digit patterns for powers of 2 will help on this problem:

$2^1 = 2$
$2^2 = 4$
$2^3 = 8$
$2^4 = 16$
$2^5 = 32$
... etc.

The units digits for powers of 2 is a repeating pattern of [2, 4, 8, 6].

If you can determine the relationship of $3a + 5b$ to a multiple of 4 (i.e., where 2^{3a+5b} is in the predictable 4-term repeating pattern of units digits), you will be able to answer the question. This question can be rephrased as, "What is the remainder when $3a + 5b$ is divided by 4?"

(1) INSUFFICIENT: If $b = 24$, then $5b$ is a multiple of 4. However, a could be any integer less than 24. Possible remainders when $3a$ is divided by 4 are 0, 1, 2, or 3.

(2) SUFFICIENT: If the greatest common factor of a and b is 12, then 12 must be a factor of both variables. That is, both a and b are multiples of 12 and thus also multiples of 4. As a result, $3a$ and $5b$ will be multiples of 4 as well, so the remainder will be 0 when $3a + 5b$ is divided by 4.

The correct answer is (B).

95. **(D) 360:** Valid codes must have a second digit that is exactly twice the first digit. There are three ways to do this with the available digits:

Scenario A: 12*XXXXX*
Scenario B: 24*XXXXX*
Scenario C: 36*XXXXX*

For each of these basic scenarios, there are 5! ways to shuffle the remaining 5 numbers (represented by *X*'s above).

Thus, the total number of valid codes is $3 \times 5! = 3 \times 120 = 360$.

The correct answer is **(D)**.

96. (A): If $x = 2$, then x is a factor of any even integer. Thus, this question can be rephrased, "Is $x = 2$ or any other factor of z?"

(1) SUFFICIENT: The statement indicates that x and y are primes. In addition, $x < y$. The factors of 57 are 1, 3, 19, and 57, all odd numbers. Because x and y sum to an odd number, one must be even and one must be odd. The number 2 is the only even prime, so x must be 2 (since it is smaller than y and z) and y must be an odd prime.

If $x = 2$, then x must be a factor of the even integer z.

(2) INSUFFICIENT: If y is not a factor of z, then $y \neq 2$. Therefore, y cannot be 1 either, as x must be positive and $x < y$. Thus, $y \geq 3$, but it isn't possible to determine the shared factors (if any) of x and z.

For example, it is possible that $x = 2$, $y = 4$, and $z = 6$. In this case, x is a factor of z, and the answer is Yes.

It is also possible that $x = 3$, $y = 5$, and $z = 8$. In this case, x is not a factor of z, and the answer is No.

The correct answer is **(A)**.

97. (B) $1, \dfrac{z}{y}, \dfrac{x+z}{w+y}, \dfrac{x}{w}, \dfrac{xz}{wy}, \dfrac{x^2}{w^2}$: It would require a lot of tricky work to solve this algebraically,

so *Test Cases* instead. Make sure to pick values for the unknowns such that $\dfrac{w}{x} < \dfrac{y}{z} < 1$ holds true.

For example, if $w = 1$, $x = 2$, $y = 3$, and $z = 4$, then $\dfrac{1}{2} < \dfrac{3}{4} < 1$ is true.

Before plugging those values in for the quantities, check the answers. All of them begin with 1 and z/y, so don't bother to test z/y. In addition, check the answer choices after each term that you evaluate.

$$\dfrac{x}{w} = \dfrac{2}{1} = 2, \quad \dfrac{x^2}{w^2} = \dfrac{2^2}{1^2} = 4, \quad \dfrac{xz}{wy} = \dfrac{(2)(4)}{(1)(3)} = \dfrac{8}{3}, \quad \text{and} \quad \dfrac{x+z}{w+y} = \dfrac{2+4}{1+3} = \dfrac{6}{4} = \dfrac{3}{2}.$$

Placed in ascending order: $1 < \dfrac{z}{y} < \dfrac{3}{2} < 2 < \dfrac{8}{3} < 4$.

The third term is $\dfrac{x+z}{w+y}$ so cross off answers (A), (C), and (D). The fourth term is $\dfrac{x}{w}$ so cross off answer (E).

The correct answer is **(B)**.

98. (C): The question asks for the absolute value of $a + b$, so try to manipulate the statements to isolate that combination of variables, $a + b$. Statement (2) looks much easier, so start there.

(2) INSUFFICIENT: This provides information about c and d, and the relationship between them, but no information about a or b.

(1) INSUFFICIENT: Manipulate the equation to group $(a + b)$ and $(c + d)$ terms:

$$(a + b + c + d)(a + b - c - d) = 16$$
$$[(a + b) + (c + d)][(a + b) - (c + d)] = 16$$

9

Note that this is of the form $(x + y)(x - y)$, where $x = (a + b)$ and $y = (c + d)$. This is the *difference of squares* special product, $(x + y)(x - y) = x^2 - y^2$. Use this to transform this expression:

$[(a + b) + (c + d)][(a + b) - (c + d)] = 16$
$(a + b)^2 - (c + d)^2 = 16$
$(a + b)^2 = 16 + (c + d)^2$

This is not enough to determine the value of $(a + b)^2$.

(1) AND (2) SUFFICIENT: From statement (2), $(a + b)^2 = 16 + (c + d)^2$. From statement (1) $c + d = 3$. You can substitute for $c + d$ and solve. The solution is shown below, but note that you don't have to do that math: the question asked for the absolute value of $a + b$, so the fact that the equation has $(a + b)^2$ doesn't matter.

$(a + b)^2 = 16 + (c + d)^2$
$(a + b)^2 = 16 + 3^2$
$(a + b)^2 = 16 + 9$
$(a + b)^2 = 25$
$(a + b) = 5$ or -5
$|a + b| = 5$

The correct answer is **(C)**.

99. **(B)** $\dfrac{1}{3}$: If y has no factor z such that $1 < z < y$, then y must be prime. Examine a few examples to see why this is true:

6 has a factor 2 such that $1 < 2 < 6$: 6 is NOT prime.
15 has a factor 5 such that $1 < 5 < 15$: 15 is NOT prime.
3 has NO factor between 1 and 3: 3 IS prime.
7 has NO factor between 1 and 7: 7 IS prime.

Because y is selected from set B, it is a prime number between 10 and 50, inclusive. The only prime number that is divisible by 3 is 3, so y is definitely not divisible by 3.

Thus, xy is only divisible by 3 if x itself is divisible by 3. Rephrase the question: "What is the probability that a multiple of 3 will be chosen randomly from set A?"

There are $21 - 10 + 1 = 12$ terms in set A. Of these, 4 terms (12, 15, 18, and 21) are divisible by 3.

Thus, the probability that x is divisible by 3 is $\dfrac{4}{12} = \dfrac{1}{3}$.

The correct answer is **(B)**.

100. **(E)** $\dfrac{(x-1)!}{(y-1)!(x-y)!}$: This problem contains variables in the answer choices, so *Choose Smart Numbers:*

$x = 8$

$y = 5$

There are 8 children at the party, and 5 will sit at the table with the cake. Sally must sit at the birthday cake table, so pick $5 - 1 = 4$ of the other $8 - 1 = 7$ children to sit at that table with her. How many different ways can you choose 4 from a group of 7? Set up an anagram grid, where *Y* means "at the cake table" and *N* means "at the other table."

A	B	C	D	E	F	G
Y	Y	Y	Y	N	N	N

Now you can calculate the number of possible groups:

$$\frac{7!}{4!3!} = \frac{(7)(6)(5)}{(3)(2)(1)} = 35$$

Note that the answer choices are in factorial form; it may be the case that you will find the unsimplified factorial form, rather than 35. Test each answer choice by plugging in $x = 8$ and $y = 5$:

(A) $\dfrac{(x-1)!}{(y-1)!(y-1)!} = \dfrac{(8-1)!}{(5-1)!(5-1)!} = \dfrac{7!}{4!4!} =$ not a match for the factorial form

(B) $\dfrac{x!}{y!(x-y)!} = \dfrac{8!}{5!(8-5)!} = \dfrac{8!}{5!3!} =$ not a match for the factorial form

(C) $\dfrac{y!}{x!(x-y)!} = \dfrac{5!}{8!(8-5)!} = \dfrac{5!}{8!3!} =$ not a match for the factorial form

(D) $\dfrac{(y-1)!}{(x-y)!(y-1)!} = \dfrac{1}{(8-5)!} =$ not a match for the factorial form

(E) $\dfrac{(x-1)!}{(x-y)!(y-1)!} = \dfrac{(8-1)!}{(8-5)!(5-1)!} = \dfrac{7!}{3!4!} =$ match!

As an alternative to testing all five choices, you could use a hybrid approach to determine the formula using variables.

The number of possible groups was $\dfrac{7!}{4!3!}$, but remember that this formula took Sally into account.

The 7 came from $8 - 1 = x - 1$.

The 4 came from $5 - 1 = y - 1$.

The 3 came from the difference between these numbers: $7 - 4 = (x - 1) - (y - 1) = (x - y)$.

Substitute these variable expressions in place of the numbers: $\dfrac{7!}{4!3!} = \dfrac{(x-1)!}{(y-1)!(x-y)!}$

The correct answer is **(E)**.

Workout Set 11

101. A casino pays players with chips that are either turquoise- or violet-colored. If each turquoise-colored chip is worth *t* dollars, and each violet-colored chip is worth *v* dollars, where *t* and *v* are integers, what is the combined value of four turquoise-colored chips and two violet-colored chips?

   (1) The combined value of six turquoise-colored chips and three violet-colored chips is 42 dollars.
   (2) The combined value of five turquoise-colored chips and seven violet-colored chips is 53 dollars.

102. John and Amanda stand at opposite ends of a straight road and start running towards each other at the same moment. Their rates are randomly selected in advance so that John runs at a constant rate of 3, 4, 5, or 6 miles per hour and Amanda runs at a constant rate of 4, 5, 6, or 7 miles per hour. What is the probability that John has traveled farther than Amanda by the time they meet?

   (A) $\dfrac{3}{16}$

   (B) $\dfrac{5}{16}$

   (C) $\dfrac{3}{8}$

   (D) $\dfrac{1}{2}$

   (E) $\dfrac{13}{16}$

103. If *p* is a positive integer, is p^2 divisible by 96?

   (1) *p* is a multiple of 8.
   (2) p^2 is a multiple of 12.

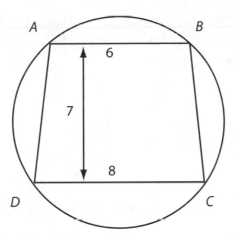

104. In the figure above, the trapezoid *ABCD* is inscribed in a circle. Parallel sides *AB* and
     CD are 7 inches apart and 6 and 8 inches long, respectively. What is the radius of the
     circle in inches?

    (A) 4
    (B) 5
    (C) 7
    (D) $4\sqrt{2}$
    (E) $5\sqrt{2}$

105. If $9^y + 3^b = 10(3^b)$, then $2y =$

    (A) $b - 2$
    (B) $b - 1$
    (C) b
    (D) $b + 1$
    (E) $b + 2$

106. The radius of a circle is *r* yards. Is the area of the circle at least *r* square yards?
     (1 yard = 3 feet)

    (1)   The diameter of the circle is more than 2 feet.
    (2)   If the radius of the same circle is *f* feet, the area of the circle is more than 2*f*
          square feet.

9

107. For a three-digit number xyz, where x, y, and z represent the digits of the number, the function $h(xyz) = 5^x 2^y 3^z$. If $h(abc) = 3 \times h(def)$, what is the value of $abc - def$, where the letters a through f represent digits as well?

    (A) 1
    (B) 2
    (C) 3
    (D) 9
    (E) 27

108. Let x and y be positive integers, and r and s be single-digit positive integers. If $\dfrac{x}{y} = r.\overline{sss}$, where the bar above the s indicates that the decimal repeats infinitely, which of the following CANNOT be true?

    (A) $y = 1.2 \times 10^a$, where a is a positive integer
    (B) $y = 1.5 \times 10^b$, where b is a positive integer
    (C) $y = 1.8 \times 10^c$, where c is a positive integer
    (D) $y = 2.5 \times 10^d$, where d is a positive integer
    (E) $y = 2.7 \times 10^e$, where e is a positive integer

109. If $m @ n$ represents the integer remainder that results when positive integer m is divided by positive integer n, what is the value of positive integer x?

    (1) $81 @ x = 1$
    (2) $x @ 40 = 0$

110. The positive integers p and r have exactly three prime factors in common: two 2's and one 3. If p has exactly one additional prime factor x and r has exactly one additional prime factor y, which of the following represents the least common multiple of p and r?

    (A) $12xy$
    (B) $6xy$
    (C) xy
    (D) 12
    (E) 6

9

MANHATTAN
PREP

Workout Set 11 Answer Key

101. (D)
102. (A)
103. (C)
104. (B)
105. (E)
106. (A)
107. (A)
108. (D)
109. (E)
110. (A)

9

Workout Set 11 Solutions

101. **(D):** The question asks for the value of $4t + 2v$, where t and v represent the values of the turquoise and violet chips, respectively. Note that the question asks for a combination of variables, or a *combo*; it may not be necessary to be able to solve for the individual values of t and v.

(1) SUFFICIENT: Translate and simplify the statement:

$$6t + 3v = 42$$
$$3(2t + v) = 42$$
$$2t + v = 14$$

You can't solve for t and v, so this statement might look sufficient—but remember what the question is asking! You need to find the value of $4t + 2v$. Multiply the equation by two: $4t + 2v = 28$.

(2) SUFFICIENT: Translate the statement:

$$5t + 7v = 53$$

There isn't a way to simplify this one, but notice all those prime numbers. Primes tend to minimize the number of allowable scenarios, especially when the question also specifies that the variables have to be integers. See what combinations of integers would actually work here.

The $5t$ term could be 5, 10, 15, 20, and so on. This term can contribute only numbers that end in 5 or 0. If that's the case, the $7v$ term must have a units digit of either 3 or 8. List out the possibilities for $7v$ and try only the ones that end in 3 or 8.

$7v$: 7, 14, 21, 28, 35, 42, 49

Only one ends in 3 or 8! If $7v = 28$, then $v = 4$ and the $5t$ term must equal 25, so $t = 5$. This one scenario works and it is the only possible scenario for this equation, given that v and t must be integers.

The correct answer is **(D)**.

102. **(A)** $\dfrac{3}{16}$: If John and Amanda run at the same rate, they will meet each other exactly in the middle. John will only run farther than Amanda if John's rate is greater than Amanda's. In math terms, distance = rate × time, and since John and Amanda run for the same time, their relative distances depend solely on their relative rates. Rephrase the question as, "what is the probability that John ran faster than Amanda?"

There are four possible rates for John (3, 4, 5, and 6) and four for Amanda (4, 5, 6, and 7). In total, there are $(4)(4) = 16$ possible rate scenarios.

MANHATTAN
PREP

Of John's four possible rates, only two (5 and 6) are greater than some of Amanda's possible rates (4 and 5). List the three rate scenarios that result in a faster speed (greater distance) for John:

> John ran 5 mph, and Amanda ran 4 mph.
> John ran 6 mph, and Amanda ran 4 mph.
> John ran 6 mph, and Amanda ran 5 mph.

Since there are 16 possible combinations of rates, the probability that John ran farther than Amanda is 3/16.

The correct answer is **(A)**.

103. **(C):** The prime factorization of 96 is $(2)(2)(2)(2)(2)(3) = (2^5)(3^1)$. In order for p^2 to be divisible by 96, p^2 would have to have the prime factors $2^5 3^1$ in its prime box. The rephrased question is therefore "Does p^2 have *at least* five 2's and one 3 in its prime box?"

(1) INSUFFICIENT: If p is a multiple of $8 = (2)(2)(2)$, p has 2^3 in its prime box. Therefore, p^2 has $(2^3)^2 = 2^6$ in its prime box, and therefore has the required five 2's. However, it is uncertain whether p^2 has at least one 3 in its prime box.

(2) INSUFFICIENT: If p^2 is a multiple of $12 = (2)(2)(3)$, p^2 has two 2's and one 3 in its prime box. It is uncertain whether p^2 has at least five 2's total, as there may or may not be three more 2's in the prime box.

(1) AND (2) SUFFICIENT: Statement (1) indicates that p^2 has 2^6 in its prime box, and statement (2) indicates that p^2 has a 3 in its prime box. Therefore, it is certain that p^2 has *at least* five 2's and one 3 in its prime box.

The correct answer is **(C)**.

104. **(B) 5:** Redraw the figure as closely to scale as possible (remember that the official scrap paper is graph paper!), labeling the known dimensions and the radius in question.

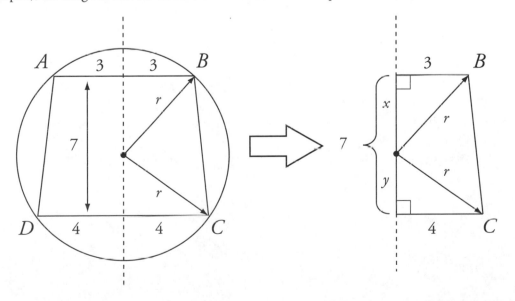

In order for the trapezoid vertices to lie on the circle, the trapezoid must be symmetrical about the dotted line, which passes through the center of the circle. Draw this vertical and the radii to points B and C to create two right triangles, allowing you to use the Pythagorean theorem.

In fact, you might play an educated hunch that the triangles are 3–4–5 common right triangles. This checks out: If hypotenuse r is 5, then each triangle has a 3 and 4 side. The unknown vertical sides are thus 4 and 3, which sum to 7 as they must.

Algebraically, set up the following equations from the picture:

$$x^2 + 3^2 = r^2$$
$$y^2 + 4^2 = r^2$$
$$x + y = 7$$

Setting the two equations for r^2 equal:

$$x^2 + 3^2 = y^2 + 4^2$$
$$x^2 - y^2 = 4^2 - 3^2$$
$$(x + y)(x - y) = 7$$

Since $(x + y)(x - y) = 7$, $(x - y) = 1$.

Solve for x and y:

$$+ \begin{array}{r} (x + y) = 7 \\ (x - y) = 1 \\ \hline 2x = 8 \\ x = 4 \\ y = 7 - x = 3 \end{array}$$

The radius of the circle is 5, because $r^2 = 3^2 + 4^2 = 25$.

The correct answer is **(B)**.

105. **(E)** $b + 2$: Manipulate:

$$9^y + 3^b = 10(3^b)$$
$$(3^2)^y + 3^b = 10(3^b)$$
$$(3^2)^y = 10(3^b) - 3^b$$
$$3^{2y} = 3^b(10 - 1)$$
$$3^{2y} = 3^b(3^2)$$
$$3^{2y} = 3^{b+2}$$
$$2y = b + 2$$

The correct answer is **(E)**.

106. (A): First, translate the question stem: Is $\pi r^2 \geq r$? Simplify:

Is $\pi r \geq 1$?
Is $r \geq 1/\pi$?

Note that the question is stated in yards, but the statements use feet, so convert the question stem to feet:

Is $r \geq 1/\pi$ yards?
If $r \geq 3/\pi$ feet?

(1) SUFFICIENT: $D > 2$ feet. Therefore, $r > 1$ foot. The value of $3/\pi$ is approximately $3/3.14$, or a little bit less than 1 so, yes, $r \geq 3/\pi$ feet.

(2) INSUFFICIENT: According to this statement, $\pi f^2 > 2f$. Simplify:

$\pi f^2 > 2f$
$\pi f > 2$
$f > 2/\pi$

In other words $f > 2/3.14$ or f is larger than approximately $2/3$. Therefore, f could be smaller than $3/\pi$ feet (just a bit smaller than 1) but it could also be larger.

The correct answer is **(A)**.

107. (A) 1: The problem indicates that:

$h(abc) = 3 \times h(def)$

$\dfrac{h(abc)}{h(def)} = 3$

$\dfrac{5^a 2^b 3^c}{5^d 2^e 3^f} = 3$

The number 3 has no factors of 5 or 2, so these factors must cancel out of the fraction on the left side, implying that $a = d$ and $b = e$.

That leaves $\dfrac{3^c}{3^f} = 3 = 3^{c-f}$, which implies that $c - f = 1$.

Since the only difference between abc and def is in the units digits, the difference between these three-digit numbers is equal to $c - f = 1$.

The correct answer is **(A)**.

108. **(D) $y = 2.5 \times 10^d$, where d is a positive integer:** Fractions that have only factors of 2 and 5 in the denominator equate to *terminating decimals*. Since $\dfrac{x}{y} = r.s\bar{s}\bar{s}$, a *non-terminating decimal*, y must contain some other prime factors besides just 2 and/or 5. Factor the answer choices to see whether any do not meet this criteria.

     (A) $y = 12, 120, 1{,}200$, etc. Prime factors of 12: (2)(2)(3)
     (B) $y = 15, 150, 1{,}500$, etc. Prime factors of 15: (3)(5)
     (C) $y = 18, 180, 1{,}800$, etc. Prime factors of 18: (2)(3)(3)
     (D) $y = 25, 250, 2{,}500$, etc. Prime factors of 25: (5)(5). CANNOT be true (only 5's and 2's)
     (E) $y = 27, 270, 2{,}700$, etc. Prime factors of 27: (3)(3)(3)

The correct answer is **(D)**.

109. **(E):** First, understand the function given in the question stem by thinking of some examples:

$16 @ 5 = 1$, since 16 divided by 5 leaves a remainder of 1.
$21 @ 3 = 0$, since 21 divided by 3 leaves a remainder of 0.
$17 @ 3 = 2$, since 17 divided by 3 leaves a remainder of 2.

(1) INSUFFICIENT: If a remainder of 1 is left when 81 is divided by x, then x divides evenly into 80. In other words, x is a factor of 80, but not of 81. Therefore, x could be 80 or any factor of 80, such as 40. Since there are multiple possible values for x, this statement is not sufficient.

(2) INSUFFICIENT: If a remainder of 0 is left when 40 is divided by x, then 40 divides evenly into x. Therefore, x could be any multiple of 40: 40, 80, 120, 160, etc.

(1) AND (2) INSUFFICIENT: x could be either 40 or 80, according to both statements.

The correct answer is **(E)**.

110. **(A) 12xy:** Draw overlapping circles in which to place the shared and non-shared *prime factors* of p and r. To find the least common multiple (LCM), multiply from left to right and include all the common factors in the product:

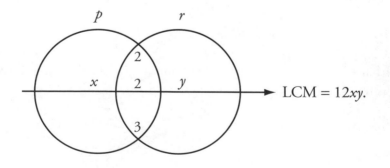

The correct answer is **(A)**.

Workout Set 12

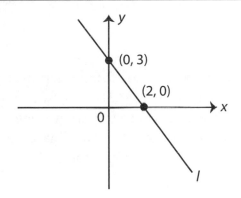

111. Which of the following equations represents a line parallel to line *l* in the figure above?

    (A) $2y - 3x = 0$
    (B) $2y + 3x = 0$
    (C) $2y - 3x = 6$
    (D) $3y + 2x = 6$
    (E) $3y - 2x = 9$

112. If $y = |x - 1|$ and $y = 3x + 3$, then x must be between which of the following values?

    (A) 2 and 3
    (B) 1 and 2
    (C) 0 and 1
    (D) −1 and 0
    (E) −2 and −1

113. An antiques dealer purchased three cabinets at three distinct costs last year and resold all three of those cabinets for three distinct prices this year. If the median price was received for the cabinet that cost the median amount, and the antiques dealer made a 10% profit on that cabinet, did the dealer make more than a 10% profit margin on any one of the three cabinet sales?

    (1) One of the cabinets sold for a price less than its original cost.
    (2) The cabinet that sold for the lowest price was the one that cost the antiques dealer the most to purchase.

9

|——————————————————— 1 mile stretch of highway ———————————————————|

black line   black line

114. A road crew painted two black lines across a road as shown in the figure above, to mark the start and end of a one-mile stretch. Between the two black lines, they will paint across the road a red line at each third of a mile, a white line at each fifth of a mile, and a blue line at each eighth of a mile. What is the smallest distance (in miles) between any of the painted lines on this stretch of highway?

   (A) 0

   (B) $\dfrac{1}{120}$

   (C) $\dfrac{1}{60}$

   (D) $\dfrac{1}{40}$

   (E) $\dfrac{1}{30}$

115. Set S consists of n consecutive integers, where $n > 1$. What is the value of n?

   (1) The sum of the integers in Set S is divisible by 7.
   (2) The sum of the integers in Set S is 14.

116. A trapezoid is symmetrical about a vertical center line. If a circle is drawn such that it is tangent to exactly three points on the trapezoid and is enclosed entirely within the trapezoid, what is the diameter of the circle?

   (1) The parallel sides of the trapezoid are 10 inches apart.
   (2) Of the parallel sides of the trapezoid, the shorter side is 15 inches long.

9

117. Three boys are ages 4, 6, and 7, respectively. Three girls are ages 5, 8, and 9, respectively. If two of the boys and two of the girls are randomly selected, and the sum of the selected children's ages is z, what is the difference between the probability that z is even and the probability that z is odd?

    (A) $\dfrac{1}{9}$

    (B) $\dfrac{1}{6}$

    (C) $\dfrac{2}{9}$

    (D) $\dfrac{1}{4}$

    (E) $\dfrac{1}{2}$

118. If the three unique positive digits A, B, and C are arranged in all possible sequences (ABC, ACB, BAC, etc ...), then the sum of all the resulting three-digit integers must be divisible by each of the following EXCEPT

    (A) 2
    (B) 3
    (C) 6
    (D) 11
    (E) 37

119. Positive integers a and b are less than or equal to 9. If a and b are assembled into the six-digit number $ababab$, which of the following must be a factor of $ababab$?

    (A) 3
    (B) 4
    (C) 5
    (D) 6
    (E) none of the above

120. The two-digit positive integer s is the sum of the two-digit positive integers m and n. Is the units digit of s less than the units digit of m?

    (1) The units digit of s is less than the units digit of n.
    (2) The tens digit of s is not equal to the sum of the tens digits of m and n.

Workout Set 12 Answer Key

111.　(B)
112.　(D)
113.　(B)
114.　(D)
115.　(E)
116.　(C)
117.　(A)
118.　(D)
119.　(A)
120.　(D)

9

Workout Set 12 Solutions

111. **(B) $2y + 3x = 0$:** Parallel lines have the same slope. The slope of line l is $\dfrac{\text{rise}}{\text{run}} = \dfrac{\text{change in } y}{\text{change in } x} = \dfrac{0-3}{2-0} = -\dfrac{3}{2}$.

Work Backwards from the answers by rearranging into slope-intercept form: $y = mx + b$ form, where the slope is m. Since only one answer can be correct, only one answer will have a slope of $-\dfrac{3}{2}$; stop when you find the one with the matching slope.

(A) $2y = 3x$	$y = \dfrac{3}{2}x$	Slope $= \dfrac{3}{2}$ INCORRECT
(B) $2y = -3x$	$y = \dfrac{-3}{2}x$	Slope $= -\dfrac{3}{2}$ CORRECT

Alternatively, use the slope to write the equation, manipulate, and look for a match:

$y = (-3/2)x + b$
$2y = -3x + b$

Only answer (B) is a match for the x and y portions.

The correct answer is **(B)**.

112. **(D) -1 and 0:** Set the two equations for y equal and algebraically solve $|x - 1| = 3x + 3$ for x. This requires two solutions: one for the case that $x - 1$ is positive, the other for the case that $x - 1$ is negative:

$x - 1$ is positive:	$x - 1$ is negative:
$(x - 1) = 3x + 3$	$-(x - 1) = 3x + 3$
$-4 = 2x$	$-x + 1 = 3x + 3$
$-2 = x$	$-2 = x$
	$-\dfrac{2}{4} = -\dfrac{1}{2} = x$

In the $x - 1$ is positive case, the answer is $x = -2$. In this case, $x - 1$ is not actually positive, so this is a false case. Discard it. As a result, there is only *one* solution: $x = -\dfrac{1}{2}$.

The correct answer is **(D)**.

113. **(B):** Call the cabinets A, B, and C, with the understanding that A cost the least and C cost the most for the dealer to purchase. The median cabinet, B, not only cost the median amount, but also was sold for the median revenue. The profit on B was 10%, so *Choose a Smart Number* and say that B cost $100 and was sold for $110. Select values for A and C relative to these values.

(1) INSUFFICIENT: Cabinet B was sold for a profit, so only cabinets A or C could have sold for less than its original cost. Try to come up with two cases: one that shows 10% was the greatest margin, and one that shows a margin greater than 10%.

Case 1: *C* sold for less than its cost, but *A* has a profit margin greater than 10%.

	A	*B*	*C*
Cost	$50	$100	$150
Revenue	$75	$110	$120
Profit margin	50%	10%	−20%

Case 2: *A* sold for less than its cost, and the maximum profit margin is 10%.

	A	*B*	*C*
Cost	$50	$100	$150
Revenue	$25	$110	$160
Profit margin	−50%	10%	<10%

It is uncertain whether the dealer made more than 10% on any one of the three cabinet sales.

(2) SUFFICIENT: Cabinet *C* sold for the least money, which implies that cabinet *A* sold for the most, because cabinet *B*'s revenue was in the middle. Relate both of these revenue possibilities to the smart number of $110 for *B*'s revenue. Put the numbers into a chart:

	A	*B*	*C*
Cost	less than $100	$100	more than $100
Revenue	more than $110	$110	less than $110
Profit margin	>10%	10%	<10%

In words, this statement indicates that the dealer paid less for *A* and sold it for more (relative to *B*), so he made a greater profit on *A* than *B*. The dealer definitely made a profit greater than 10% on the sale of one of the cabinets.

The correct answer is **(B)**.

114. **(D)** $\frac{1}{40}$: When comparing fractional pieces of a whole, find a common denominator. In this case, the one-mile stretch is divided into thirds, fifths, and eighths. The smallest common denominator of 3, 5, and 8 is 120. If the one-mile highway is divided into 120 equal increments, where will the red, white, and blue marks fall?

Red (thirds): 40, 80 (out of 120 increments)

White (fifths): 24, 48, 72, 96 (out of 120 increments)

Blue (eighths): 15, 30, 45, 60, 75, 90, 105 (out of 120 increments)

The smallest distance between two marks is 75 − 72 = 3 or 48 − 45 = 3. This equates to 3/120, or 1/40 miles.

The correct answer is **(D)**.

115. **(E):** Both statements provide information about the sum of the set, so rephrase with this in mind:

> Sum of Consecutive Set = (Median)(Number of Terms)
> Sum of Consecutive Set = (Median)(n)

For n = odd, the median is the middle term, an integer. For n = even, the median is the average of the two middle terms, a non-integer of the form "integer + 0.5." You can determine n if you can determine both the median of Set S and the sum of the integers in Set S.

Next, glance at the statements. Statement (2) is actually a subset of statement (1): if the sum is exactly 14, then the sum is divisible by 7. As a result, the answer can't be (A), because if statement (1) is sufficient, then statement (2) would also have to be sufficient. The answer also can't be (C), because statement (2) doesn't add new information to statement (1). Cross off answers (A) and (C) and start with statement (2).

(2) INSUFFICIENT: Since n must be an integer, use divisibility rules to narrow down possible median values.

$$\text{Sum of Consecutive Set} = (\text{Median})(n)$$
$$14 = (\text{Median})(n)$$
$$(2)(7) = (\text{Median})(n)$$

Check some possible median and n values (remember that $n > 1$):

> $n = 2$ and Median = 7: Set S can't have an integer median if there are only 2 terms. IGNORE.
> $n = 7$ and Median = 2: Set S is {−1, 0, 1, 2, 3, 4, 5}, which has a sum of 14. OK.
> $n = 4$ and Median = 3.5: Set S is {2, 3, 4, 5}, which has a sum of 14. OK.

There are at least two possible values for n.

(1) INSUFFICIENT: The two possible cases for statement (2) also apply to statement (1), since the numbers chosen for statement (2) must also work in statement (1).

(1) AND (2) INSUFFICIENT: As noted, the final two cases tested for statement (2) are also allowed by statement (1), so there are still at least two possible values for n.

The correct answer is **(E)**.

9

116. **(C):** There are four basic ways this picture could look, as there are four sides of the trapezoid that could serve as the non-tangent side:

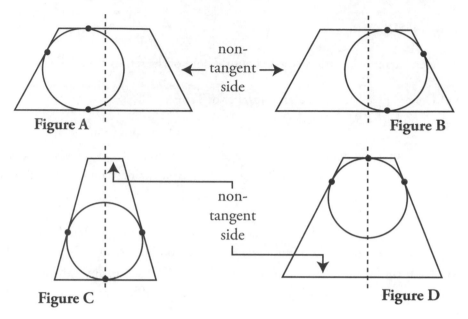

(1) INSUFFICIENT: If the circle is tangent to both of the parallel sides (Figure A or B), then the diameter must be 10. If the circle is tangent to only one of the parallel sides (Figure C or D), then the diameter is less than 10. Since there are multiple possibilities for the diameter of the circle, statement (1) does not contain enough information to answer the original question.

(2) INSUFFICIENT: Just knowing the length of the shorter parallel side is not enough to determine which of the basic figures above describes the correct situation. If Figure A or B represents the correct situation, the diameter of the circle is determined solely by the distance between the parallel sides; the diameter is independent of the length of the shorter parallel side. If Figure C or D describes the correct situation, then the diameter would depend on not only the 15-inch side but also the longer parallel side, which has an unknown length.

(1) AND (2) SUFFICIENT: In Figures C and D, the diameter must be less than 10 but also greater than the length of the smaller parallel side. If the length of the smaller parallel side is 15, then the diameter would have to be greater than 15 for Figures C and D, but this is impossible (since the diameter has to be less than 10). Therefore, Figure A or B represents the correct situation and the diameter of the circle must equal 10.

Alternatively, notice that Figure D could not represent the situation, since the circle would have to have a diameter larger than 15 inches in order to be tangent to the short parallel side and the non-parallel sides of the trapezoid. The parallel sides of the trapezoid are only 10 inches apart, so the circle would be too large to be drawn entirely within the trapezoid as required. Similar logic explains why Figure C is also impossible when considering (1) and (2) together.

The correct answer is **(C)**.

117. **(A)** $\frac{1}{9}$: List the possible cases. Wherever possible, avoid computing: use *Odd & Even* principles to reduce your computation.

Boys	Girls	Sum *z*
4, 6 = even	5, 8 = odd	E + O = O
4, 6 = even	5, 9 = even	E + E = E
4, 6 = even	8, 9 = odd	E + O = O
4, 7 = odd	5, 8 = odd	O + O = E
4, 7 = odd	5, 9 = even	O + E = O
4, 7 = odd	8, 9 = odd	O + O = E
6, 7 = odd	5, 8 = odd	O + O = E
6, 7 = odd	5, 9 = even	O + E = O
6, 7 = odd	8, 9 = odd	O + O = E

Of the 9 scenarios listed, 5 yield an even *z* and 4 yield an odd *z*.

The difference between the probability that *z* is even and the probability that *z* is odd is therefore $5/9 - 4/9 = 1/9$.

The correct answer is **(A)**.

118. **(D)** 11: First, consider a random three-digit number as an example: $375 = 100(3) + 10(7) + 1(5)$, because 3 is in the hundreds place, 7 is in the tens place, and 5 is in the ones place. More generally, $ABC = 100(A) + 10(B) + 1(C)$. For digit problems, particularly those that involve "shuffling" or permutations of digits, think about place value.

Since there are three unique digits, the number of possible sequences will be 3! or 6. Write them out to see a pattern:

ABC
ACB
BAC
BCA
CAB
CBA

Notice that each unique digit appears exactly twice in each column, so each column individually sums to $2(A + B + C)$.

Sum of the hundreds column: $100 \times 2(A + B + C) = 200(A + B + C)$
Sum of the tens column: $100 \times 2(A + B + C) = 20(A + B + C)$
Sum of the ones column: $1 \times 2(A + B + C) = 2(A + B + C)$
Altogether, the sum of the three-digit numbers is $(200 + 20 + 2)(A + B + C) = 222(A + B + C)$.

Regardless of the values of *A*, *B*, and *C*, the sum of the three-digit numbers must be divisible by 222 and all of its factors: 1, 2, 3, 6, 37, 74, 111, and 222. The only answer choice that is not among these is 11.

The correct answer is **(D)**.

119. **(A) 3:** This problem is most efficiently solved by *Working Backwards* from the answers.

(A)   3: The sum of the digits of *ababab* is 3(*a* + *b*). This must be a multiple of 3.
      On the test, stop here and select answer (A). Below, you'll find explanations for the other answers.

(B)   4: An integer is divisible by 4 if its last two digits represent a two-digit number that is itself divisible by 4. It is uncertain whether the two-digit integer *ab* is divisible by 4.

(C)   5: An integer is divisible by 5 if the last digit is 0 or 5. It is uncertain whether the positive integer *b* is 5.

(D)   6: An integer is divisible by 6 if it is even and divisible by 3. Answer (A) established that *ababab* is divisible by 3, but it is uncertain whether the last digit *b* is even, a requirement for *ababab* to be even. Note that you can also use logic to eliminate this answer. If *ababab* were divisible by 6, it would also have to be divisible by 3, but that would lead to two correct answers!

The correct answer is **(A)**.

120. **(D):** Try out a few randomly-chosen numbers to help you understand the question.

If *m* = 10 and *n* = 10, then *s* = 20 and the units digits of *m* and *s* are equal.
If *m* = 11 and *n* = 12, then *s* = 23 and the units digit of *s* is greater than the units digit of *m*.
If *m* = 19 and *n* = 11, then *s* = 30 and the units digit of *s* is less than the units digit of *m*.

What's going on with all of these cases? Basically, if the units digits of *m* and *n* are small enough, then the units digit of *s* will be equal to or greater than the units digit of *m* (and of *n*).

On the other hand, if the units digits of *m* and *n* are large enough to cause you to "carry over" a 1 to the tens digit, then the units digit of *s* will end up being smaller than the units digit of *m* (and of *n*).

(1) SUFFICIENT: If the units digit of *s* is definitely less than the units digits of one of the smaller numbers, then the "carry over" situation must apply, in which case the units digits of both *m* and *n* must be larger than the units digit of *s*.

(2) SUFFICIENT: There are only two ways in which the tens digit will not equal the tens digits of the two smaller numbers:

Case 1: The tens digits of the two smaller numbers result in a number that needs to carry over into the hundreds digit. This is impossible for this problem because *s* is also a two-digit number.

Case 2: The units digits of the two smaller numbers result in a number that carries over into the tens digit. This must be what is happening in this case. If so, then the units digit of the larger number, *s*, must be smaller than the units digits of the two smaller numbers, *m* and *n*.

The correct answer is **(D)**.

Workout Set 13

121. If $p^2 - 13p + 40 = q$, and p is equally likely to be *any* positive integer between 1 and 10, inclusive, what is the probability that $q < 0$?

    (A) $\dfrac{1}{10}$

    (B) $\dfrac{1}{5}$

    (C) $\dfrac{2}{5}$

    (D) $\dfrac{3}{5}$

    (E) $\dfrac{3}{10}$

122. If the number 200! is written in the form $p \times 10^q$, where p and q are integers, what is the maximum possible value of q?

    (A) 40
    (B) 48
    (C) 49
    (D) 55
    (E) 64

123. If x and y are integers, and $x \neq 0$, what is the value of x^y?

    (1) $|x| = 2$
    (2) $64^x 6^{2x+y} = 48^{2x}$

124. The three sides of a triangle have lengths p, q, and r, each an integer. Is this triangle a right triangle?

    (1) The perimeter of the triangle is an odd integer.
    (2) If the triangle's area is doubled, the result is not an integer.

125. If x is positive, what is the least possible value of $\dfrac{x}{2} + \dfrac{2}{x}$?

    (A) $\dfrac{1}{2}$

    (B) 1
    (C) 2
    (D) 3
    (E) 4

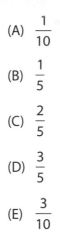

126. The average (arithmetic mean) cost of three computer models is $900. If no two computers cost the same amount, does the most expensive model cost more than $1,000?

    (1)   The most expensive model costs 25% more than the model with the median cost.
    (2)   The most expensive model costs $210 more than the model with the median cost.

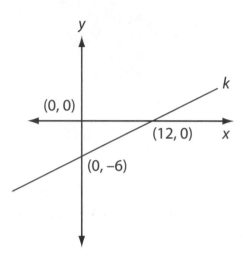

127. Which of the following equations represents a line perpendicular to line k in the figure above?

    (A) $3y + 2x = -12$
    (B) $2y + x = 0$
    (C) $2y - x = 0$
    (D) $y + 2x = 12$
    (E) $y - 2x = 12$

128. Is $x > 0$?

    (1) $|2x - 12| < 10$
    (2) $x^2 - 10x \geq -21$

129. K-numbers are positive integers with only 2's as their digits. For example, 2, 22, and 222 are K-numbers. The K-weight of a number n is the minimum number of K-numbers that must be added together to equal n. For example, the K-weight of 50 is 5, because $50 = 22 + 22 + 2 + 2 + 2$. What is the K-weight of 600?

    (A) 10
    (B) 11
    (C) 12
    (D) 13
    (E) 14

130. If the reciprocals of two consecutive positive integers are added together, what is the sum in terms of the greater integer x?

   (A) $\dfrac{3}{x}$

   (B) $x^2 - x$

   (C) $2x - 1$

   (D) $\dfrac{2x-1}{x^2+x}$

   (E) $\dfrac{2x-1}{x^2-x}$

9

Workout Set 13 Answer Key

121. (B)
122. (C)
123. (B)
124. (D)
125. (C)
126. (D)
127. (D)
128. (A)
129. (A)
130. (E)

9

Workout Set 13 Solutions

121. **(B)** $\dfrac{1}{5}$: Factor the quadratic:

$$p^2 - 13p + 40 = q$$
$$(p - 8)(p - 5) = q$$

For $p = 5$ and $p = 8$, $q = 0$. Between $p = 5$ and $p = 8$, q is negative, as $(p - 8)$ is negative and $(p - 5)$ is positive. With a total of 10 possible integer p values, only two ($p = 6$ and $p = 7$) fall in the range $5 < p < 8$, so the probability is 2/10 or 1/5.

The correct answer is **(B)**.

122. **(C) 49:** To maximize the value of q, you would need to constrain p to NOT be a multiple of 10. In other words, q should count *every* factor of 10 in 200!, and p would be the product of the remaining factors of 200!.

To count factors of 10 in 200!, you could start by counting the multiples of 10 between 1 and 200, inclusive. But this method would undercount the number of 10's that are factors of 200! because it would miss other pairs that can create 10, such as:

> 200! has 2 and 5 as factors, which multiply to 10, and thus another factor of 10.
> 200! has 6 and 15 as factors, which multiply to 90, and thus another factor of 10.

Therefore, this problem is really about counting the number of 2×5 factor pairs that can be made from the factors of 200.

Of 2 and 5, there will be fewer 5's overall, so count the number of 5's found among the factors of 200!:

	Number of multiples between 1 and 200, inclusive
Multiples of 5 ($= 5^1$)	200/5 = 40
Multiples of 25 ($= 5^2$)	200/25 = 8
Multiples of 125 ($= 5^3$)	125 is the only one: 1

The higher multiples contribute *more than one* factor of 5 to the total.

There are eight multiples of 25 in the range (namely, 25, 50, 75, 100, 125, 150, 175, and 200). Each of these is also a multiple of 5, so each has already been counted once, and thus each of the eight multiples of 25 contributes one *additional* factor of 5. Finally, 125 contributes a total of three 5's to the count—but two have already been counted, leaving only one *additional* factor of 5 to include.

Therefore, the prime factorization for 200! includes $40 + 8 + 1 = 49$ factors of 5.

The correct answer is **(C)**.

123. **(B):** Since $x \neq 0$, x^y does not equal 0^y or 0.

(1) INSUFFICIENT: This statement indicates that x is equal to 2 or -2. The statement indicates nothing about y.

(2) SUFFICIENT: Simplify using exponent rules, noting the common factors of 6 and 8 on each side of the equation:

$$64^x 6^{2x+y} = 48^{2x}$$
$$(8^2)^x 6^{2x+y} = (6 \times 8)^{2x}$$
$$8^{2x} 6^{2x} 6^y = 6^{2x} 8^{2x}$$
$$6^y = 1$$
$$y = 0$$

Since $y = 0$ and $x \neq 0$ (as stated in the question stem), this information is sufficient to conclude that $x^y = x^0 = 1$.

The correct answer is **(B)**.

124. **(D):** The question stem specifies that the triangle's sides all have integer lengths.

(1) SUFFICIENT: Perimeter is calculated by summing the three side lengths. In order for that sum to be odd, either all three numbers have to be odd or one of the three numbers has to be odd:

$$O + O + O = \text{odd}$$
$$O + E + E = \text{odd}$$

If the triangle is a right triangle, then the Pythagorean theorem ($a^2 + b^2 = c^2$) holds. If all three side lengths are odd, this would mean odd^2 + odd^2 = odd^2. This is impossible, however; odd + odd = even.

If one side length is odd and the other two are even, then there are two possibilities:

$$\text{odd}^2 + \text{even}^2 = \text{even}^2 \text{ (impossible: odd + even = odd)}$$
$$\text{even}^2 + \text{even}^2 = \text{odd}^2 \text{ (also impossible: even + even = even)}$$

Every "right triangle" possibility is impossible, so the triangle cannot be a right triangle.

(2) SUFFICIENT: $A = \dfrac{1}{2}bh$, or $2A = bh$. If, as this statement indicates, $2A$ is not an integer, then A itself is not an integer. As a result, at least one of b and h is also not an integer.

For right triangles, b and h are the two shorter sides of the triangle. The question stem specifies that all three sides are integers, so if the triangle were a right triangle, then b and h would both have to be integers. This is impossible, so the triangle cannot be a right triangle.

The correct answer is **(D)**.

125. **(C):** The problem specifies that x has to be positive, so try some small positive integers to see how the expression $\frac{x}{2} + \frac{2}{x}$ works.

If $x = 1$, then the expression becomes $1/2 + 2 = 2.5$. If $x = 2$, then the expression becomes $1 + 1 = 2$. Since x can equal 2, eliminate answers (D) and (E).

What if x is a fraction, such as 1/2? In that case, the expression becomes $\frac{\frac{1}{2}}{2} + \frac{2}{\frac{1}{2}}$ or $\frac{1}{4} + 4$ ... interesting. It's even bigger than the integer options above. How come?

The expressions $\frac{x}{2}$ and $\frac{2}{x}$ are reciprocals of each other. As long as x is positive, there are two broad scenarios possible:

(1) If one expression is less than 1, then the other has to be greater than 1;

(2) If one expression equals 1, then the other also equals 1.

Answers (A) and (B), then, are impossible.

The correct answer is **(C)**.

126. **(D):** If the average of the cost of the three models is $900, then the sum is $2,700. Call the three models a, b, and c, in order from least expensive to most.

(1) SUFFICIENT: The statement indicates that $c = 1.25b$, so $a + b + 1.25b = 2,700$. This isn't enough to solve for specific values, but it might be enough to tell whether $c > \$1,000$. Keep working.

$$a + b + 1.25b = \$2,700$$
$$a + 2.25b = \$2,700$$

By definition, $a < b$, so plug LTb (less than b) into the equation for a:

$$\text{LT}b + 2.25b = 2,700$$

$$\text{LT}3.25b = 2,700$$

$$\text{LT}b = \frac{2,700}{3.25}$$

$$\text{LT}b - \frac{2,700}{\frac{13}{4}}$$

$$\text{LT}b = 2,700\left(\frac{4}{13}\right)$$

From here, estimate: 13 goes into 2,600 a total of 200 times, and it goes into 100 approximately 7 times. Therefore, LT$b = (207)(4) = 828$.

If b is approximately 830, then 125% of b is definitely larger than 1,000. Therefore, the most expensive model does cost more than \$1,000.

(2) SUFFICIENT: Follow a similar path: $c = b + 210$.

$$LTb + b + (b + 210) = 2{,}700$$
$$LTb + 2b = 2{,}490$$
$$LT3b = 2{,}490$$
$$LTb = 830$$

If b is a bit more than 830, then $b + 210$ is definitely over 1,000. Therefore, the most expensive model does cost more than \$1,000.

The correct answer is **(D)**.

127. **(D):** The product of the slopes of two perpendicular lines is -1. The slope of line k is:

$$\frac{\text{rise}}{\text{run}} = \frac{\text{change in } y}{\text{change in } x} = \frac{0 - (-6)}{12 - 0} = \frac{6}{12} = \frac{1}{2}.$$

Thus, the slope of a line perpendicular to k is -2.

Use the desired slope to create a slope-intercept equation and look for a match among the answers:

$$y = -2x + b$$
$$y + 2x = b$$

Only answer (D) offers a match for the left side of the equation.

Alternatively, put each choice in slope-intercept form: $y = mx + b$, where the slope is m. Stop when you find the right answer.

(A) $3y + 2x = -12$	$y = \dfrac{-2}{3}x - 4$	Slope $= -\dfrac{2}{3}$	INCORRECT
(B) $2y + x = 0$	$y = \dfrac{-1}{2}x$	Slope $= -\dfrac{1}{2}$	INCORRECT
(C) $2y - x = 0$	$y = \dfrac{1}{2}x$	Slope $= \dfrac{1}{2}$	INCORRECT
(D) $y + 2x = 12$	$y = -2x + 12$	Slope $= -2$	CORRECT

The correct answer is **(D)**.

128. (A):

(1) SUFFICIENT: Manipulate the absolute value expression to represent this inequality on a number line:

$$|2x - 12| < 10$$
$$|2(x - 6)| < 10$$
$$2|x - 6| < 10$$
$$|x - 6| < 5$$

This can be interpreted as "The distance between x and 6 is less than 5." On a number line, this is the region between 1 and 11:

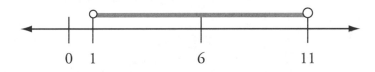

All possible values for x are positive, so the answer to the question is a definite "Yes."

(2) INSUFFICIENT: Manipulate the inequality to get 0 on one side, then factor the resulting quadratic:

$$x^2 - 10x \geq -21$$
$$x^2 - 10x + 21 \geq 0$$
$$(x - 7)(x - 3) \geq 0$$

The factored quadratic on the left side will equal 0 when $x = 3$ and 7. These are the boundary points. On a number line, check the regions on either side of these boundary points to determine the valid region(s) for x:

Note that when $3 < x < 7$, $(x - 7)(x - 3) =$ (neg)(pos) = neg.

Since both positive and negative values are possible for x, the answer is "Maybe."

The correct answer is **(A)**.

129. (A): Since you are looking for the *minimum* number of *K*-numbers that sum to 600, a practical place to start is with the *largest K*-number less than 600, or 222. There are between two and three multiples of 222 in 600, so subtract out the two whole multiples!

$$\begin{array}{r} 600 \\ \underline{-444} \, (= 2 \times 222) \\ 156 \end{array}$$

9

Now, the next largest *K*-number is 22. Again subtract as many whole multiples as possible:

$$\begin{array}{r} 156 \\ -\,154 \ (= 7 \times 22) \\ \hline 2 \end{array}$$

The next largest *K*-number is obviously 2:

$$\begin{array}{r} 2 \\ -\,2 \ (= 1 \times 2) \\ \hline 0 \end{array}$$

Thus, $600 = 222(2) + 22(7) + 2(1)$, and the *K*-weight of 600 is $2 + 7 + 1 = 10$.

The correct answer is **(A)**.

130. **(E):** If the greater of the two integers is x, then the two integers can be expressed as $x - 1$ and x. The sum of the reciprocals would therefore be:

$$\frac{1}{x-1} + \frac{1}{x} = \frac{x + (x-1)}{(x-1)x}$$

$$= \frac{2x-1}{x^2-x}$$

Alternatively, *Choose Smart Numbers*. For example, let the larger number $x = 3$. The smaller number would therefore be $3 - 1 = 2$. The sum of the reciprocals would be:

$$\frac{1}{3} + \frac{1}{2} = \frac{2}{6} + \frac{3}{6} = \frac{5}{6}$$

Plug $x = 3$ into the answers and find the one that equals $\dfrac{5}{6}$.

(A) $\dfrac{3}{x} = \dfrac{3}{3} = 1$

(B) $x^2 - x =$ an integer, not a fraction

(C) $2x - 1 =$ an integer, not a fraction

(D) $\dfrac{2x-1}{x^2+x} = \dfrac{5}{9+3} = \dfrac{5}{12}$

(E) $\dfrac{2x-1}{x^2-x} = \dfrac{6-1}{9-3} = \dfrac{5}{6}$

The correct answer is **(E)**.

9

Workout Set 14

131. The sequence A is defined by the following relationship: $A_n = A_{n-1} + (-1)^{n+1}(n^2)$ for all integer values $n > 1$. If $A_1 = 1$, what is $A_{15} - A_{13}$?

    (A)   14
    (B)   29
    (C)   169
    (D)   196
    (E)   421

132. If d represents the hundredths digit and e represents the thousandths digit in the decimal $0.4de$, what is the value of this decimal rounded to the nearest tenth?

    (1) $d - e$ is a positive perfect square.
    (2) $\sqrt{d} > e^2$

133. If n is a three-digit positive integer, what is the tens digit of n?

    (1)   Dividing n by 4 gives the same remainder as does dividing n by 25.
    (2)   Dividing n by 16 gives the same remainder as does dividing n by 25.

134. A chain is comprised of 10 identical links, each of which independently has a 1% chance of breaking under a certain load. If the failure of any individual link means the failure of the entire chain, what is the probability that the chain will fail under the load?

    (A) $(0.01)^{10}$
    (B) $10(0.01)^{10}$
    (C) $1 - (0.10)(0.99)^{10}$
    (D) $1 - (0.99)^{10}$
    (E) $1 - (0.99)^{(10 \times 9)}$

135. If y^4 is divisible by 60, what is the minimum number of distinct factors that positive integer y must have?

    (A)   2
    (B)   6
    (C)   8
    (D)   10
    (E)   12

9

136. Are the positive integers x and y consecutive?

    (1) $x^2 - y^2 = 2y + 1$
    (2) $x^2 - xy - x = 0$

137. What is the value of $y - x^2 - x$?

    (1) $y = -3x$
    (2) $y = -4(x + 1)$

138. The vertical position of an object can be approximated at any given time by the function $p(t) = rt - 5t^2 + b$, where $p(t)$ is the vertical position in meters, t is the time in seconds, and r and b are constants. If $p(2) = 41$ and $p(5) = 26$, what is $p(4)$?

    (A) 24
    (B) 26
    (C) 39
    (D) 41
    (E) 45

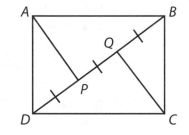

139. In the figure above, $ABCD$ is a rectangle, and each of AP and CQ is perpendicular to BD. If $DP = PQ = QB$, what is the ratio of AB to AD?

    (A) $\sqrt{2}$ to 1
    (B) $\sqrt{3}$ to 1
    (C) $\sqrt{3}$ to $\sqrt{2}$
    (D) 2 to 1
    (E) 2 to $\sqrt{3}$

9

MANHATTAN
PREP

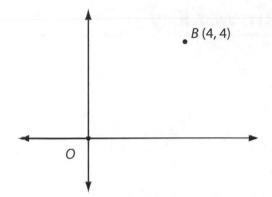

140. In the rectangular coordinate system above, if point *A* (not shown) is equidistant from points *O* and *B* and the area of triangle *OAB* is 16, which of the following are the possible coordinates of point *A*?

    (A) (−2, 6)
    (B) (0, 4)
    (C) (2, −6)
    (D) (2, 6)
    (E) (4, 0)

Workout Set 14 Answer Key

131.   (B)
132.   (E)
133.   (A)
134.   (D)
135.   (C)
136.   (D)
137.   (C)
138.   (D)
139.   (A)
140.   (A)

Workout Set 14 Solutions

131. **(B) 29:** Generate the first several values of the sequence, using the given relationship. Notice that a component such as $(-1)^{n+1}$ simply switches the sign of the additive term back and forth. Use a table to keep your work organized:

n	$A_n = A_{n-1} + (-1)^{n+1}(n^2)$
1	1
2	$1 + (-1)^{2+1}(2^2) = 1 - 4 = -3$
3	$-3 + (-1)^{3+1}(3^2) = -3 + 9 = 6$
4	$6 + (-1)^{4+1}(4^2) = 6 - 16 = -10$
5	$-10 + (-1)^{5+1}(5^2) = -10 + 25 = 15$
6	$15 + (-1)^{6+1}(6^2) = -15 - 36 = -21$

What is the pattern? The sign alternates between positive and negative. Ignoring the sign of the terms (taking absolute values) might help to determine the full pattern:

n	$A_n = A_{n-1} + (-1)^{n+1}(n^2)$	$|A_n|$	Change from previous term
1	1	1	
2	-3	3	$+2$
3	6	6	$+3$
4	-10	10	$+4$
5	15	15	$+5$
6	-21	21	$+6$

That is, the absolute value of each term equals the absolute value of the previous term plus n. Following this pattern, $|A_{15}|$ is 15 greater than $|A_{14}|$, and $|A_{14}|$ is 14 greater than $|A_{13}|$. Thus, $|A_{15}| - |A_{13}| = +15 + 14 = 29$.

Since the odd-numbered terms in the original sequence are positive, the absolute value of any odd-numbered term equals the term itself, so $|A_{15}| - |A_{13}| = A_{15} - A_{13} = 29$.

The correct answer is **(B)**.

132. **(E):** When rounding to the nearest tenth, use the hundredths digit, or d in this case. If $d \geq 5$, the decimal $0.4de$ is rounded up to 0.5. If $d \leq 4$, the decimal $0.4de$ is rounded down to 0.4. Thus, a rephrase of this question is "Is $d < 5$ (or, equivalently, is $d \geq 5$)?"

(1) INSUFFICIENT: Since $d - e$ is positive, $d > e$. Since d and e are digits (i.e., 0, 1, 2, ..., 7, 8, 9), there is a maximum value for the difference: $d - e \leq 9$. There are only three perfect squares less than or equal to 9: $d - e = 1$, 4, or 9:

d	e	$d - e = $ **perfect square**	**Is $d < 5$?**
9	0	$9 - 0 = 9$ ✓	No
1	0	$1 - 0 = 1$ ✓	Yes

It is possible for d to round up or down, so this statement isn't sufficient.

(2) INSUFFICIENT: Since d and e are positive, you can square each side of the inequality without worrying about flipping the sign: $d > e^4$. Since d and e are digits (i.e., 0, 1, 2, ..., 7, 8, 9), $9 \geq d > e^4$, which means that e can only be 0 or 1. (Note that $2^4 = 16$, which is too large.) Test cases again; whenever possible, reuse numbers that you tried in the last statement, assuming those numbers are allowed by the new statement.

d	e	$\sqrt{d} > e^2$	**Is $d < 5$?**
9	0	$3 > 0$ ✓	No
1	0	$\sqrt{1} > 0$ ✓	Yes

It is again possible for d to round up or down, so this statement isn't sufficient.

(1) AND (2) INSUFFICIENT: Taking both statements together, e must be 0 or 1 and that $d - e$ is equal to 9, 4 or 1.

You've already tested the $d = 9$ and $d = 1$ scenarios for both of the statements individually, so you don't need to re-test them here. Even together, the two statements allow d to round up or down.

The correct answer is **(E)**.

133. **(A):** The question asks only for the tens digit of n, not the value of n. It would be enough to know that the tens digit is consistently the same number, even if n could be multiple numbers.

(1) SUFFICIENT: Dividing by 4 allows four possible remainders: 0, 1, 2, or 3. Dividing by 25 would allow remainders from 0 to 24, but only the remainders 0, 1, 2, and 3 are applicable, since n also has to be divided by 4.

Call the common remainder r. You can express n in two ways:

$n = r +$ a multiple of 4, and
$n = r +$ a multiple of 25

In other words $n - r$ is a multiple of both 4 and 25, or $n - r$ is a multiple of 100.

$n - r =$ a multiple of 100
$n =$ a multiple of $100 + r$

Because r can be 0, 1, 2, or 3, n could be 100, 101, 102, or 103. It could also be 200, 201, 202, or 203, and so on, up to 900, 901, 902, and 903. In all cases, the tens digit of n is 0.

(2) INSUFFICIENT: Dividing by 16 allows sixteen possible remainders: 0, 1, 2, ... 15. Using the same reasoning as for statement (1), $n - r +$ a multiple of (16)(25), or $n - r$ is a multiple of 400. Again using the same reasoning, $n =$ multiple of $400 + r$, and $0 \leq r \leq 15$, so n could be 401, 402, ... 415. The tens digit could be 0 or 1.

The correct answer is **(A)**.

134. **(D)** $1 - (0.99)^{10}$: Qualitatively, many failure scenarios could occur:

- None of the links will fail.
- Exactly one of the links will fail.
- Exactly two of the links will fail.
- etc.

Given the complexity of the failure scenarios, it is easier to look at the opposite scenario:

probability that at least one link will fail $= 1 -$ probability that <u>no</u> links will fail

For each of the links, the probability that it will not fail is $1 - 0.01 = 0.99$. The probability that all 10 will not fail is thus $(0.99)^{10}$, since the probability that all 10 will not fail equals the product of the probabilities of the individual links not failing.

Therefore, the probability that at least one link will fail $= 1 - (0.99)^{10}$.

The correct answer is **(D)**.

135. **(C) 8:** The prime factorization of 60 is $(2)(2)(3)(5) = 2^2 3^1 5^1$. Thus, $y^4 = 2^2 3^1 5^1 x$, where x is some integer.

Assign the factors of y^4 to the prime boxes of y to see what the factors of y could be:

y^4			
y	y	y	y
2	2	(2)	(2)
3	(3)	(3)	(3)
5	(5)	(5)	(5)
?	?	?	?

The prime factors in parentheses above are factors not explicitly given for y^4, but which must exist. y^4 is the 4th power of an integer, which must have must have "quadruples" of the prime factors of y. Since y^4 has a factor of 2^2, y has a factor of 2. Since y^4 has factors of 3 and 5 among its factors, y has factors of 3 and 5.

Thus y is a multiple of $(2)(3)(5) = 30$, and at the very least y has 1, 2, 3, 5, 6, 10, 15, and 30 as factors, or at least eight distinct factors.

Alternatively, you could use the exponent method of calculating the number of factors:

y contains $(2^1)(3^1)(5^1)$. There are two ways to include a factor of 2: 2^0 and 2^1. There are also two ways to include a factor of 3 and two ways to include a factor of 5. There are, therefore $2 \times 2 \times 2 = 8$ different ways to combine the possible factors.

The correct answer is **(C)**.

136. **(D):** Consecutive integers differ by exactly 1. For x and y to be consecutive, either $x = y + 1$ or $x = y - 1$. Rephrase the question as, "Does x equal either $(y + 1)$ or $(y - 1)$?"

(1) SUFFICIENT: There's only one term with x but a couple with y, so it is easiest to solve for x:

$$x^2 - y^2 = 2y + 1$$
$$x^2 = y^2 + 2y + 1$$
$$x^2 = (y + 1)^2$$
$$\sqrt{x^2} = \sqrt{(y + 1)^2}$$
$$|x| = y + 1$$

x and y are both positive, so you can drop the absolute value signs and conclude that $x = y + 1$.

MANHATTAN
PREP

(2) SUFFICIENT: Factor out a common term:

$$x^2 - xy - x = 0$$
$$x(x - y - 1) = 0$$

Therefore, $x = 0$ or $x - y - 1 = 0$. The question stem indicates that x is positive, so x cannot equal 0. As a result, it must be the case that $x - y - 1 = 0$, or $x = y + 1$. The two integers are consecutive.

The correct answer is **(D)**.

137. **(C):**

(1) INSUFFICIENT: Solve for the expression in question by adding $(-x^2 - x)$ to both sides:

$$y = -3x$$
$$y + (-x^2 - x) = -3x + (-x^2 - x)$$
$$y - x^2 - x = -x^2 - 4x$$

The answer depends on the value of x, which is not given.

(2) INSUFFICIENT: Solve for the expression in question by adding $(-x^2 - x)$ to both sides:

$$y = -4(x + 1)$$
$$y + (-x^2 - x) = -4(x + 1) + (-x^2 - x)$$
$$y - x^2 - x = -4x - 4 - x^2 - x$$
$$y - x^2 - x = -x^2 - 5x - 4$$

The answer depends on the value of x, which is not given.

(1) and (2) SUFFICIENT: Each statement provides a different expression equal to $y - x^2 - x$. Set these two equal to each other:

$$-x^2 - 5x - 4 = -x^2 - 4x$$
$$-5x - 4 = -4x \qquad \text{Once the squared terms drop out, the equation is solvable.}$$
$$5x + 4 = 4x \qquad \text{Stop when you know you can solve!}$$
$$x = -4$$

The correct answer is **(C)**.

9

138. **(D) 41:** The question gives a function with two unknown constants and two data points. In order to solve for $p(4)$, first solve for the constants r and b by creating two equations from the two data points given:

$$p(2) = 41 = r(2) - 5(2)^2 + b$$
$$41 = 2r + b - 20$$
$$61 = 2r + b$$

$$p(5) = 26 = r(5) - 5(5)^2 + b$$
$$26 = 5r + b - 125$$
$$151 = 5r + b$$

Now, solve these equations for r and b by subtracting one from the other to cancel the b's:

$$151 = 5r + b$$
$$\underline{- (61 = 2r + b)}$$
$$90 = 3r$$
$$30 = r$$

Substitute back in to one of the equations to find b:

$$61 = 2r + b$$
$$61 = 2(30) + b$$
$$1 = b$$

Rewrite the original function and plug in $t = 4$ to find the answer:

$$p(t) = 30t - 5t^2 + 1$$

$$p(4) = 30(4) - 5(4)^2 + 1$$
$$= 120 - 80 + 1$$
$$= 41$$

9

The correct answer is **(D)**.

139. **(A) $\sqrt{2}$ to 1:** The problem presents everything in terms of ratios, not real numbers, so *Choose a Smart Number* to make the math easier. Set each of the three equal segments DP, PQ, and QB equal to 1.

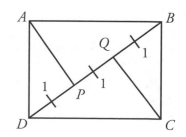

The two triangles PAD and PBA are similar triangles because all three angles are the same. First, they each have one right angle. Next, angle ADP and angle ABP are the same according to parallel line rules. If two angles are the same, then the third angle also has to be the same.

Since the triangles are similar, the sides have to be in the same ratio. The sides line up as follows:

	Triangle *PAD*	Triangle *PBA*
Shortest side	side *PD*	side *AP*
Middle side	side *AP*	side *BP*
Longest side	side *AD*	side *AB*

Since $PD = 1$, $BP = 2$, and $AP = AP$, you can set up a proportion to find the length of side AP:

$$\frac{1}{AP} = \frac{AP}{2}$$
$$2 = (AP)^2$$
$$AP = \sqrt{2}$$

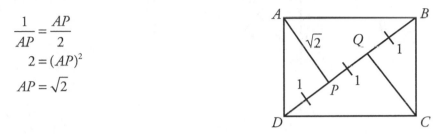

Finally, use the Pythagorean theorem to determine the lengths of AD and AB:

$$AD^2 = (1)^2 + (\sqrt{2})^2 \qquad AB^2 = (\sqrt{2})^2 + (2)^2$$
$$AD = \sqrt{3} \qquad\qquad AB = \sqrt{6}$$

The ratio of AB to AD is $\sqrt{6} : \sqrt{3}$ or $\sqrt{2} : 1$.

Alternatively, since the diagram is drawn to scale, you can try to estimate. Side AB looks approximately 1.5 times as long as side AD, which would result in a ratio of 1.5 : 1. Check the answers:

(A) $\sqrt{2}$ to 1 = 1.4 to 1
(B) $\sqrt{3}$ to 1 = 1.7 to 1
(C) $\sqrt{3}$ to $\sqrt{2}$ = 1.7 to 1.4   too small
(D)   2 to 1 = too big
(E)   2 to $\sqrt{3}$ = 2 to 1.7   too small

Only answers (A) and (B) are close to the right number.

The correct answer is **(A)**.

9

140. **(A) (–2, 6):** First draw a "rubber band" picture:

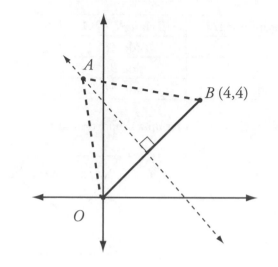

You could *Work Backwards* from the answers. Plot the five answer choices on the coordinate plane.

Points (C) and (D) aren't even on the line, so eliminate them. Answers (A), (B), and (E) do fall on the line, so check their areas. (Note: If you happen to notice that (0, 4) and (4, 0) are symmetrical, and therefore will have the same area, you can eliminate them, since you can't have two correct answers.)

First, line OB is the hypotenuse of a 45–45–90 triangle with legs 4 and 4. Therefore, $OB = 4\sqrt{2}$. This is the base for the area formula.

The height to point (–2, 6) can be calculated using the Pythagorean theorem: $4^2 + 4^2 = c^2$, or $32 = c^2$ and $c = 4\sqrt{2}$. This is the height. The area is $(1/2)bh = (1/2)(4\sqrt{2})(4\sqrt{2}) = 16$. This is the correct area.

If you've already found that answer (A) works, you don't need to calculate the area for the other two points. If you did, you would discover that the area is 8.

Alternatively, you could solve algebraically. Segment OB has a slope of +1, which means that OB is essentially the diagonal of a 4 by 4 square in the xy-coordinate system, so $OB = 4\sqrt{2}$.

Since A must be equidistant from O and B, it must lie on the dashed line with slope –1 that passes through (2, 2); that is, it must lie on the perpendicular bisector of OB. The area of triangle OAB grows as A moves away from OB. Thus, this question is indirectly asking "Exactly how far away must A be from OB to make the area of triangle $OAB = 16$?"

$$\text{Area } OAB = \frac{1}{2}bh$$

$$16 = \frac{1}{2}\left(4\sqrt{2}\right)h$$

$$16 = \left(2\sqrt{2}\right)h$$

$$\frac{16}{2\sqrt{2}} = h$$

$$\frac{16}{\left(2\sqrt{2}\right)}\frac{\sqrt{2}}{\sqrt{2}} = h$$

$$4\sqrt{2} = h$$

Since the dashed line for A has a slope of -1, you might again recognize $4\sqrt{2}$ as the diagonal of a 4 by 4 square in the xy-coordinate system. Thus A, must be 4 units left and 4 units up from $(2, 2)$, or 4 units right and 4 units down from $(2, 2)$.

Possible coordinates for A are thus:

$(2 - 4, 2 + 4)$ or $(2 + 4, 2 - 4)$
$(-2, 6)$ or $(6, -2)$

The correct answer is **(A)**.

9

Workout Set 15

141. If $\dfrac{(ab)^2+3ab-18}{(a-1)(a+2)}=0$, where a and b are integers and a does not equal 1 or -2, which of the following could be the value of b?

    I.   1
    II.   2
    III.   3

(A) I only
(B) II only
(C) I and II only
(D) I and III only
(E) I, II, and III

142. Set S contains exactly four distinct positive integers. Is the mean of S equal to the median of S?

    (1)   The smallest term in S is equal to the sum of the two middle terms minus the largest term in S.
    (2)   When the range of S is added to the sum of all the terms in S, the resulting sum is equal to the smallest term in S plus three times the largest term in S.

143. What is the area of the quadrilateral bounded by the lines $y=\dfrac{3}{4}x+6$, $y=\dfrac{3}{4}x-6$, $y=-\dfrac{3}{4}x+6$, and $y=-\dfrac{3}{4}x-6$?

(A) 48
(B) 64
(C) 96
(D) 100
(E) 140

144. Each digit 1 through 5 is used exactly once to create a 5-digit integer. If the 3 and the 4 cannot be adjacent digits in the integer, how many 5-digit integers are possible?

(A) 48
(B) 66
(C) 72
(D) 78
(E) 90

MANHATTAN
PREP

145. *a*, *b*, *c*, and *d* are positive integers. If the remainder is 9 when *a* is divided by *b*, and the remainder is 5 when *c* is divided by *d*, which of the following is NOT a possible value for *b* + *d*?

     (A) 20
     (B) 19
     (C) 18
     (D) 16
     (E) 15

146. The ratio of cupcakes to children at a party is 27 to 7. Each child at the party eats exactly *x* whole cupcakes, after which a total of *y* whole cupcakes remain uneaten. If *y* is less than the number of children at the birthday party, which of the following must be true?

        I.   *y* is a multiple of 2.
      II.   *y* is a multiple of 3.
    III.   *y* is a multiple of 7.

     (A) I only
     (B) II only
     (C) III only
     (D) I and II only
     (E) I, II and III

147. What is the units digit of the positive integer *x*?

     (1) $\dfrac{x}{5} = y.2$, where *y* is a positive integer.

     (2) $\dfrac{x}{2} = z.5$, where *z* is a positive integer.

148. If *x* and *y* are positive integers, what is the value of (*x* + *y*)?

     (1) $(x + y - 1)! < 100$
     (2) $y = x^2 - x + 1$

9

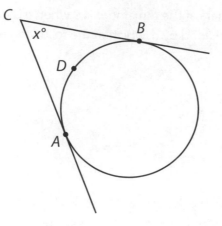

149. In the figure above, two lines are tangent to a circle at points A and B. What is x?

    (1) The area of the circle is 81π.
    (2) The length of arc ADB is 7π.

150. For all n such that n is a positive integer, the terms of a certain sequence B are given by the following rules:

    $B_n = B_{n-1} + 5$ if n is odd and greater than 1;
    $B_n = -B_{n-1}$ if n is even;
    $B_1 = 3$

    What is the sum of the first 65 terms in the sequence?

    (A) −5
    (B)   0
    (C)   3
    (D)   5
    (E)   8

9

MANHATTAN
PREP

Workout Set 15 Answer Key

141. (C)
142. (D)
143. (C)
144. (C)
145. (E)
146. (D)
147. (C)
148. (E)
149. (C)
150. (C)

9

Workout Set 15 Solutions

141. **(C) I and II only:** Factor the numerator:

$$\frac{(ab)^2 + 3ab - 18}{(a-1)(a+2)} = \frac{(ab+6)(ab-3)}{(a-1)(a+2)} = 0$$

Since the fraction equals 0, either $ab + 6 = 0$ or $ab - 3 = 0$. Thus $ab = -6$ or 3. Since a and b are integers, and $ab = -6$ or $ab = 3$, it must be the case that b is a factor of either -6 or 3. Note that $a \neq 1$ and $a \neq -2$.

   I.   POSSIBLE: If $b = 1$, then $a = -6$ or $a = 3$, which are both allowed.

   II. POSSIBLE: If $b = 2$, then $a = -3$ or $a = \dfrac{3}{2}$. One of those ($a = -3$) is allowed.

   III. IMPOSSIBLE: If $b = 3$, then $a = -2$ or $a = 1$, neither of which is allowed.

The correct answer is **(C)**.

142. **(D):** Since the four integers in the set are distinct positive integers, give them distinct ordered variables to represent their relative sizes: a, b, c, and d are the terms of set S, such that $a < b < c < d$.

The mean of S is $\dfrac{a+b+c+d}{4}$. The median of S is the average of the two middle terms, $\dfrac{b+c}{2}$.

Express the question algebraically:

$$\frac{a+b+c+d}{4} = \frac{b+c}{2}?$$

$$2(a + b + c + d) = 4(b + c)?$$
$$(a + b + c + d) = 2(b + c)?$$
$$a + b + c + d = 2b + 2c$$
$$a + d = b + c?$$

In words, this question has been rephrased as, "Is the sum of the largest and smallest terms in S equal to the sum of the two middle terms?"

(1) SUFFICIENT: If the smallest term is equal to the sum of the two middle terms minus the largest term, then the question is satisfied:

$$a = b + c - d$$
$$a + d = b + c$$

The answer to the rephrased question is a definite "Yes."

MANHATTAN
PREP

(2) SUFFICIENT: If the sum of the range of S and all the terms in S is equal to the smallest term in S plus three times the largest term in S, then:

$$(d - a) + (a + b + c + d) = a + 3d$$
$$b + c + 2d = a + 3d$$
$$b + c = a + d$$

The answer to the rephrased question is a definite "Yes."

The correct answer is **(D)**.

143. **(C) 96:** All of these line equations are of the form $y = mx + b$, where m is the slope and b is the y-intercept. Two of these lines have a slope of 3/4 and are thus parallel to each other. The other two lines are parallel to one another with a slope of $-3/4$. Two of the lines have a y-intercept of 6 while the other two lines have a y-intercept of -6.

Sketch the lines:

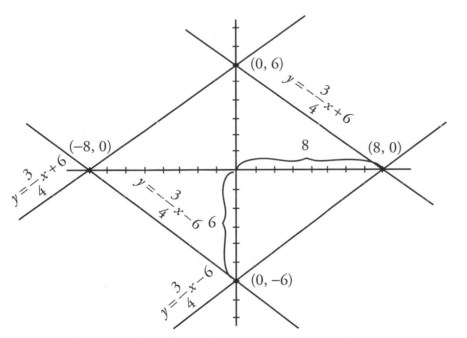

In *each* quadrant, there is a triangle with the dimensions 6−8−10, a multiple of the common 3−4−5 right triangle:

$$Area = 4\left(\frac{1}{2}bh\right)$$
$$= 2bh$$
$$= 2(6)(6)$$
$$= 96$$

Alternatively, recognize that the quadrilateral is a rhombus (four equal sides of length 10), and use the formula for the area of a rhombus: $\frac{D_1 \times D_2}{2}$, where D indicates the length of the diagonals:

$$Area = \frac{12 \times 16}{2} = 96.$$

The correct answer is **(C)**.

144. **(C) 72:** In a constrained combinatorics question such as this one, it is often easier to consider the "violating" cases instead of the "OK" cases:

> \# of permutations that obey the constraint = \# of permutations total − \# of permutations that violate the constraint.

At first glance, ignore the constraint that 3 and 4 cannot be adjacent to determine the total number of 5-digit integers possible:

> \# of permutations total = 5! = (5)(4)(3)(2)(1) = 120.

Now consider the basic ways that 3 and 4 might be adjacent to each other in a 5-digit number:

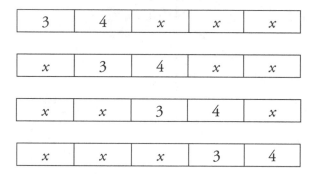

For each of these four base cases, there are two ways to order the 3 and 4 (3–4 and 4–3), as well as 3! ways the other digits (1, 2, and 5) can be arranged in the *x* positions. Thus,

> \# of permutations that violate the constraint = 4 × 2 × 3! = (4)(2)(3)(2)(1) = 48.

Therefore, the number of permutations that do not violate the constraint equals 120 − 48 = 72.

The correct answer is **(C)**.

145. **(E) 15:** To answer, recognize an important rule: *the divisor must be greater than the remainder.* Here are a few examples:

> 10 ÷ 4 = 2 remainder 2 (divisor 4 is greater than remainder 2)
> 23 ÷ 6 = 3 remainder 5 (divisor 6 is greater than remainder 5)

MANHATTAN
PREP

If the divisor weren't greater than the remainder, the divisor would be able to divide into the dividend *at least one more time*. Let's take an incorrect example to illustrate:

$$23 \div 6 = 2 \text{ remainder } 11 \quad \text{INCORRECT}$$

In this case, the divisor is LESS than the remainder (6 is less than 11). In fact, 6 actually goes into 23 three times. The remainder is what is left over when the divisor has been divided into the dividend *as many times as possible*.

Therefore, if a divided by b gives a remainder of 9, then b is greater than 9: $b \geq 10$.
Likewise, if c divided by d gives a remainder of 5, then d is greater than 5: $d \geq 6$.

Therefore, the minimum sum is $b + d \geq 16$.

Only 15 is too small.

The correct answer is **(E)**.

146. **(D) I and II only:** $\dfrac{\text{cupcakes}}{\text{children}} = \dfrac{22}{7}$, so cupcakes = $27a$ and children = $7a$, where a is a positive integer. The problem also specifies that each child eats x cupcakes.

cupcakes eaten = (children)$x = 7ax$

cupcakes leftover = total cupcakes − cupcakes eaten

$$y = 27a - 7ax$$

$0 \leq$ cupcakes leftover $<$ children
$0 \leq 27a - 7ax < 7a$
$0 \leq 27 - 7x < 7$
$-27 \leq -7x < -20$
$27 \geq 7x > 20$

Since x is an integer, and the only multiple of 7 between 20 and 27 is 21, $7x$ must equal 21.

Therefore,
$y = 27a - 7ax$
$= 27a - a(7x)$
$= 27a - 21a$
$= 6a$

  I.   TRUE: $6a$ is a multiple of 2.
  II. TRUE: $6a$ is a multiple of 3.
 III. MAYBE: $6a$ could be a multiple of 7, but only when a is a multiple of 7.

The correct answer is **(D)**.

147. **(C):**

(1) INSUFFICIENT: Manipulate the statement:

$$\frac{x}{5} = y.2$$

$$\frac{x}{5} = y + 0.2$$

$$x = 5(y + 0.2)$$

$$x = 5y + 1$$

Thus, x is 1 greater than a multiple of 5. Since all multiples of 5 end in either 0 or 5, x must end in either 1 or 6.

Alternatively, you could list numbers. Since y is a positive integer, $5y$ could be 5, 10, 15, 20, etc. Thus, x could be 6, 11, 16, 21, etc. The units digit of x could be 1 or 6.

(2) INSUFFICIENT: Manipulate the statement:

$$\frac{x}{2} = z.5$$

$$\frac{x}{2} = z + 0.5$$

$$x = 2(z + 0.5)$$

$$x = 2z + 1$$

This indicates that x is odd, because $2z$ is an even number. Any odd single-digit integer is a possible units digit for x: 1, 3, 5, 7, or 9.

(1) AND (2) SUFFICIENT: Statement (1) indicates that x must end in either 1 or 6. Because statement (2) indicates that x is odd, x must end in 1, and cannot end in 6.

The correct answer is **(C)**.

148. **(E):**

(1) INSUFFICIENT: $(x + y - 1)! < 100$. To see the possible values of $(x + y - 1)$, list the factorials of the first few integers:

$$1! = 1$$
$$2! = 2$$
$$3! = 6$$
$$4! = 24$$
$$5! = 120 \text{ (too large)}$$

So, $(x + y - 1) \le 4$, and $(x + y) \le 5$.

(2) INSUFFICIENT: Add x to both sides of $y = x^2 - x + 1$ to create $(x + y)$ on one side of the equation:

$$y = x^2 - x + 1$$
$$x + y = x + x^2 - x + 1$$
$$x + y = x^2 + 1$$

The exact value of $(x + y)$ is unknown, as it depends on the value of x^2, which could be any positive integer.

(1) AND (2) INSUFFICIENT: $(x + y) \leq 5$ and $x + y = x^2 + 1$ combine to indicate that $x^2 + 1 \leq 5$. There are two integer solutions: $x = 1$ or $x = 2$.

> If $x = 1$, then $y = 1^2 - 1 + 1 = 1$ and $x + y = 1 + 1 = 2$.
> If $x = 2$, then $y = 2^2 - 2 + 1 = 3$ and $x + y = 2 + 3 = 5$.

The correct answer is **(E)**.

149. **(C):** The size of the angle depends on two things:

The size of the circle

The distance of *C* from the circle
(inversely related to arc length ADB)

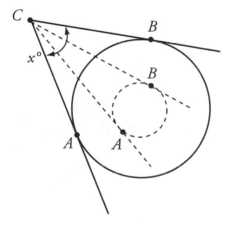

Larger circle ➔ Larger *x*

Farther *C* ➔ smaller *x*
Larger arc *ADB* ➔ smaller *x*

(1) INSUFFICIENT: The rubber band picture on the right indicates that for a circle of fixed size, *x* can still vary with the length of arc *ADB* (i.e., *x* varies with the placement of *C*).

(2) **INSUFFICIENT:** Draw some cases to prove that x can vary for a given arc *ADB*:

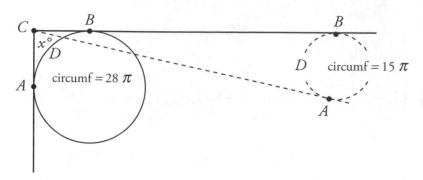

For a circle with circumference 28π, the arc *ADB* is 1/4 ($= 7\pi/28\pi$) of the circle, so x is 90°. For a circle with circumference 15π, the arc *ADB* is nearly half of the circle ($= 7\pi/15\pi$), and the lines tangent to the circle at *A* and *B* will join at a smaller angle x.

(1) AND (2) **SUFFICIENT:** If the area of the circle is $\pi r^2 = 81\pi$, then $r = 9$. The circumference of the circle is $2\pi r = 18$. Thus, arc *ADB* is 7/18 ($= 7\pi/18\pi$) of the circumference of the circle. There is only one way to draw the lines tangent to the circle at *A* and *B*, so x must be one specific value.

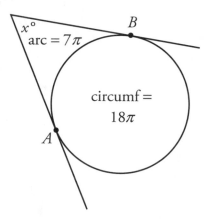

The correct answer is **(C)**.

150. **(C) 3:** List the first few terms of the sequence according to the given rules:

$B_1 = 3$
$B_2 = -B_1 = -3$
$B_3 = B_2 + 5 = -3 + 5 = 2$
$B_4 = -B_3 = -2$
$B_5 = B_4 + 5 = -2 + 5 = 3$
… etc.

MANHATTAN
PREP

Note that the pattern is a four-term repeat: 3, −3, 2, −2. Also note that the sum of this repeating group is (3) + (−3) + (2) + (−2) = 0. This repeating group will occur 16 times through term number 64. (Note: Because the sum of the four terms is 0, you don't actually have to figure out how many times the pattern repeats.) Thus, the sum of the first 64 terms will be 0. This leaves the 65th term, which will have the same value as B_1: 3. Therefore, the sum of the first 65 terms is 3.

The correct answer is **(C)**.

GO BEYOND BOOKS.
TRY A FREE CLASS NOW.

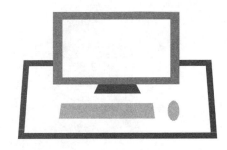

IN-PERSON COURSE

Find a GMAT course near you and attend the first session free, no strings attached. You'll meet your instructor, learn how the GMAT is scored, review strategies for Data Sufficiency, dive into Sentence Correction, and gain insights into a wide array of GMAT principles and strategies.

**Find your city at
manhattanprep.com/gmat/classes**

ONLINE COURSE

Enjoy the flexibility of prepping from home or the office with our online course. Your instructor will cover all the same content and strategies as an in-person course, while giving you the freedom to prep where you want. Attend the first session free to check out our cutting-edge online classroom.

**See the full schedule at
manhattanprep.com/gmat/classes**

GMAT® INTERACT™

GMAT Interact is a comprehensive self-study program that is fun, intuitive, and driven by you. Each interactive video lesson is taught by an expert instructor and can be accessed on your computer or mobile device. Lessons are personalized for you based on the choices you make.

**Try 5 full lessons for free at
manhattanprep.com/gmat/interact**

Not sure which is right for you? Try all three!
Or give us a call and we'll help you figure out
which program fits you best.

Toll-Free U.S. Number (800) 576-4628 | International 001 (212) 721-7400 | Email gmat@manhattanprep.com

PREP MADE PERSONAL

Whether you want quick coaching
in a particular GMAT subject area
or a comprehensive study plan developed
around your goals, we've got you covered.
Our expert, 99th percentile GMAT tutors
can help you hit your top score.

CHECK OUT THESE REVIEWS FROM MANHATTAN PREP TUTORING STUDENTS.

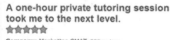

CALL OR EMAIL US AT **800-576-4628** OR **GMAT@MANHATTANPREP.COM**
FOR INFORMATION ON RATES AND TO GET PAIRED WITH YOUR GMAT TUTOR.